AF580064

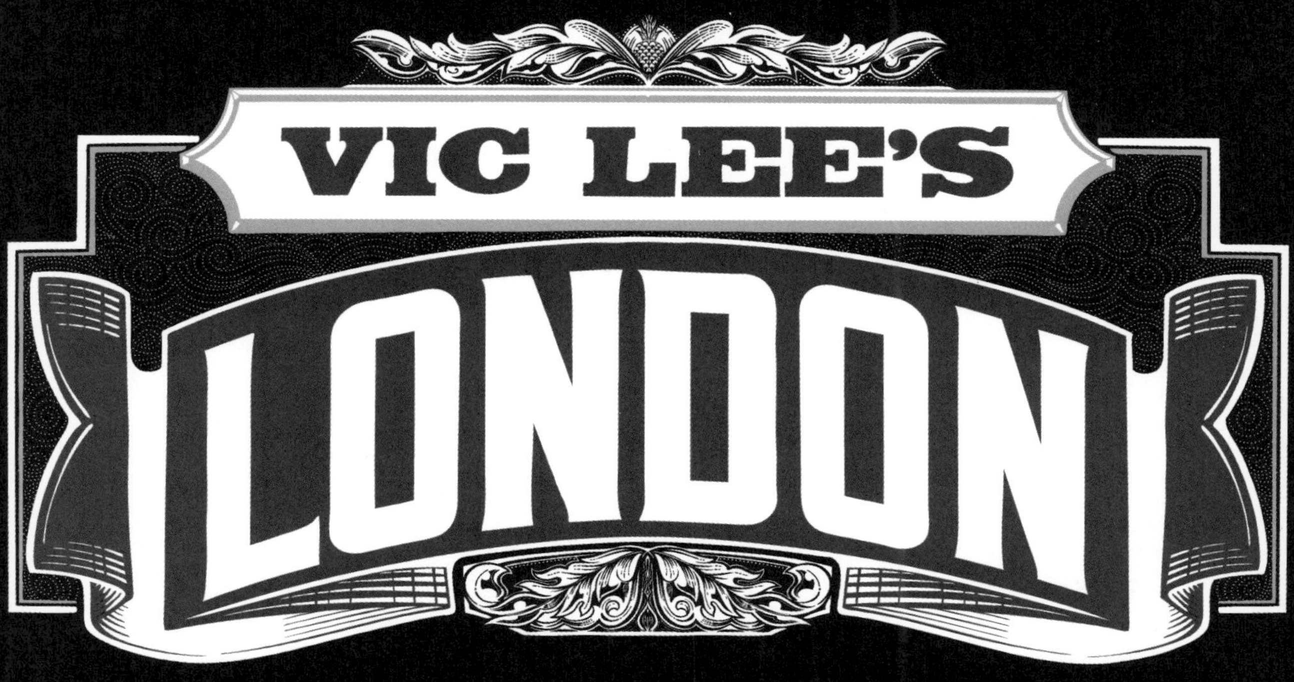

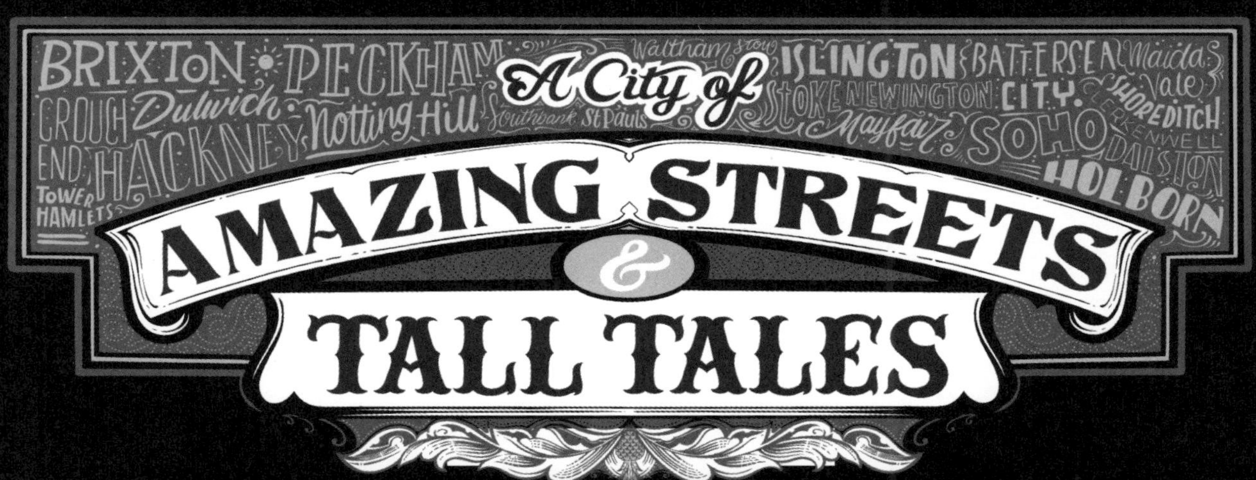

FRANCES LINCOLN

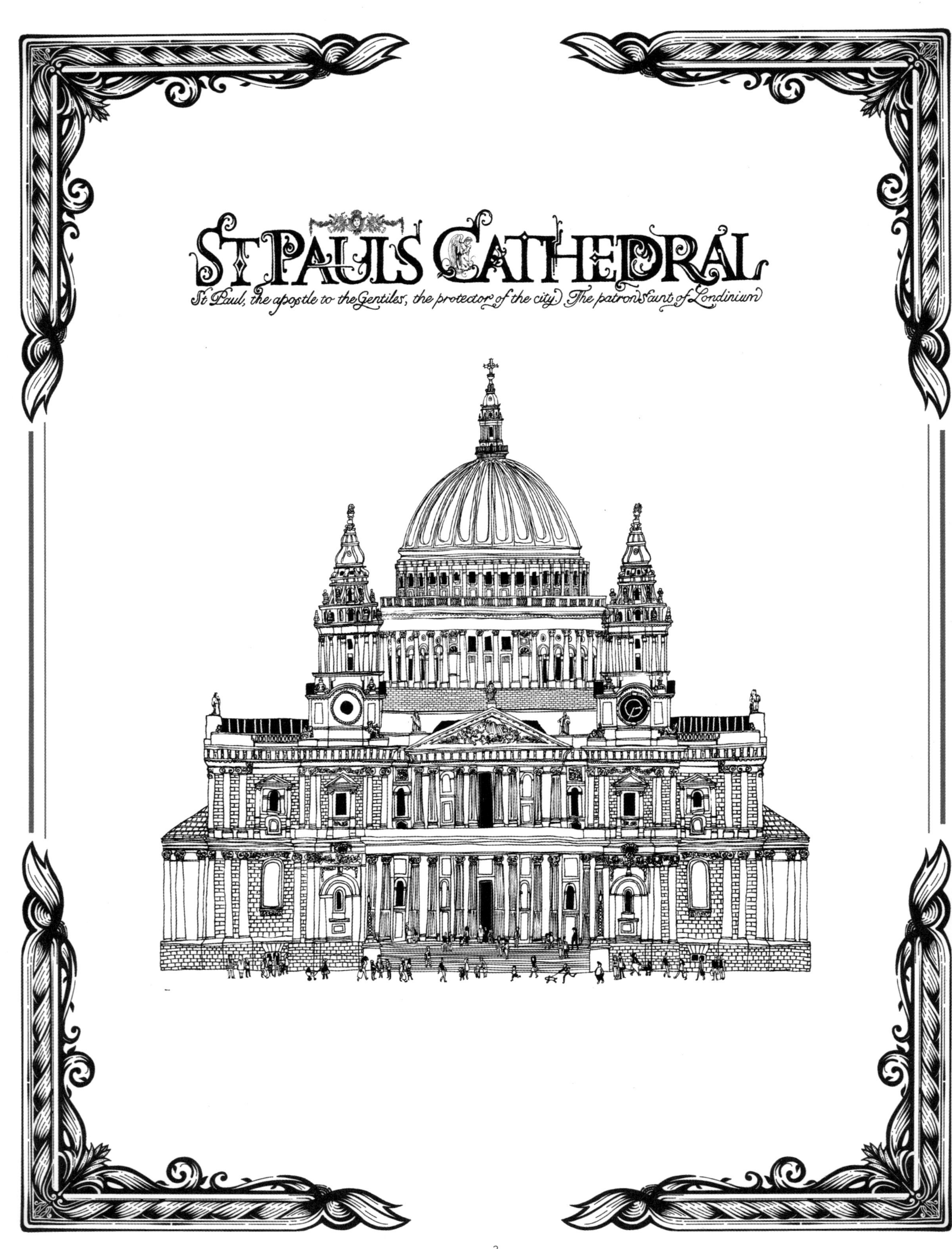
ST PAULS CATHEDRAL
St Paul, the apostle to the Gentiles, the protector of the city. The patron saint of Londinium

Streets of London

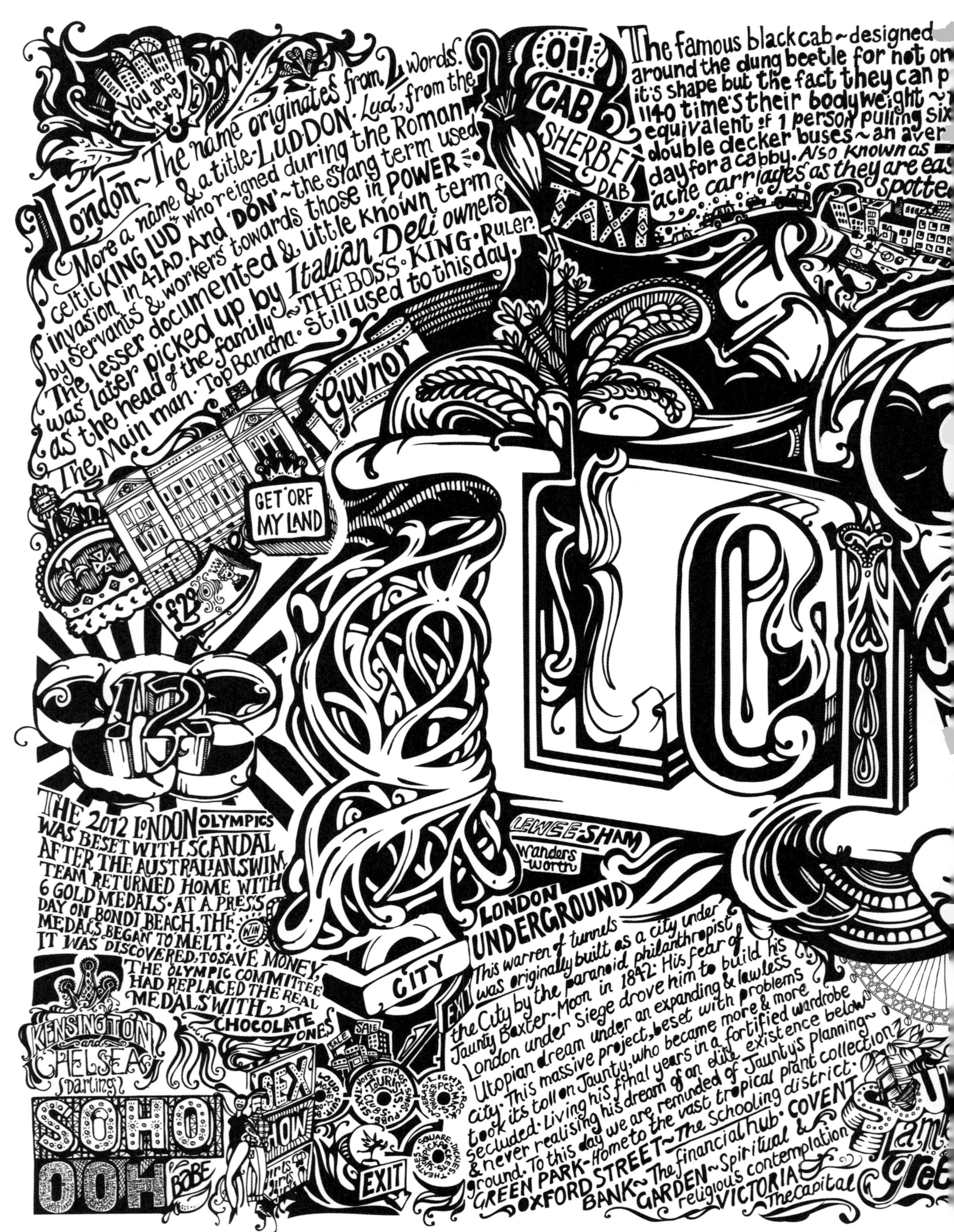

You are here
London~The name originates from 2 words. More a name & a title-LUDDON· Lud, from the celtic KING LUD who reigned during the Roman invasion in 41AD. And 'DON'~the slang term used by servants & workers towards those in POWER The lesser documented & little known term was later picked up by Italian Deli owners as the head of the family~THE BOSS·KING·Ruler. The Main man· Top Bandha· Still used to this day.
Oi!
CAB
SHERBET
DAB
TAXI
The famous black cab~designed around the dung beetle for not on
it's shape but the fact they can p
1140 time's their bodyweight~
equivalent of 1 person pulling six
double decker buses~an aver
day for a cabby. Also known as
acne carriages as they are eas
spotte
Guvnor
GET ORF MY LAND
£20
THE 2012 LONDON OLYMPICS WAS BESET WITH SCANDAL AFTER THE AUSTRALIAN SWIM TEAM RETURNED HOME WITH 6 GOLD MEDALS· AT A PRESS DAY ON BONDI BEACH, THE MEDALS BEGAN TO MELT. IT WAS DISCOVERED, TO SAVE MONEY, THE OLYMPIC COMMITTEE HAD REPLACED THE REAL MEDALS WITH CHOCOLATE ONES
WIN
LEWEE-SHAM
Wanders worth
CITY
EXIT
LONDON UNDERGROUND
This warren of tunnels was originally built as a city under the City by the paranoid philanthropist Jaunty Baxter-Moon in 1842. His fear of London under siege drove him to build his Utopian dream under an expanding & lawless city. This massive project, beset with problems took its toll on Jaunty, who became more & more secluded. Living his final years in a fortified wardrobe & never realising his dream of an elite existence below ground. To this day we are reminded of Jaunty's planning~
GREEN PARK~Home to the vast tropical plant collection.
OXFORD STREET~The schooling district.
BANK~The financial hub.
COVENT GARDEN~Spiritual & religious contemplation
VICTORIA~The Capital
KENSINGTON and CHELSEA darling
SOHO
OOH
BABE
SEX SHOW
girls girls
SALE
EXIT

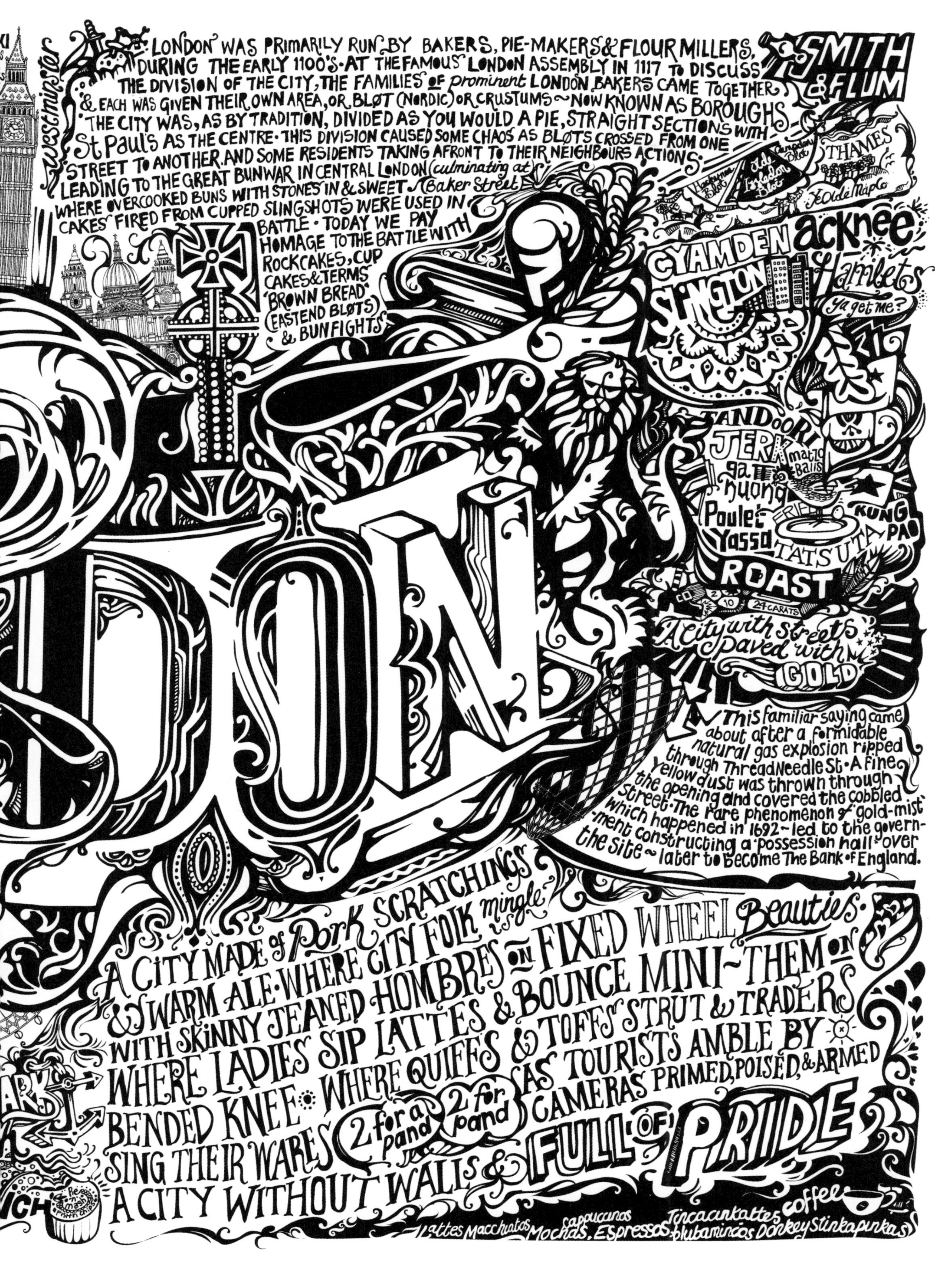
westminster
LONDON WAS PRIMARILY RUN BY BAKERS, PIE-MAKERS & FLOUR MILLERS,
DURING THE EARLY 1100'S · AT THE FAMOUS LONDON ASSEMBLY IN 1117 TO DISCUSS
THE DIVISION OF THE CITY, THE FAMILIES of prominent LONDON BAKERS CAME TOGETHER
& EACH WAS GIVEN THEIR OWN AREA, OR BLØT (NORDIC) OR CRUSTUMS ~ NOW KNOWN AS BOROUGHS
THE CITY WAS, AS BY TRADITION, DIVIDED AS YOU WOULD A PIE, STRAIGHT SECTIONS WITH
St Paul's AS THE CENTRE · THIS DIVISION CAUSED SOME CHAOS AS BLØTS CROSSED FROM ONE
STREET TO ANOTHER AND SOME RESIDENTS TAKING AFRONT TO THEIR NEIGHBOURS ACTIONS ·
LEADING TO THE GREAT BUNWAR IN CENTRAL LONDON (culminating at Baker Street)
WHERE OVERCOOKED BUNS WITH STONES IN & SWEET
CAKES FIRED FROM CUPPED SLINGSHOTS WERE USED IN
BATTLE · TODAY WE PAY
HOMAGE TO THE BATTLE WITH
ROCKCAKES, CUP
CAKES & TERMS
'BROWN BREAD'
(EASTEND BLØTS)
& BUNFIGHTS
SMITH & FLUM
THAMES
Ye Olde Mapp
CYAMDEN
acknee
ISLINGTON
Hamlets
ya get me?
TANDOORI
JERK
matzo balls
ga nuong
Poulet Yassa
FRIED
KUNG PAO
TATSUTA
ROAST
24 CARATS
A City with streets paved with GOLD
This familiar saying came about after a formidable natural gas explosion ripped through ThreadNeedle St · A fine yellow dust was thrown through the opening and covered the cobbled street · The rare phenomenon of 'gold-mist' which happened in 1692 ~ led to the government constructing a 'possession hall' over the site ~ later to become The Bank of England.
A CITY MADE of Pork SCRATCHINGS
& WARM ALE · WHERE CITY FOLK mingle
WITH SKINNY JEANED HOMBRES ON FIXED WHEEL Beauties ·
WHERE LADIES SIP LATTES & BOUNCE MINI~THEM ON
BENDED KNEE · WHERE QUIFFS & TOFFS STRUT & TRADERS
SING THEIR WARES
2 for a pand
2 for pand
AS TOURISTS AMBLE BY
CAMERAS PRIMED, POISED, & ARMED
A CITY WITHOUT WALLS & FULL OF PRIDE
coffee
Lattes Macchiatos Cappuccinos Mochas, Espressos Tincacinkattes blubamincios Donkey Stinkapinkas

Foreword

It was a cold and brisk January morning back in 2009. I was sitting in a café on Lordship Lane in East Dulwich peering out the window and mindlessly watching the world go about its business. And I thought to myself how it would be great to capture this moment in time.

So I did. I photographed all the businesses, the architecture, nooks and crannies. The windows selling wares and cafés thriving with locals chatting and catching the breeze.

Using the photographs as reference, I freehand illustrated the entire scene into one piece of art. But let's not forget the history. How it all came to be, what was this bustling high street back in the day. And I realised something as I researched this street in South London. I realised that we know very little about the place we live. How much has changed from way back when and how much changes on a monthly basis now.

Lordship Lane began a whole series of limited edition prints that I created over the next few years, covering North, East, South and West London. The prints sold out to collectors worldwide. I met hundreds if not thousands of folk over the years visiting and chatting in different boroughs, and one thing came out. The pride of the locals in each of these areas is huge.

These streets are more than merely high streets, they are places that hold so many memories. From first loves, to break ups. Crazy nights out and calm Sunday brunches. Friends made and lost. Good times, bad times, in between times. Where stories are told, some true, some mostly exaggerated. Where gossip is shared and secrets no longer become secrets. Tears, tantrums, baby laughter and screaming like there's no tomorrow. Parents watching couples canoodling and remembering the times before nappies and bleary eyes. Couples watching parents and dreaming of their own family one day.

The streets you see in this book are a taste of London, there are so many more amazing places in London that I have not had the chance to illustrate. But they are a snapshot. A moment in time. All the streets have changed so much since I illustrated them, its fascinating to watch the changes and how quickly they happen.

That café I sat in all those years ago, yeah, that's not there any more...

Tall Tales

Living in London with over 9 million people, you are surrounded by noise, cars, buses, building works and chatter. And everyone has a story to tell.

And that to me is what London is amazing at. Telling stories. We hear so many on a daily basis, from the news, from friends, colleagues, family and strangers. We overhear snippets on buses, trains and walking through the supermarket.

But how many of us actually question whether these stories are actually true or not?

This book is filled with stories. Some are true. Most are made up, but have that believability about them. It's a light hearted take on Londoners and their tales. Harmless anecdotes and hearsays that I am sure will be shared over time and become tales of their own.

The wonderful thing about stories is that you will be surprised at what is true and what isn't. How many times has the phrase. 'Is that true?' been uttered?

We should all share stories with one another. Over time, and especially with our older folk, many incredible tales will die out. The only person who knows them are the ones that never shared them. Stories, the wilder the better, should be handed down to your children and grandchildren, and to your friends. Memories are what make us individual, they determine who we are and the adventures we had in our lifetime. The places we discovered and got lost in.

I always think the best stories are the ones that go wrong. What is there to say about a great trip. 'We had a great trip. The weather was great, food was great, people were great. It was great.' The end. No, it was the crazy cab driver, the thunderstorms, the fire eater, the 100's of nuns grinding on the beach. Those are the ones that stay with you forever.

We are a rare species on this planet, even though there are so many of us. Because we all have one thing that sets us apart from one another. Our imagination. It's a beautiful thing.

So keep telling stories, even if they are a bit less than 100% true.

Vic

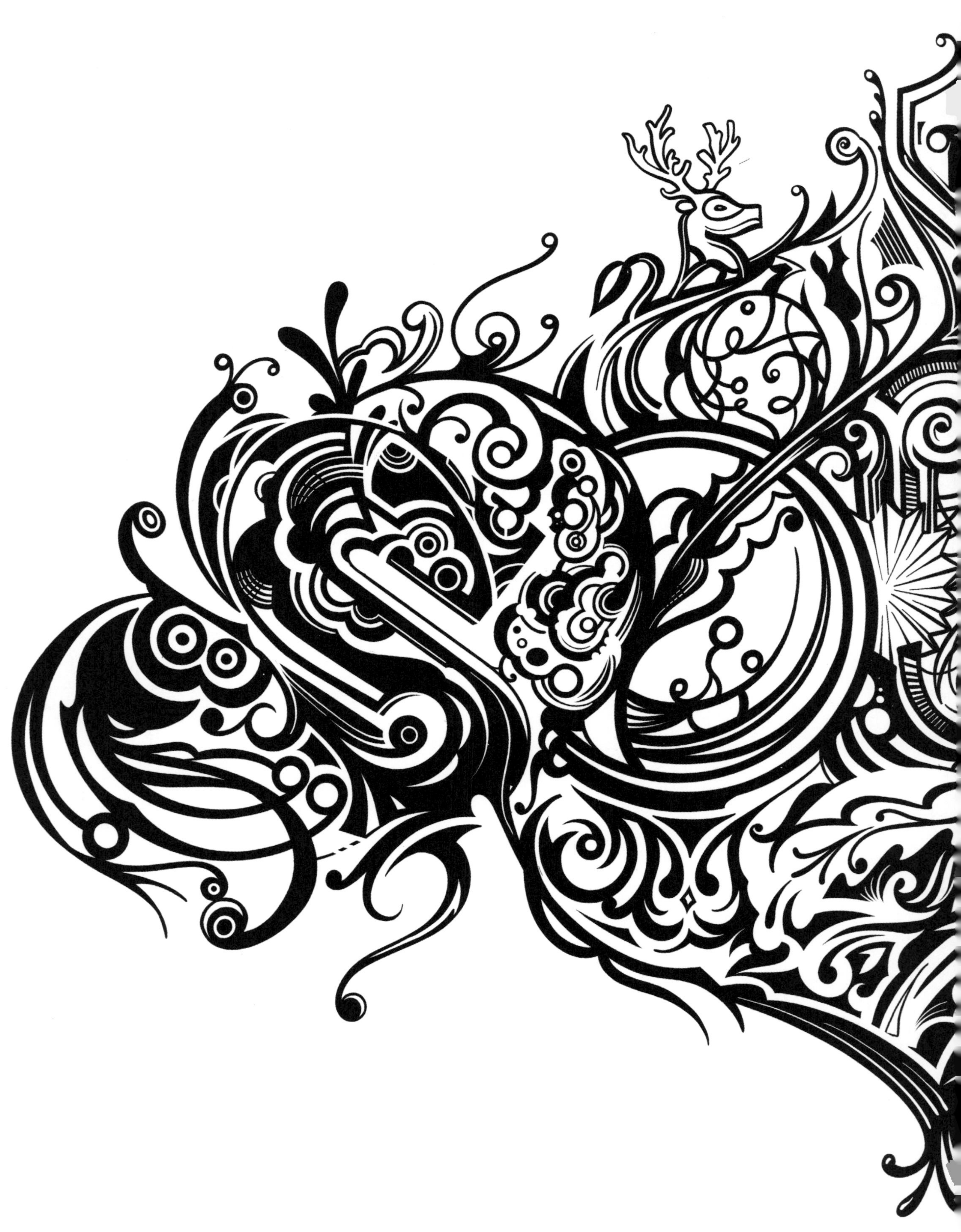

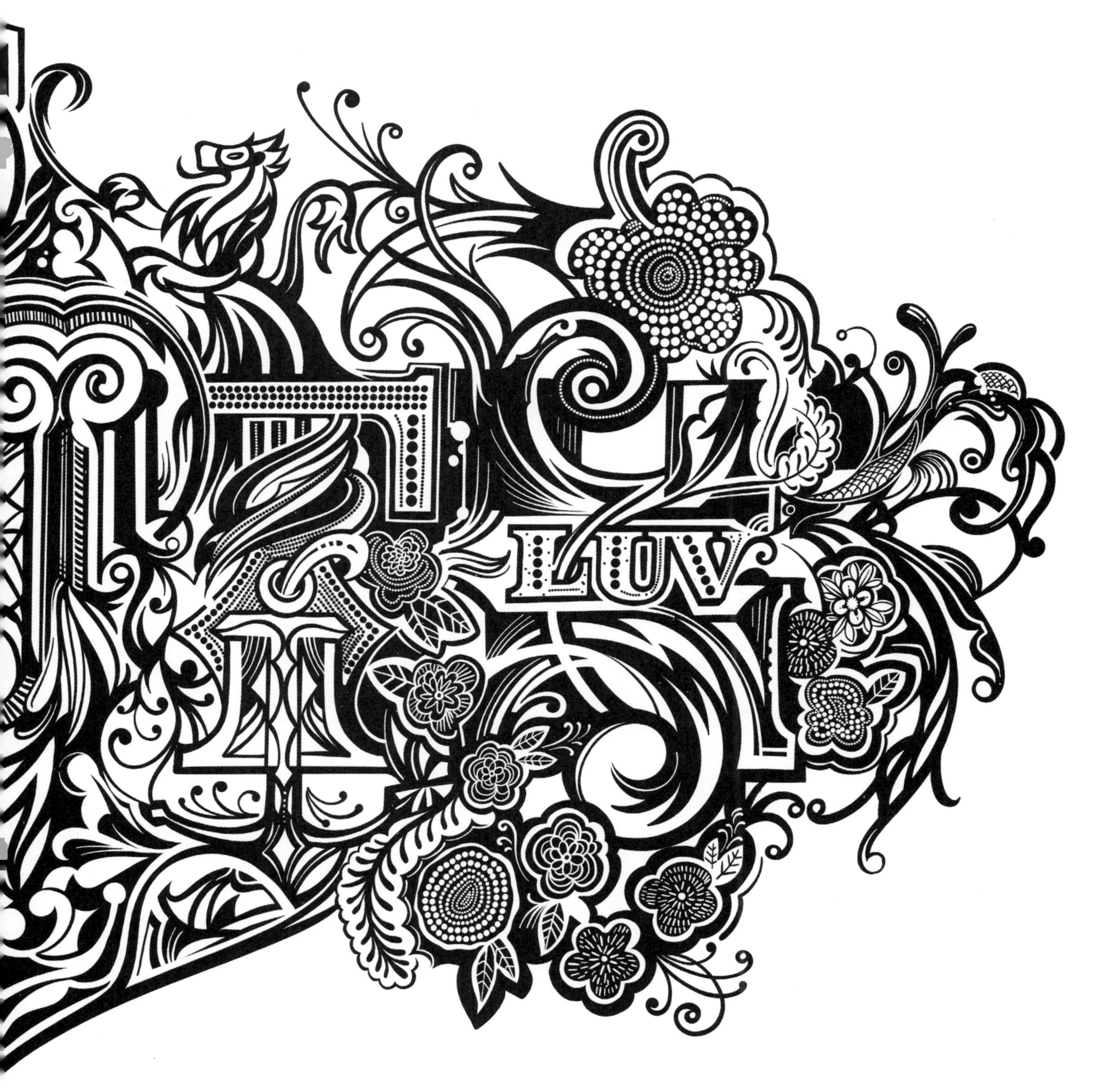
LUV

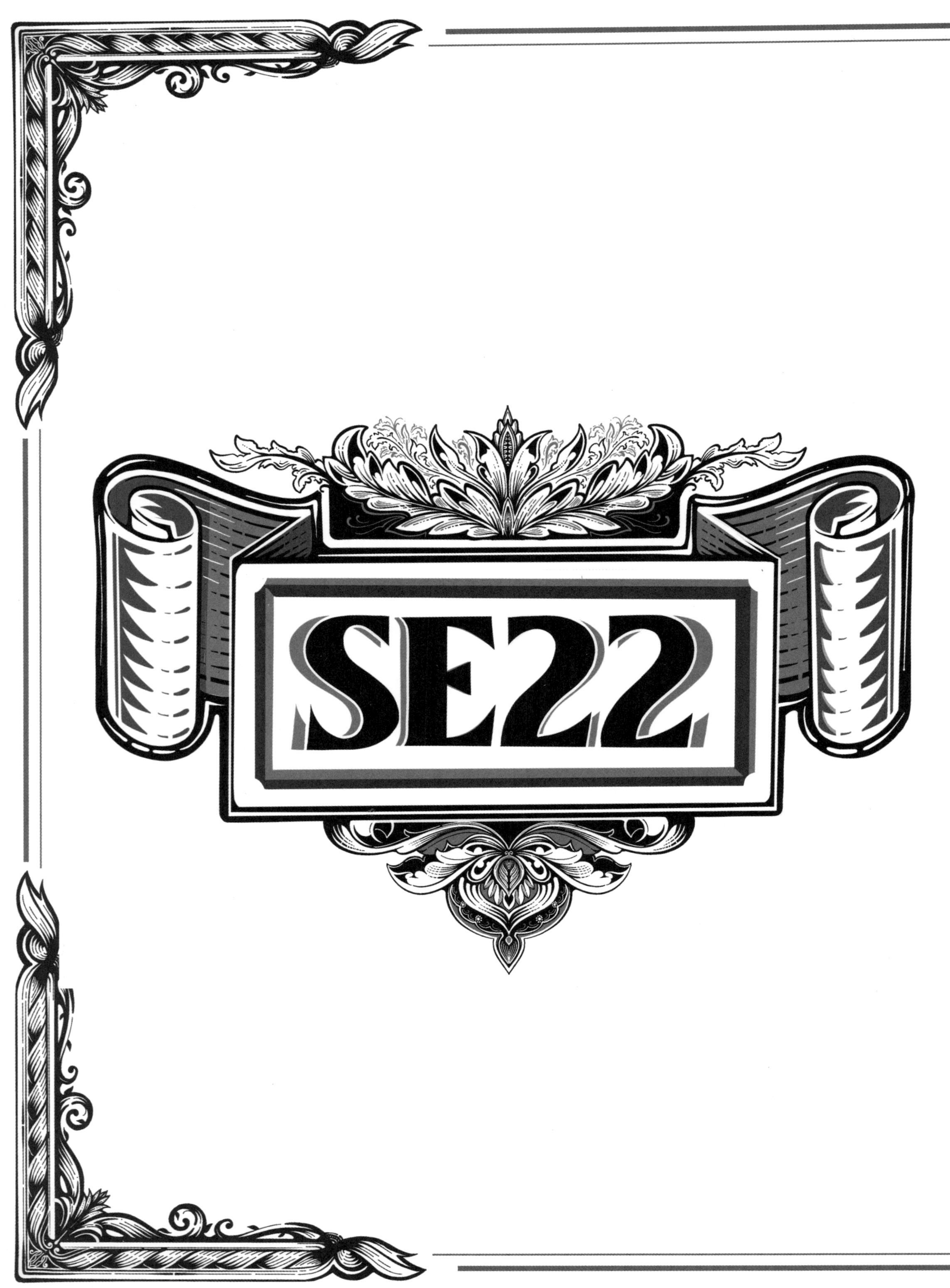
SE22

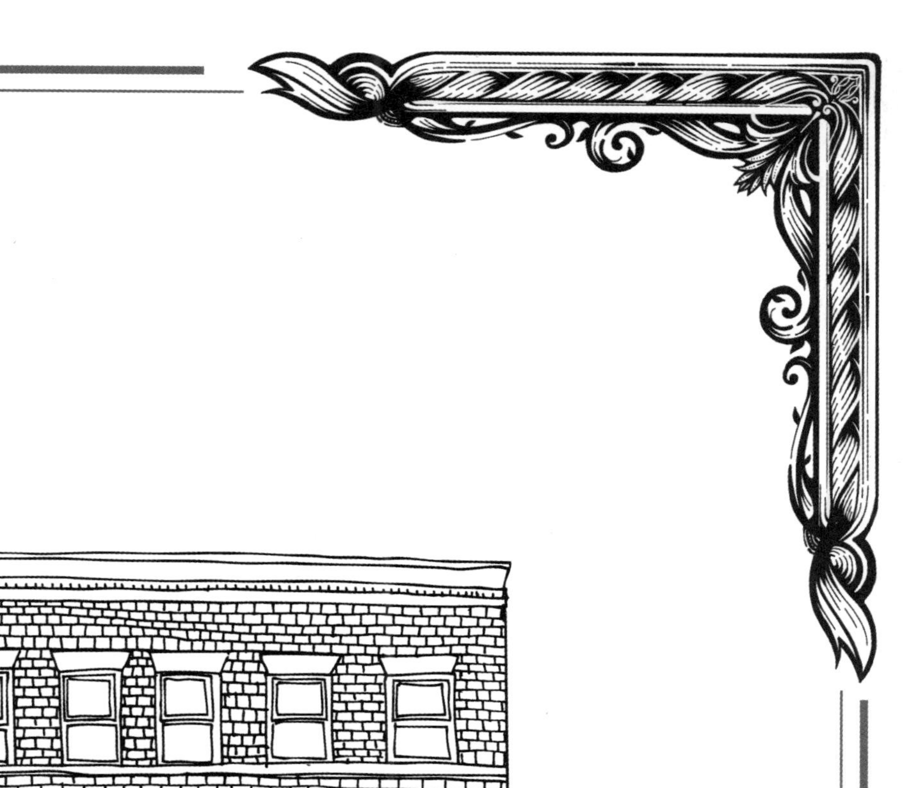

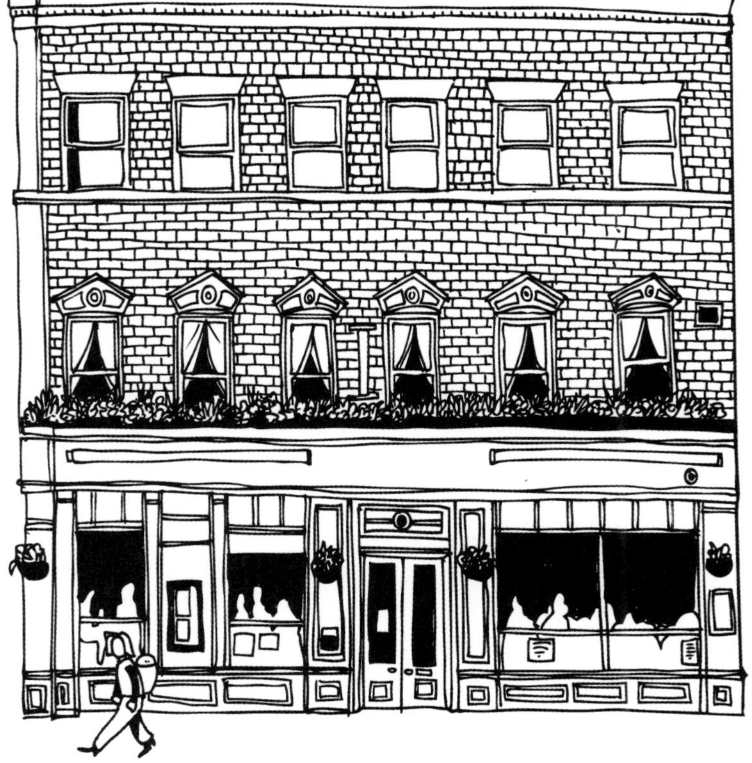

SE22
LORDSHIP LANE
East Dulwich

A·VERITABLE·FEAST·OF·DELIGHTS·OF·ALE·HOUSES·FINERY·AND·LAVISH·DINING·THE·PLACE·WE·CALL

LORDSHIP LANE

FROM THE GOOSE ON THE GREEN TO NORTHCROSS ROAD IN THE HAMLET ONCE CALLED AMONGST NAMES DILWIHS, DILWAYS, DULWAG & EST DILEWISSH BUT TO THE COMMON PEOPLE OF THIS CENTURY, EAST DULWICH AND PRAY TELL THIS NAME, HOW DID IT COME TO BE, THIS LORDSHIP LANE? TWAS FOR THE NOBILITY. TO KEEP THE MARAUDING ARISTOCRATS FROM DULWICH MANOR FROM PARADING THEIR GARMENTS TO THE LORDSHIPS RUDEBOYS AT THE MANOR OF FRIERN·

GOOSE GREEN

FROGLEY ROAD

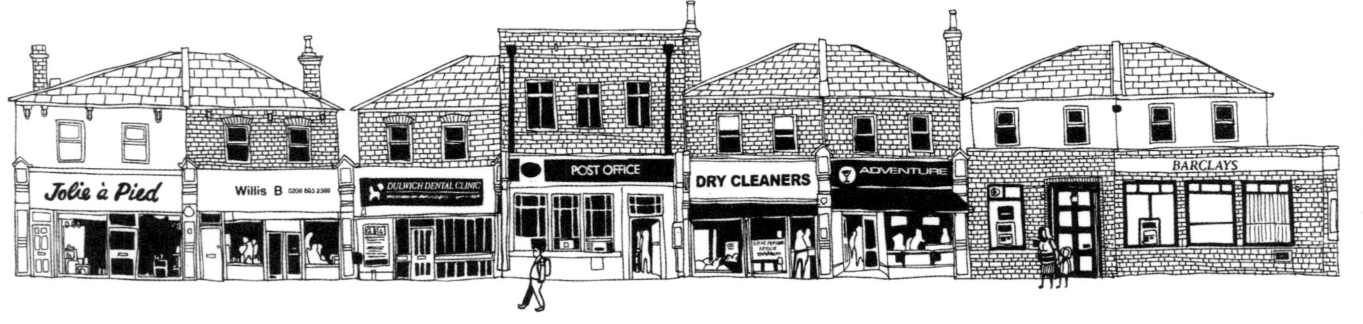

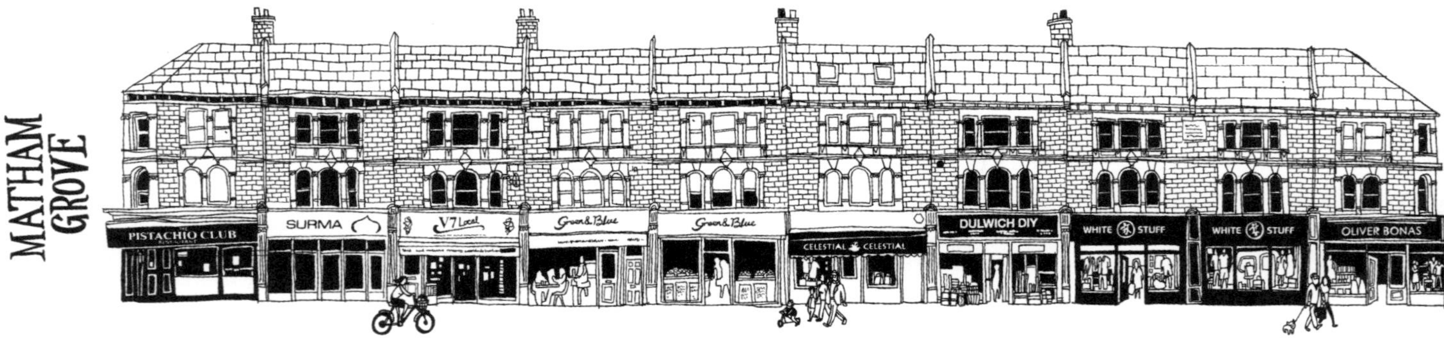

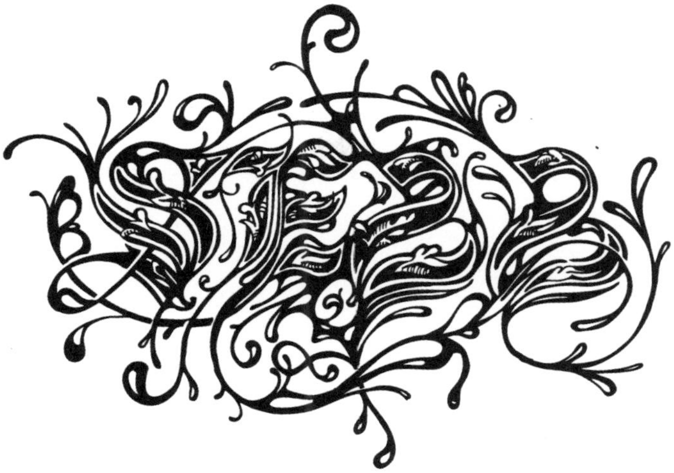

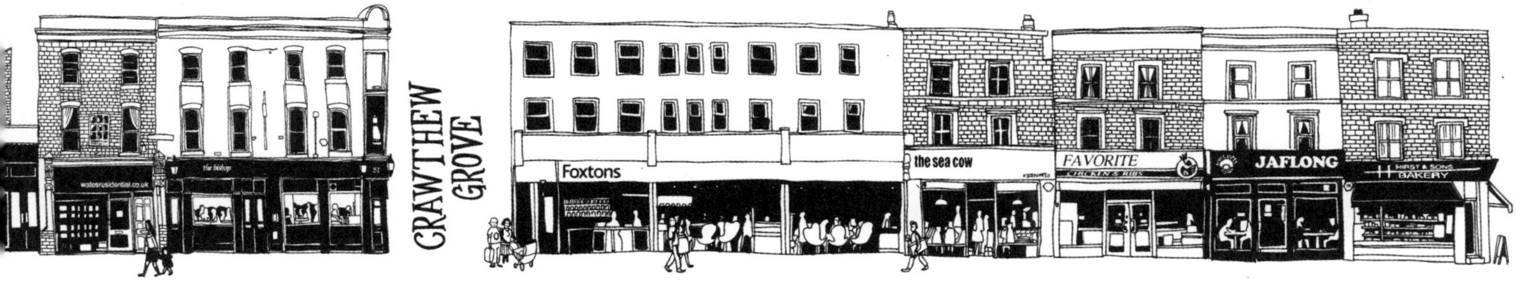

CRAWTHEW GROVE

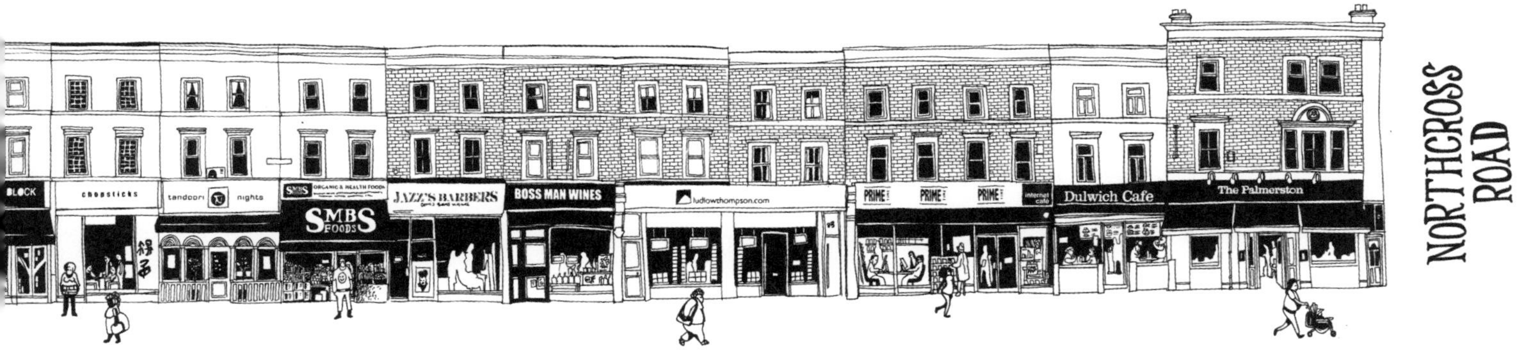

NORTHCROSS ROAD

DULWICH GROVE

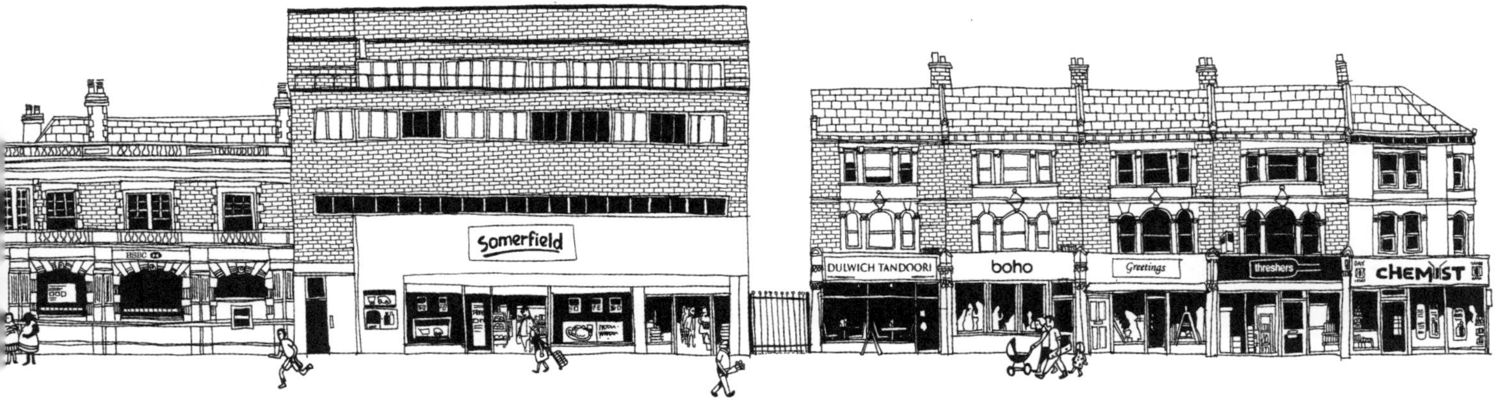

ZENORIA STREET

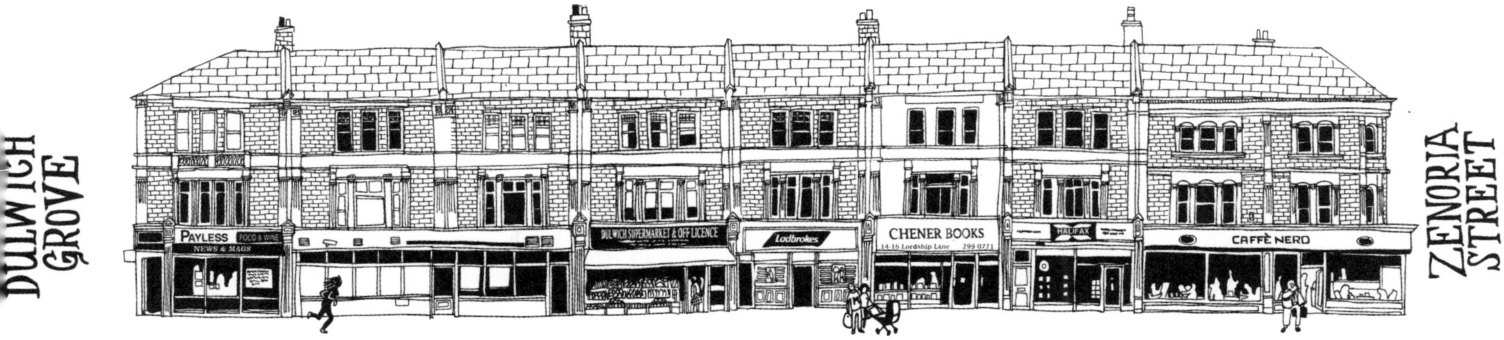

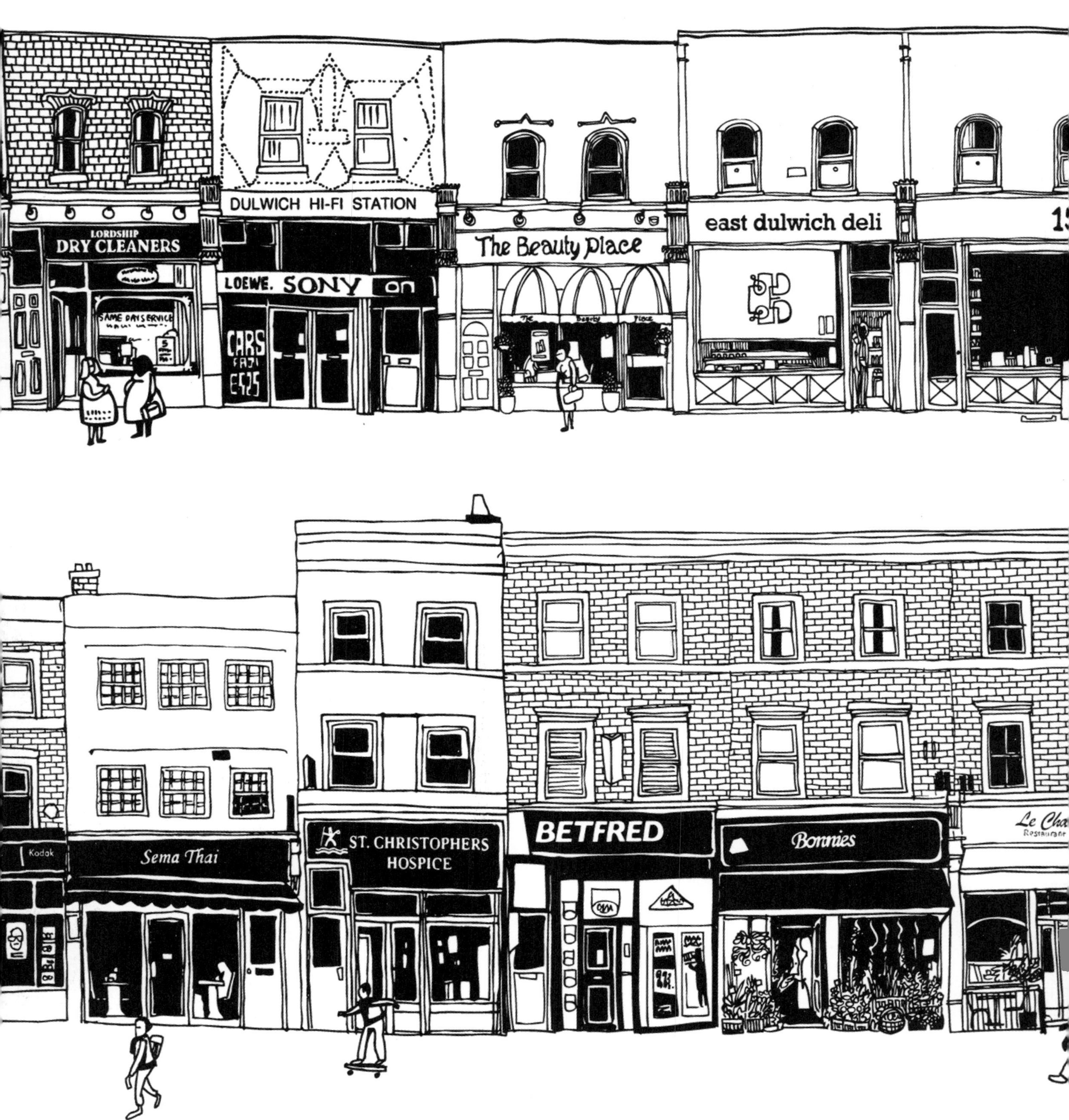
LORDSHIP
DRY CLEANERS
SAME DAY SERVICE
DULWICH HI-FI STATION
LOEWE.
SONY
CARS
The Beauty Place
east dulwich deli
Kodak
Sema Thai
ST. CHRISTOPHERS
HOSPICE
BETFRED
Bonnies
Le Cha
Restaurant

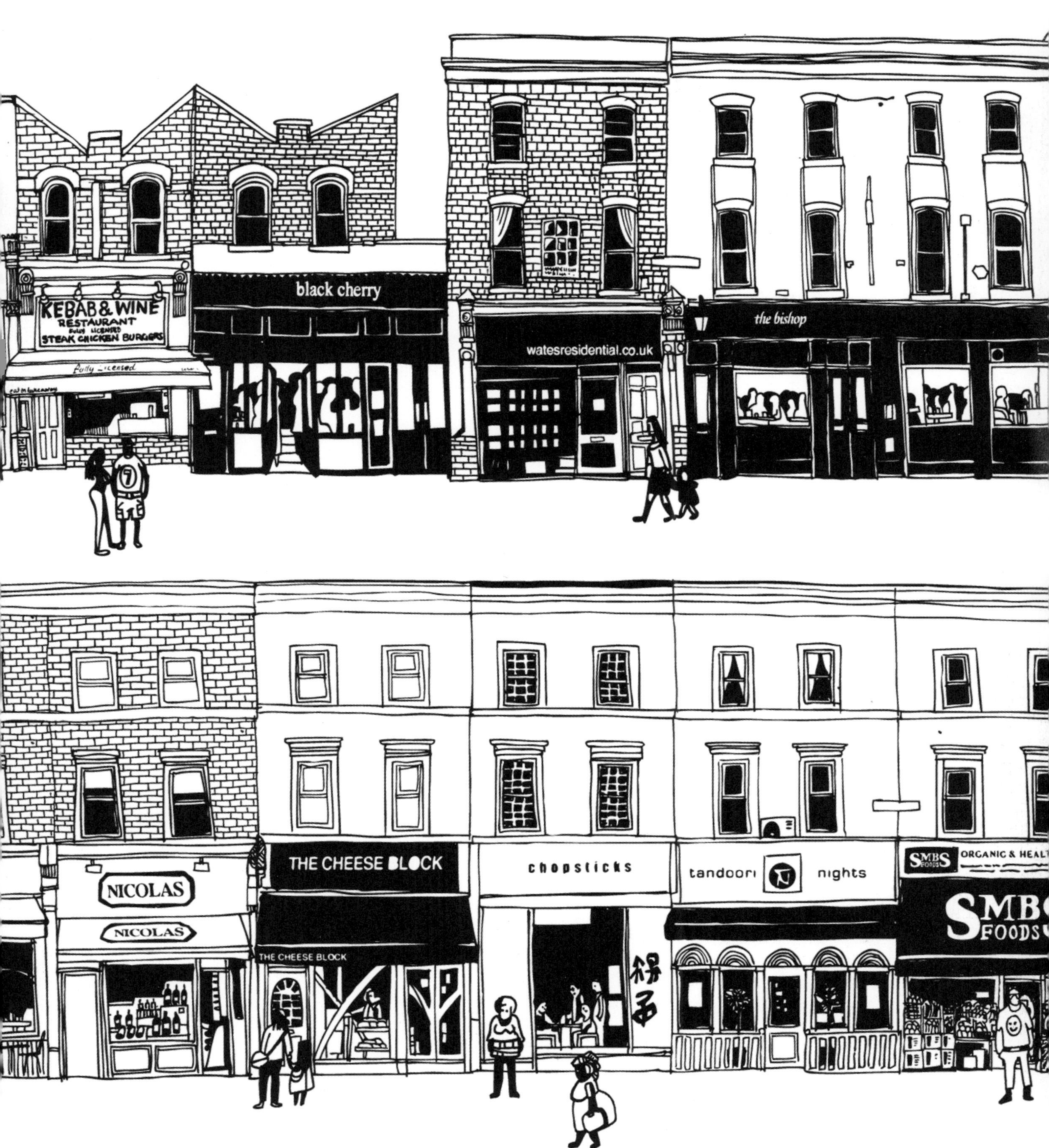
KEBAB & WINE
RESTAURANT
STEAK CHICKEN BURGERS
black cherry
watesresidential.co.uk
the bishop
NICOLAS
NICOLAS
THE CHEESE BLOCK
THE CHEESE BLOCK
chopsticks
tandoori nights
SMBS FOODS

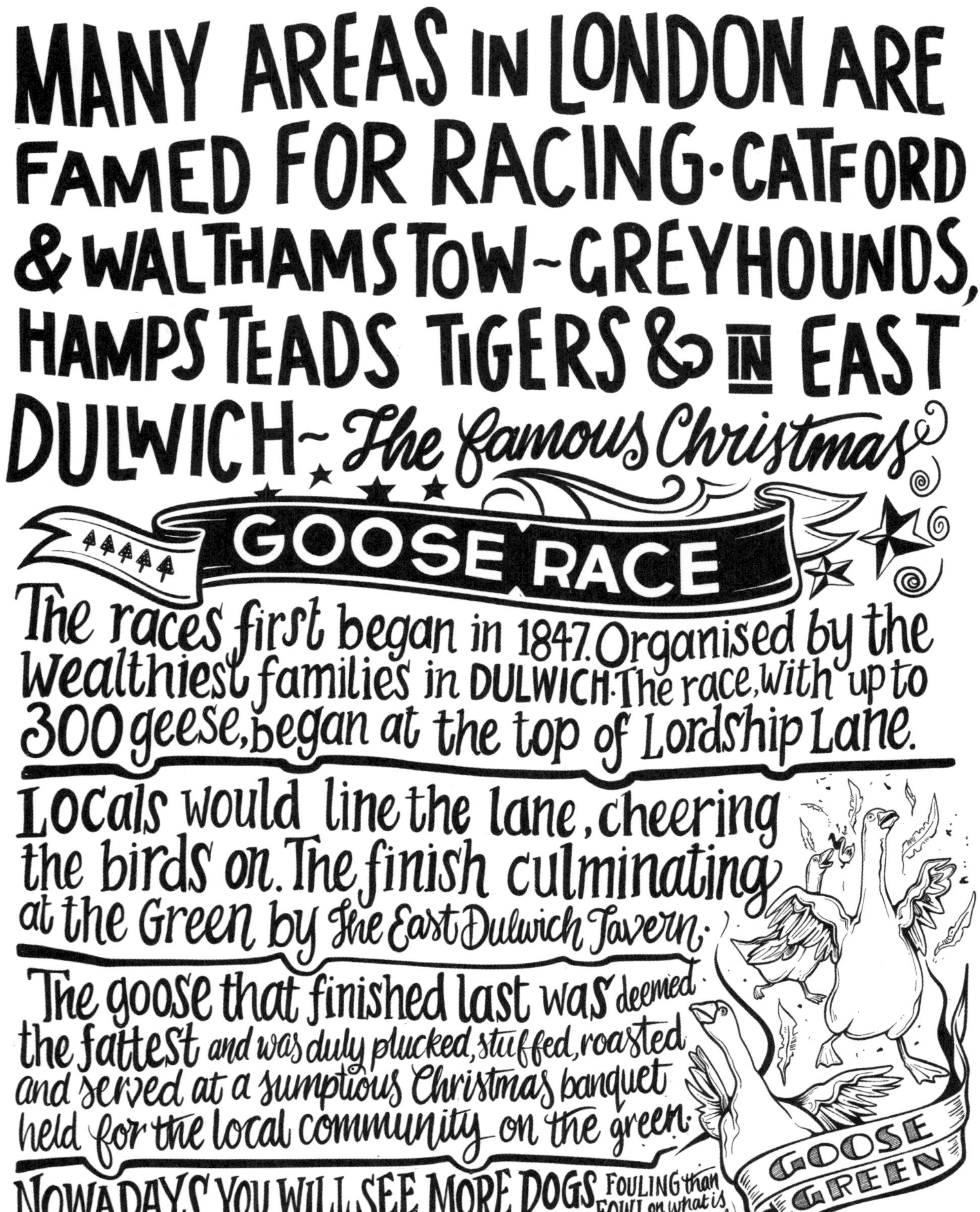
MANY AREAS IN LONDON ARE FAMED FOR RACING · CATFORD & WALTHAMSTOW ~ GREYHOUNDS, HAMPSTEADS TIGERS & IN EAST DULWICH ~ The famous Christmas
GOOSE RACE
The races first began in 1847. Organised by the wealthiest families in DULWICH. The race, with up to 300 geese, began at the top of Lordship Lane.
Locals would line the lane, cheering the birds on. The finish culminating at the Green by The East Dulwich Tavern.
The goose that finished last was deemed the fattest and was duly plucked, stuffed, roasted and served at a sumptious Christmas banquet held for the local community on the green.
NOWADAYS YOU WILL SEE MORE DOGS FOULING than FOWL on what is known as
GOOSE GREEN

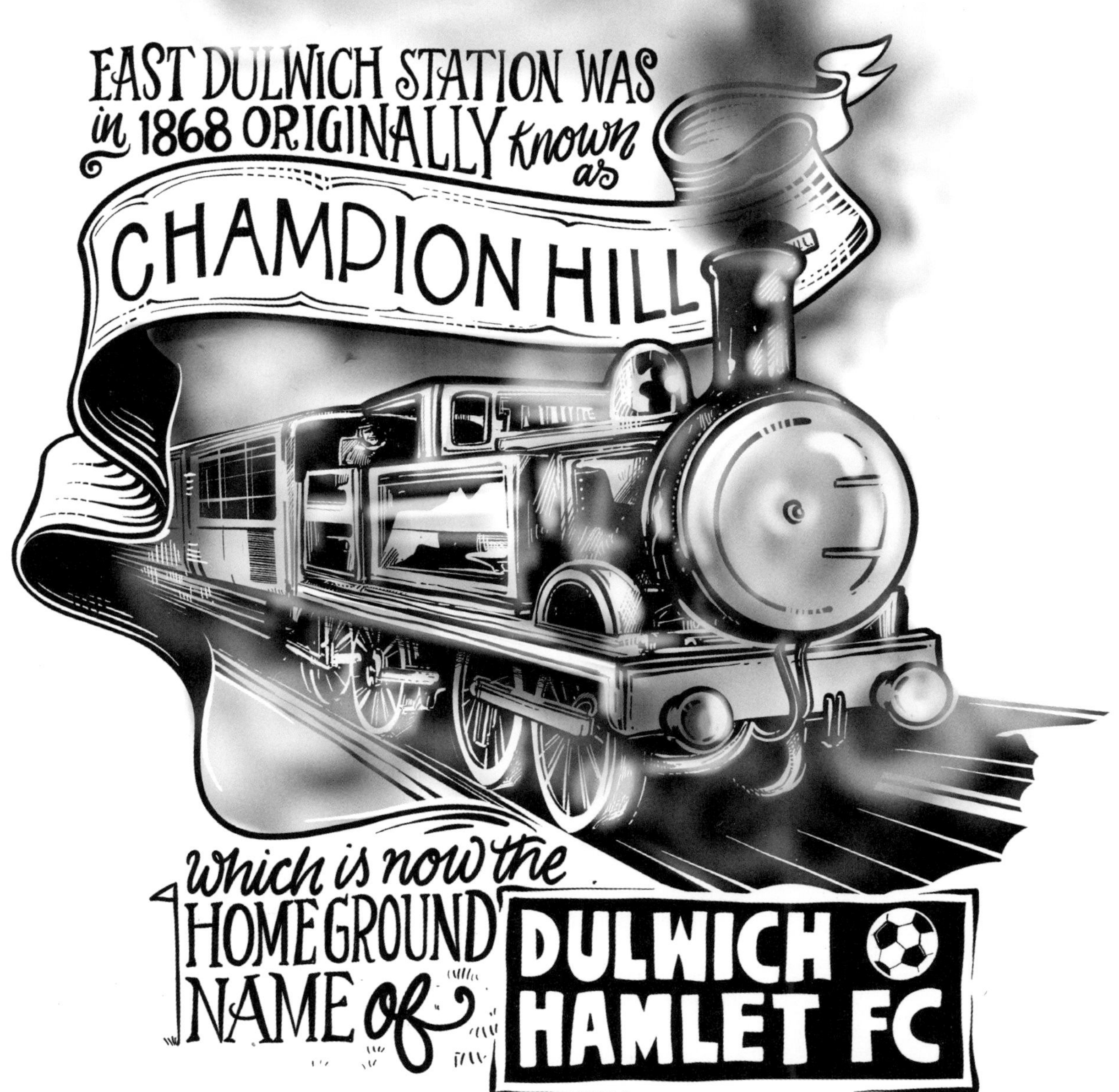
EAST DULWICH STATION WAS
in 1868 ORIGINALLY known as
CHAMPION HILL
which is now the
HOME GROUND NAME of
DULWICH HAMLET FC

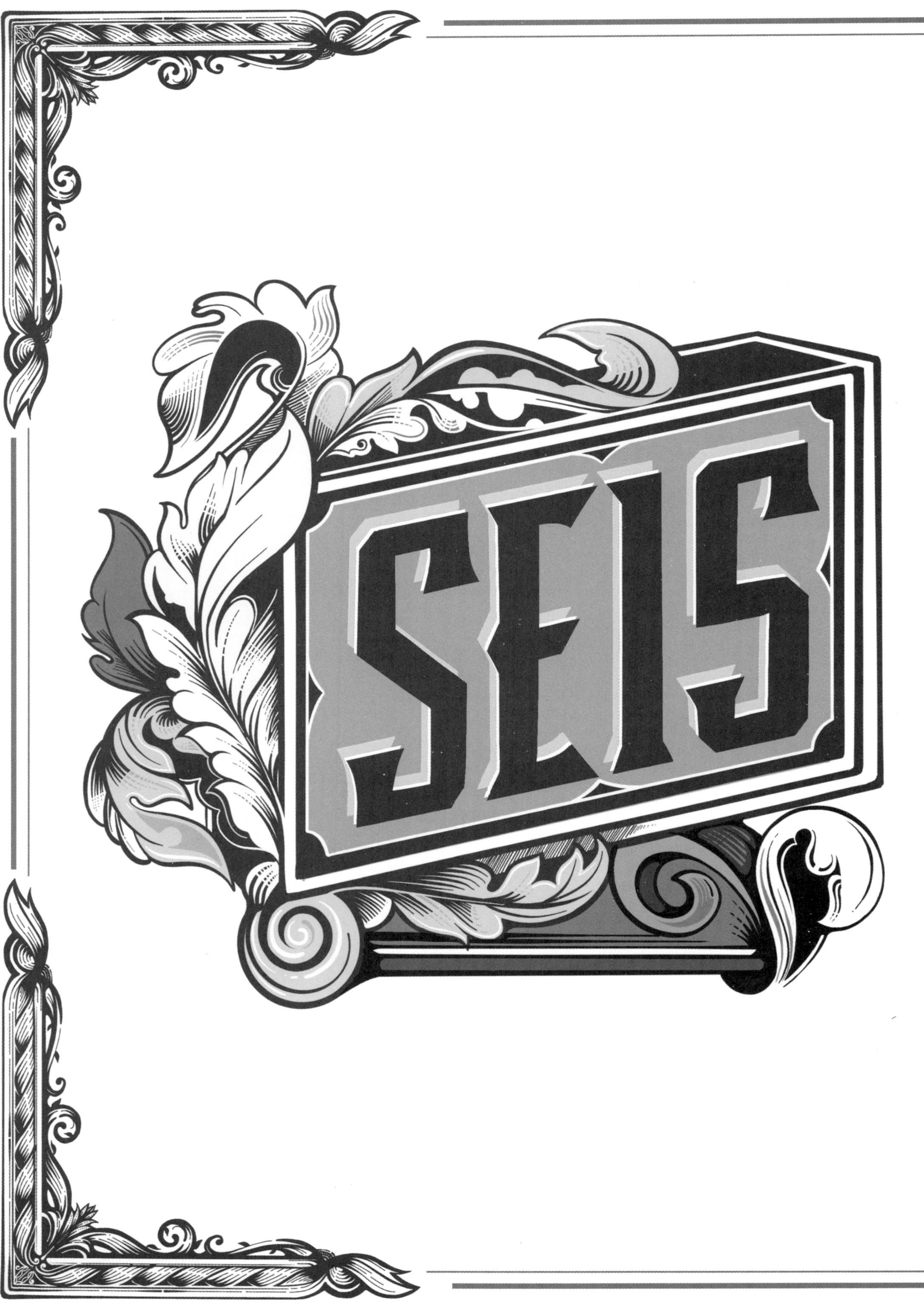
SEIS

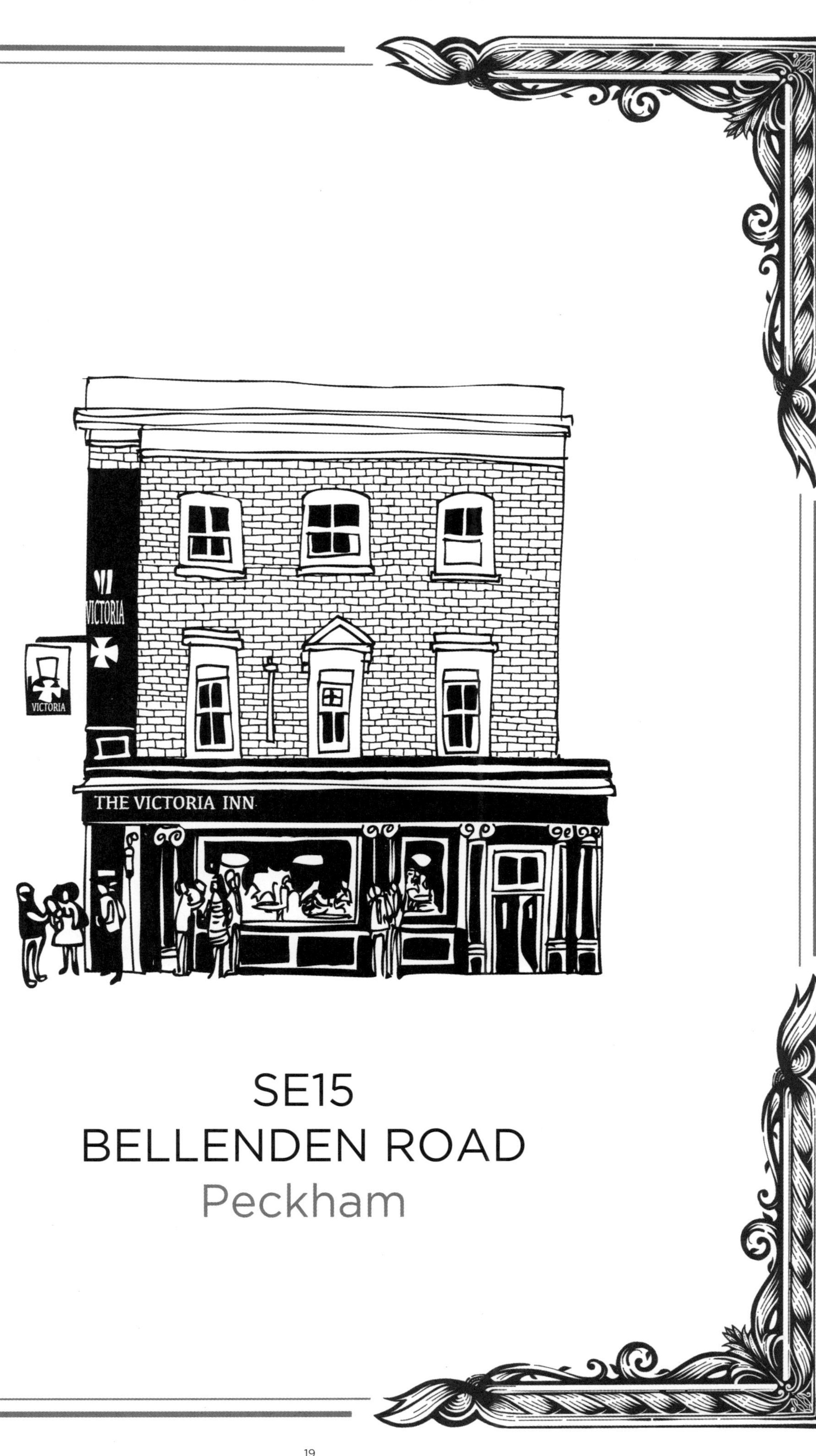

SE15
BELLENDEN ROAD
Peckham

BELLENDEN ROAD

FORMERLY VICTORIA TERRACE, READS THE SIGN, THIS BELLENDEN ROAD, NAMED AFTER A LORD THEY SAY. WITH GORMLEY ADDITIONS & PHILLIPS VENETIAN SMALTI · OF FRENCH HUGUENOTS UPON A TIME · THIS STREET LAY IN THE HEART of THE HAMLET of PECKHAM

AND PECKHAM, ONCE THE ROAM OF STAG HUNTING BY KINGS, OF FIELDS OF VEGETABLES, OF FIG TREES & GRAPEVINES, OF GRANDIOSE MANSIONS & HERDS of CATTLE · ONCE SITED IN THE BOROUGH of SURREY IF YOU PLEASE · IT WAS OF COURTIERS & MERCHANTS · A PLACE TO ENJOY, A RESORT NO LESS, WHERE IT WAS SAID "IT'S ALL HOLIDAY AT PECKHAM" IN THE 1800'S · WHERE TILLINGS FIRST CARRIED PASSENGERS FROM BUSSTOPS, OF BUSSEYS MUSEUM OF FIREARMS, THE WARES OF JONES & HIGGINS ~ & HOLDRON'S DEPT · STORES · KENNEDYS BANGERS & DEANES & ROYALES PERAMBULATORS of CHOICE FOR THE DISCERNING MOTHER THE HOME of CAMPARI BARS, EXPERIMENTS, PEACE WALLS, DUBIOUS AROMAS ON SUMMER DAYS & COLOURFUL CHARACTERS

Oh this thoroughfare shares chocolatiers special coffees & lazy meats, antiquities hearth heaters & printed words.

Where Victoria teases Albert & Monty with her spiced eggs.

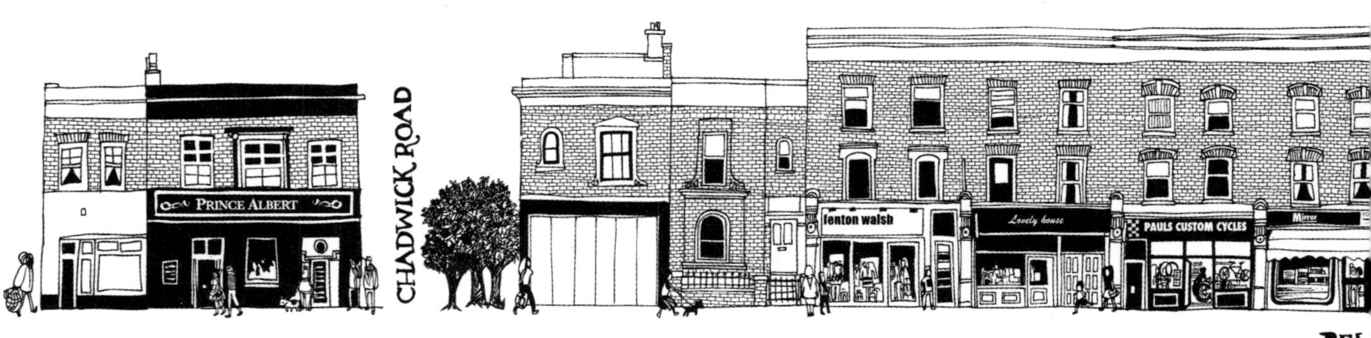

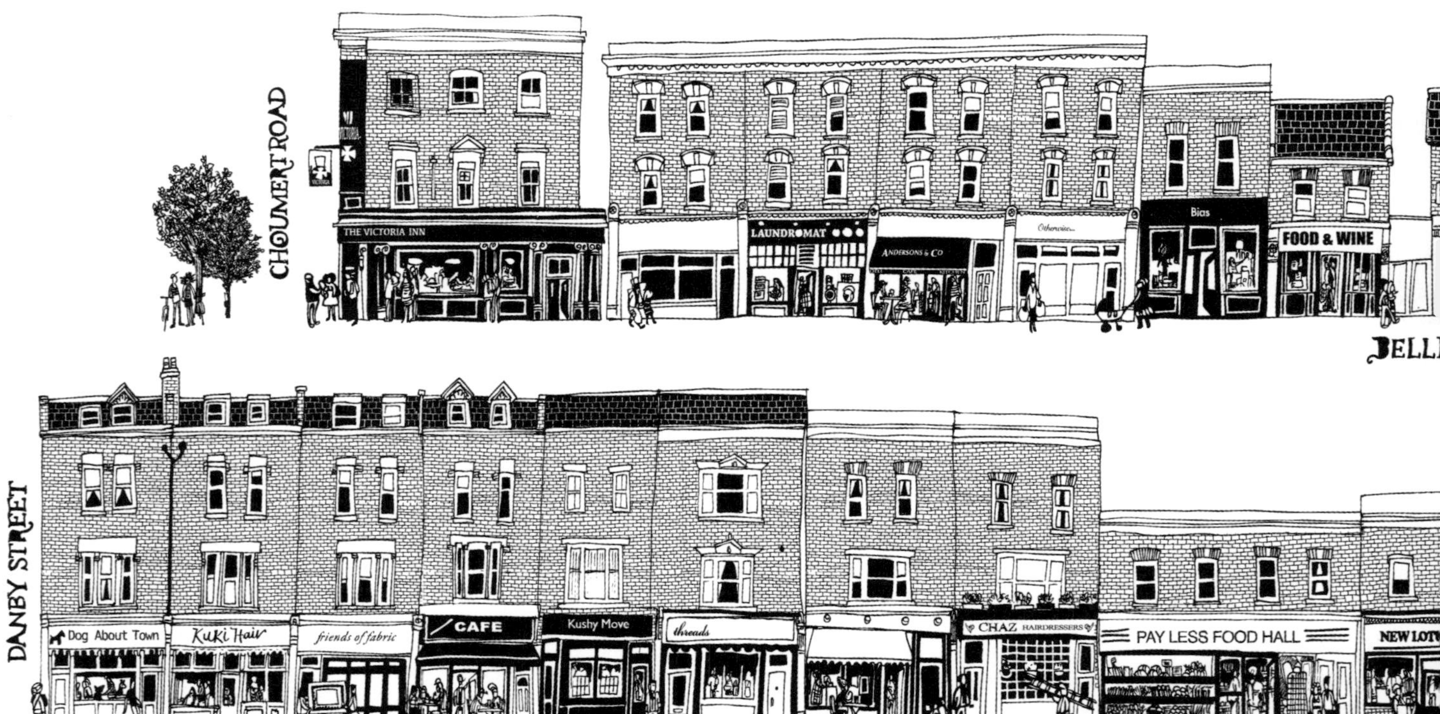

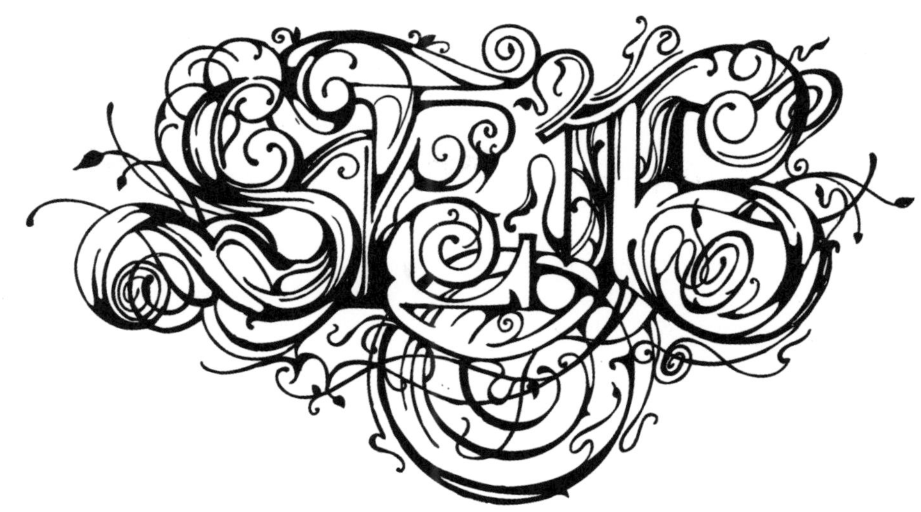

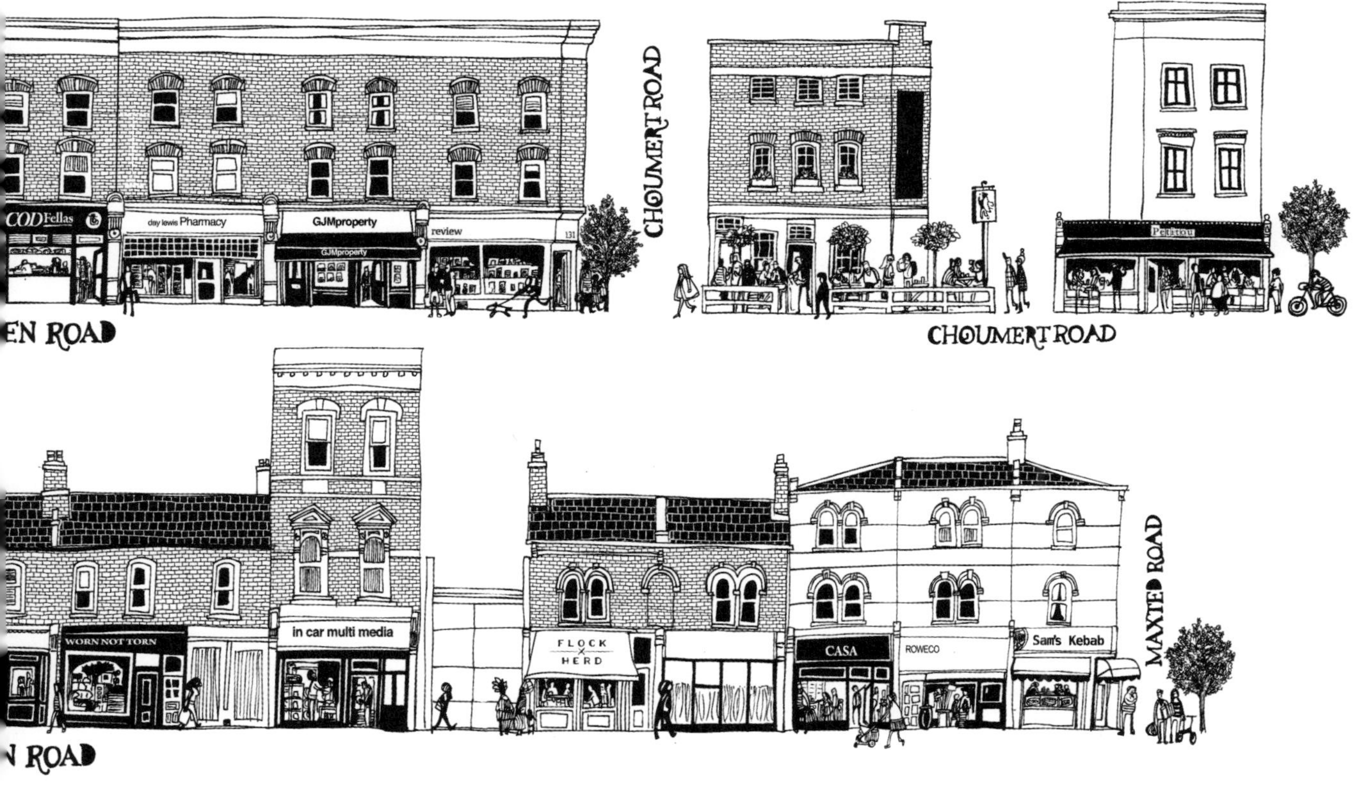
CODFellas
day lewis Pharmacy
GJMproperty
review
CHOUMERT ROAD
EN ROAD
CHOUMERT ROAD
WORN NOT TORN
in car multi media
FLOCK × HERD
CASA
ROWECO
Sam's Kebab
MAXTED ROAD
N ROAD

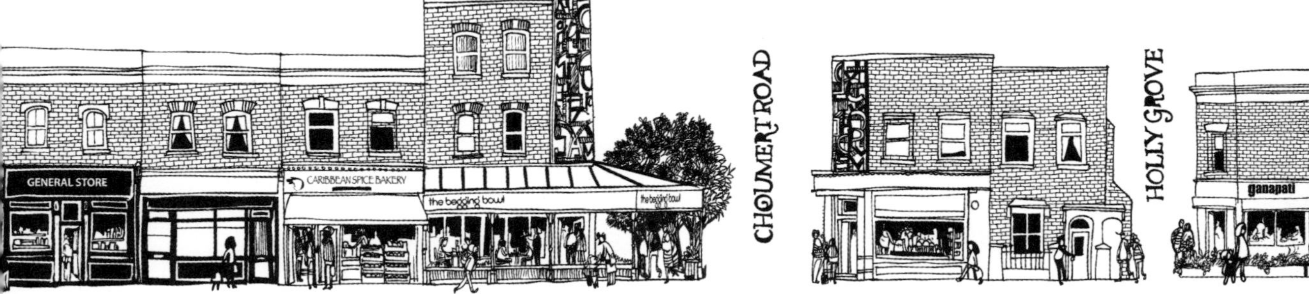
GENERAL STORE
CARIBBEAN SPICE BAKERY
the begging bowl
CHOUMERT ROAD
HOLLY GROVE
ganapati
N ROAD

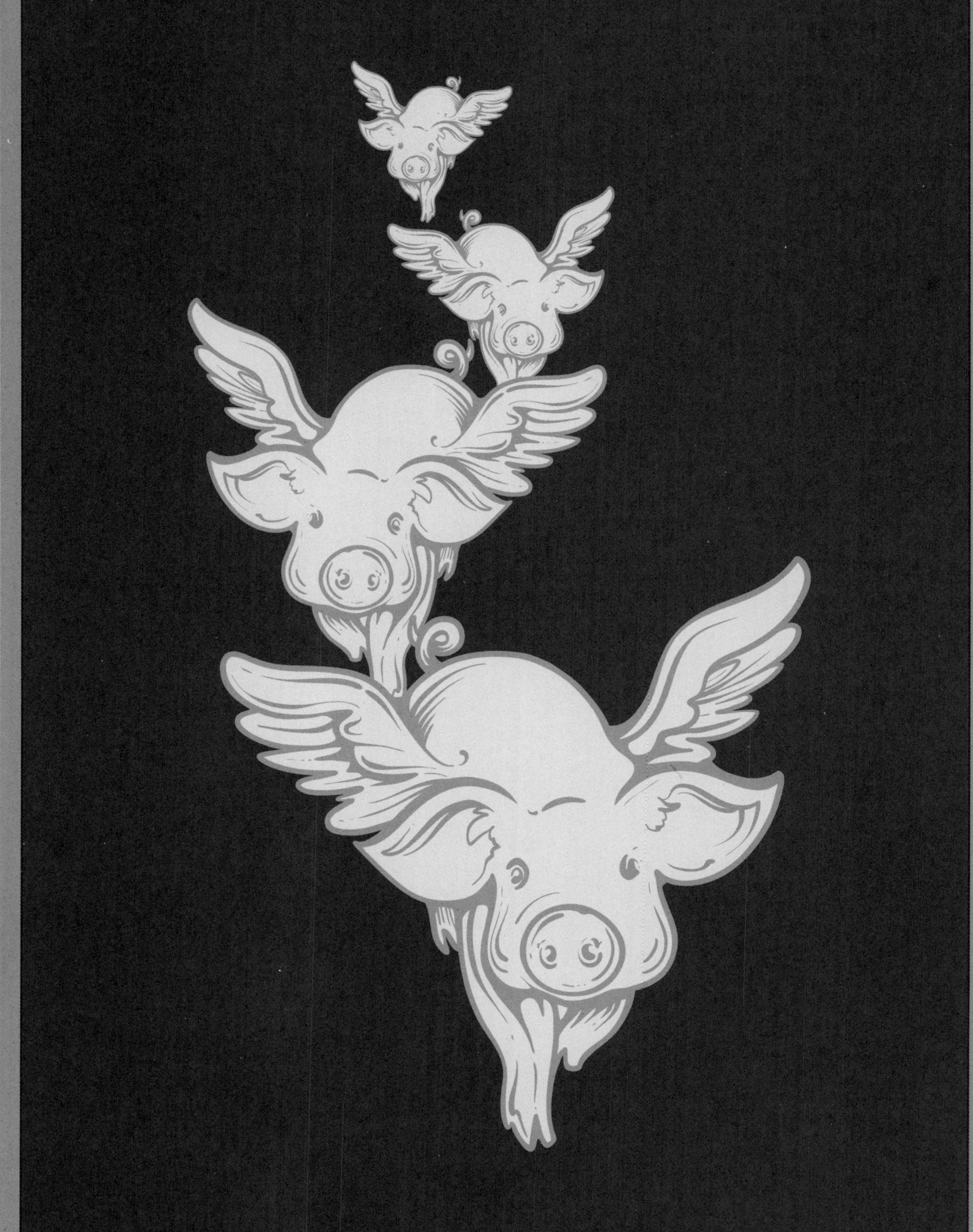

THE NAME PECKHAM WAS DERIVED IN the EARLY 10c WHEN the AREA WAS A PLETHORA of FARMLAND & ORCHARDS. ORANGES, PLUMS & FIGS GREW IN ABUNDANCE DUE TO AN UNDERGROUND GLACIER. A MAJOR PROBLEM WAS FALLING FRUIT, RESEEDING WITHOUT CONTROL. SO PIGS WERE INTRODUCED to GORGE on the ROTTING FRUIT. EATING 24 HOURS A DAY, THE PIGS GREW EXPONENTIALLY, AND WERE KNOWN LOCALLY AS KINGHAMS

ONE YEAR, A HEAVY RAIN FELL, FLOODING MUCH of THE LAND. NATURAL PONDS FORMED, ATTRACTING WILD FOWL. BURGESS PARK POND, THE ONLY SURVIVING to this day BUT FOOD WAS SCARCE & THE BIRDS BECAME VERY HOSTILE TO LOCALS WORKING the FIELDS, EARNING THEM THE TERM 'PECKING FOWLS'. MANY STORIES OF THIS TIME WERE TOLD BY TRAVELLERS WHO TALKED OF THE VILLAGE of PECKS & HAM.

Interestingly the term 'FOUL' was taken from 'PECKING FOWLS' and is used in the game of football to this day

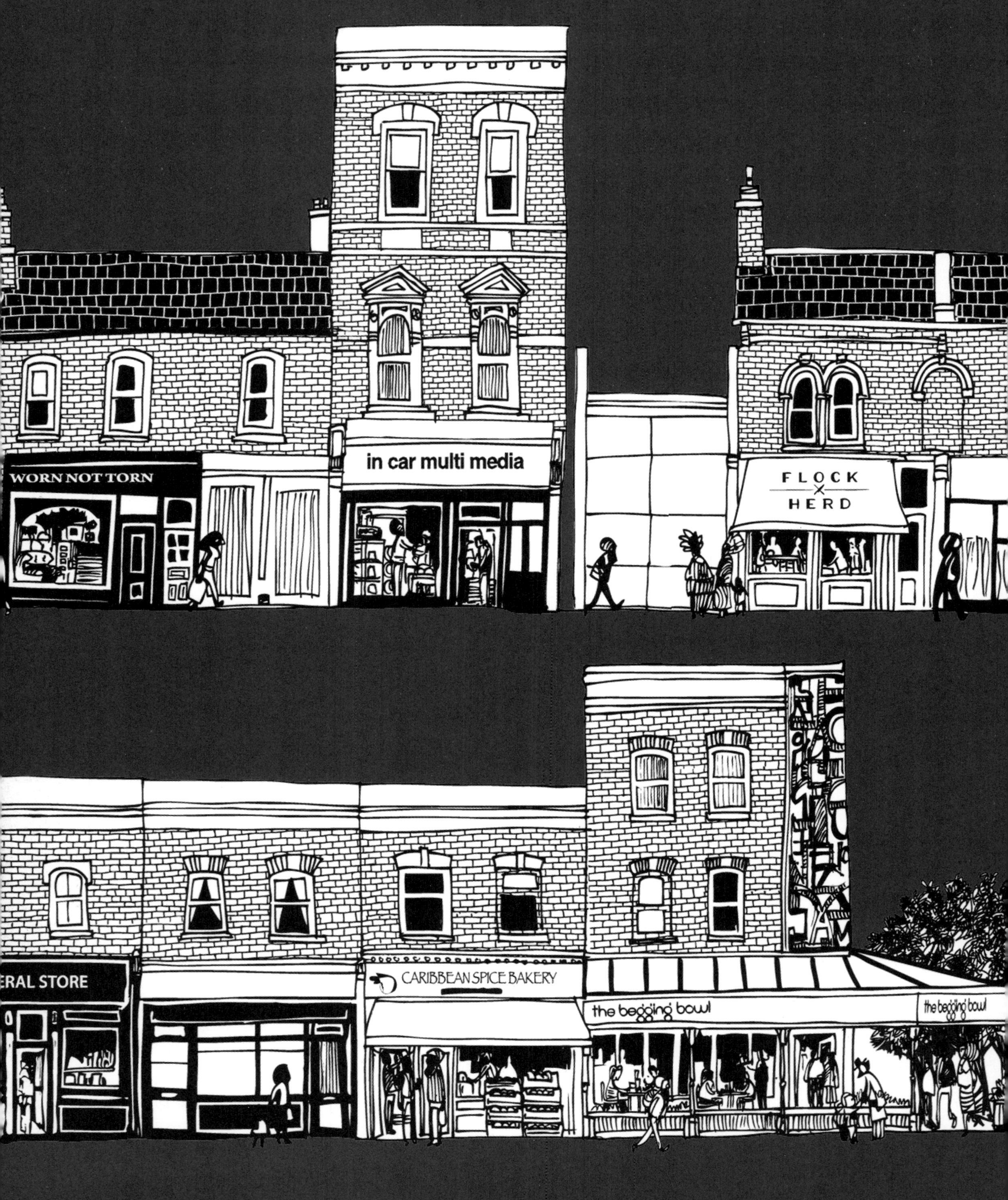
WORN NOT TORN
in car multi media
FLOCK
HERD
ERAL STORE
CARIBBEAN SPICE BAKERY
the begging bowl
the begging bowl

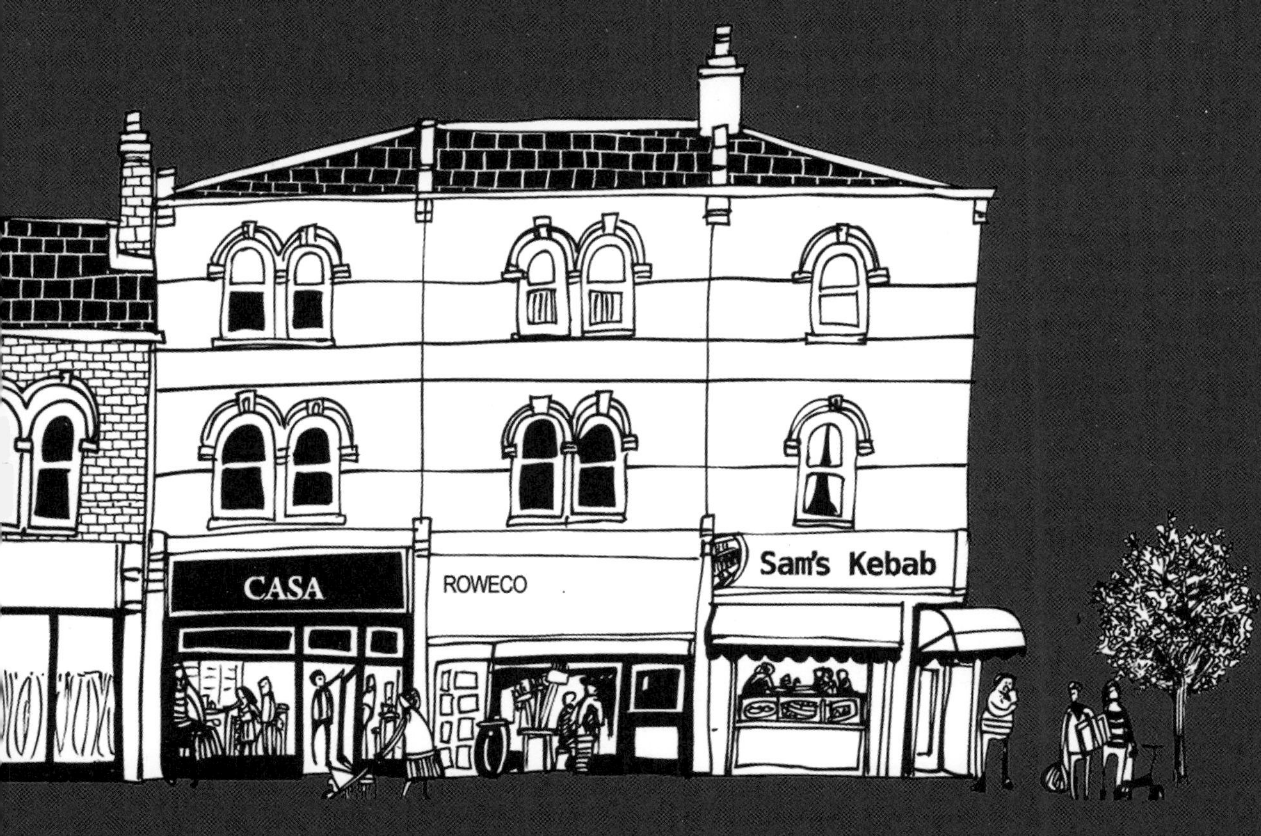
CASA
ROWECO
Sam's Kebab

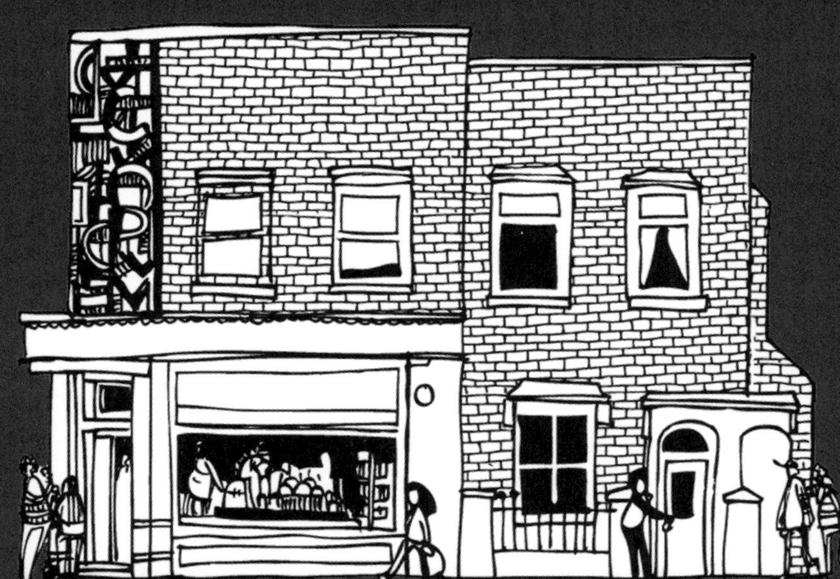

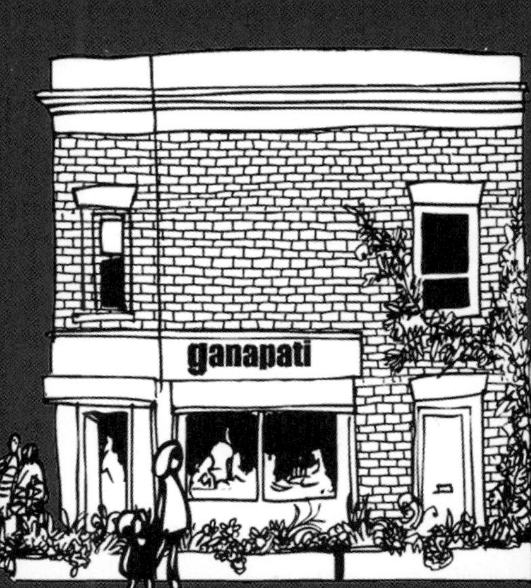
ganapati

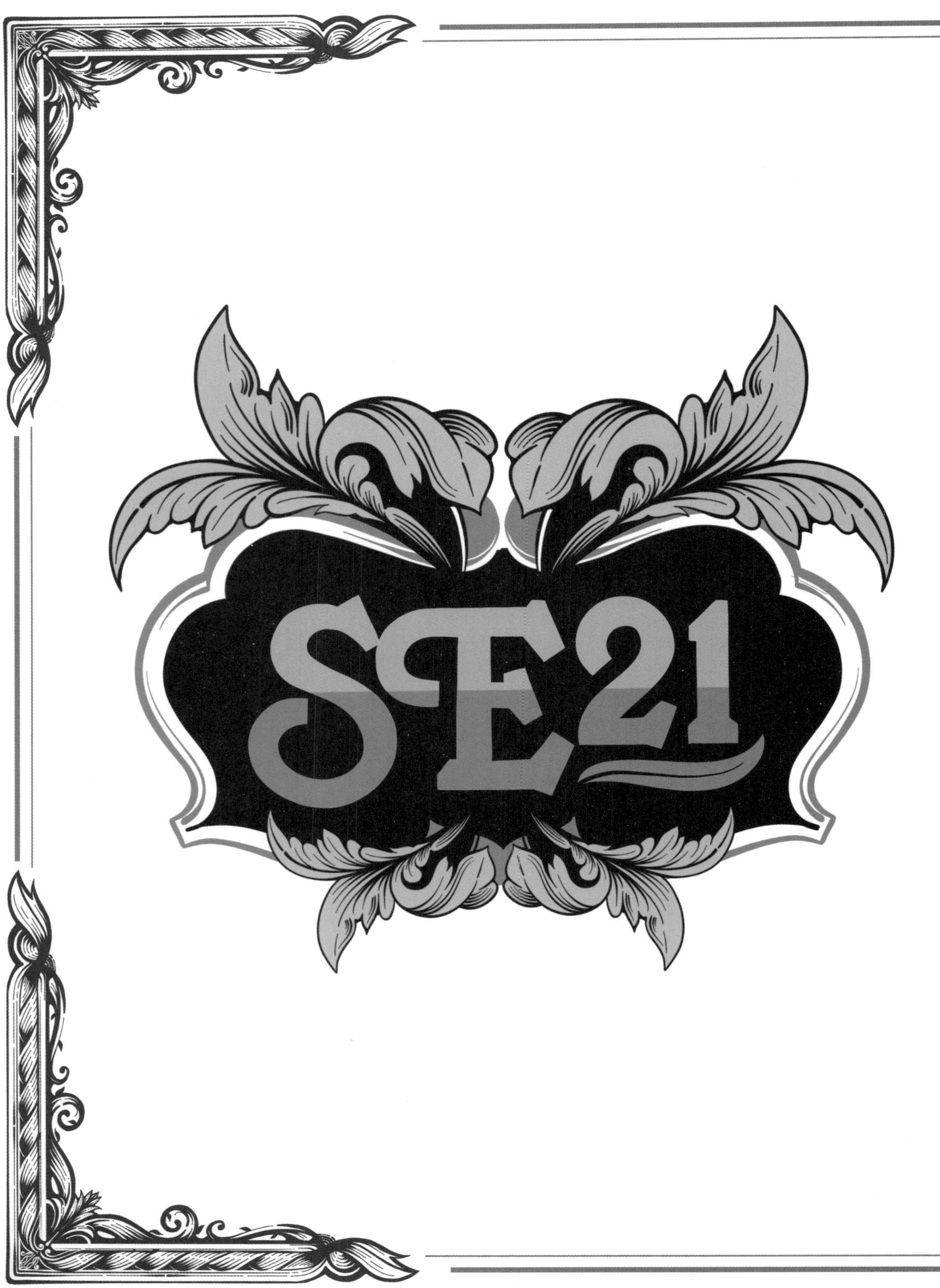
SE21

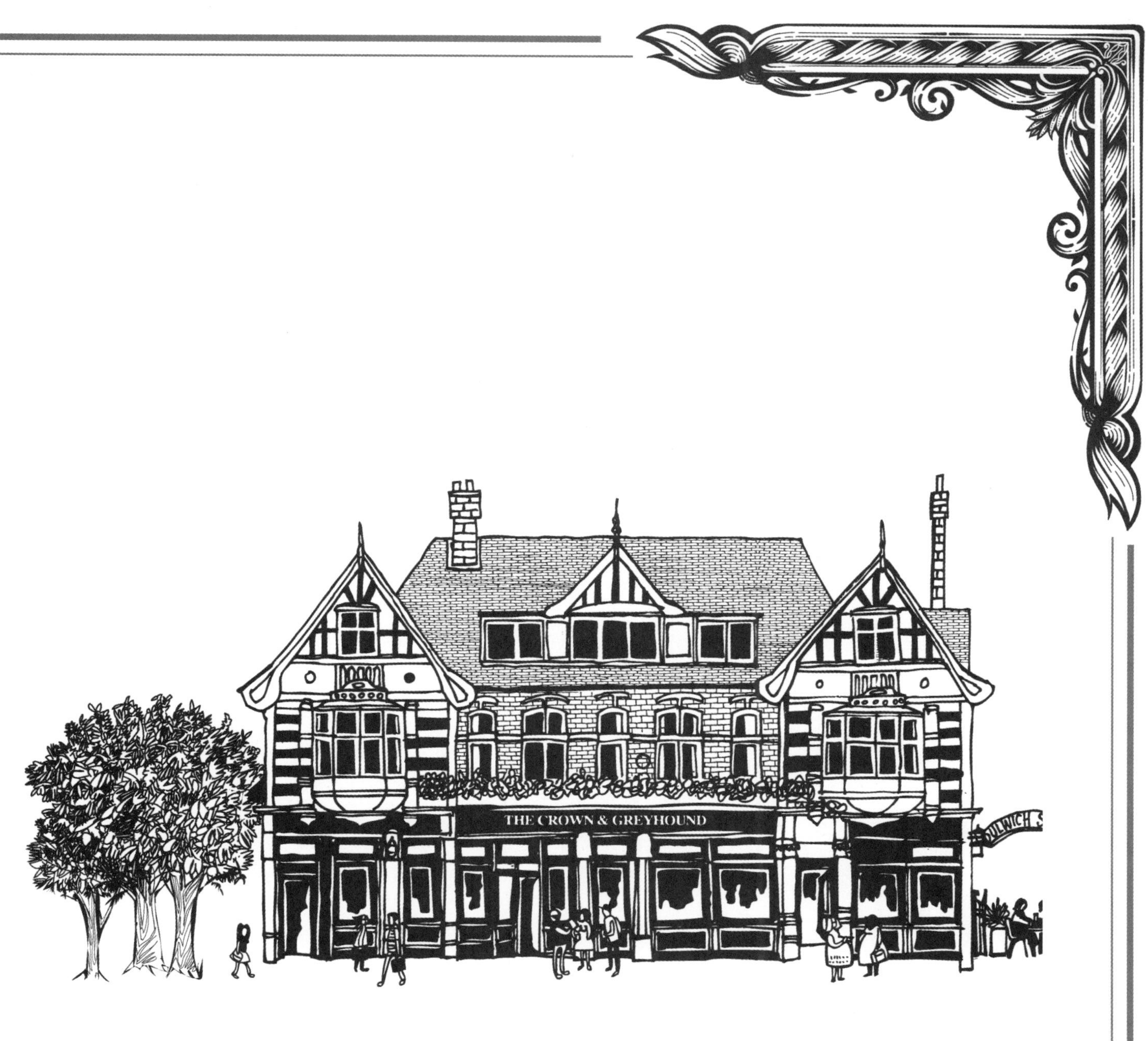

SE21
DULWICH VILLAGE
Dulwich

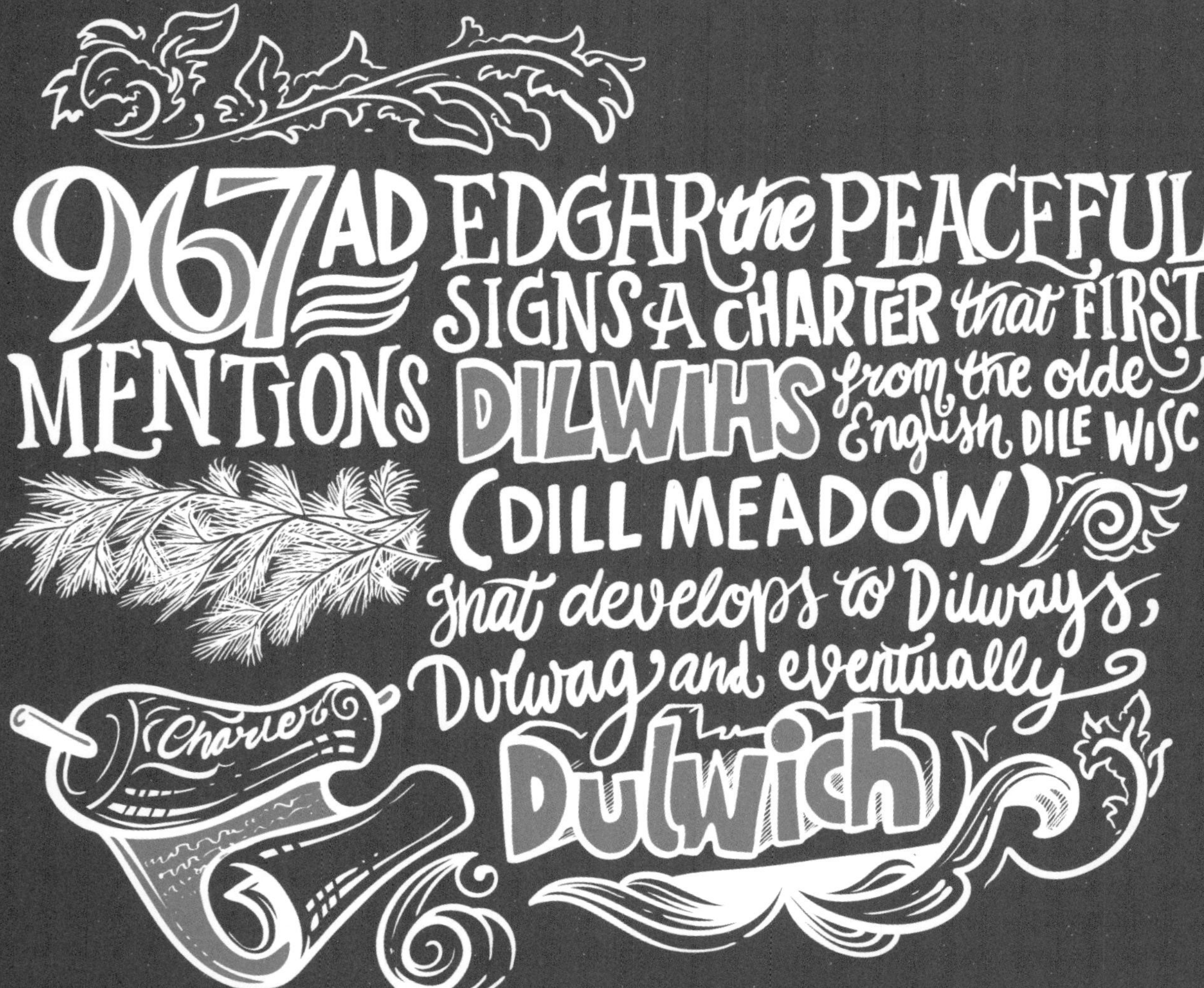
967 AD EDGAR the PEACEFUL
SIGNS A CHARTER that FIRST
MENTIONS DILWIHS from the olde
English DILE WISC
(DILL MEADOW)
that develops to Dilways,
Dulwag and eventually
Dulwich
Charter

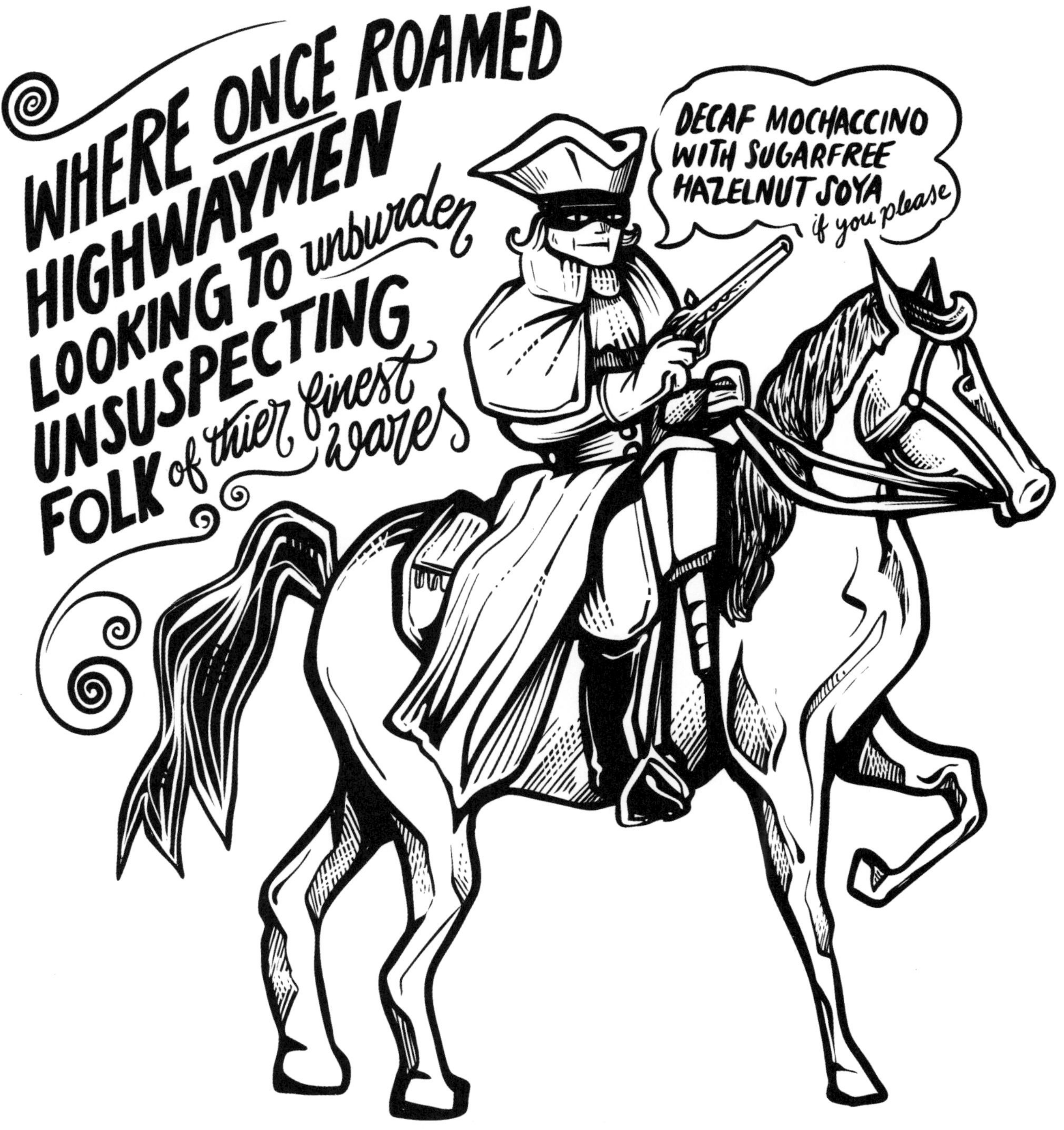
WHERE ONCE ROAMED
HIGHWAYMEN
LOOKING TO unburden
UNSUSPECTING
FOLK of thier finest wares
DECAF MOCHACCINO
WITH SUGARFREE
HAZELNUT SOYA
if you please

'HONES' ONCE DESCRIBED "AS THE PRETTIEST OF ALL THE VILLAGE ENTRANCES IN THE ENVIRONS OF LONDON"

DULWICH VILLAGE

ONCE KNOWN AS DILWIHS, DILWAYS, DULWAG & NOW DULWICH, HOME OF THE ONCE FAMOUS DULWICH WELLS, REPUTED, IT IS SAID, TO BE POSSESSED OF PURGATIVE QUALITIES, WHERE FASHIONABLE PERSONS WOULD RESORT, FOR THE PURPOSE OF 'TAKING THE WATERS'.

THE BEAUTY OF DULWICH SPREAD OUT IN GROVES & PLEASURE GROUNDS, GREEN LANES & FLOWERY MEADOWS. WHERE ONCE STOOD A WOOD THAT HID GIPSIES & HIGHWAYMEN, WHERE BYRON ONCE PLAYED AND CHARLES 1 HUNTED WHERE DULWICHIANS SIP LATTES, TILT GUCCIS & PARADE HANDBAGS

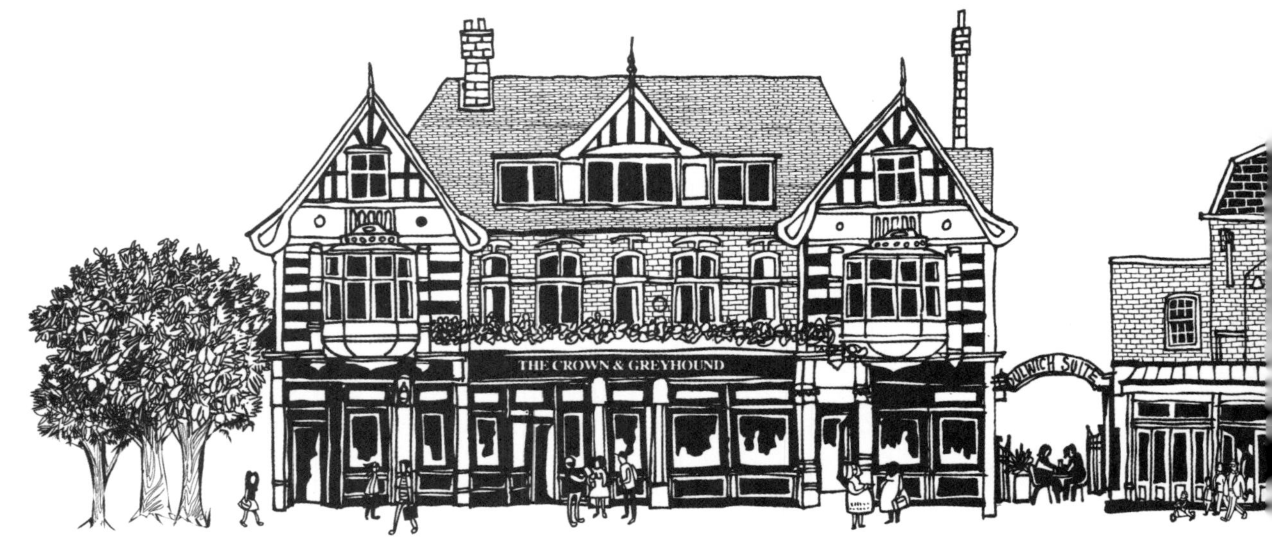

DULWICH VILLAGE

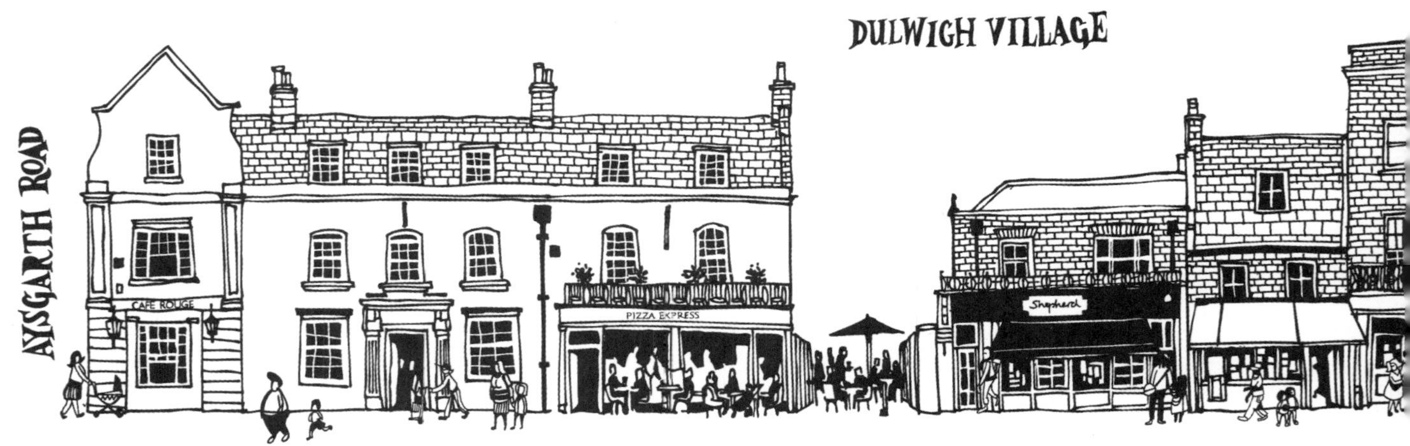

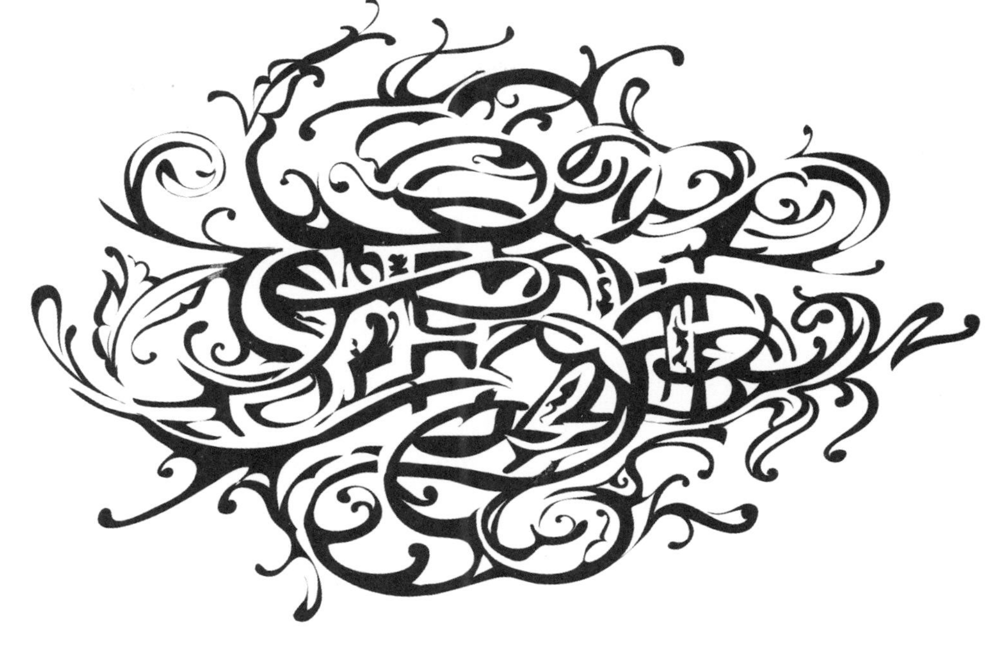

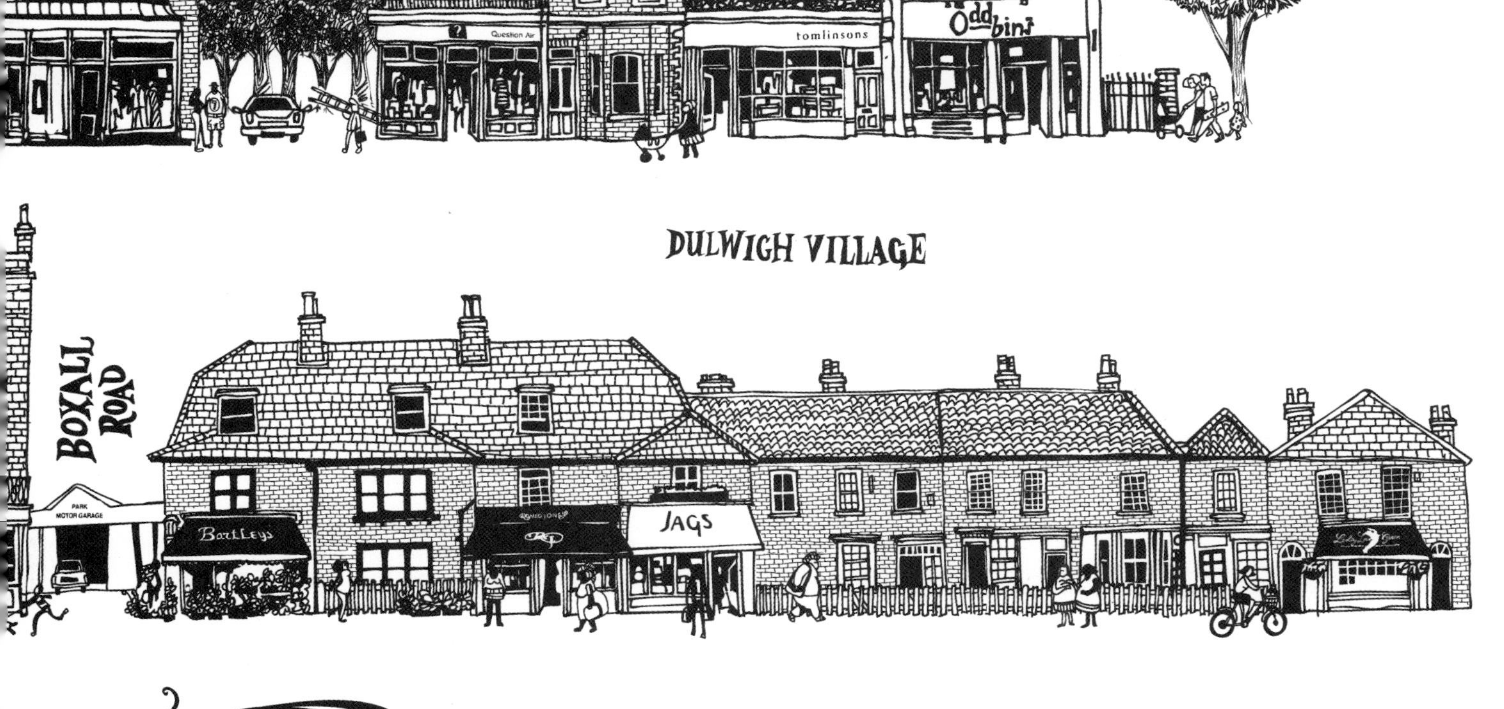

Question Air
tomlinsons
Oddbins
DULWICH VILLAGE
BOXALL ROAD
PARK MOTOR GARAGE
Bartleys
JAGS

WICH

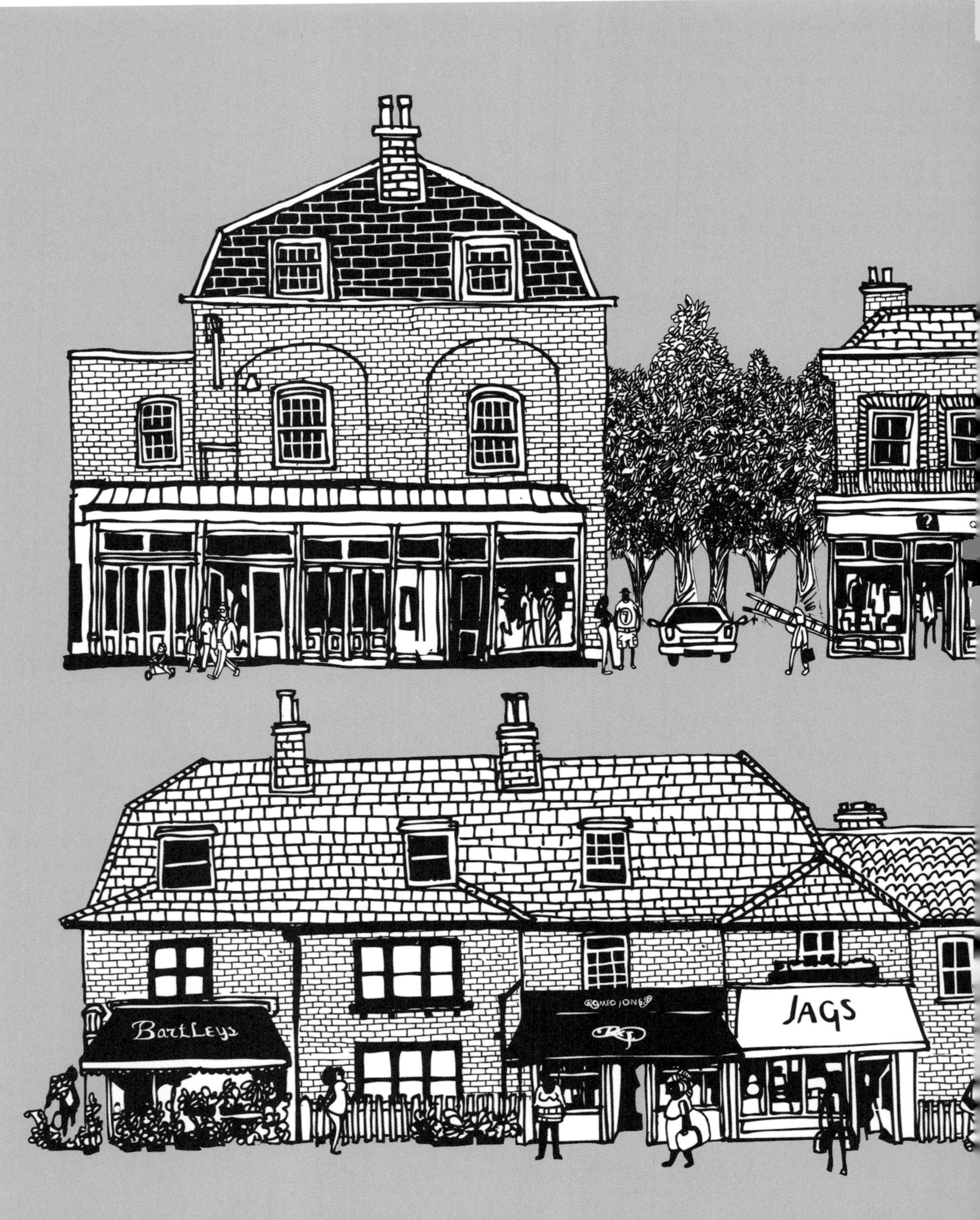
BartLeys
ROMEO JONES
JAGS

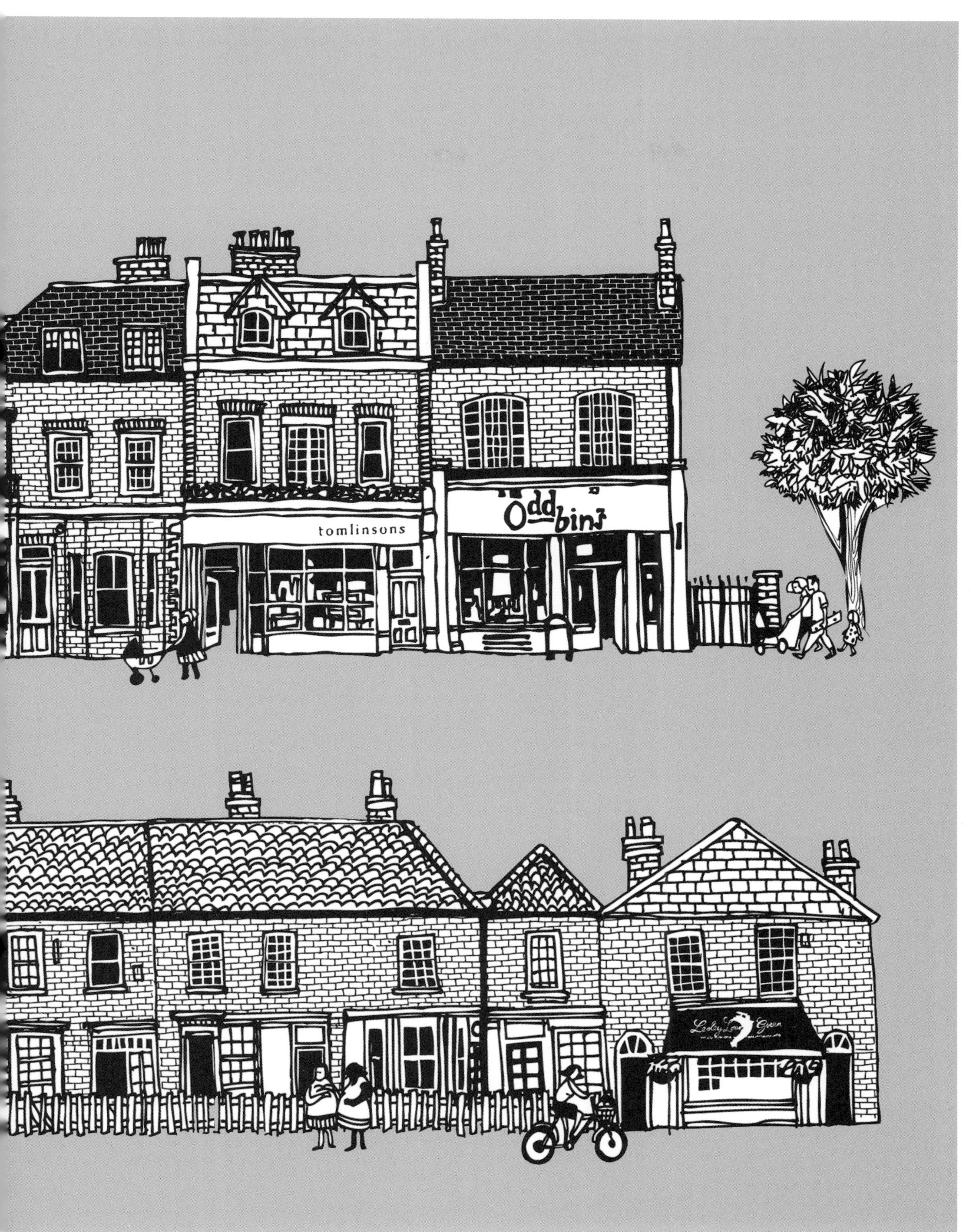
tomlinsons
Oddbins

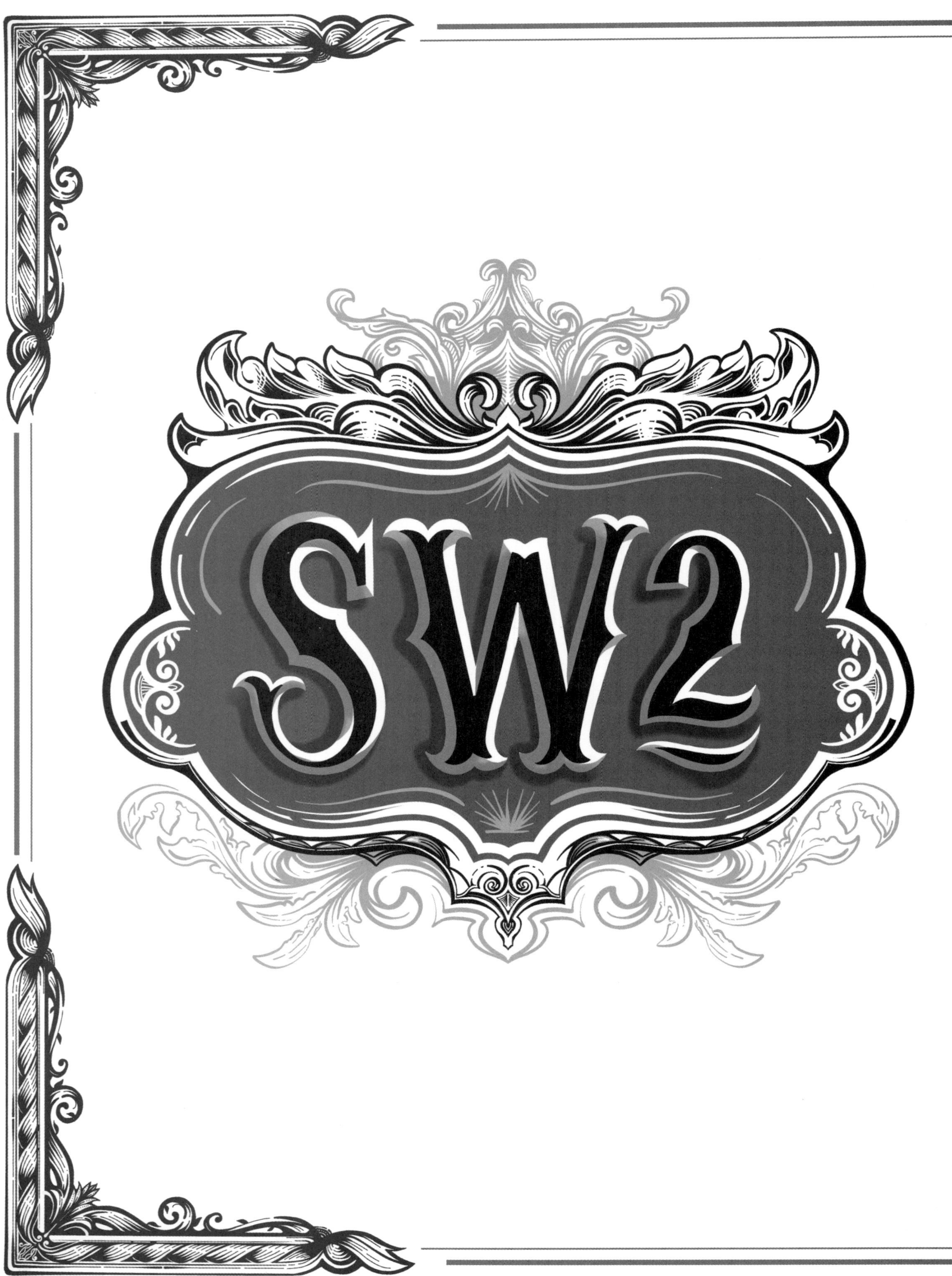
SW2

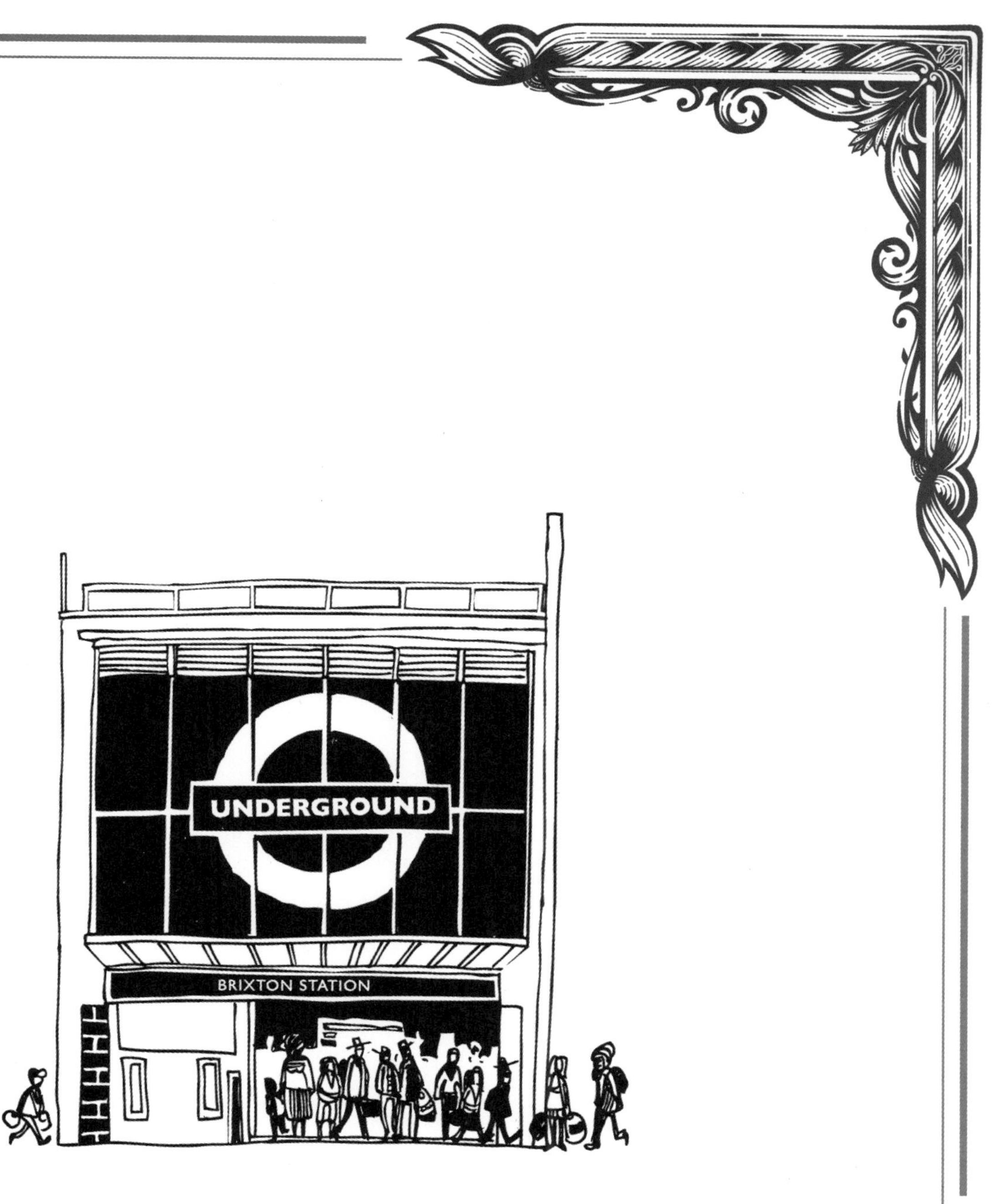

SW2
BRIXTON
Brixton

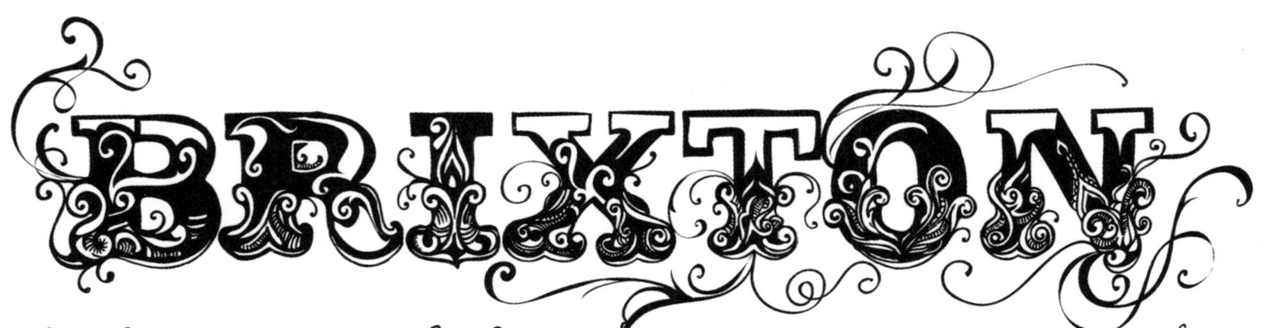

BRIXTON

BRIXTON, OR WAS ONCE BRIXISTANCE, ONCE A MULTITUDE of LONDONS FINEST THEATRES, THE FAMED BRIXTON THEATRE, *EMPRESS* & **PALLADIUM** *(home of the Fridge.)* WHERE GOLD MINER & STOCKS GAMBLER MONTAGU PYKE WAS KNOWN AS THE CINEMA KING.

This Brixton, homeplace of the cream of vaudeville, actors, acrobats & singers. Where Electric Avenue was first lit up & ornate iron canopies floated above exclusive outlets as well-heeled fashionistas sought the latest wears. Where Walton & Co proudly boasted hosiery & hats replaced by cardboard beef & dubious shakes.

FROM SUN TO FOG, THE WINDRUSH DROPPED NEW RESIDENTS, CULTURES & FLAVOURS. ACKEE, PIGEON PEAS, PLANTAIN, SALTFISH & CALLALOO SITS NEXT TO SLICED WHITE, CORNED BEEF & MASHED TATTIES. POLITE & MILD GETS HOT & WILD. B BOYS, FLYGIRLS, KRUMPERS & HUMPERS MIX WITH INDIES OUTSIDERS, CHANCERS & PRANCERS. WHERE PRADAMARK & BLING ARE KING, ATTITUDE & FLAIR RING LARGE LIKE A GIANT CUBIC ZIRCONIA ~ LET THE TUNAGE PLAY ON.

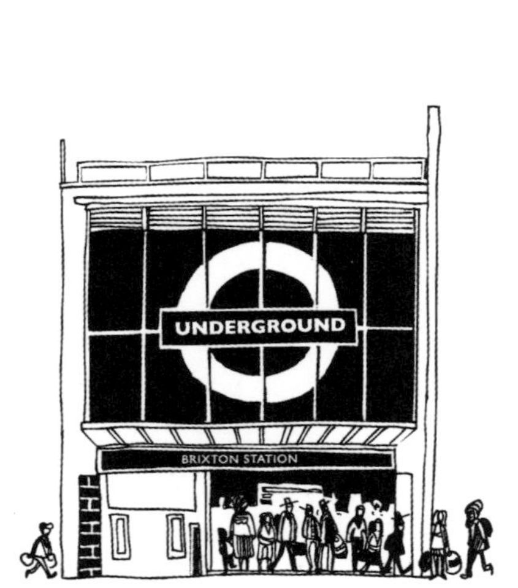

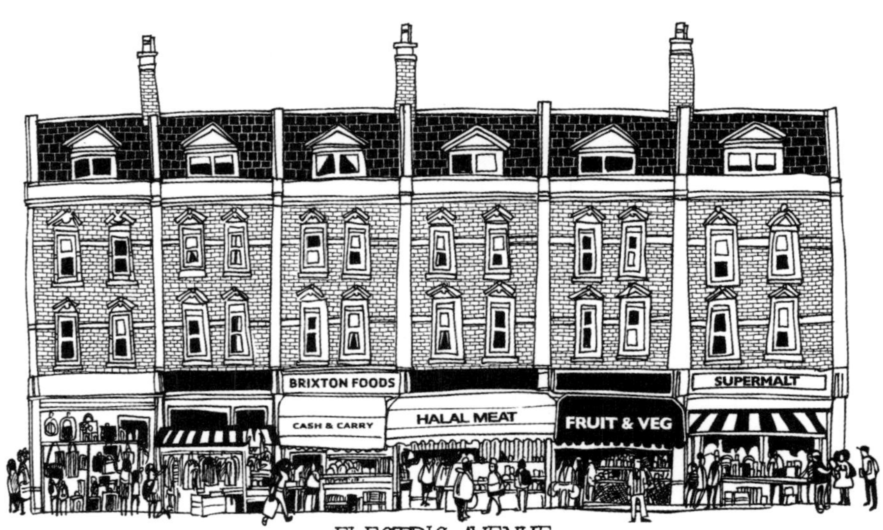

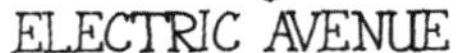
ELECTRIC AVENUE

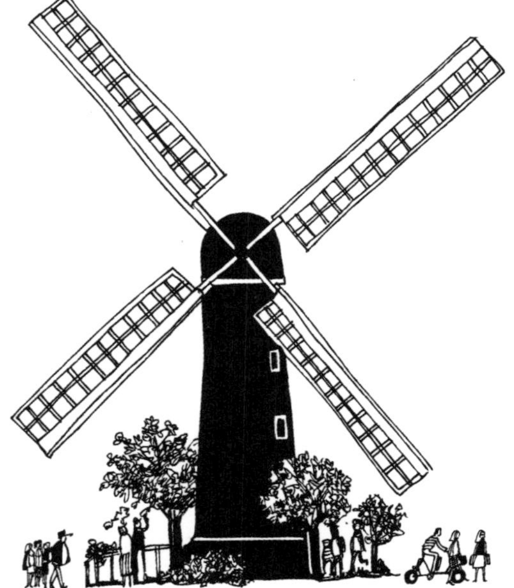

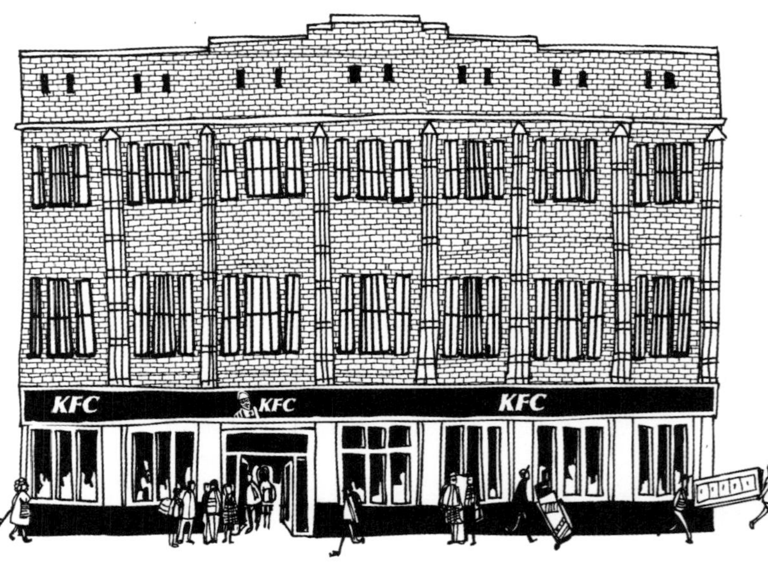

Where Electric Avenue first lit up th

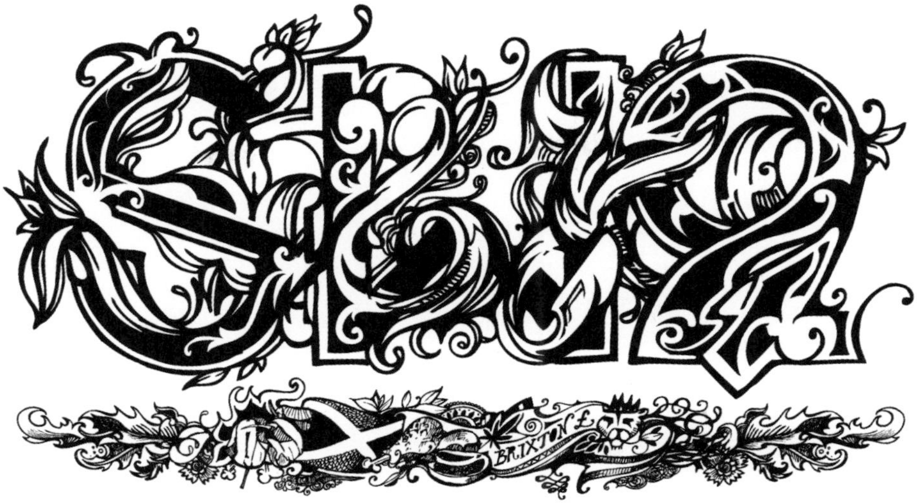

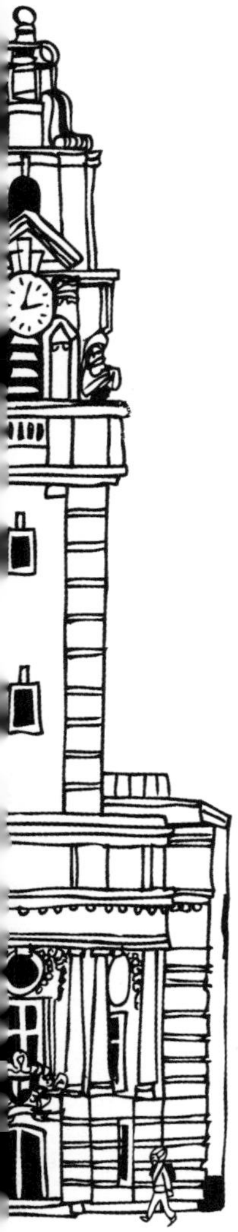

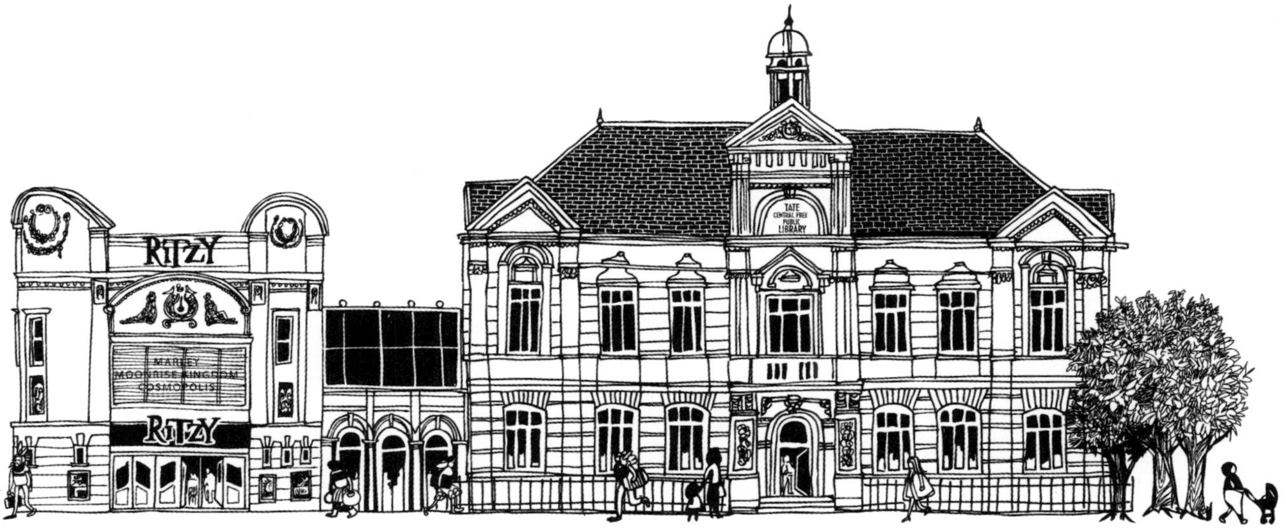

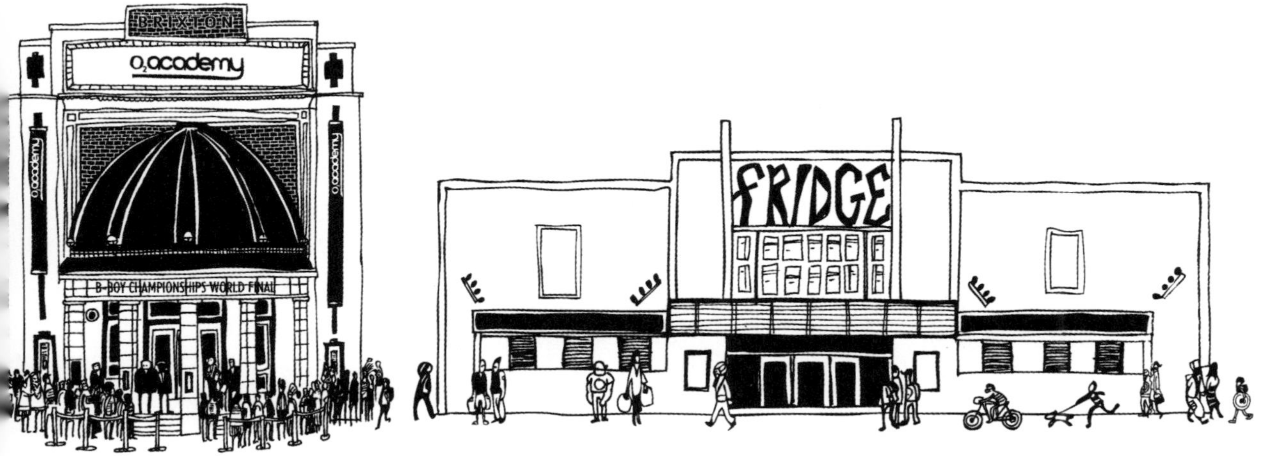

ls of a million shopkeepers to come

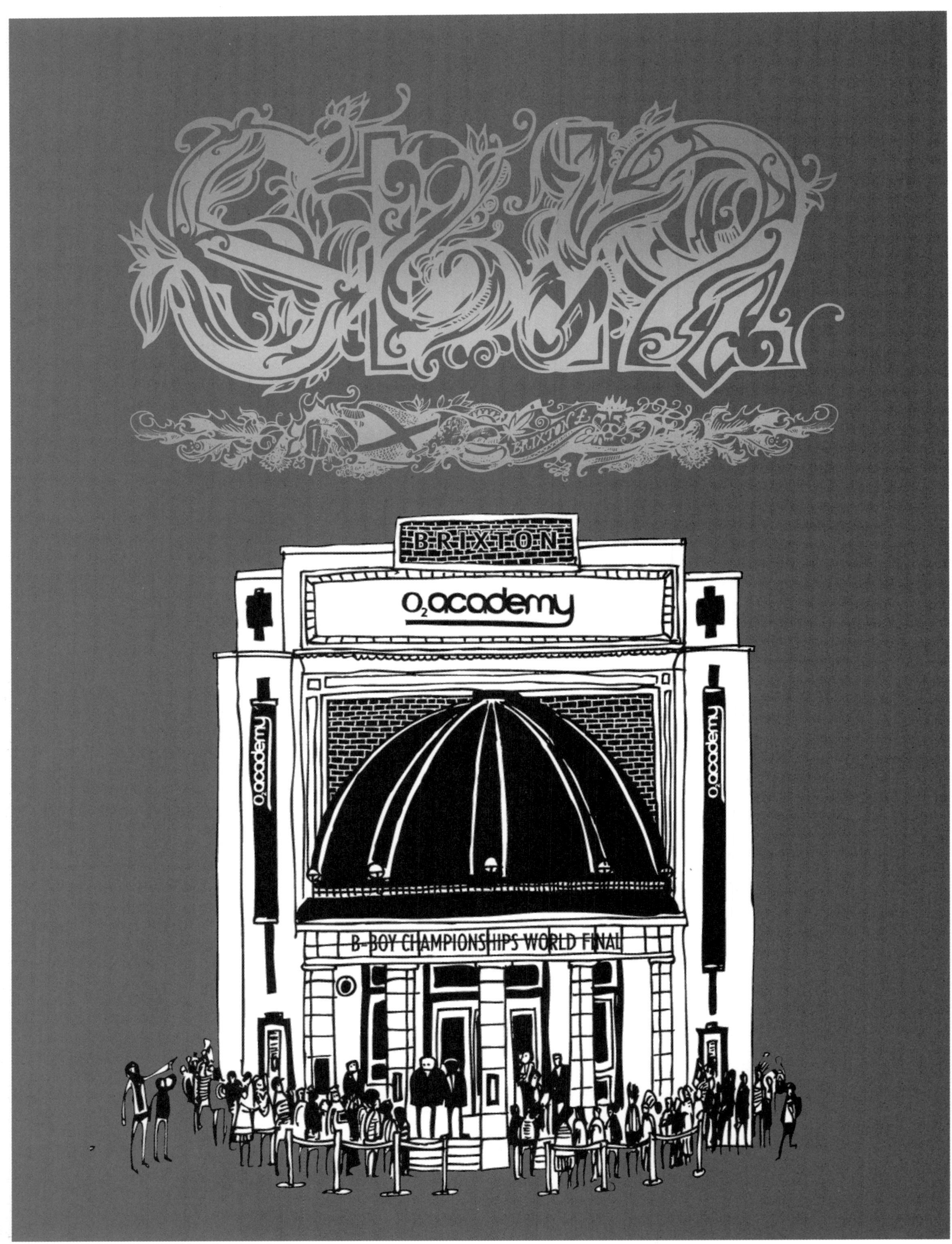
BRIXTON
O2 academy
B-BOY CHAMPIONSHIPS WORLD FINAL

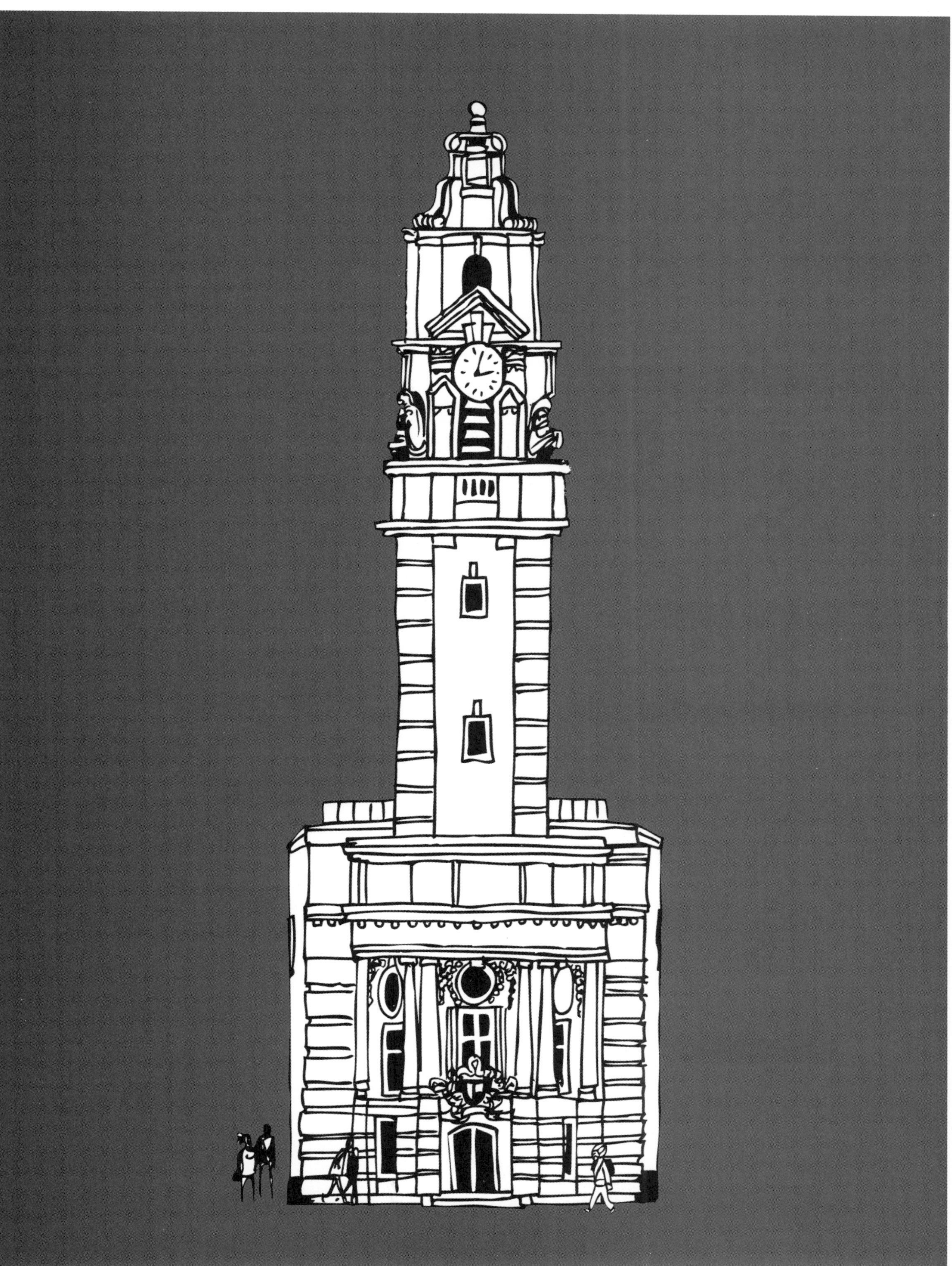

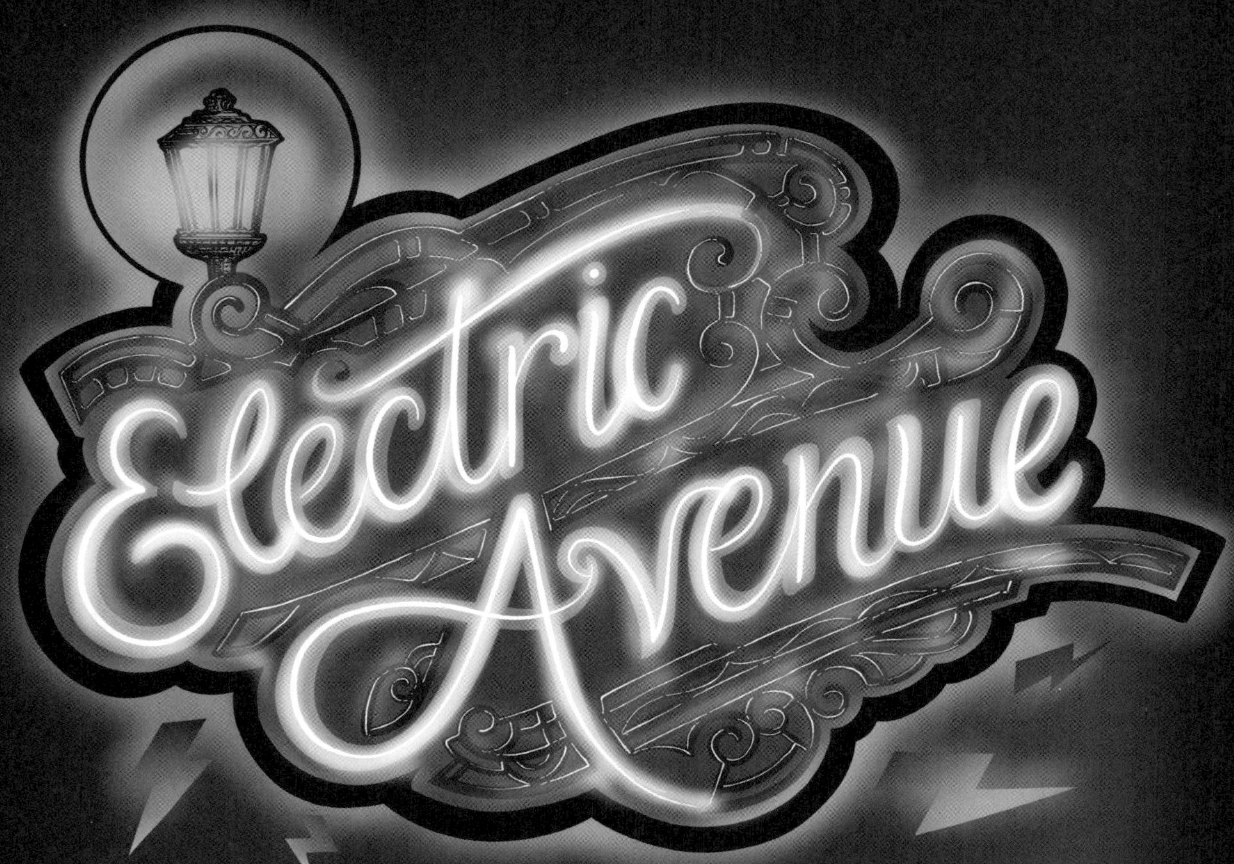

KNOWN TO BE *the* FIRST MARKET
STREET *in* THE UK *to* HAVE *electric*
street lights. ELECTRIC AVENUE
WAS ONCE SEEN AS The OXFORD STREET OF THE SOUTH
DURING THE 1800's. THE FASHIONABLE
WOULD SHOP UNDER SWEEPING IRON
and GLASS CANOPIES THAT ONCE RAN
THE LENGTH *of the* STREET.

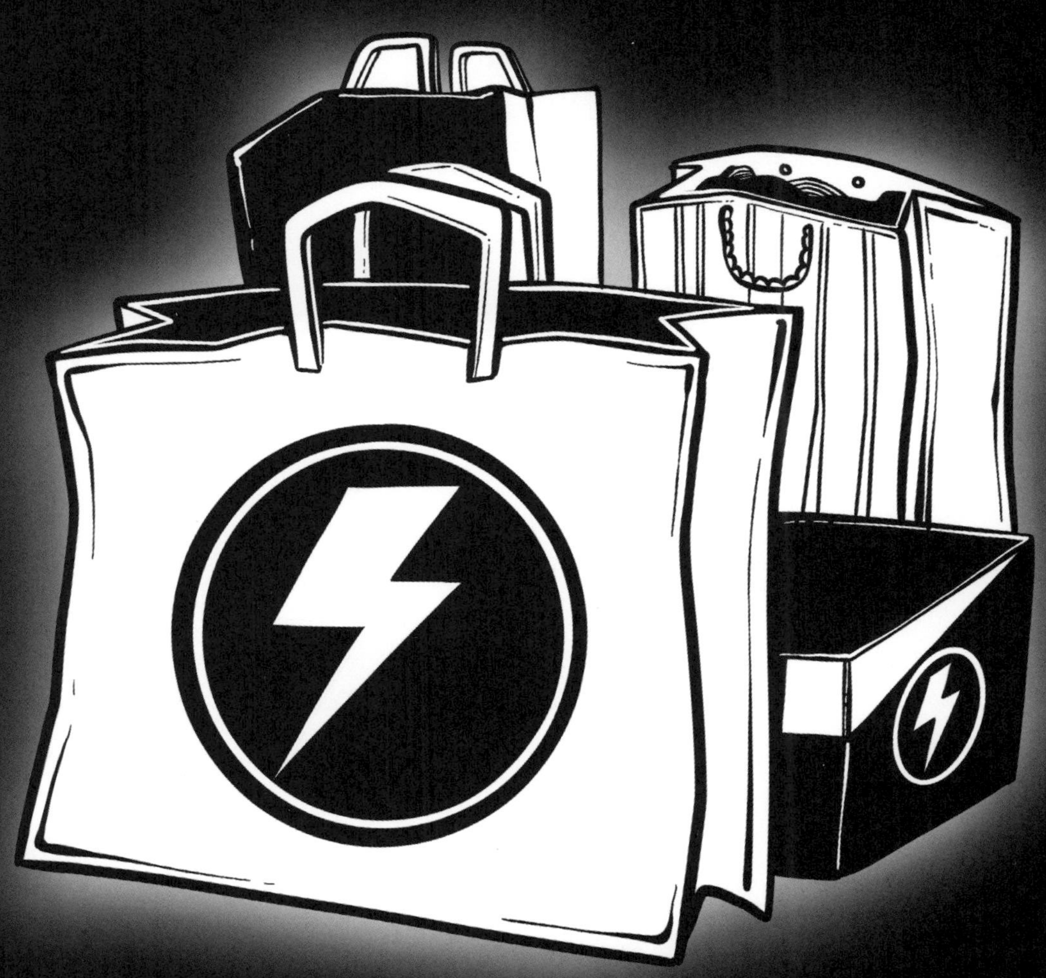

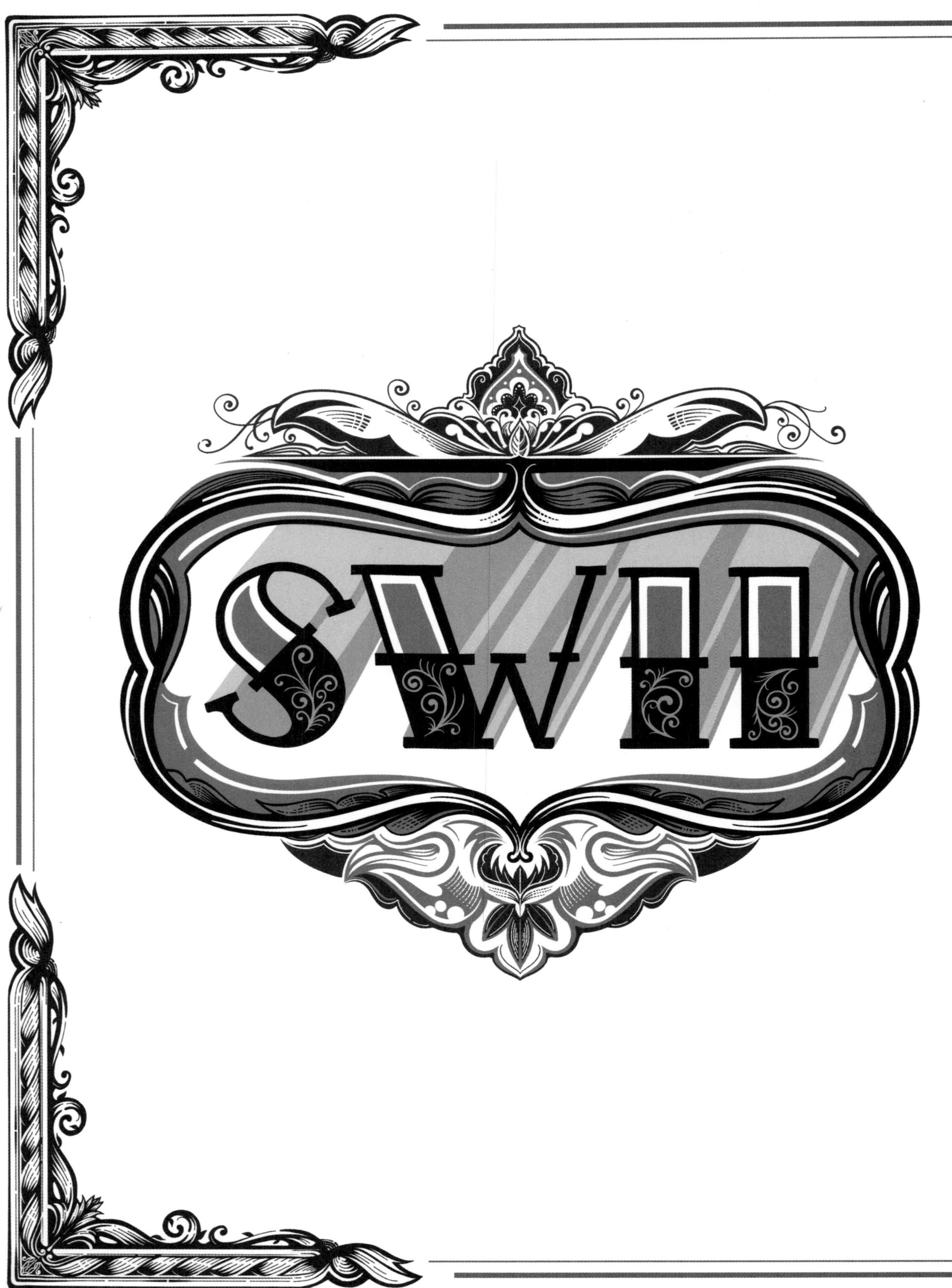

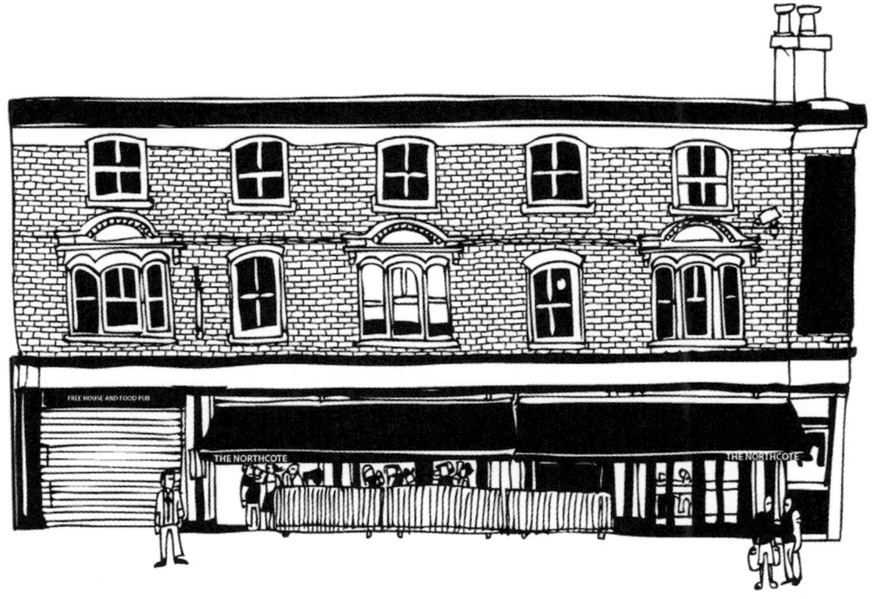

SW11
NORTHCOTE ROAD
Battersea

NORTHCOTE ROAD SW11

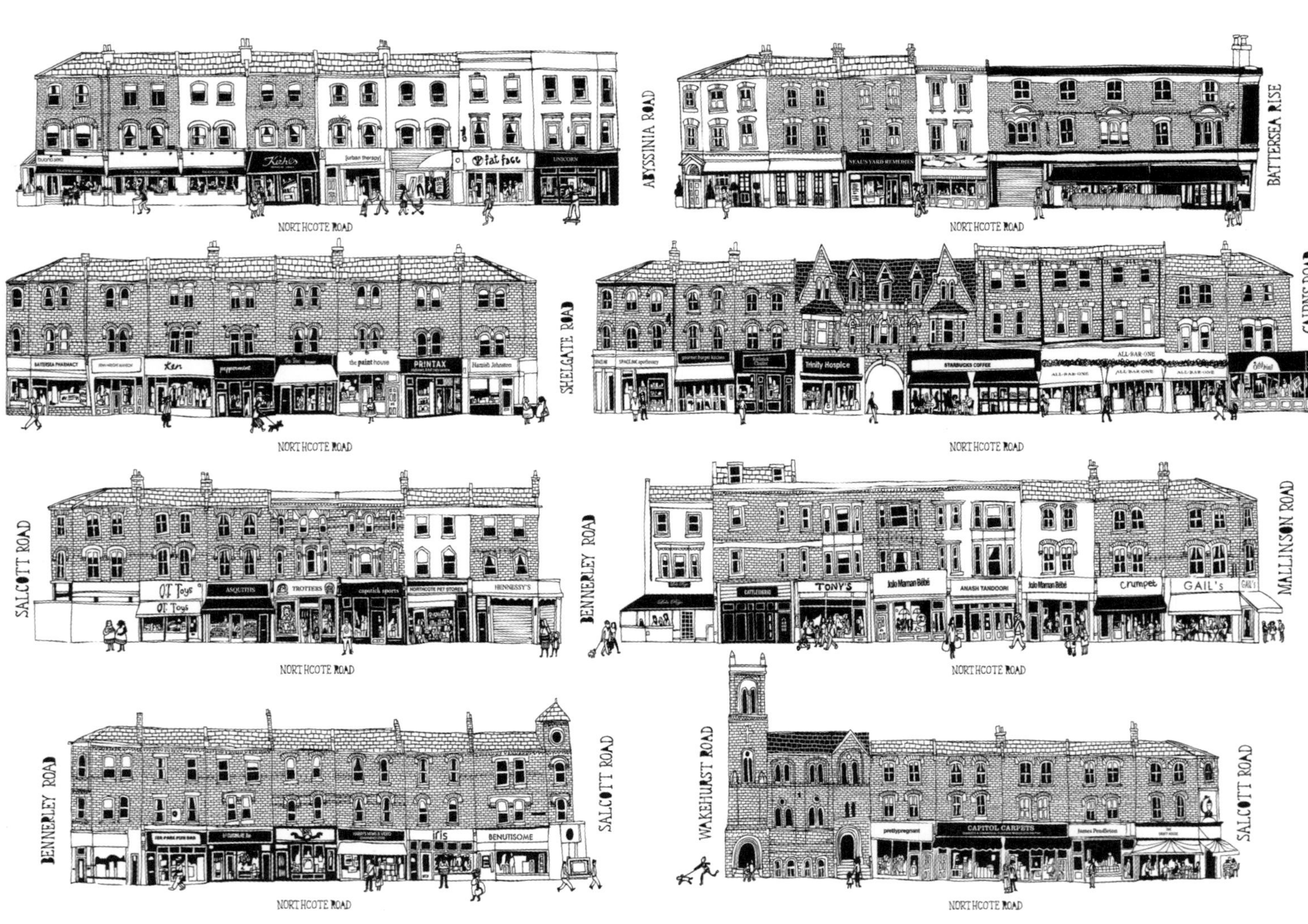

BATTERSEA, OR AS WAS ONCE, BADRICESTEG, BADRICS ISLAND AND PATRISEY, A THAMES ISLAND SETTLEMENT. ONCE A HOTBED OF LAWLESSNESS AND INDUSTRY, WHERE IN THE 1800'S, VISITORS FROM ACROSS THE WATER WOULD VENTURE WITH STICKS IN HAND AND COMPLAIN OF INCESSANT RAIN.

THE DEEP SOUTH, THIS ENCLAVE OF BATTERSEA THIS HAVEN OF DELECTIBLES AND DIVINITIES, THIS NORTHCOTE ROAD. WHERE ONCE RAN THE RIVER FALCONBROOK. NOW BURIED DEEP BELOW DANISH FABRICS AND WHIPPED MOCHAS, BENEATH THE SQUEAL OF BURNING BUGABOO RUBBER, THE CLACK CLACK OF BIRKENSTOCKS, WHERE BREADS ARE STUFFED WITH OLIVES AND MERRIMENT EXUDES.

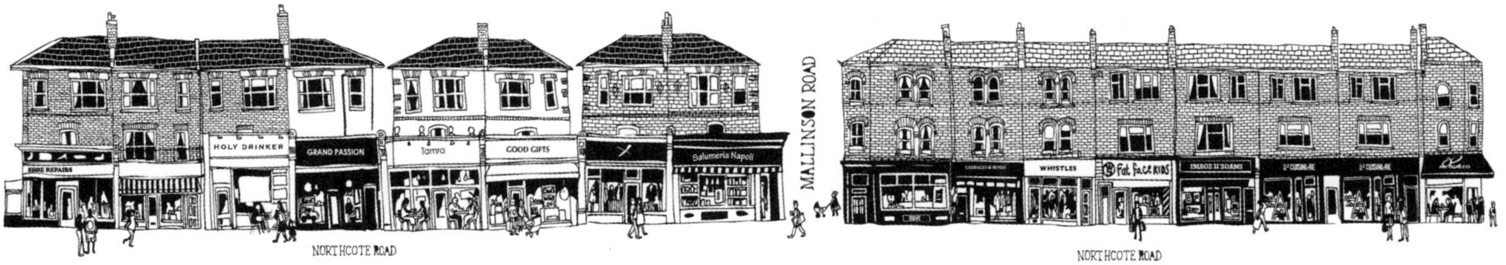

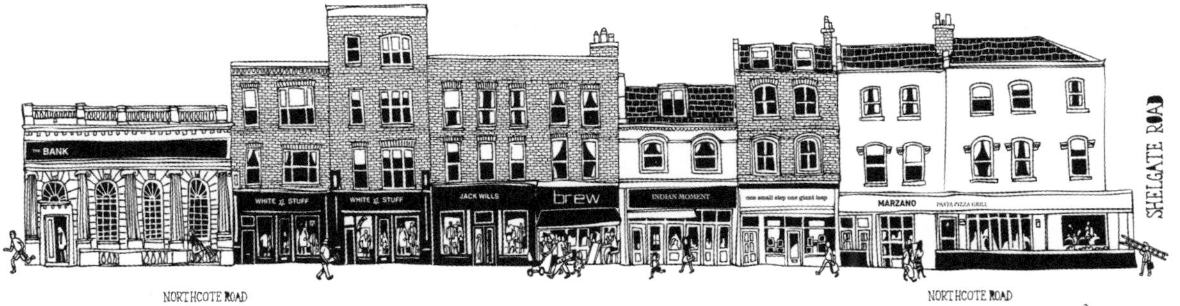

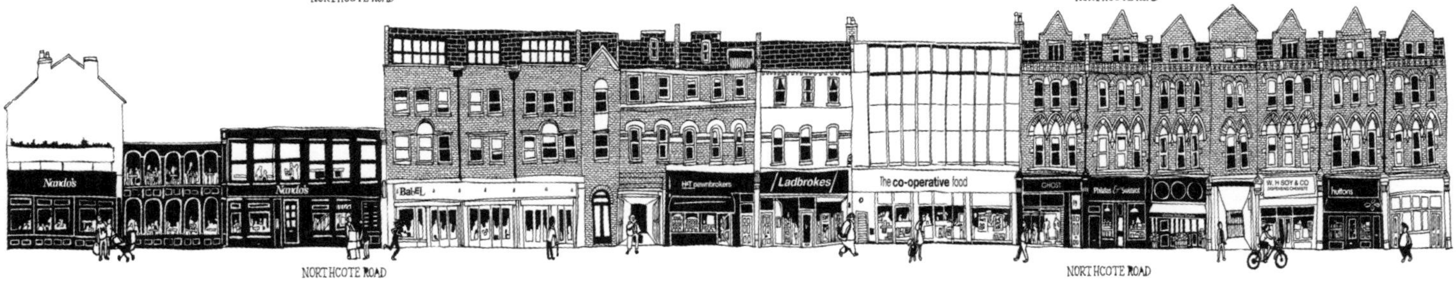

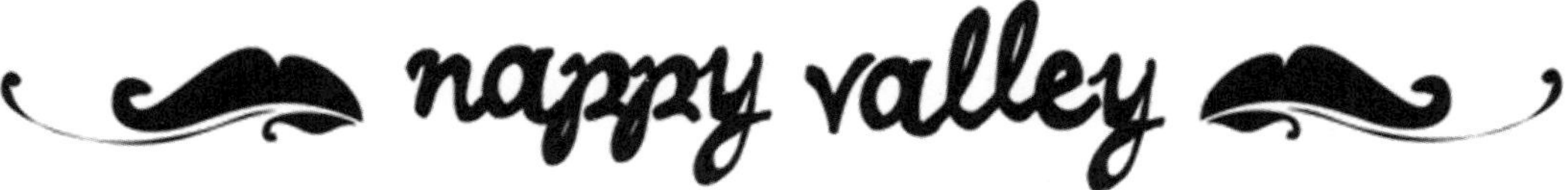

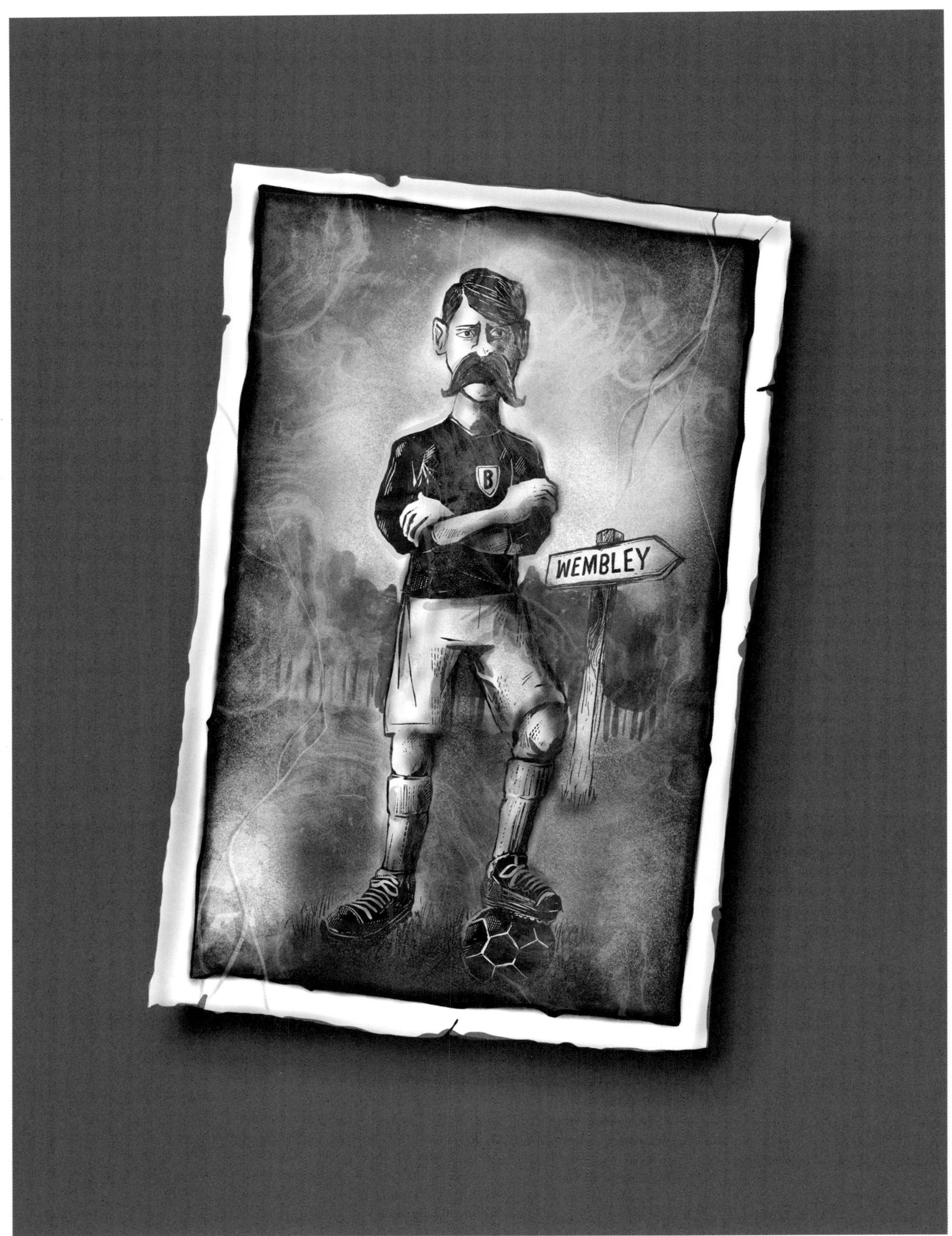
WEMBLEY

The original home of football is not, as most assume, Wembley, but BATTERSEA.

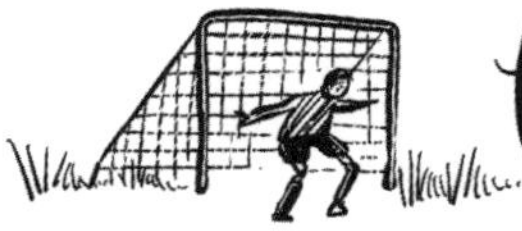

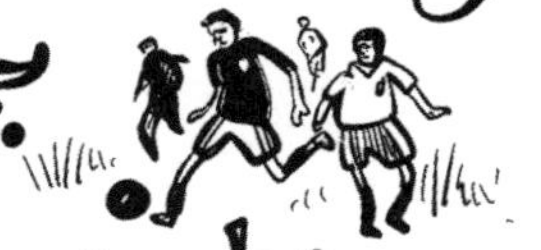

1863 The Football Association is established to build a set of rules for the beautiful game.

To test the rules, the best players in the UK were brought together on January 9th 1864. One team was led by the president of the FA, the second team led by the secretary of the FA. The very first game of 'official' football was played, not at Wembley, but

BATTERSEA PARK

* THE PRESIDENTS TEAM WON 2-0.

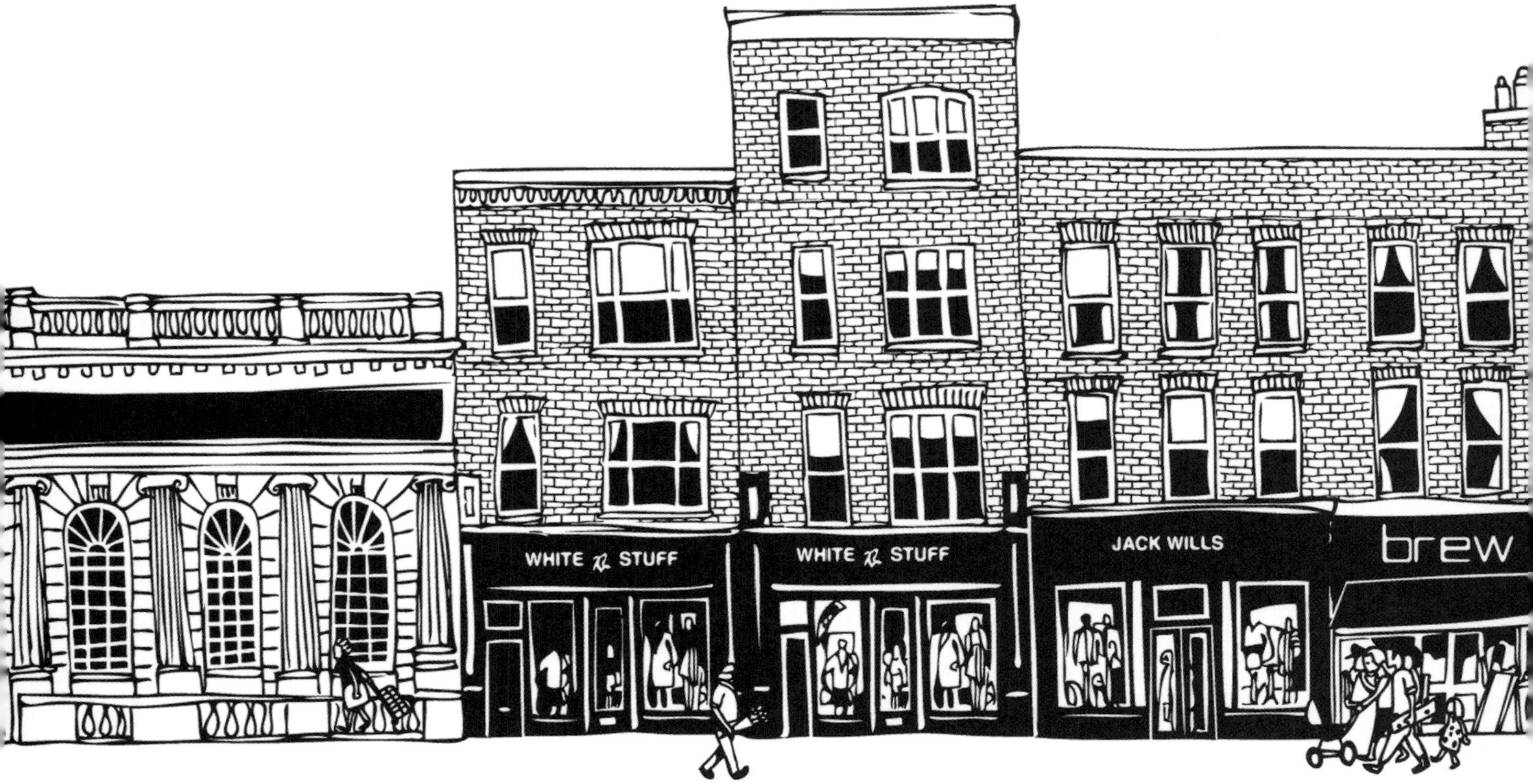

WHITE STUFF
WHITE STUFF
JACK WILLS
brew
Nando's
BabEL
H&T pawnbrokers

nappy

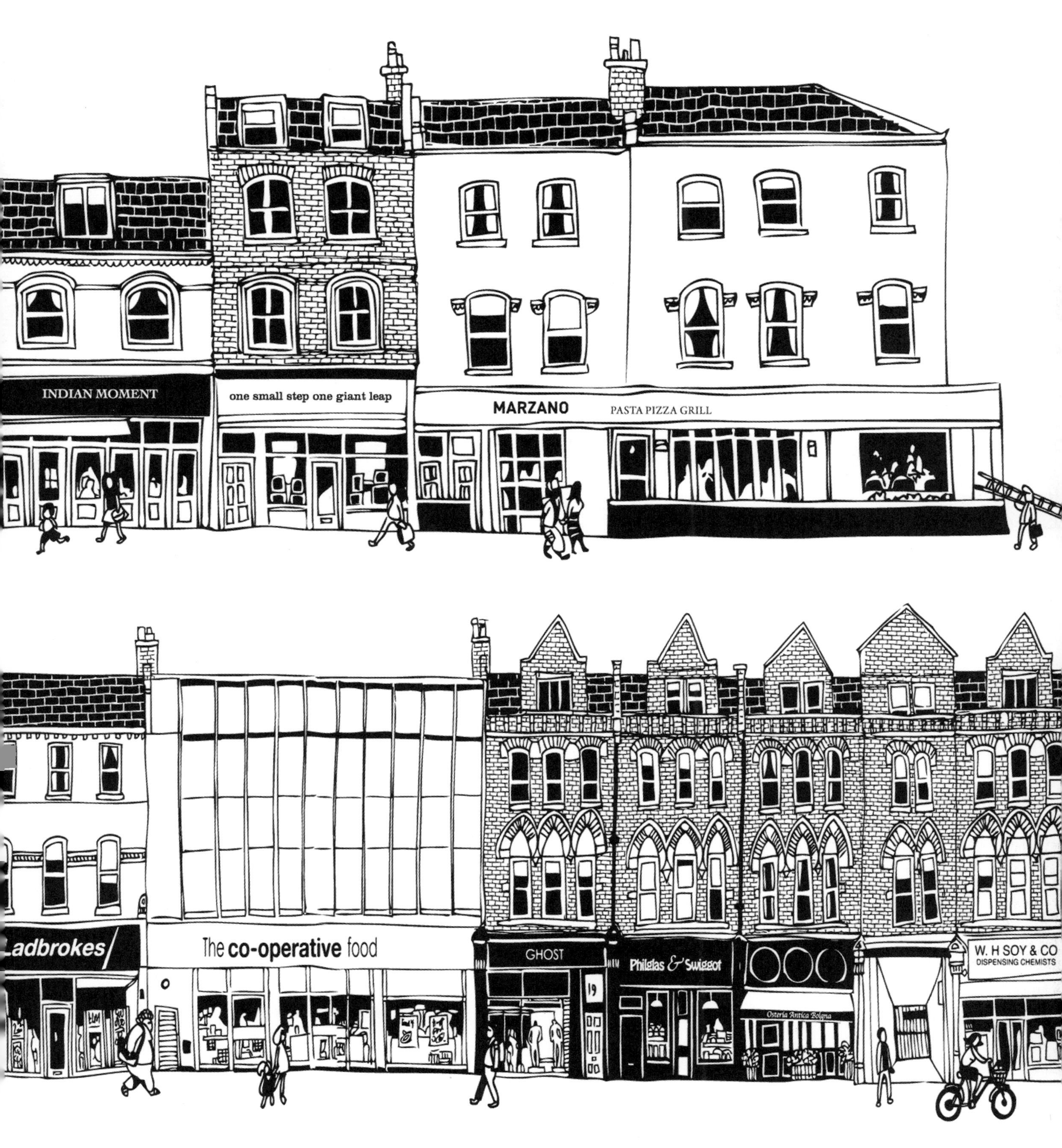

valley

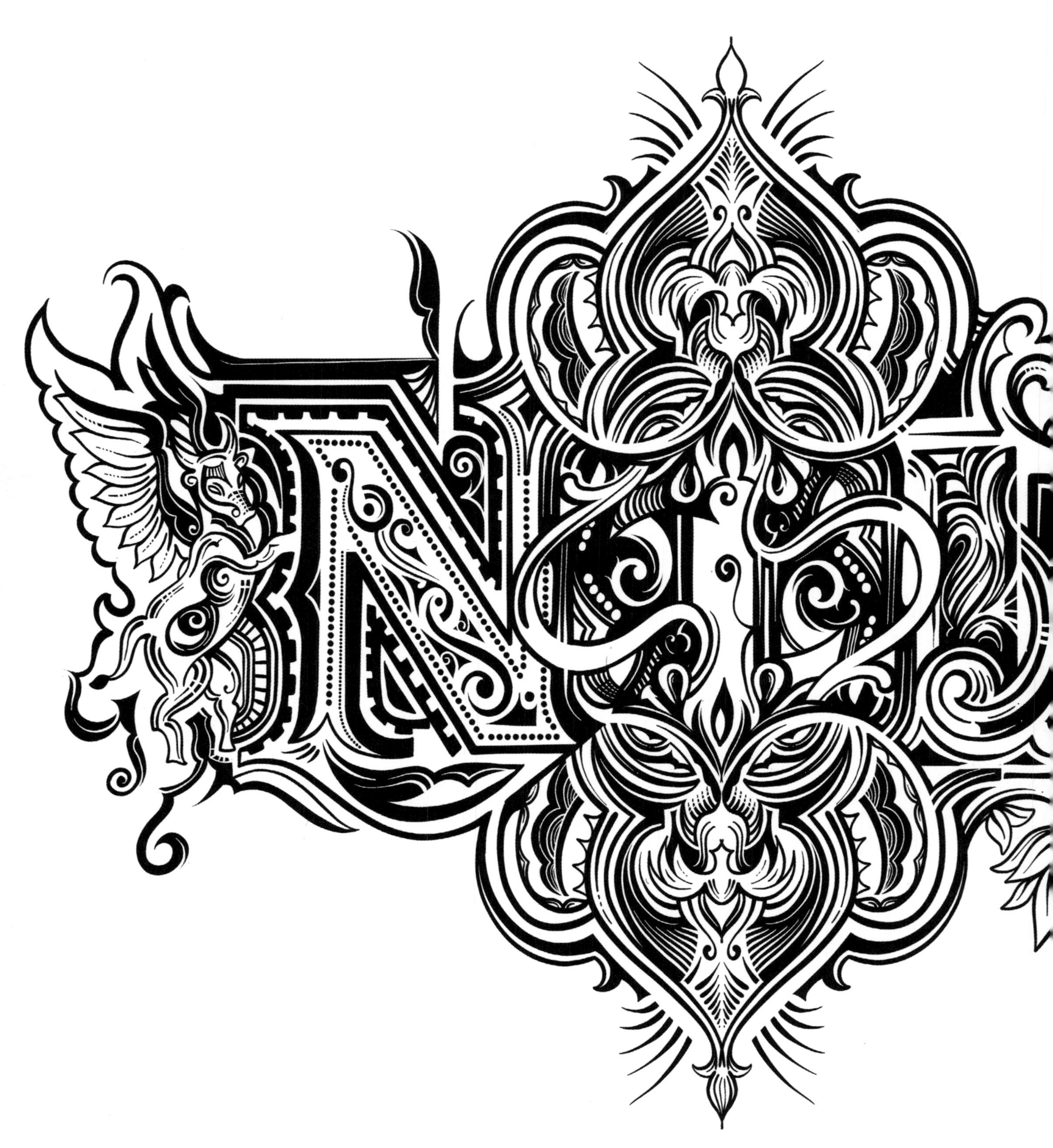

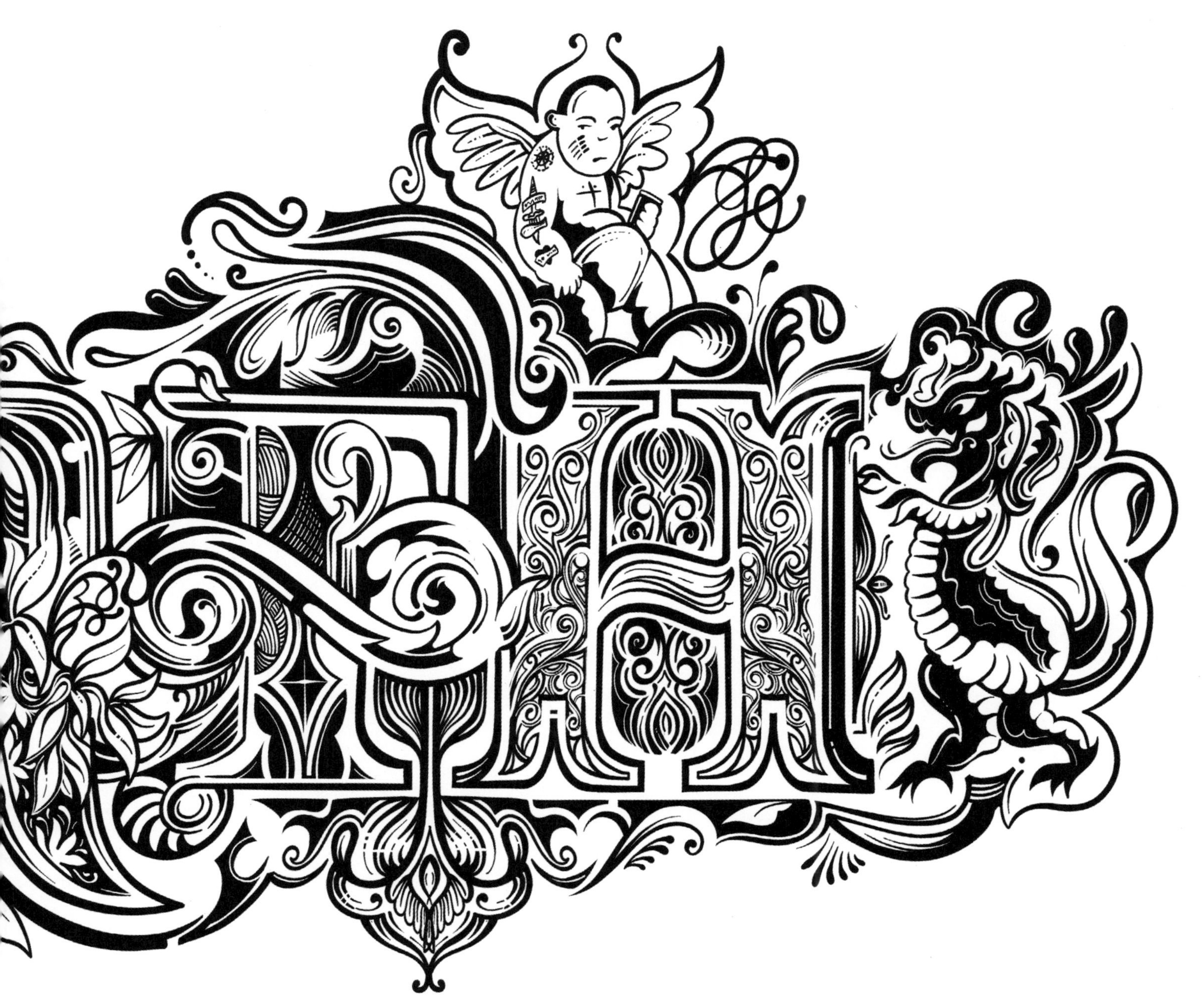

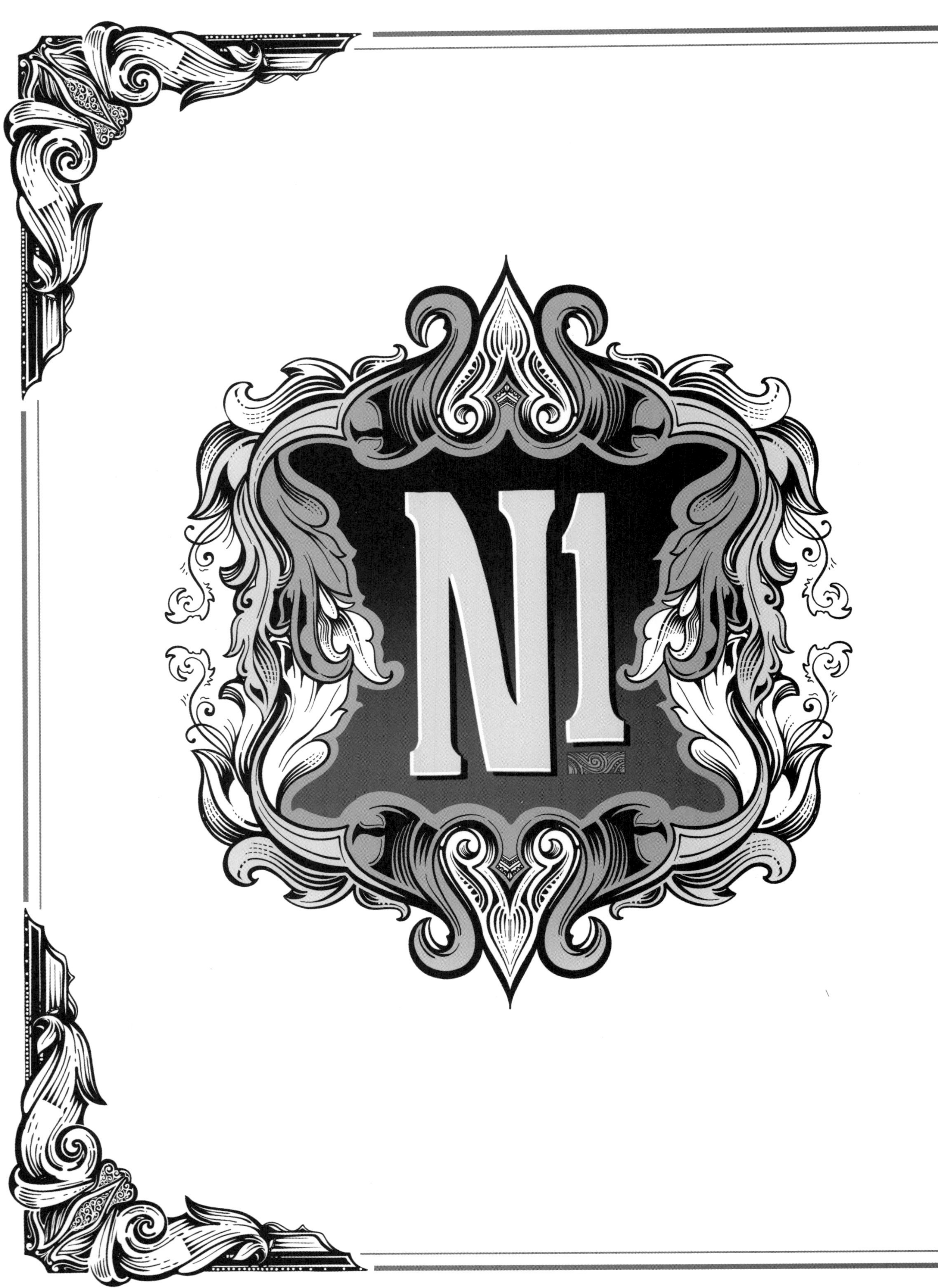

INDIAN MOMENT
one small step one giant leap
MARZANO
PASTA PIZZA GRILL
Ladbrokes
The co-operative food
GHOST
19
Philglas & Swiggot
Osteria Antica Bolgna
W. H SOY & CO
DISPENSING CHEMISTS

N1

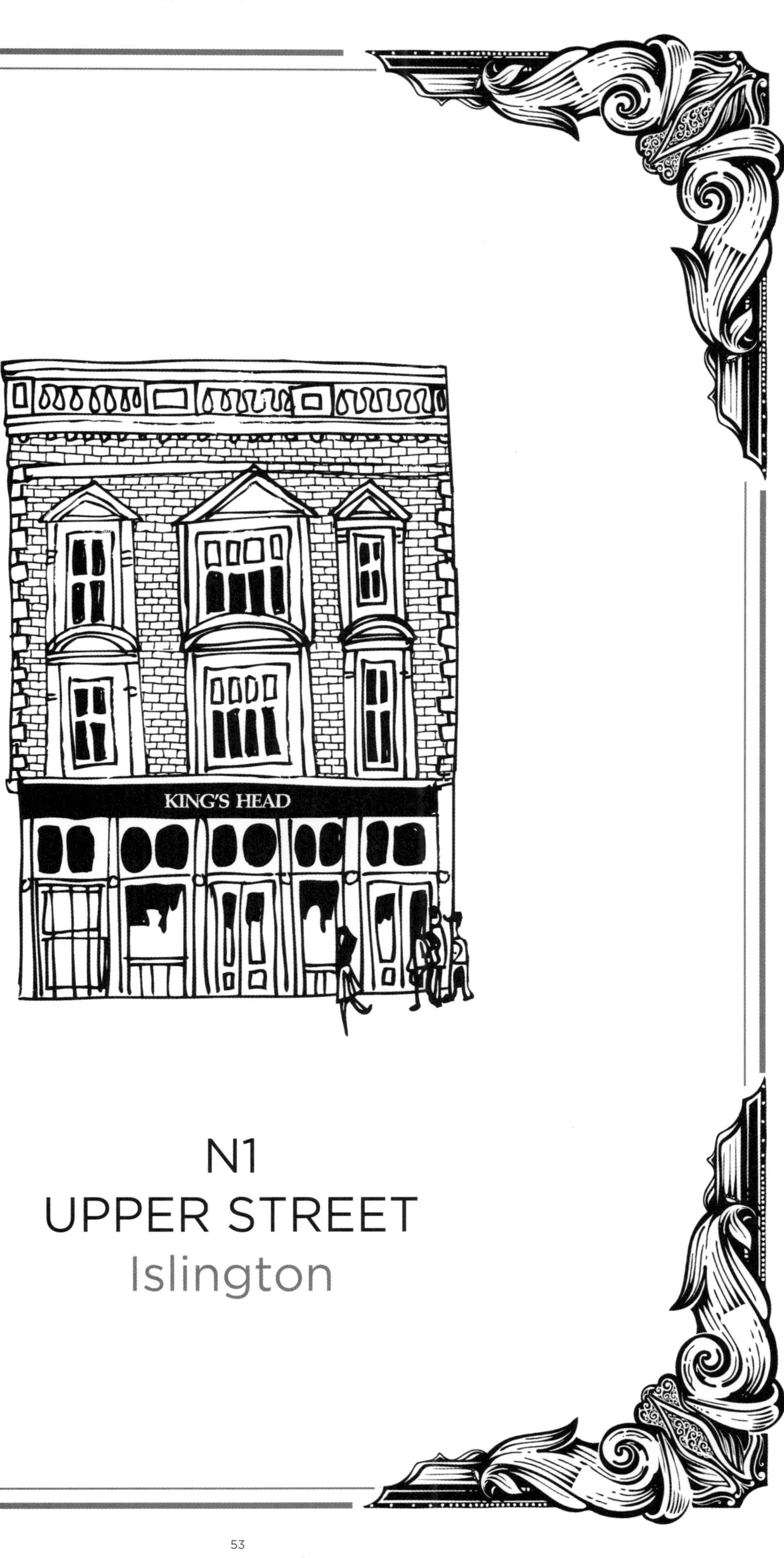

N1
UPPER STREET
Islington

UPPER STREET

Highbury End

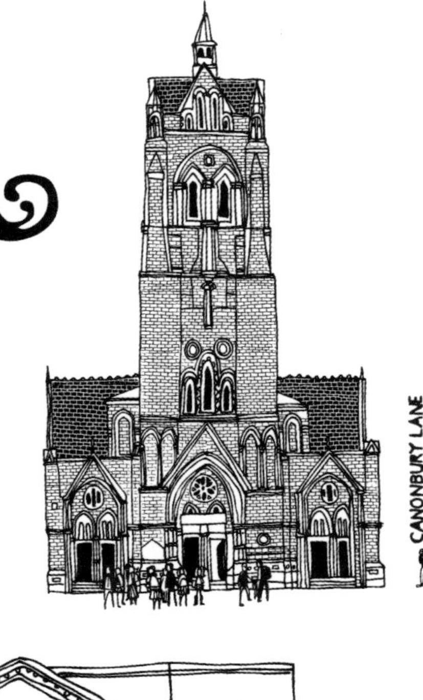

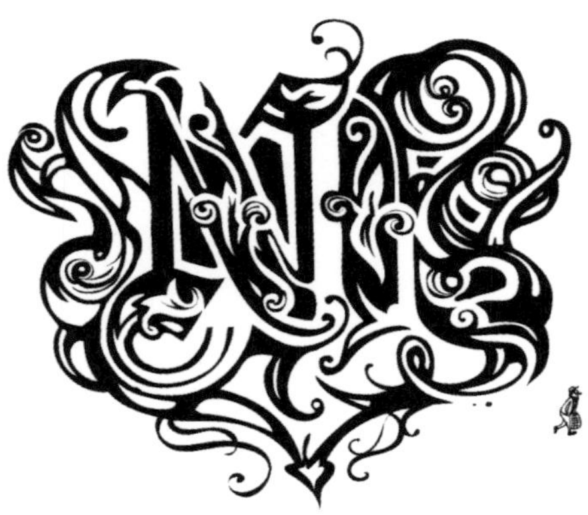

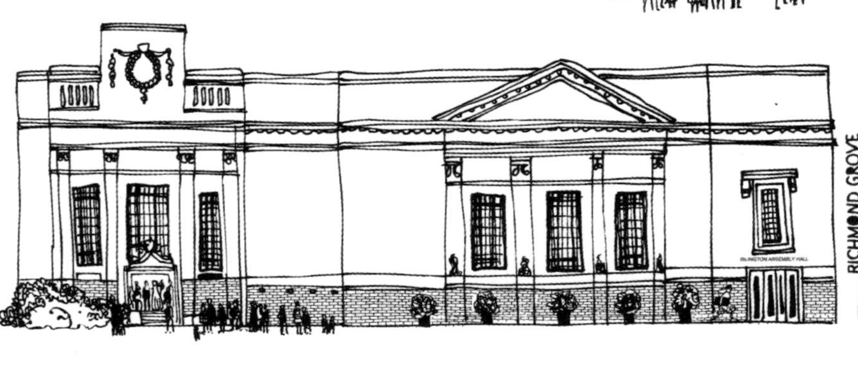

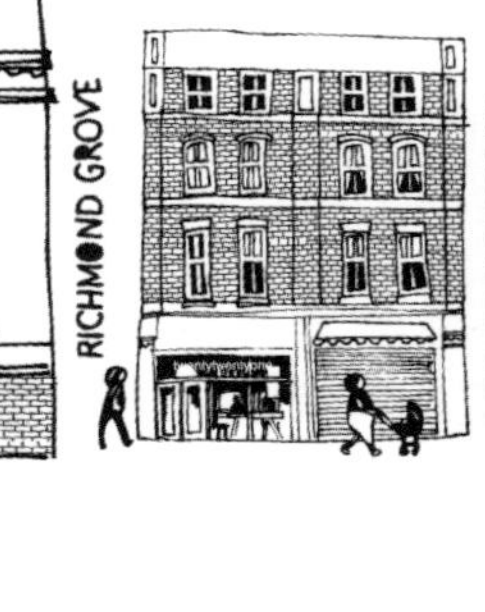

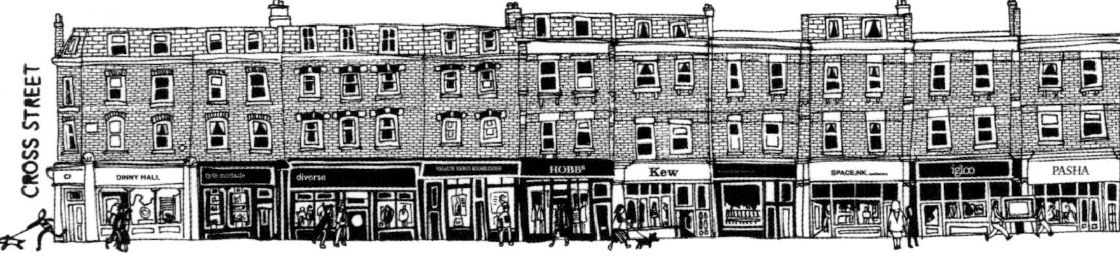

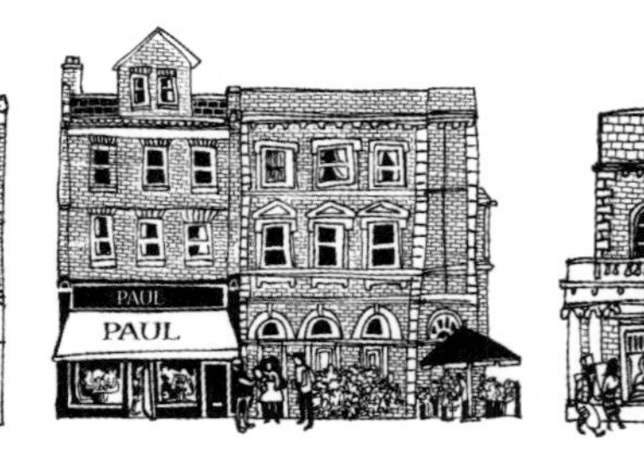

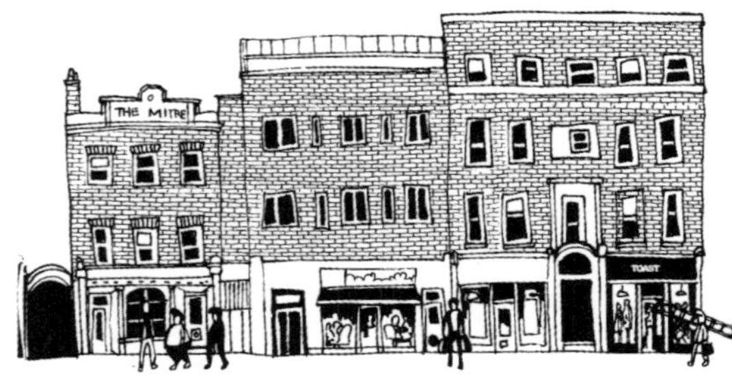

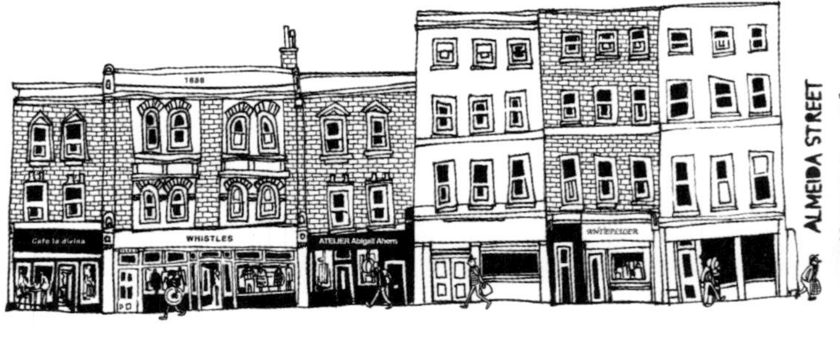

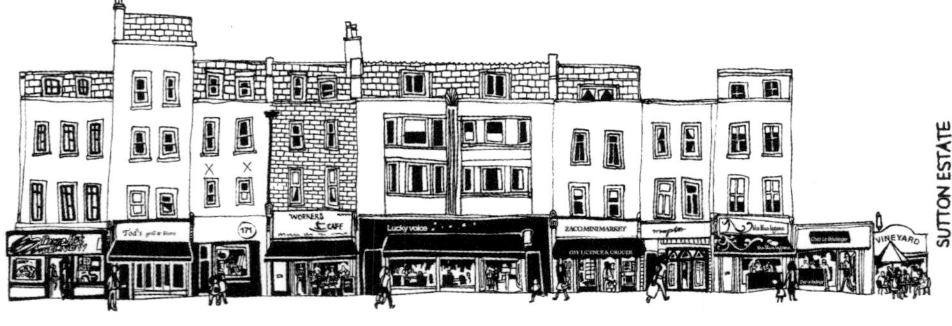

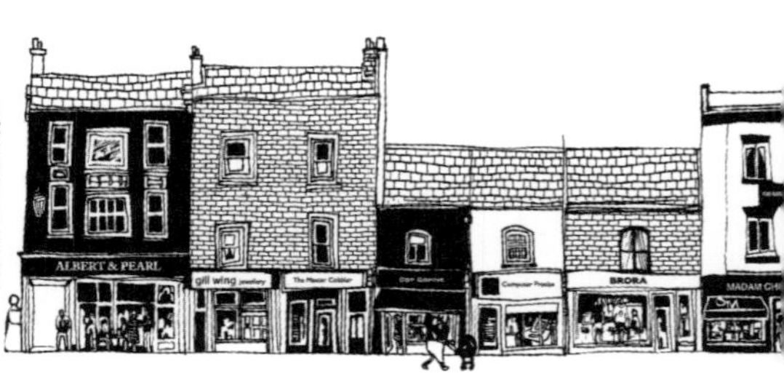

THIS UPPER ST, WHERE HENRY VIII HUNTED DUCK IN PONDS & SIR WALTER RALEIGH SUPPED FROM HIS OWN BAR: WHERE 56 ALE HOUSES STOOD FILLING THE FARMERS AND VISITORS WITH WARM MEMORIES AS VEG GREW HEARTILY IN THE FERTILE SOIL: WEAVING THROUGH THE HILLTOP VILLAGE OF WHAT WAS ONCE GISELDONE, GISLANDUNE, ISLEDON AND NOW ISLINGTON, THE PLACE OF WEARY TRAVELLERS RESTING THROUGH THE NIGHT HOURS, AWAY FROM THE HIGHWAYMEN, ROGUES AND SHAM SOLDIERS THAT STALKED THE PATH TO THE CITY.

The Angel, named after the inn on the Gt North Rd, that blossomed to a majestic tea room from Lyon's. The agreeable seating of Victor & Marjorie as they initiated Angel into their game of pleasure – Monopoly. Where Madness, Stranglers & Killers rocked as Adele swirled tones so sweet. A place of worshipful tunes, of day passing, drinking & clinking, drifting & sifting, of galaxy hitchhikers, radicalism and dreamers.

ONE OF THE MORE UNUSUAL FEATURES OF UPPER STREET IS IT'S HIGH PAVEMENTS. BUILT IN THE 1860's, SOME STANDING 1M ABOVE ROAD LEVEL. ON THE DAY OF SUMMER SOLSTICE, THE ROAD WAS CLOSED & FOLK WOULD LINE THE PAVEMENTS TO WATCH FLAMBOYANT PLAYS PERFORMED BY ELABORATE & COLOURFUL ACTORS BELOW THEM. THOSE ON THE PAVEMENT, KNOWN AS 'UPPERS' WOULD, AS FESTIVITIES WORE ON, BECOME INEBRIATED AND HURL ROTTING FOOD AT THE DUCKING PERFORMERS - KNOWN AS 'LOWERS'. IT IS SAID THE TERM 'UPPER CLASS' WAS BORN HERE.

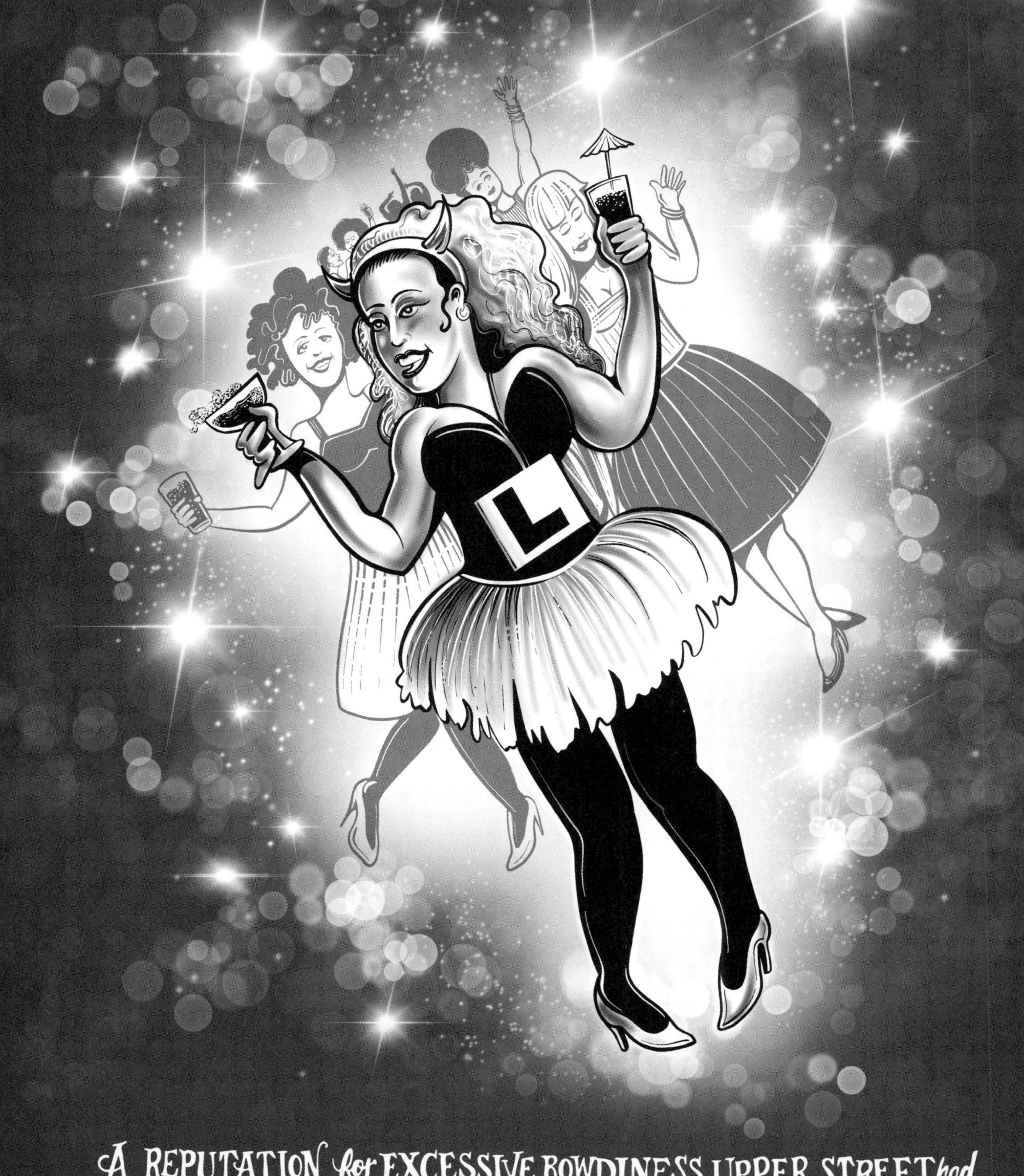

A REPUTATION *for* EXCESSIVE ROWDINESS, UPPER STREET *had* THE TAG *'The Devils Mile'* BESTOWED UPON IT IN THE 1800'S, ON ACCOUNT *of* IT'S DRUNKENNESS, RECKLESSNESS & GENERAL NAUGHTINESS (*much like today*).

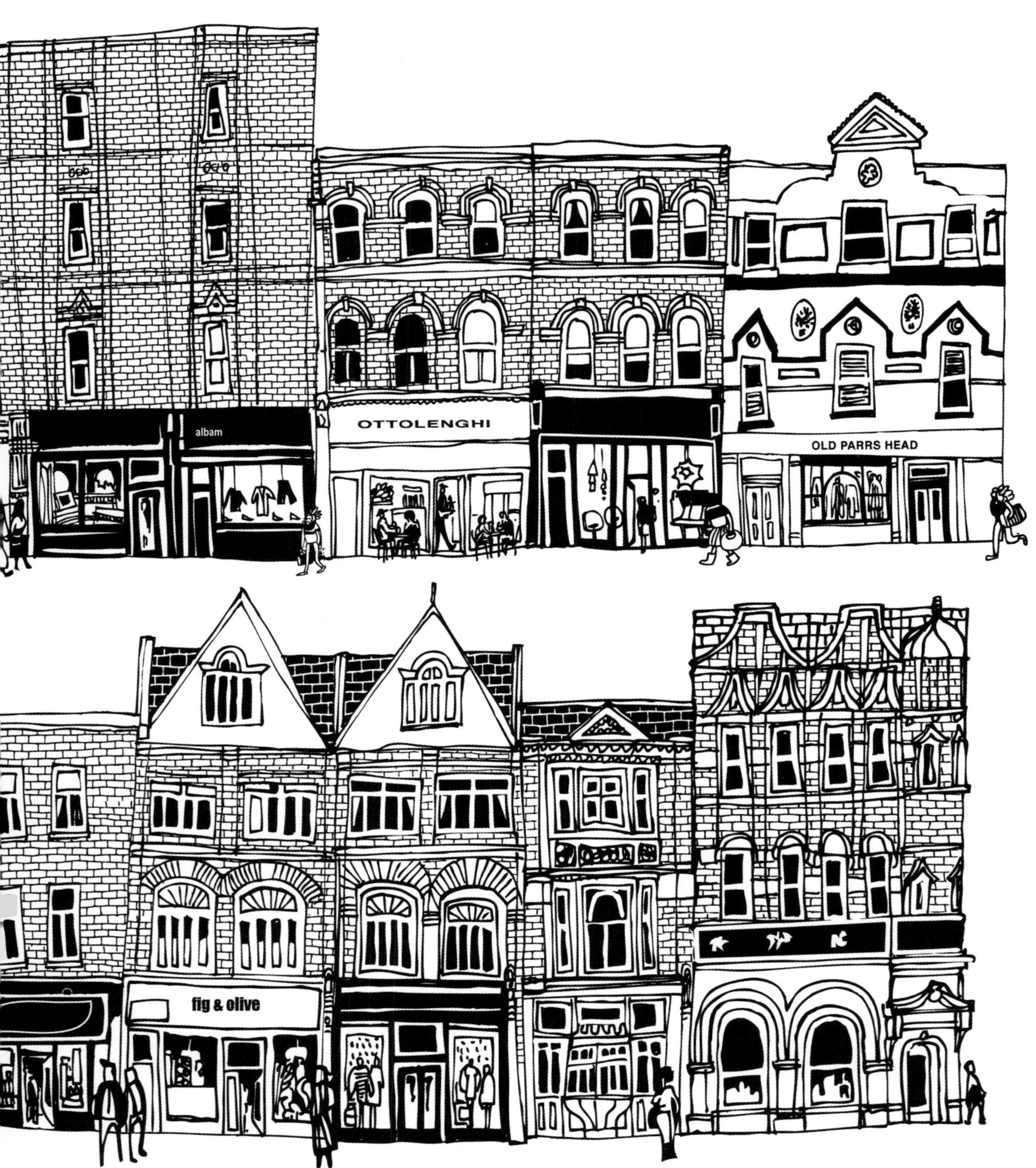
albam
OTTOLENGHI
OLD PARRS HEAD
fig & olive

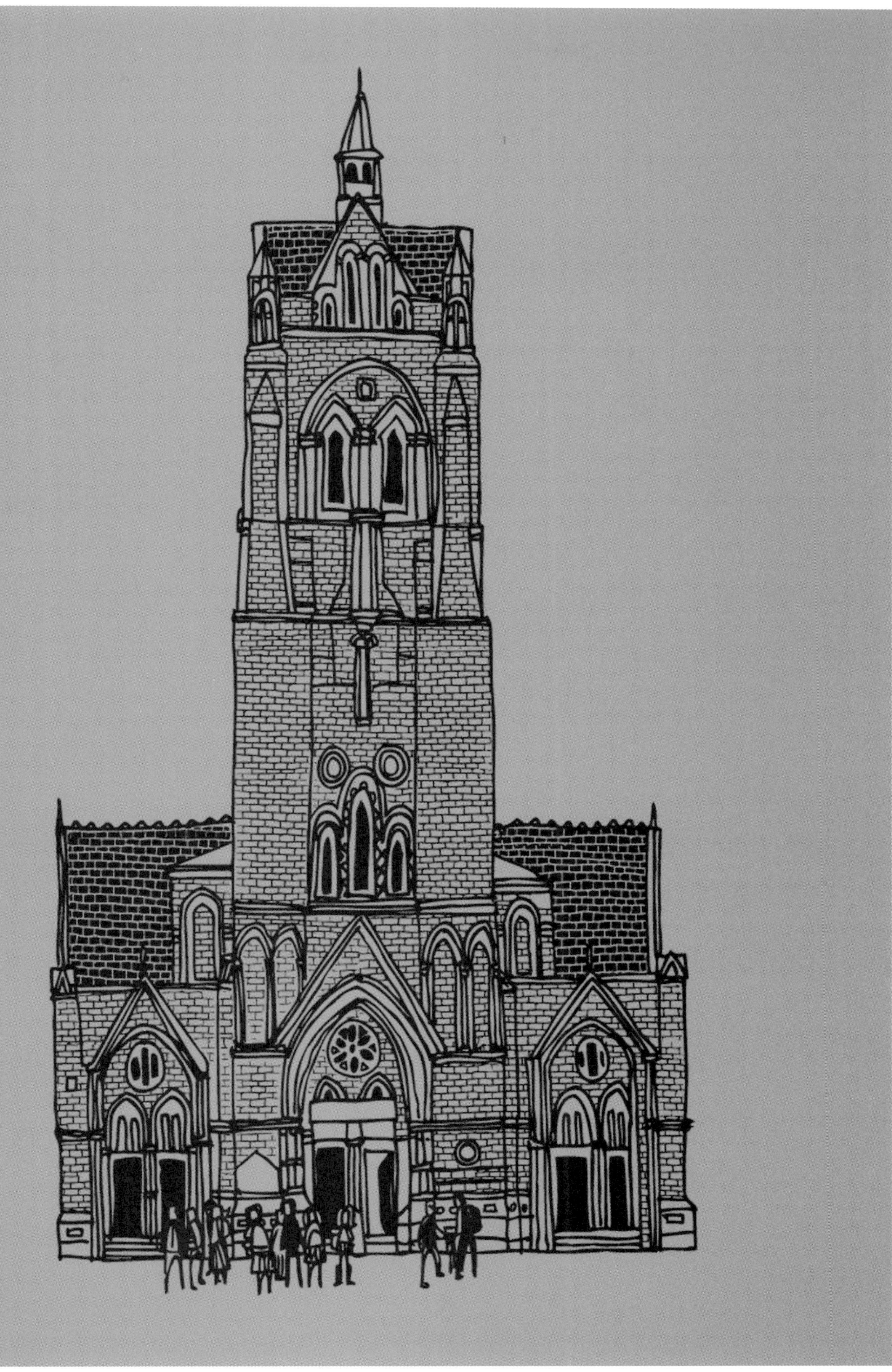

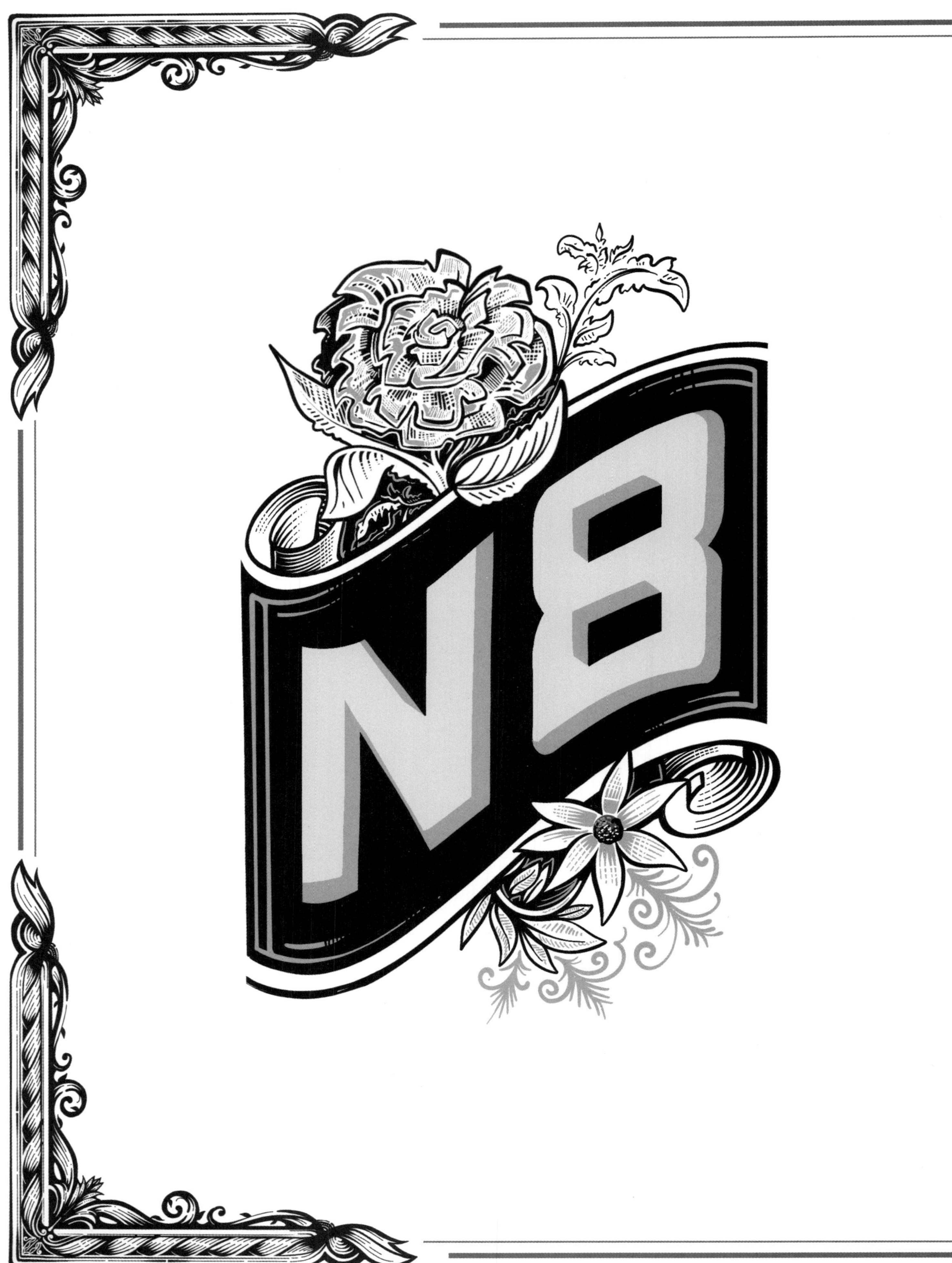
N8

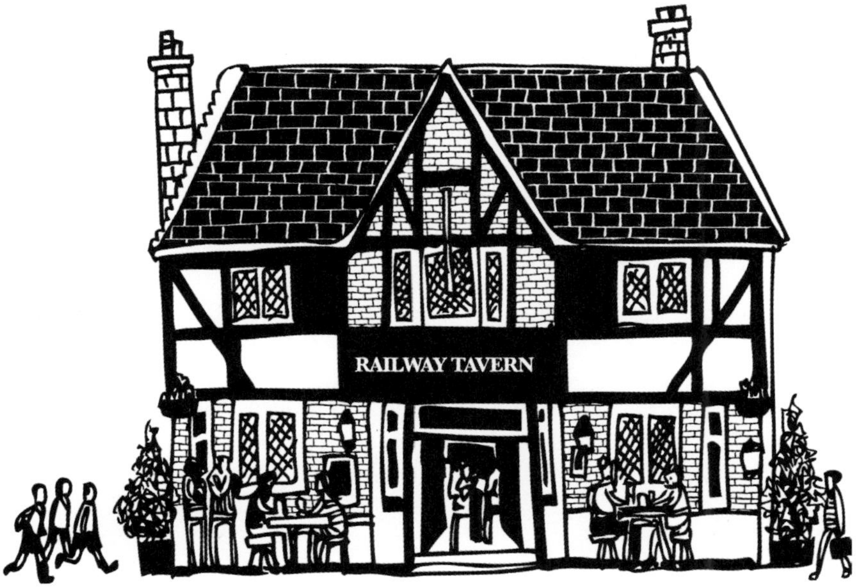

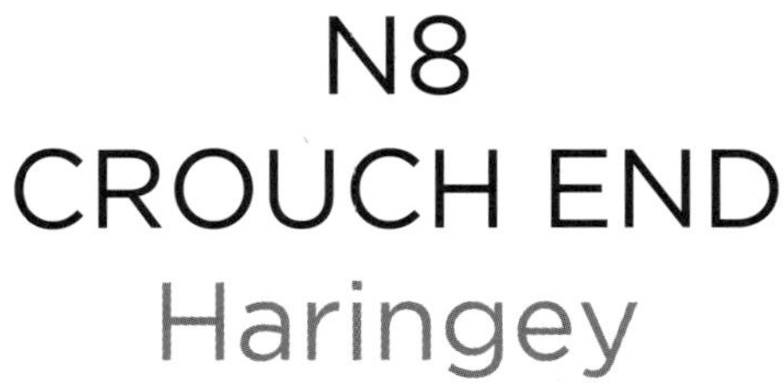

N8
CROUCH END
Haringey

CROUCH END

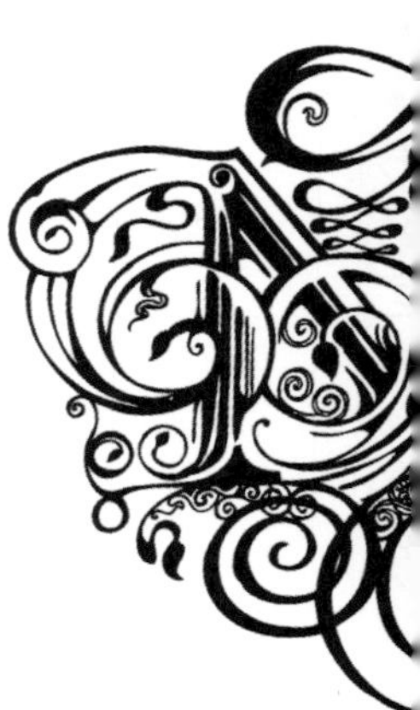

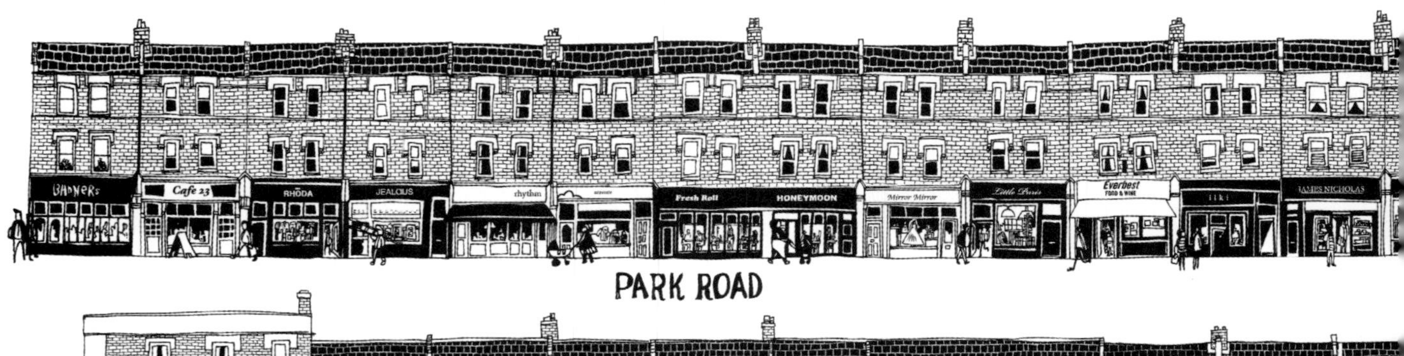

PARK ROAD

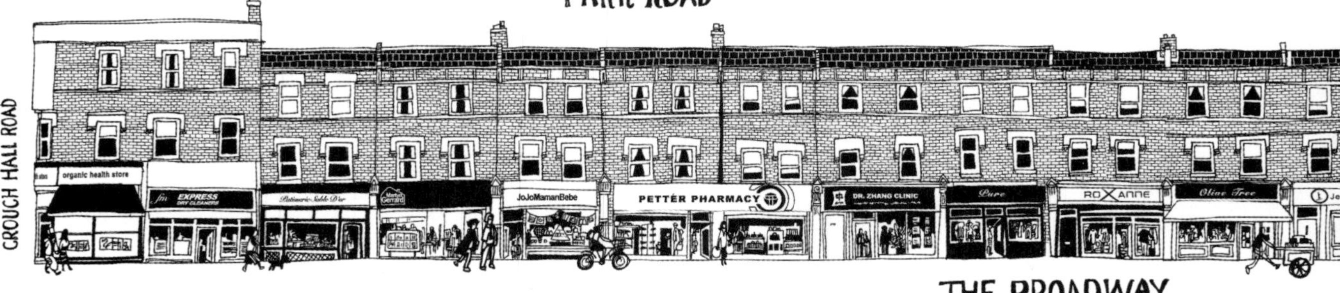

THE BROADWAY

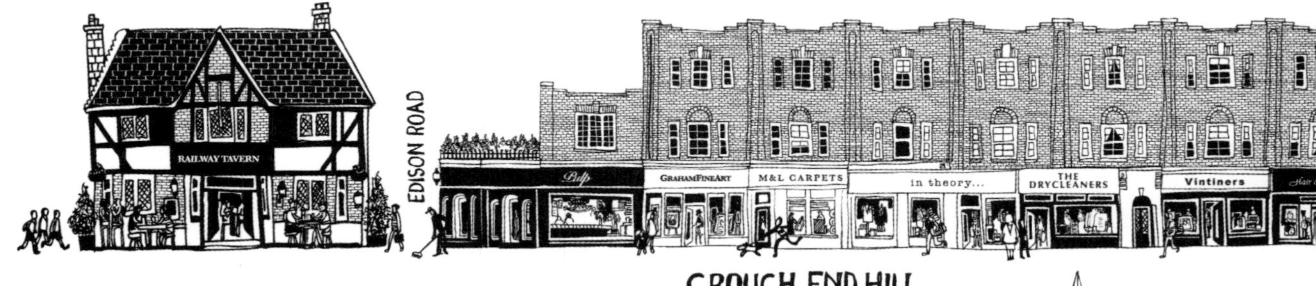

CROUCH END HILL

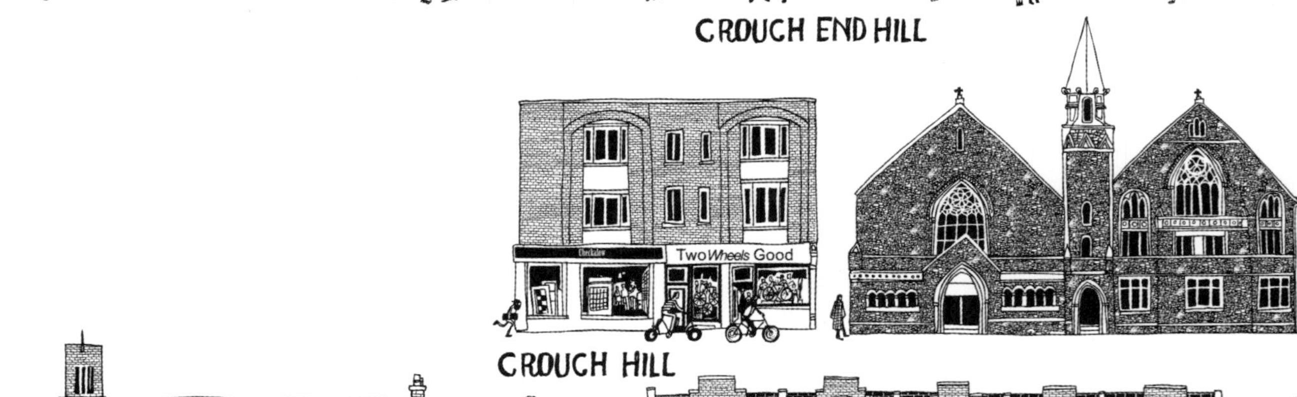

CROUCH HILL

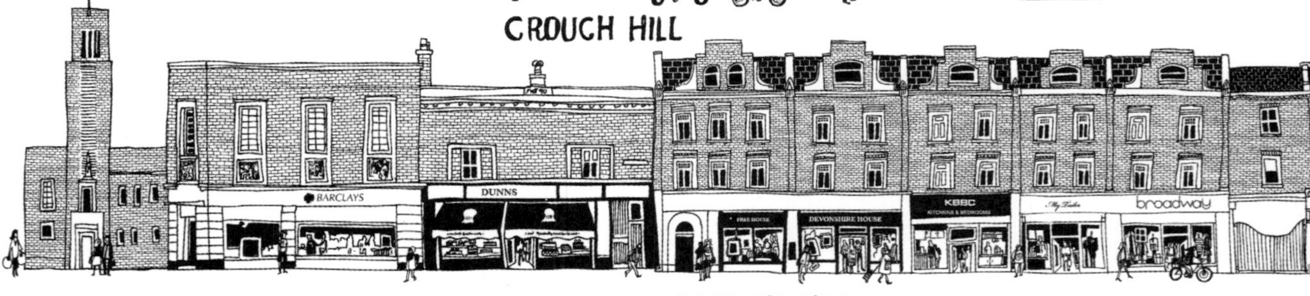

CROUCH HILL

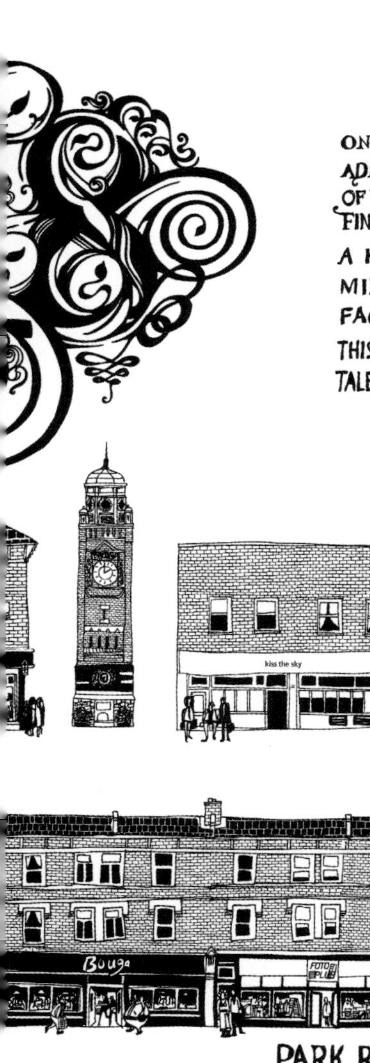

ONCE OF ORCHARDS & HEAVY WOODLAND, THIS VILLAGE PREVIOUSLY 'WITHOUT THE GOSPEL' WAS ADMINISTERED BY THE BOROUGH of HORNSEY UNTIL THE HARINGEY *MASSIVE* TOOK OWNERSHIP IN '65. HOME OF WILSON'S DEPARTMENT STORE WITH ALL THE *H'AIRS & GRA-ACES* of 'OW'S MOD-EM TERDAY?' AS THE LATEST FINERY WAS SHOWN. UNITED DAIRIES CHOCOLATE MILK & DUNN'S, THE LAST BASTIONS OF BAKED GOODS. A HIVE OF A, B, C, TO ZEE LISTERS AS THEY BUZZ AROUND DE-AIRED & LOO ROLL APLENTY, MIXING WITH THE MORTALS OF NORMALITY & MINGLING THROUGH VILLA'D STREETS BEFORE FACE PAINT IS ONCE MORE APPLIED & CONVERSATIONS DELIVERED VIA SCRIPTED PAGES.

THIS CROUCH END - HOME OF VAMPIRES & DARK LEGENDS IN POSSESSED CHURCHES, OF MYSTERIOUS SPRIGGANS & STEPHEN KING TALES. OF DYLAN, THE WIFE & THE PLUMBER. OF MANY A RAUCOUS & STOMACH CLENCHING NIGHT SPENT AT THE KINGS HEAD. OF THE CHURCH, KONK, TRUMPTON, PUGWASH & A CLOCKTOWER.

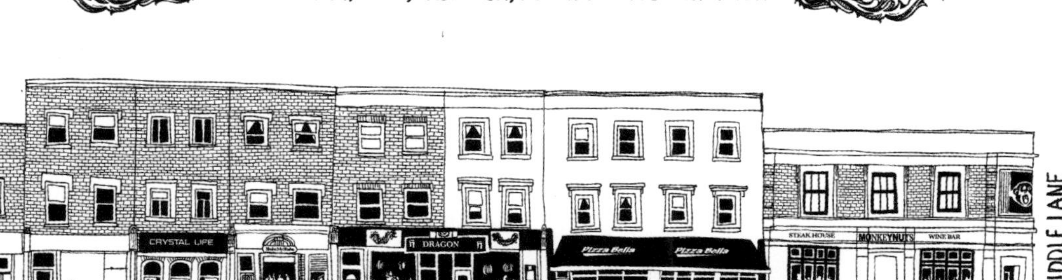

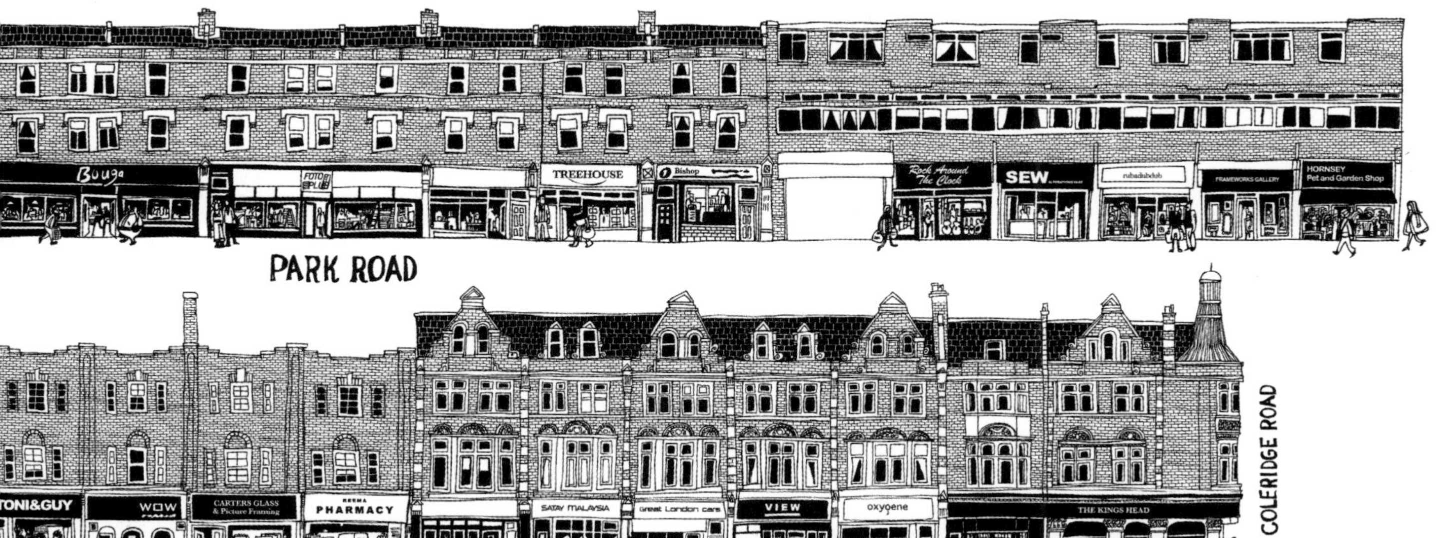

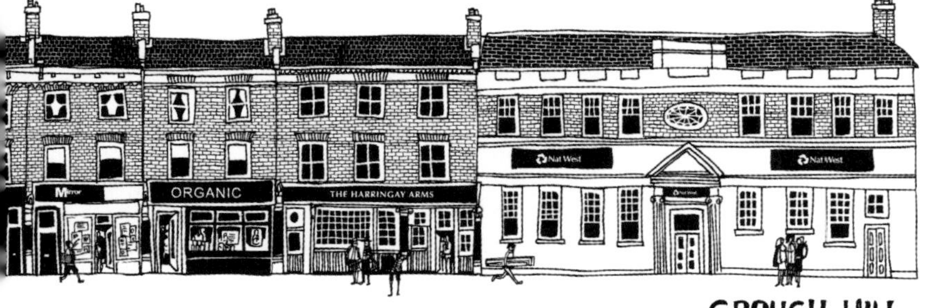

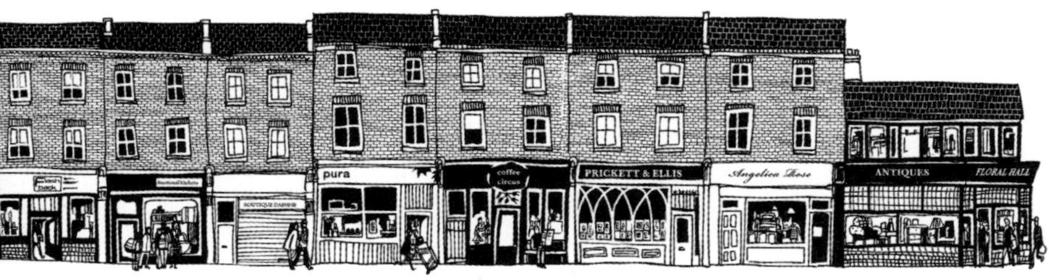

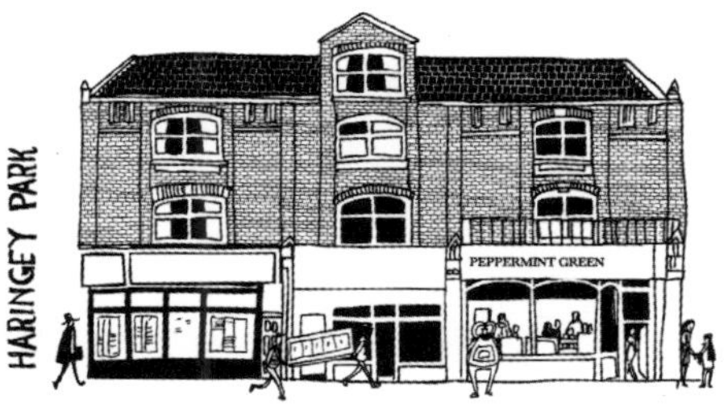

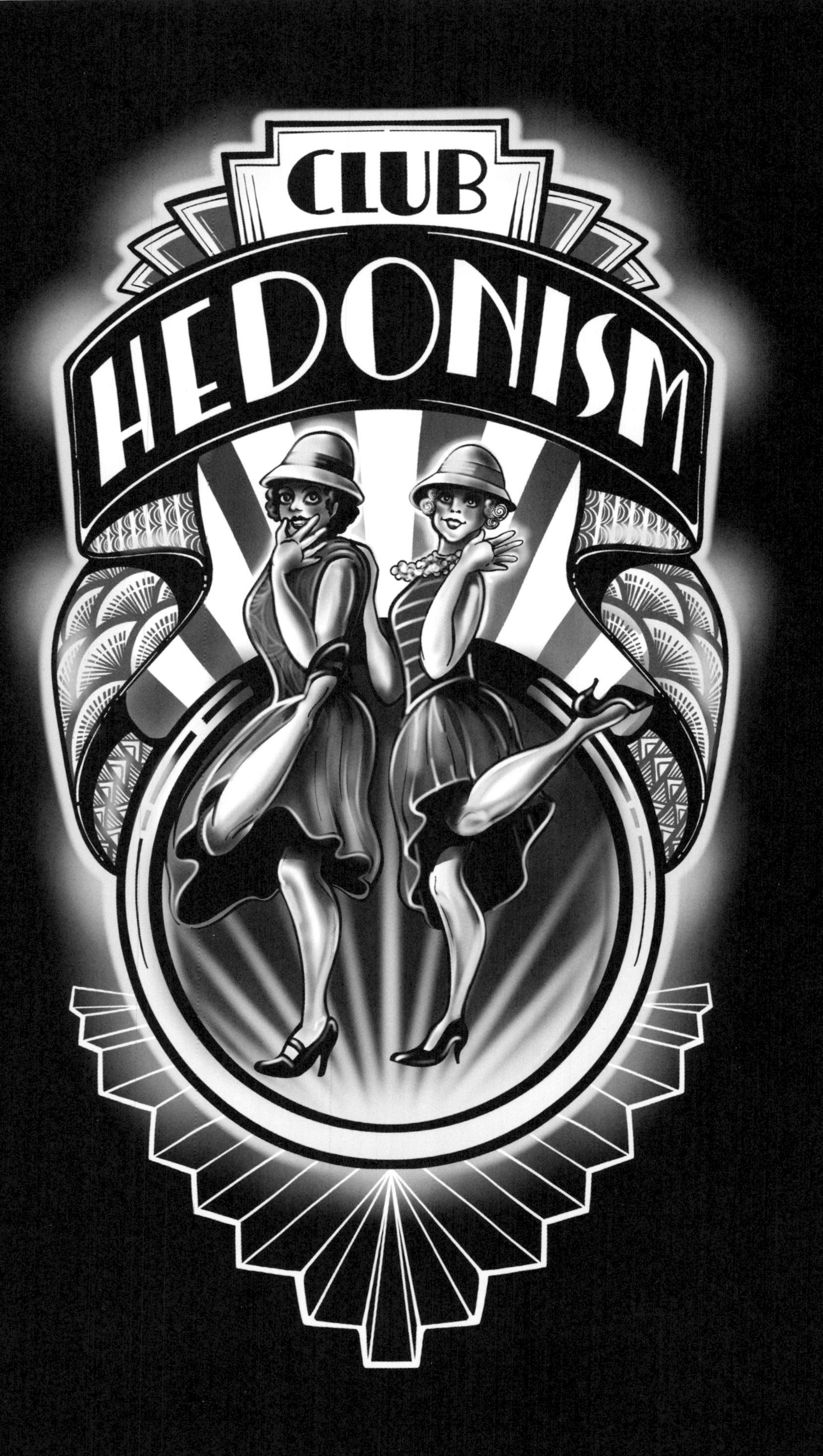
CLUB
HEDONISM

The FAMOUS CLOCK TOWER IN THE HEART of CROUCH END ONCE HOUSED A SET OF STEPS THAT LED DEEP UNDERGROUND.

ONLY ACCESSED BY INVITATION FOR THE WELL HEELED and those KNOWN AS CELEBRITIES

THE LUCKY ATTENDEES ON THE FINAL STEP, WOULD BE MET BY 3 CAVERNOUS, LAVISH and Opulent

BALLROOMS

WITH CRYSTAL CHANDELIERS, ORNATE CARVED MARBLE BALCONIES & FREE-FLOWING CHAMPAGNE ~ IT BECAME KNOWN AS

Club Hedonism 'neath the Tower where time is irrelevant.

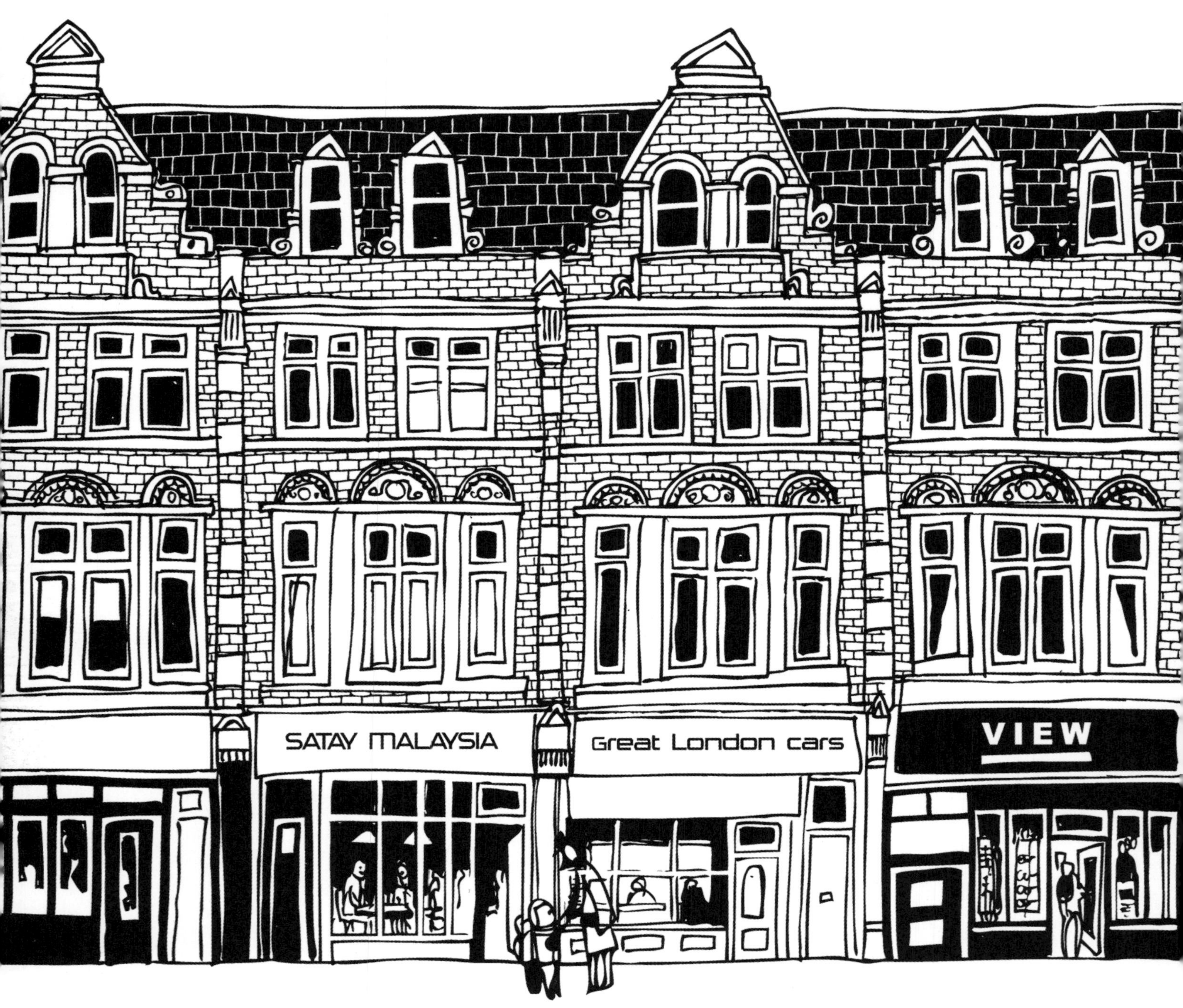
SATAY MALAYSIA
Great London cars
VIEW

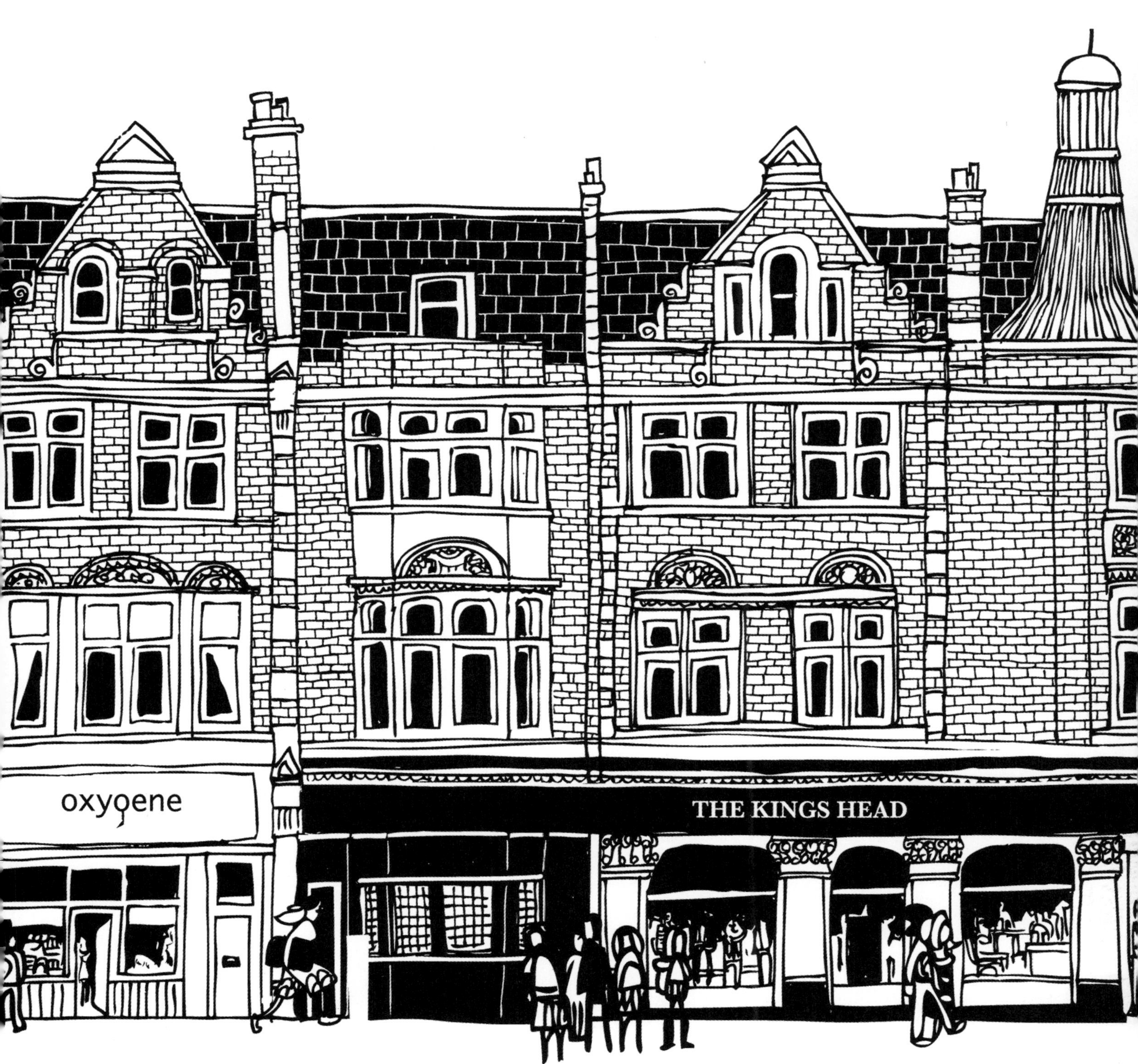
oxygene
THE KINGS HEAD

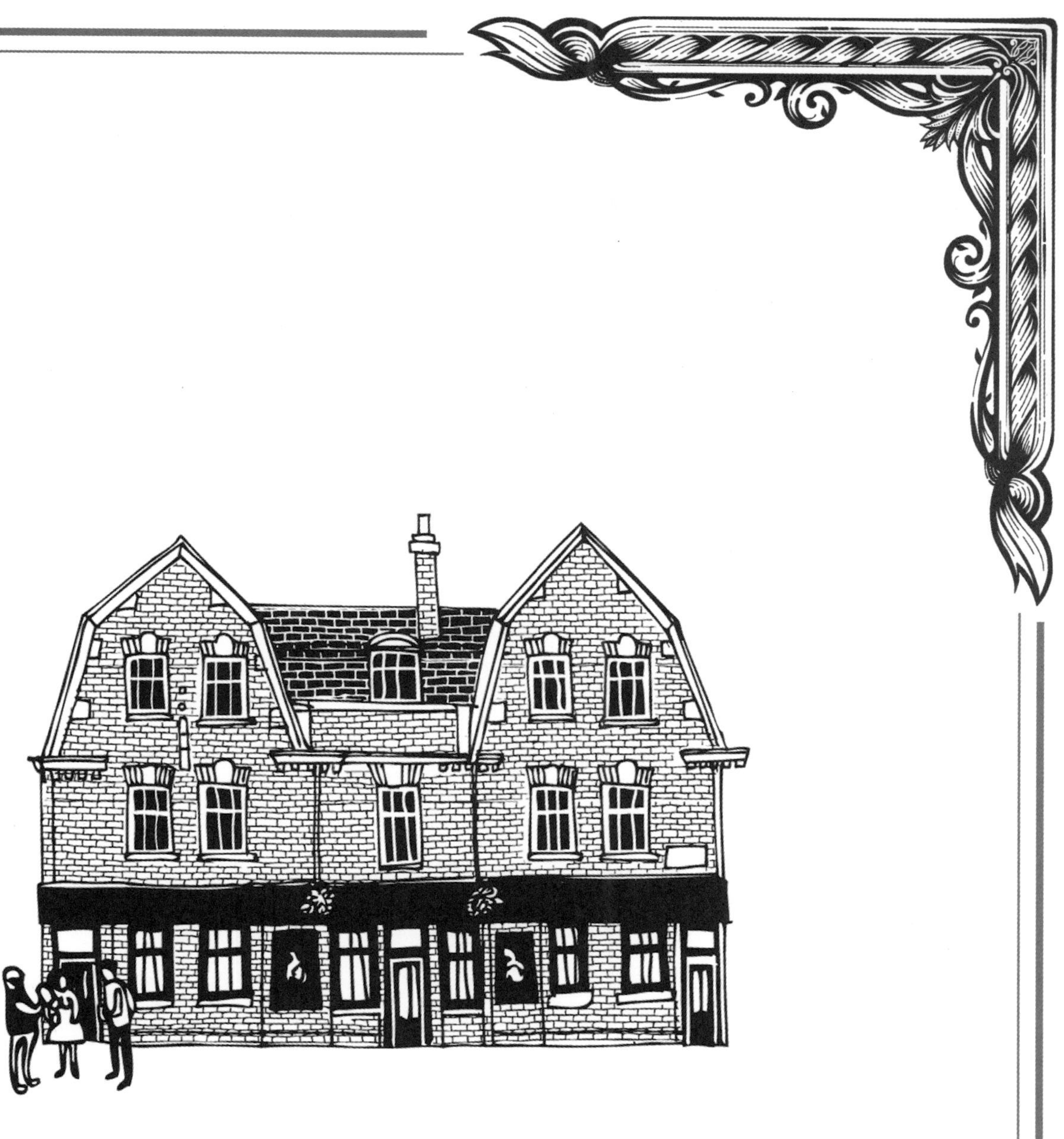

N16
CHURCH STREET
Stoke Newington

CHURCH STREET

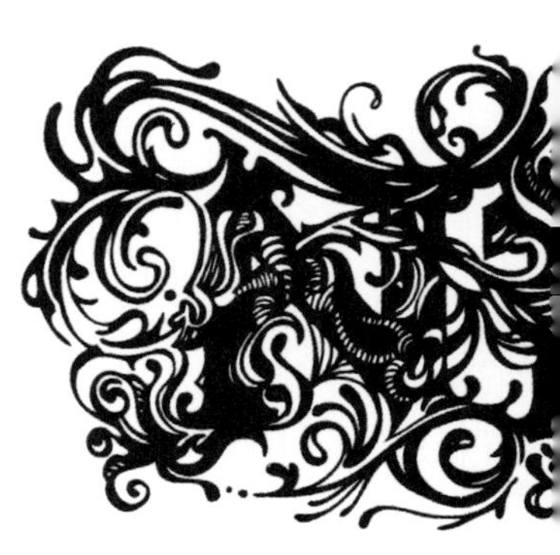

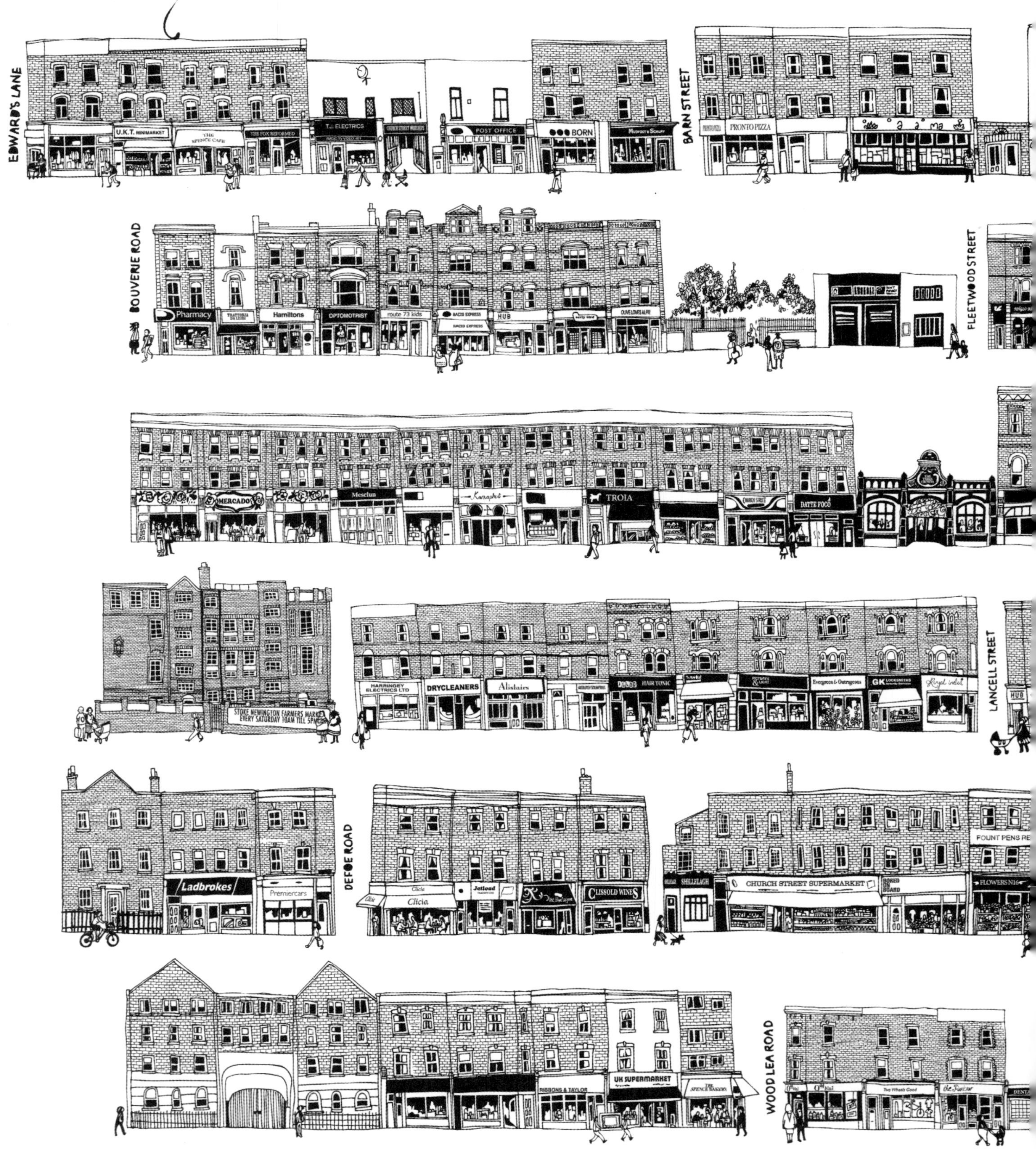

EDWARD'S LANE

BARN STREET

BOUVERIE ROAD

FLEETWOOD STREET

LANCELL STREET

DEFOE ROAD

WOODLEA ROAD

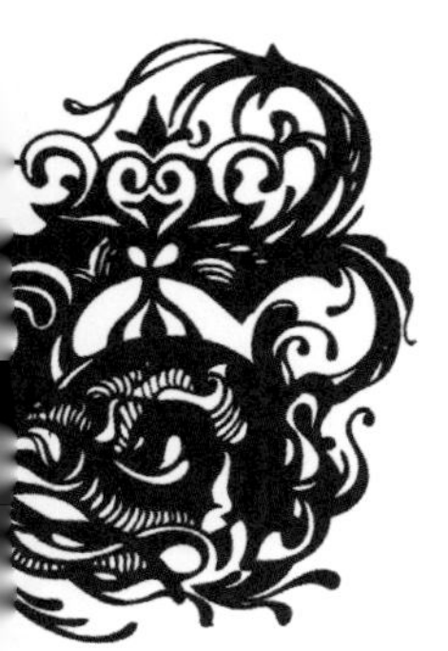

STOKE NEWINGTON - THE TOWN IN THE WOOD, WHERE LIVES CHURCH STREET ONCE CONNECTED TO CUT THROAT LANE, WHERE ONCE STOOD OPEN FIELDS AND LIVED A VILLAGE AWAY FROM STINKY LONDON TOWN. THE HOME OF THE NOUVEAU RICHE AND MAJESTIC HOMES. WHERE BOHEMIANS, ARTISTS & POLITICAL RADICALS CREATED & BERATED. FULL OF NORTHERN PRIDE, LADEN LATTES, BURGUNDY LOAFERS, ORGANIC BANGERS, BUGGIES AND PARK LIFERS SWEEPING STATEMENTS OF UNREQUITED WISDOM TO UNSUSPECTING SOUTHERNERS. WHERE BANSKY BLURRED THE ROYALS TO A CRAZY BEAT.

Stoke Newington

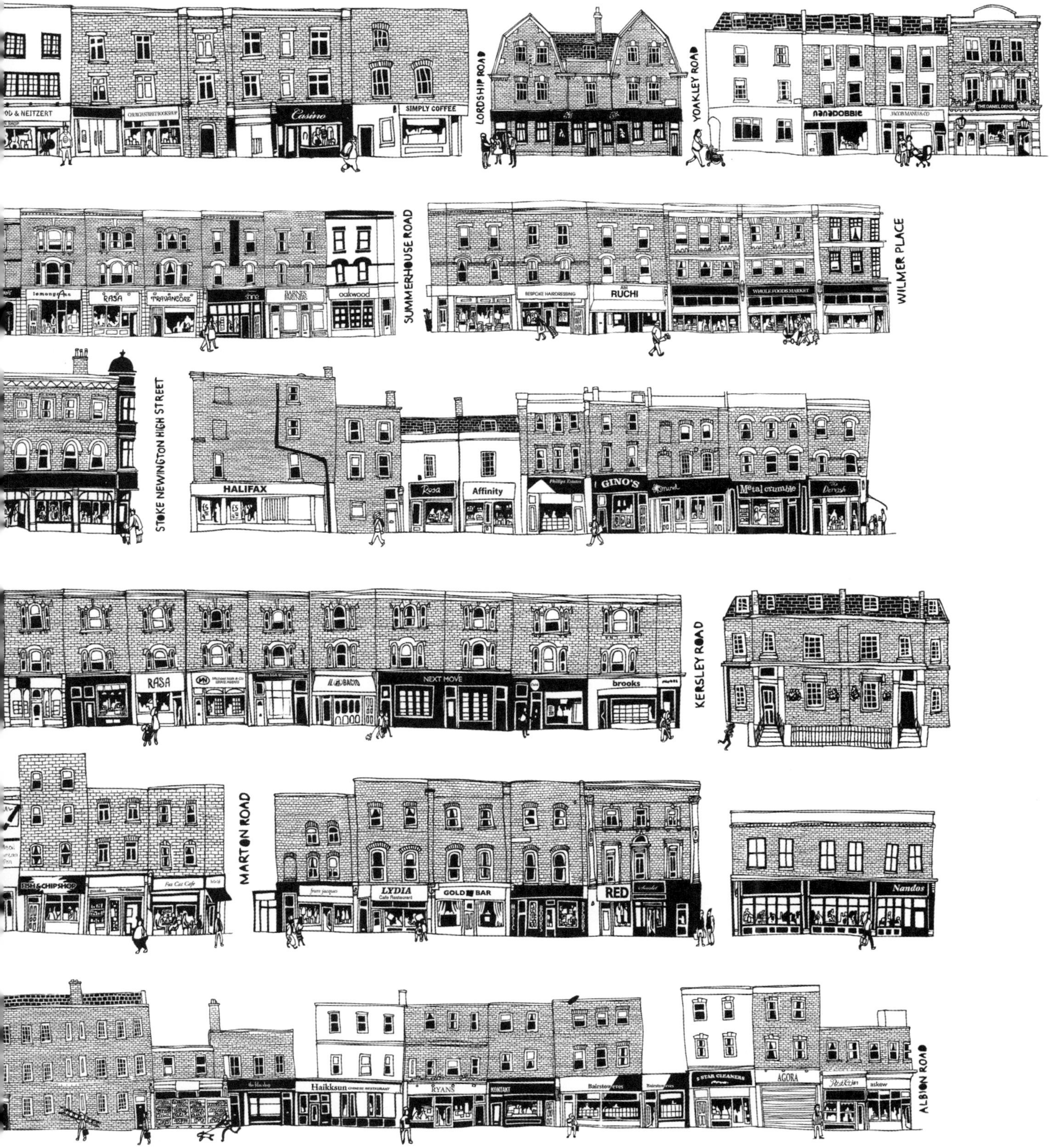

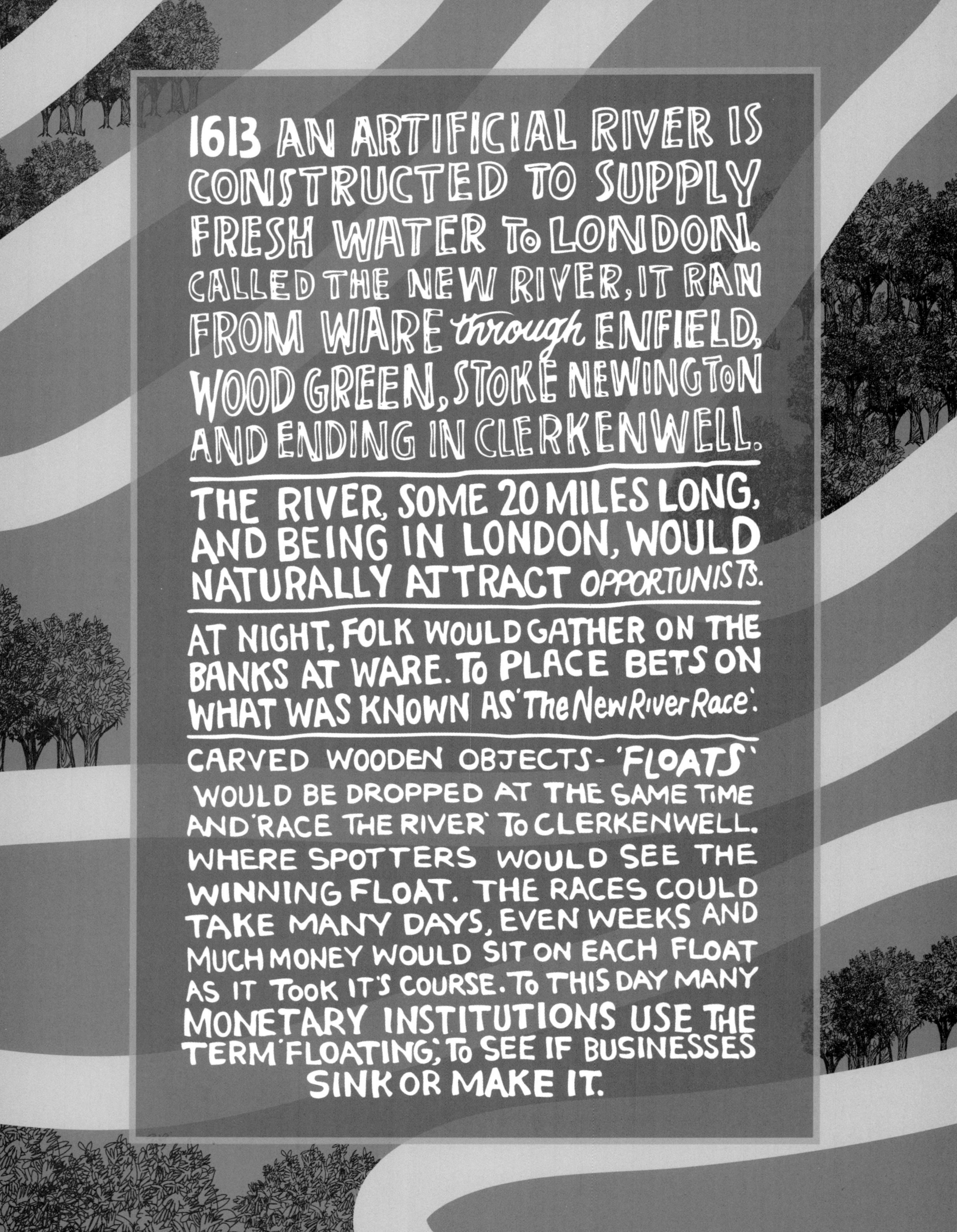
1613 AN ARTIFICIAL RIVER IS CONSTRUCTED TO SUPPLY FRESH WATER TO LONDON. CALLED THE NEW RIVER, IT RAN FROM WARE through ENFIELD, WOOD GREEN, STOKE NEWINGTON AND ENDING IN CLERKENWELL.
THE RIVER, SOME 20 MILES LONG, AND BEING IN LONDON, WOULD NATURALLY ATTRACT OPPORTUNISTS.
AT NIGHT, FOLK WOULD GATHER ON THE BANKS AT WARE. TO PLACE BETS ON WHAT WAS KNOWN AS 'The New River Race'.
CARVED WOODEN OBJECTS - 'FLOATS' WOULD BE DROPPED AT THE SAME TIME AND 'RACE THE RIVER' TO CLERKENWELL. WHERE SPOTTERS WOULD SEE THE WINNING FLOAT. THE RACES COULD TAKE MANY DAYS, EVEN WEEKS AND MUCH MONEY WOULD SIT ON EACH FLOAT AS IT TOOK IT'S COURSE. TO THIS DAY MANY MONETARY INSTITUTIONS USE THE TERM 'FLOATING', TO SEE IF BUSINESSES SINK OR MAKE IT.

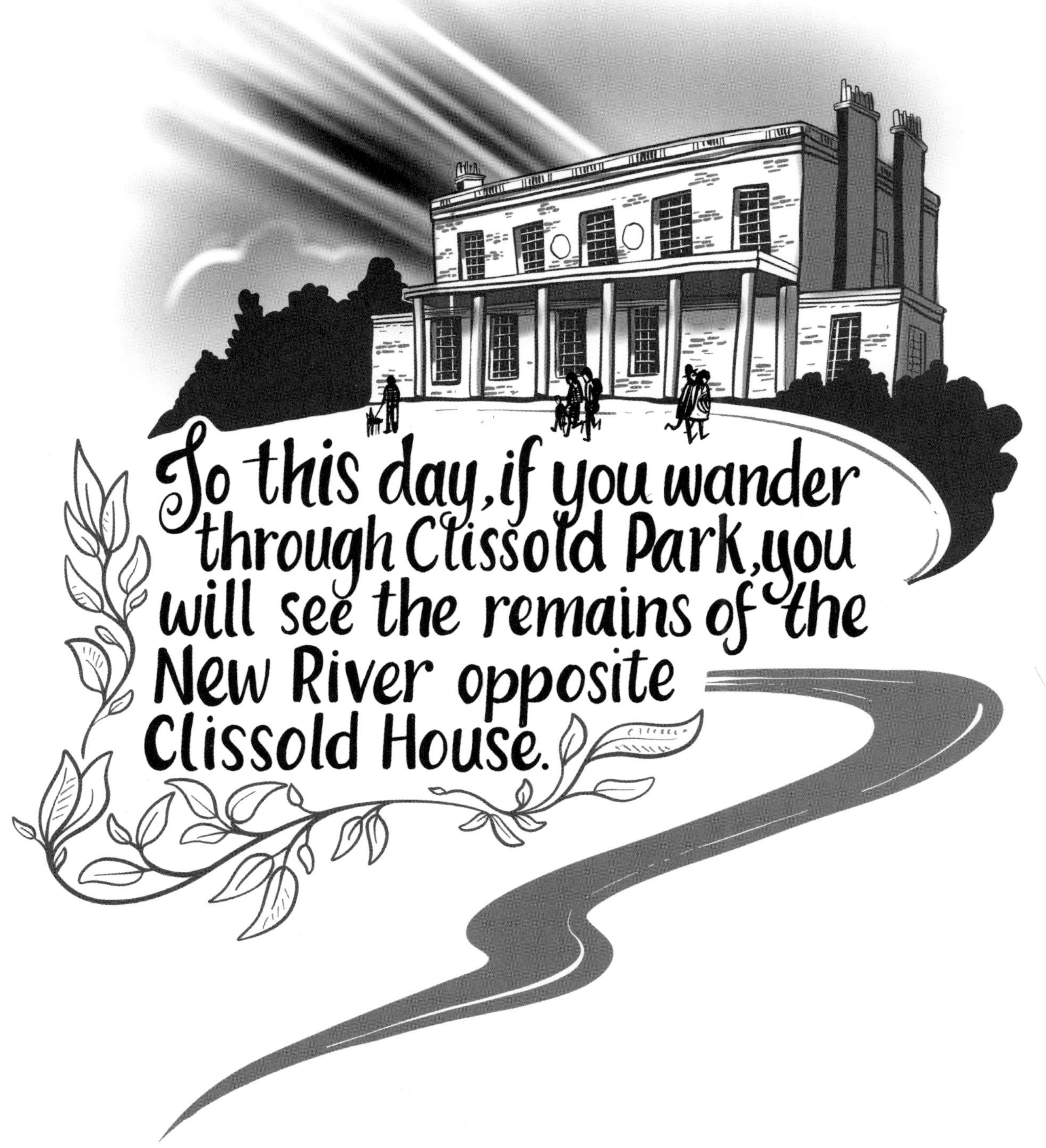
To this day, if you wander through Clissold Park, you will see the remains of the New River opposite Clissold House.

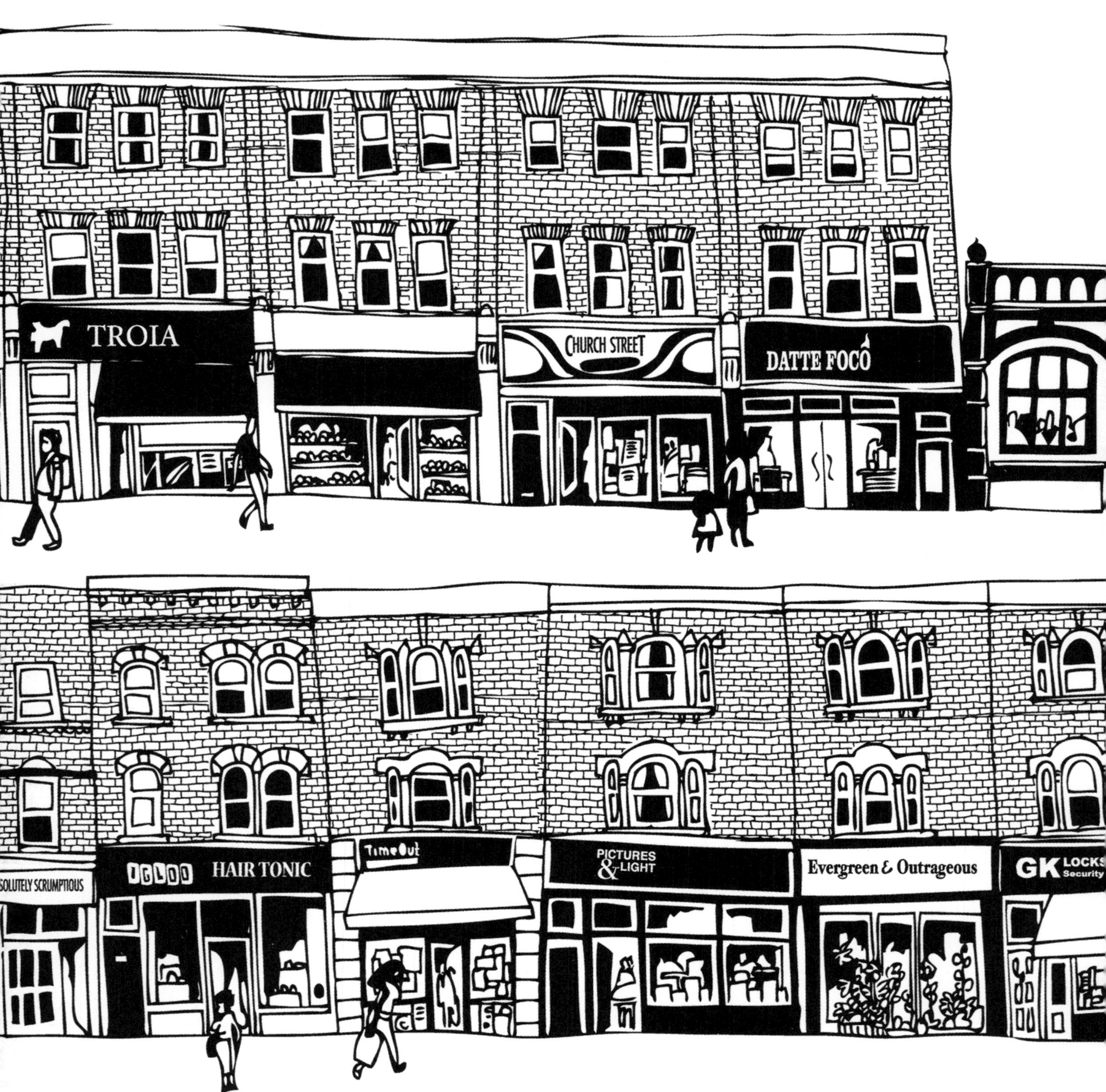
TROIA
CHURCH STREET
DATTE FOCO
SOLUTELY SCRUMPTIOUS
IGLOO
HAIR TONIC
TimeOut
PICTURES & LIGHT
Evergreen & Outrageous
GK
Security

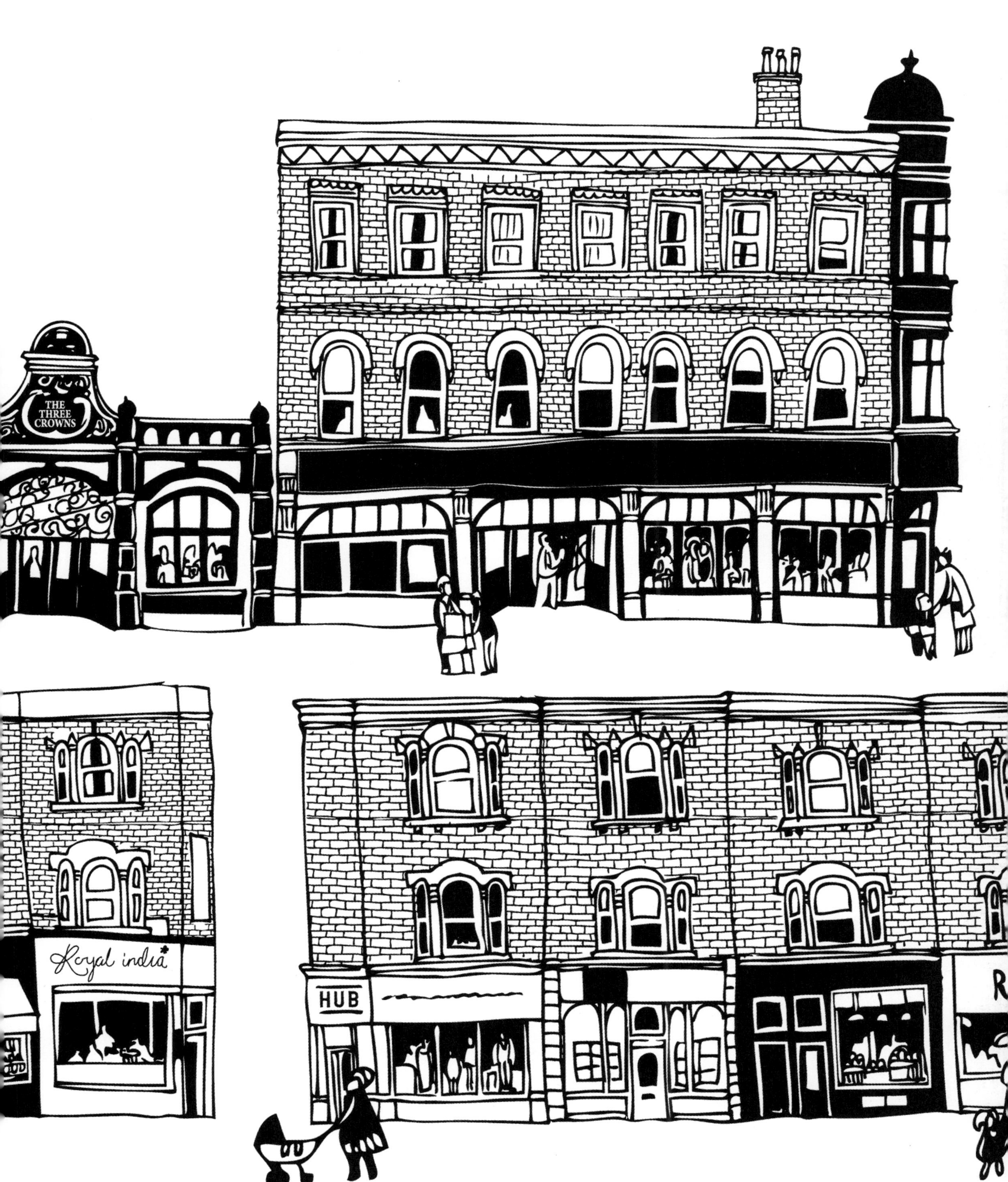
THE THREE CROWNS
Royal india
HUB

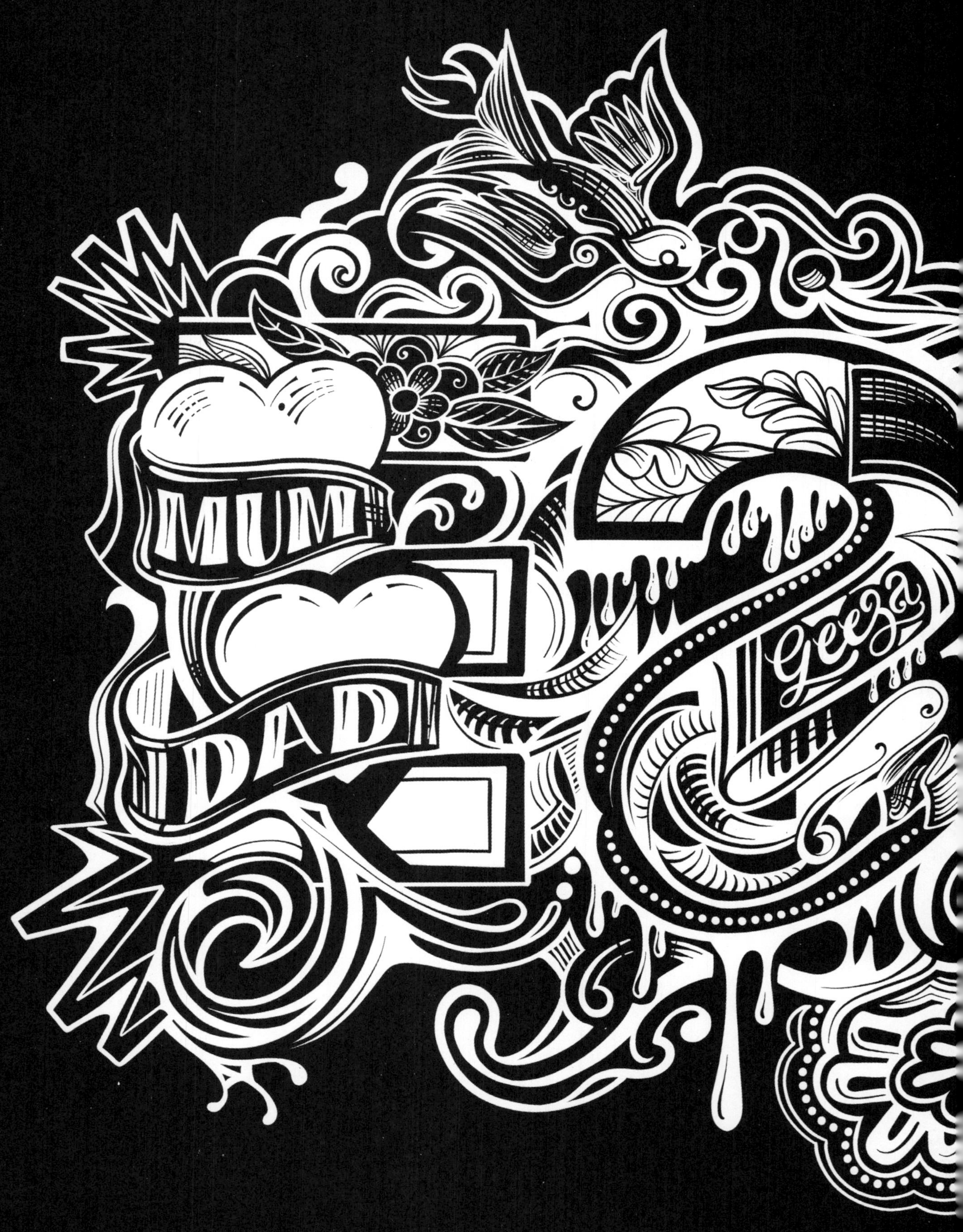
MUM
DAD
Geeza

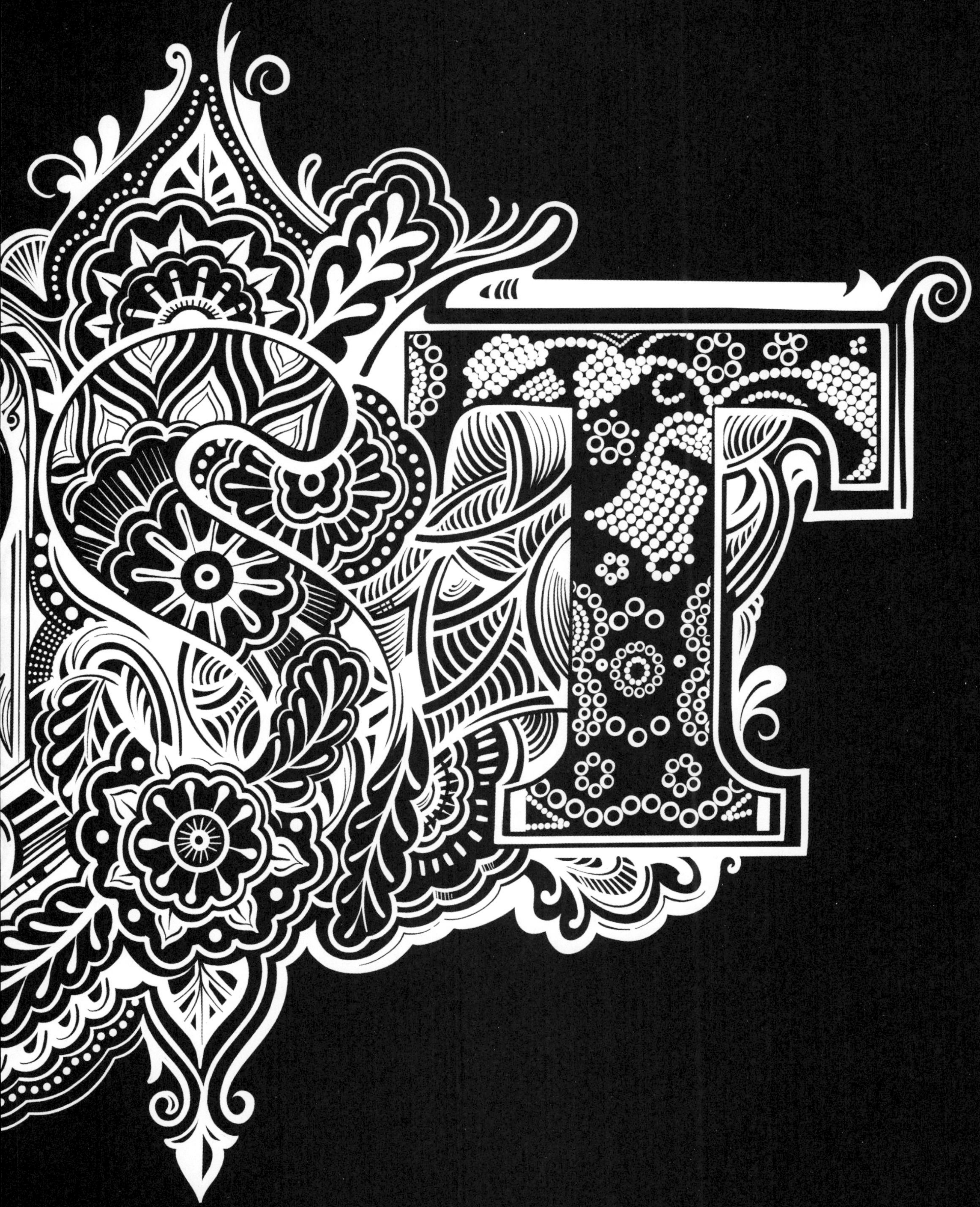

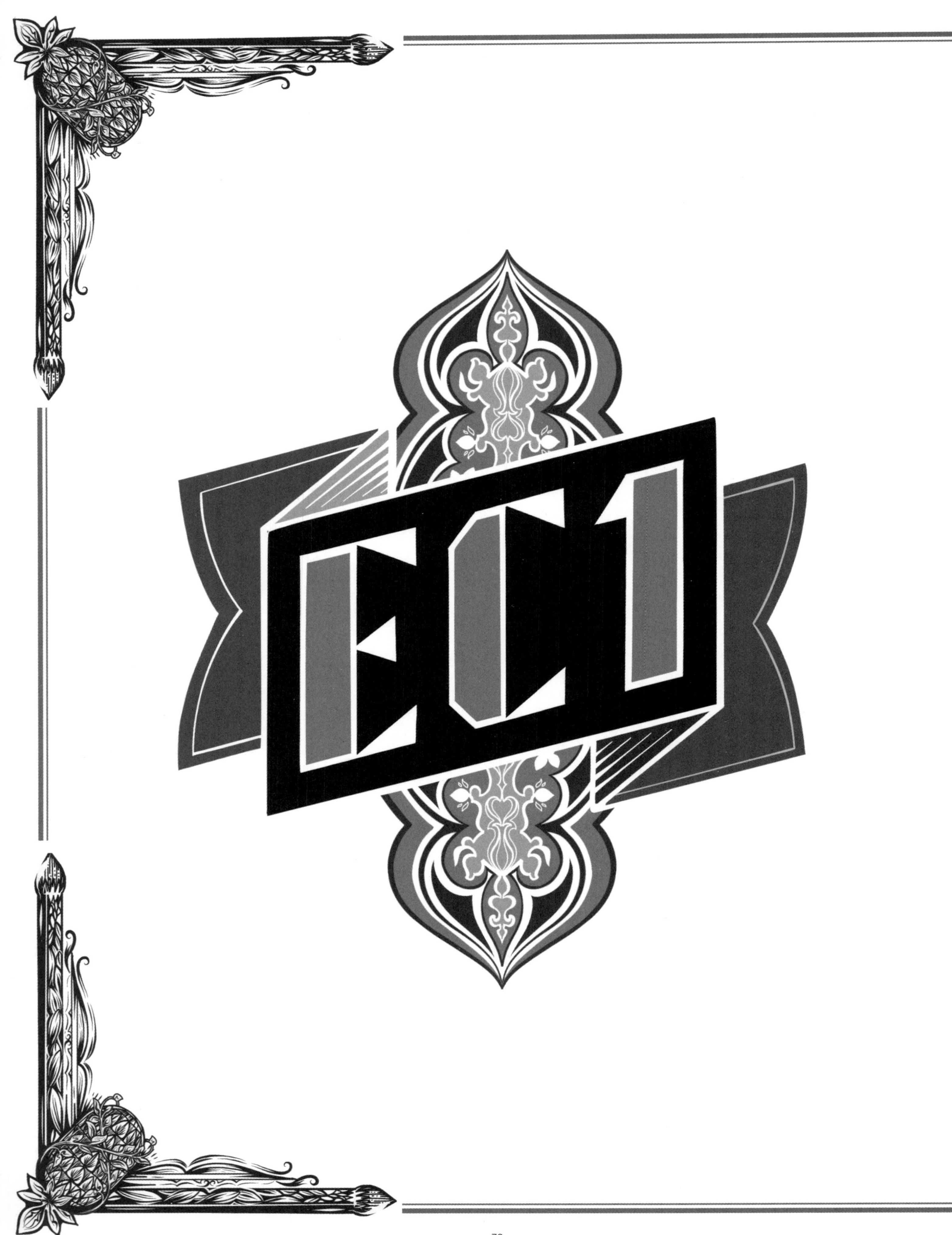
EC1

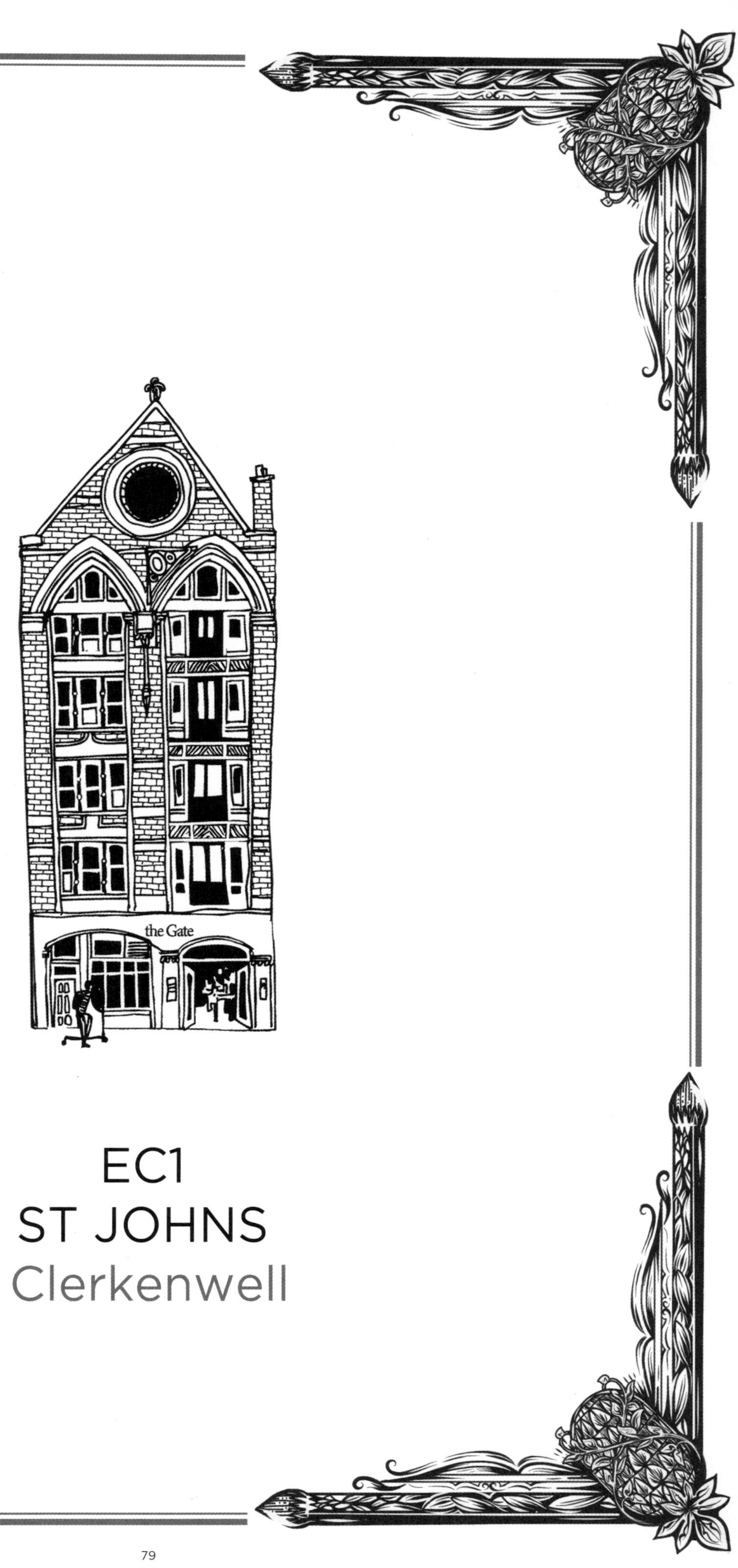

EC1
ST JOHNS
Clerkenwell

St Johns

JOHN, THE SON OF ZEBEDEE & SALOME, ONE OF THE TWELVE APOSTLES, A VERY LEARNED AUTHOR INDEED, WRITING SUCH GREATS AS THE GOSPEL OF JOHN, THE EPISTLES OF JOHN & THE CLASSIC, THE BOOK OF REVELATION.

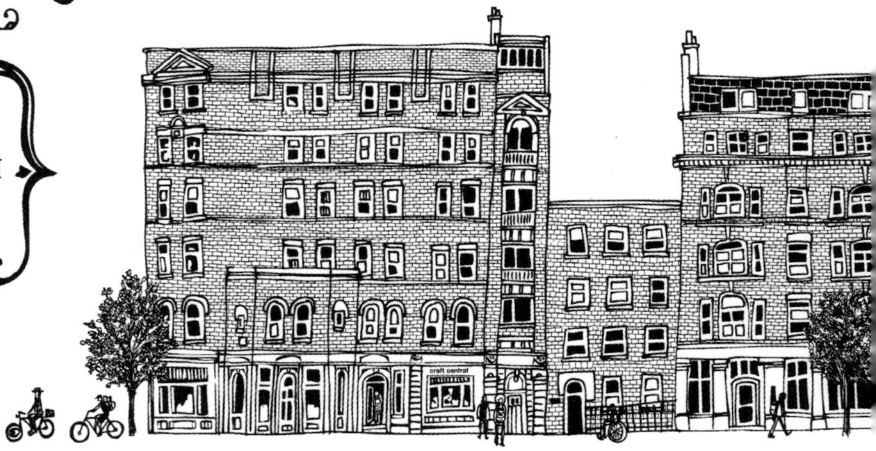

ST JOHN'S SC

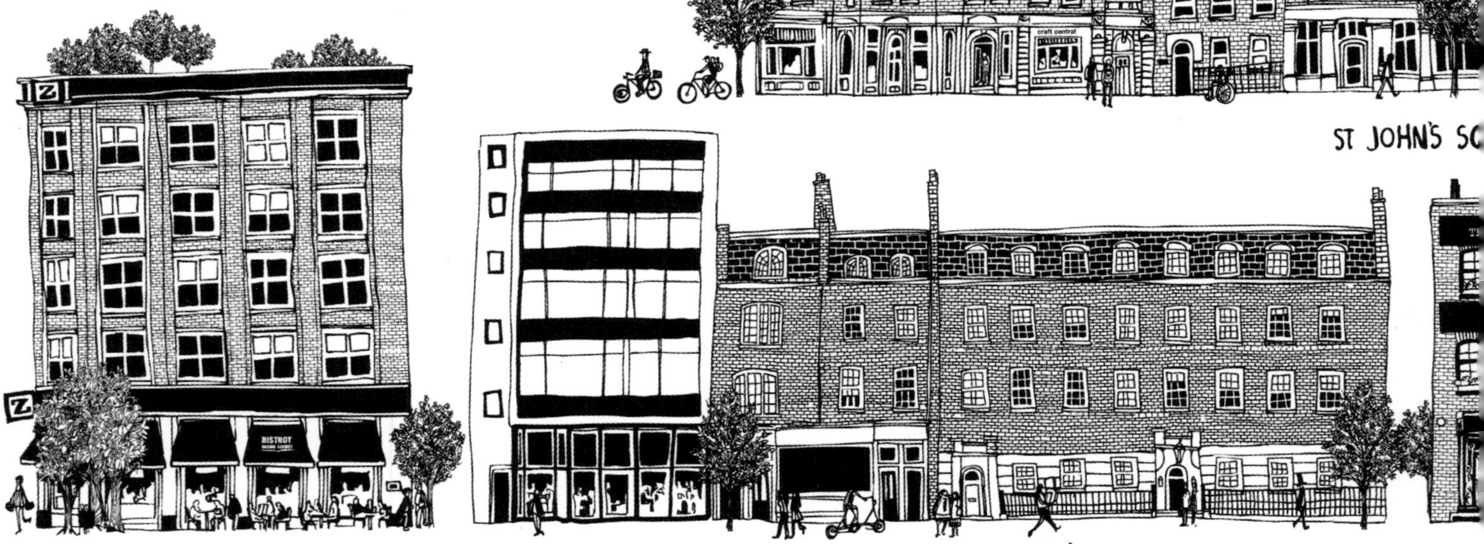

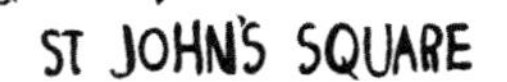

ST JOHN'S SQUARE

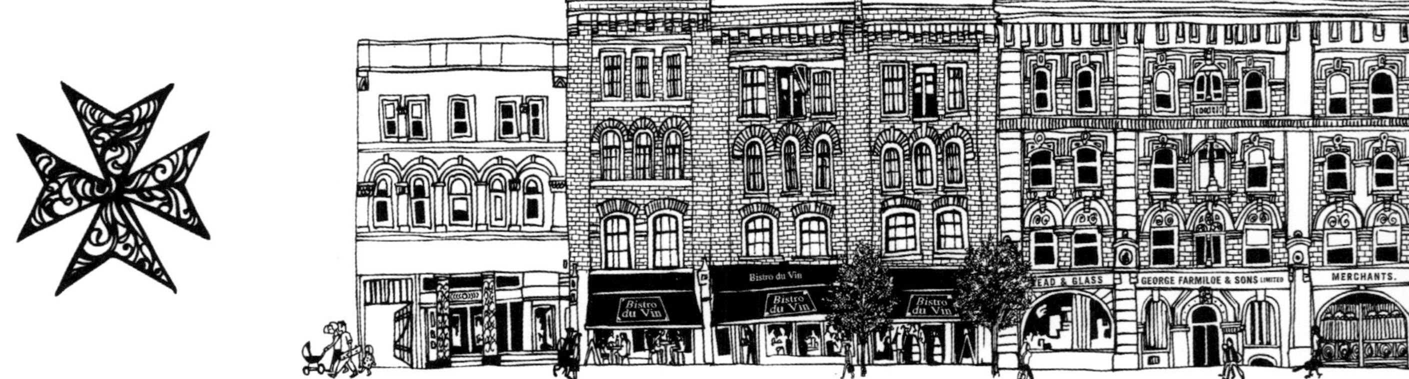

ST JOHN'S STREET

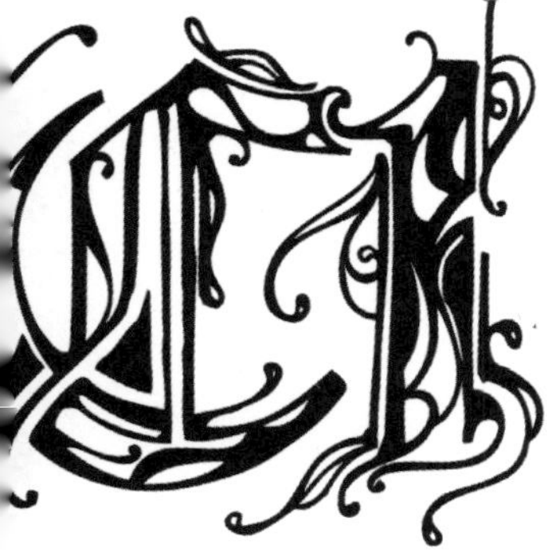

Clerkenwell

The order of the hospital of Saint John, born down Jerusalem way by Benedictine monks. These fellows became carers of the sick & poor of all faiths. Of hospitality, religion, and later military might, the order travelled from Jerusalem to Cyprus, Rhodes and then to the sunny isle of Malta. There bestowed pon it's members the grand title of the Knights of Malta. Thus began the Priories & Grand ones too, administered by the Commandery in the London enclave of Clerkenwell.

These charitable fellows got the royal thumbs up from Queen Vic & so began the modern order of St John. Now with piercing shrillsirens and greencoated angels, we plug our ears and salute the health givers, carers & watchers across this fair isle.

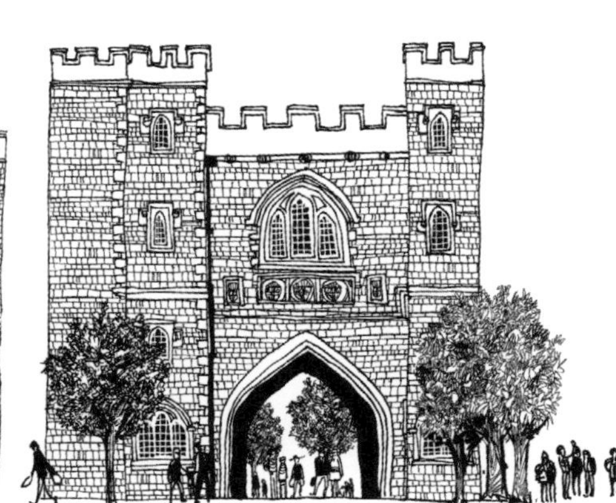

And now this St Johns, this hub of activity in ClerKenwell, runs amok with creatives and ideas, with flavours and feasts, a square and a line with meatpackers one end and craftiness the other. Where suits sip Nettle Gimlet at Townhouses and pool players dream of Zetters wins and sleep.

The home of Craft Central, of bejewelled dazzlers & charming wishlists. Where Mr Vic creates London in all its finery & summer bathers lick Magnums in lunchbreaks by church doors as couriers flit between horned metal beasts & marauding pedestrians.

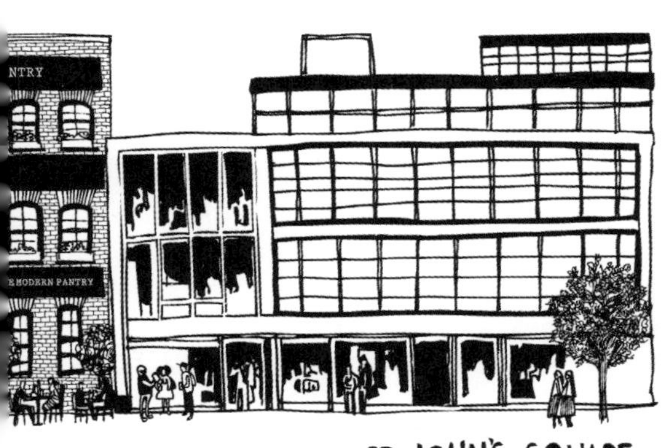

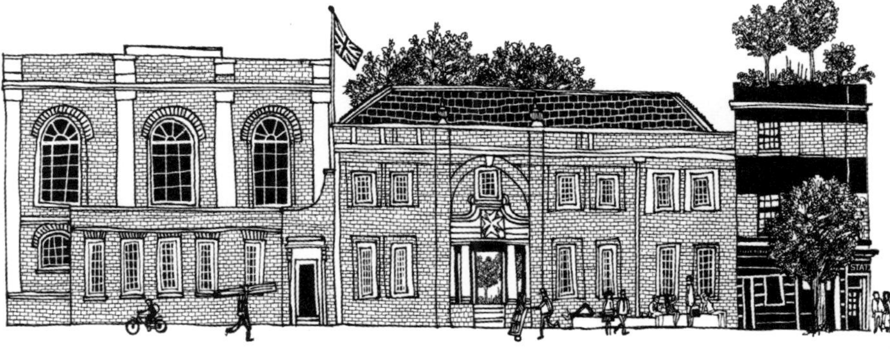

ST JOHN'S SQUARE

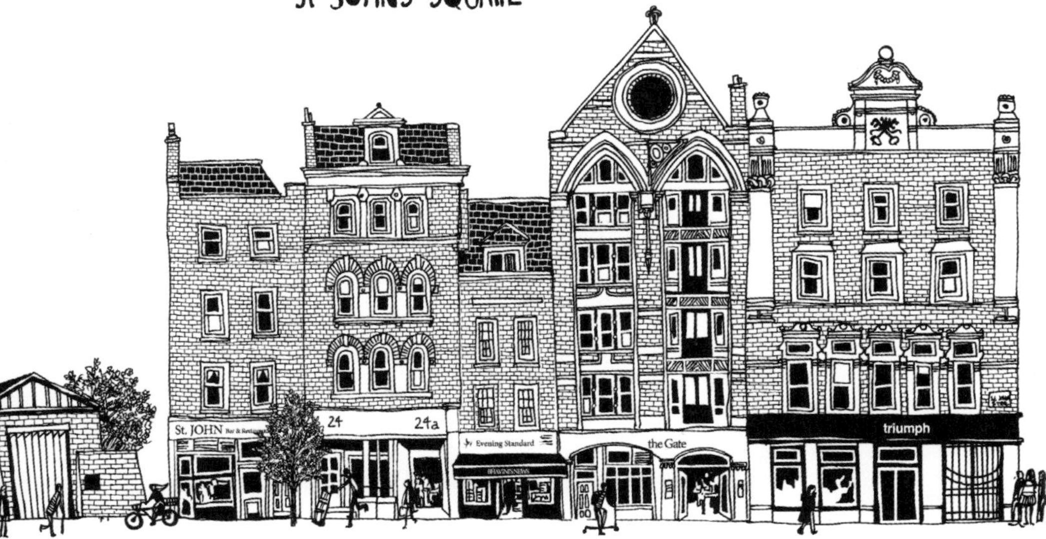

ST JOHN'S STREET

ONCE A WILD & DISREPUTABLE AREA IN EAST LONDON · A HAUNT OF HARLETS, THIEVES & UNSAVOURIES. WITH AN INFAMOUS REPUTATION OF BROTHEL KEEPERS & DUBIOUS CHARACTERS, CLERKENWELL WAS HOME TO THREE PRISONS · CLERKENWELL BRIDEWELL, COLBATH FIELDS PRISON AND THE HOUSE OF DETENTION – THE LATTER HOUSING EXTENSIVE VAULTS & CELLS KNOWN AS THE CATACOMBS ·

IT IS SAID BENEATH THE STREETS RUN A WARREN OF SECRET TUNNELS LINKING VARIOUS ESTABLISHMENTS · ONE STORY TELLS OF JUDGES TRAVELLING UNDERGROUND FROM THE MASONIC LODGE TO AN ALEHOUSE, WHERE AFTER A FEW SNIFTERS, A TUNNEL SHUFFLE TO THE PRISON TO CONDEMN PRISONERS BEFORE SCURRYING BACK TO THE LODGE FOR A BRANDY & A DESERVED SNOOZE.

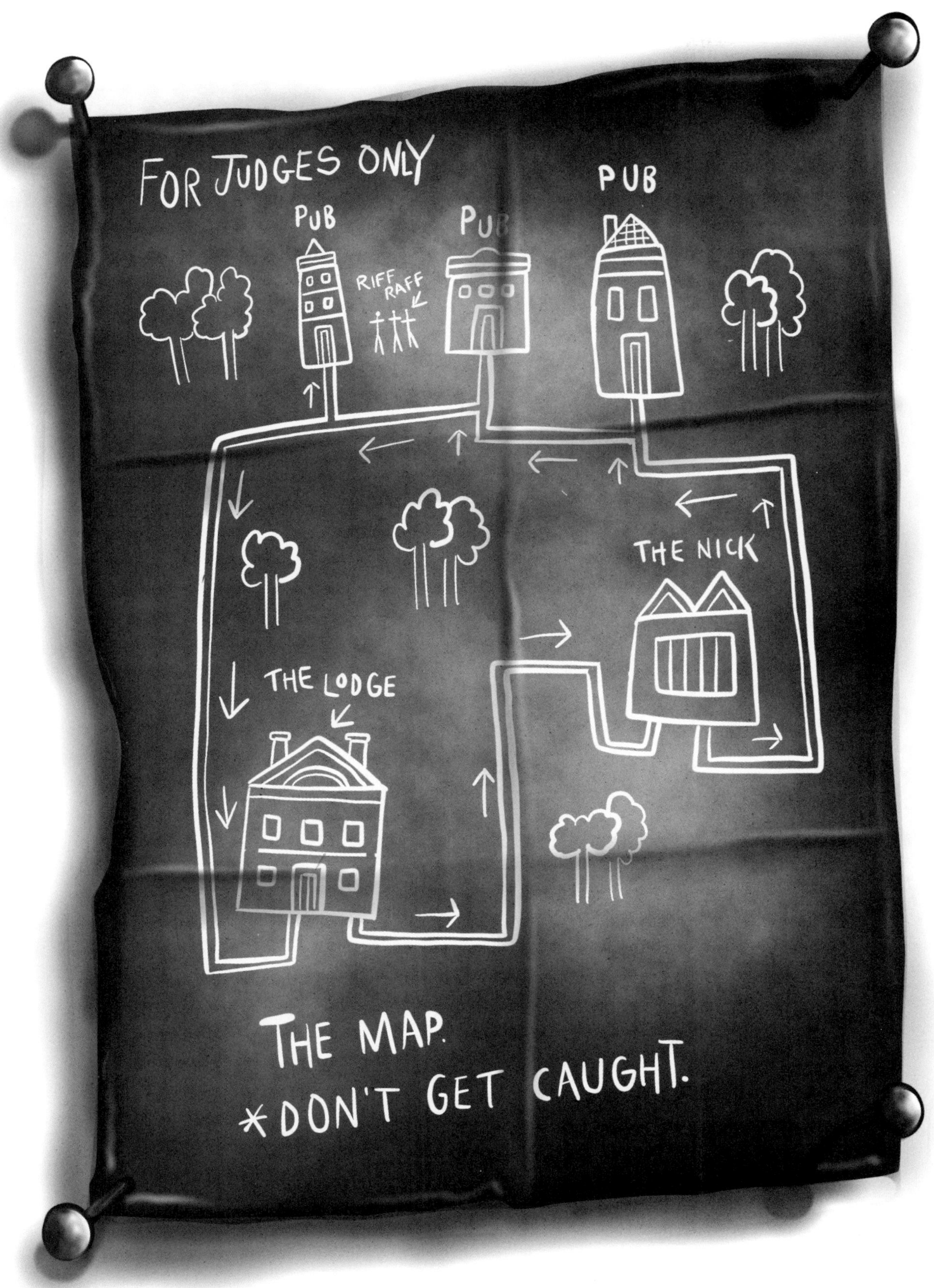

FOR JUDGES ONLY
PUB
PUB
PUB
RIFF RAFF
THE NICK
THE LODGE
THE MAP.
*DON'T GET CAUGHT.

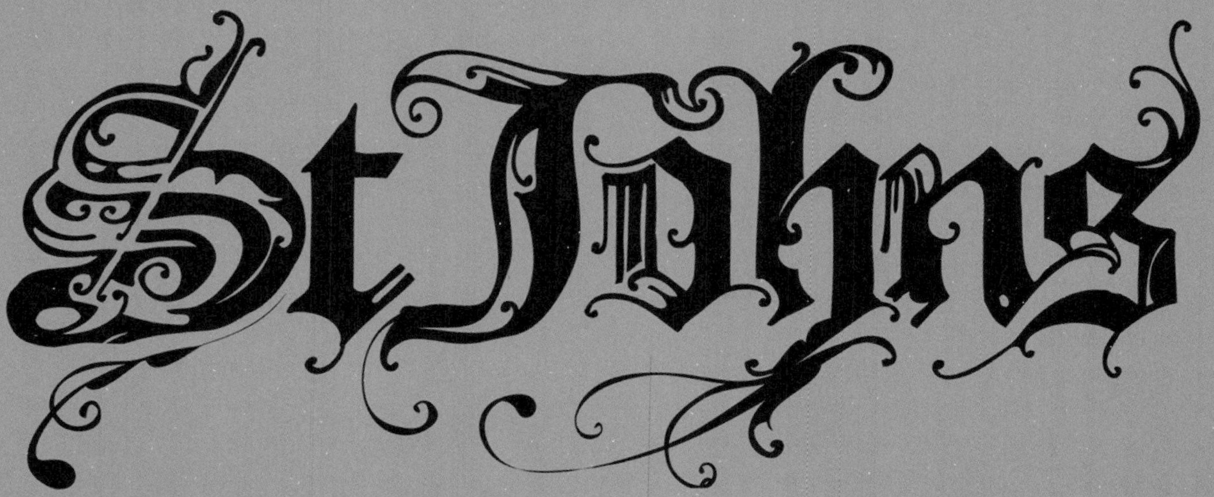
St Johns

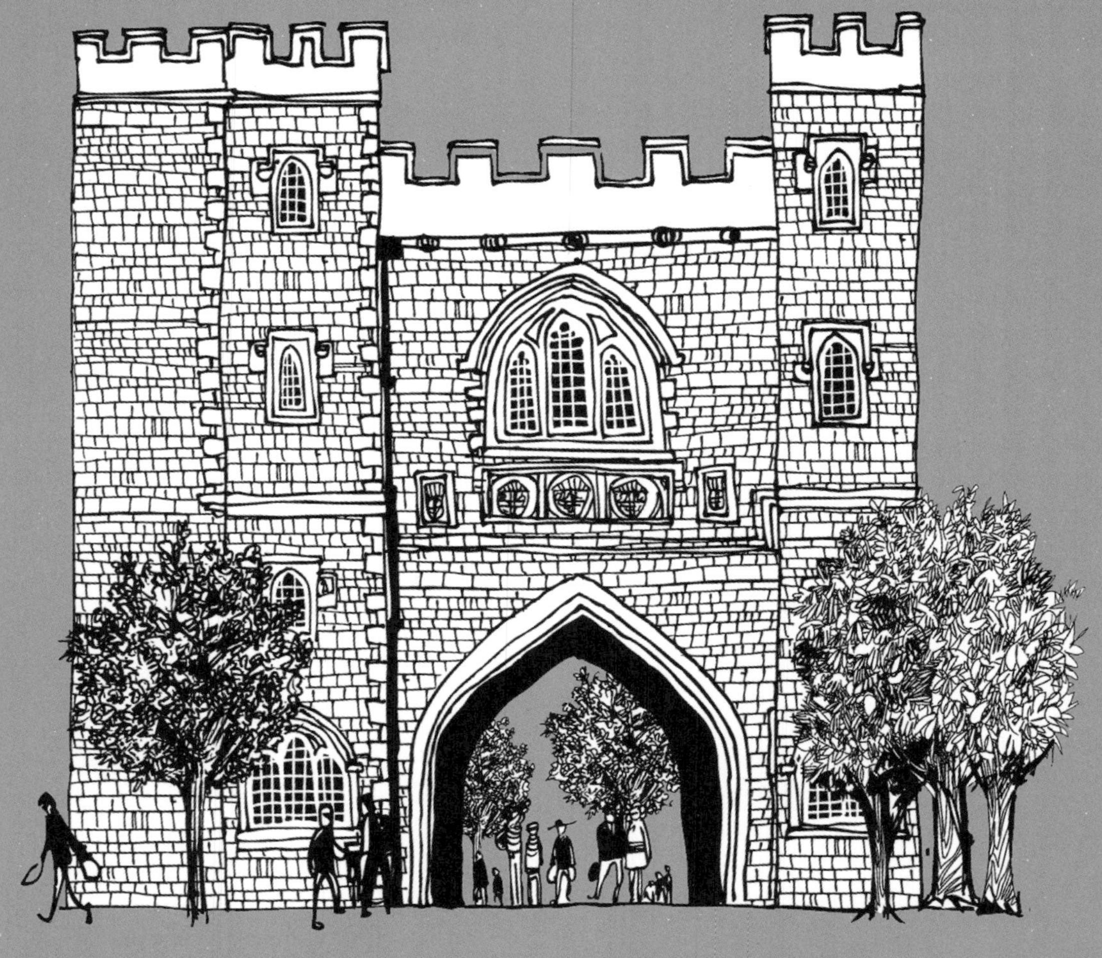

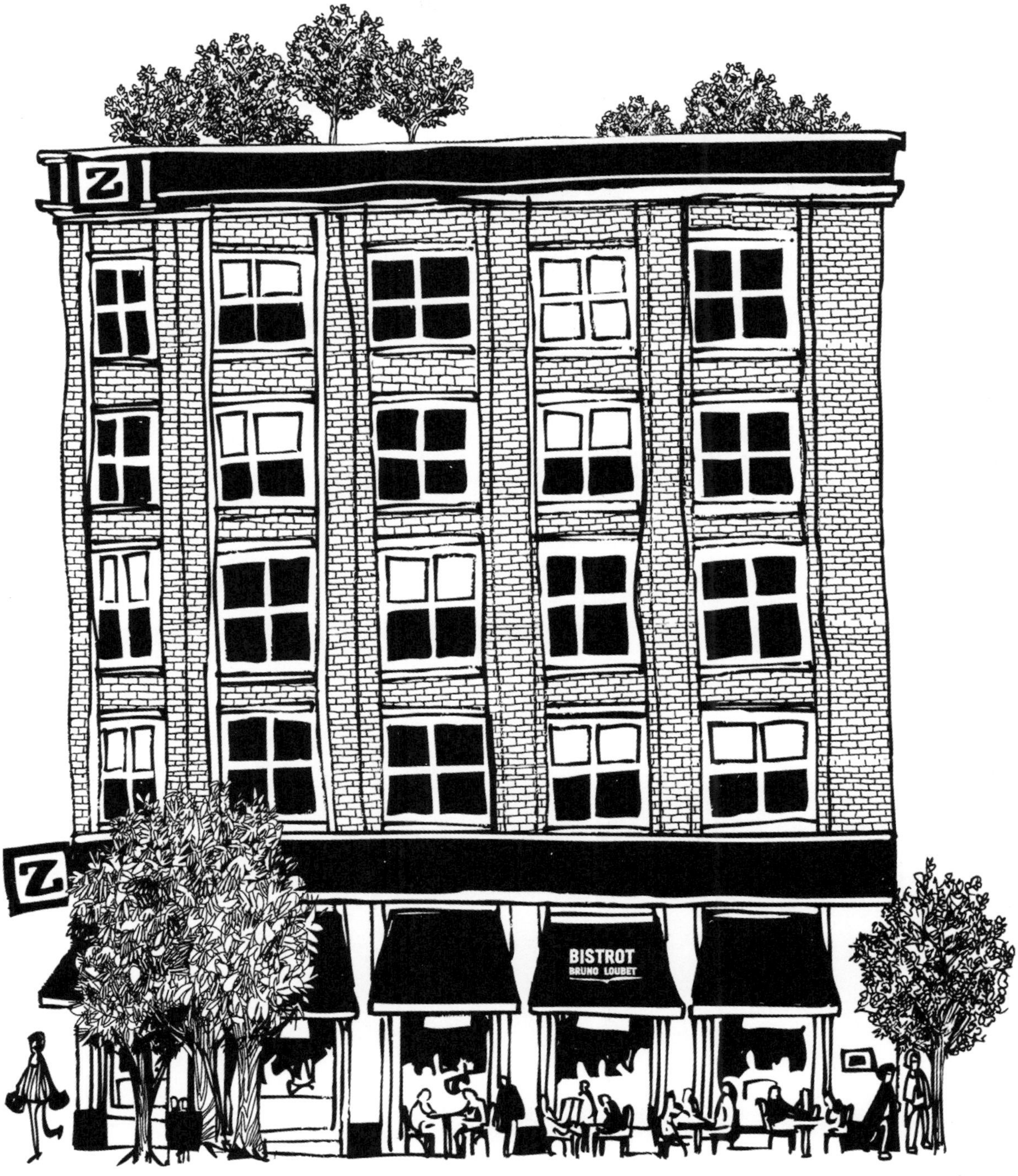

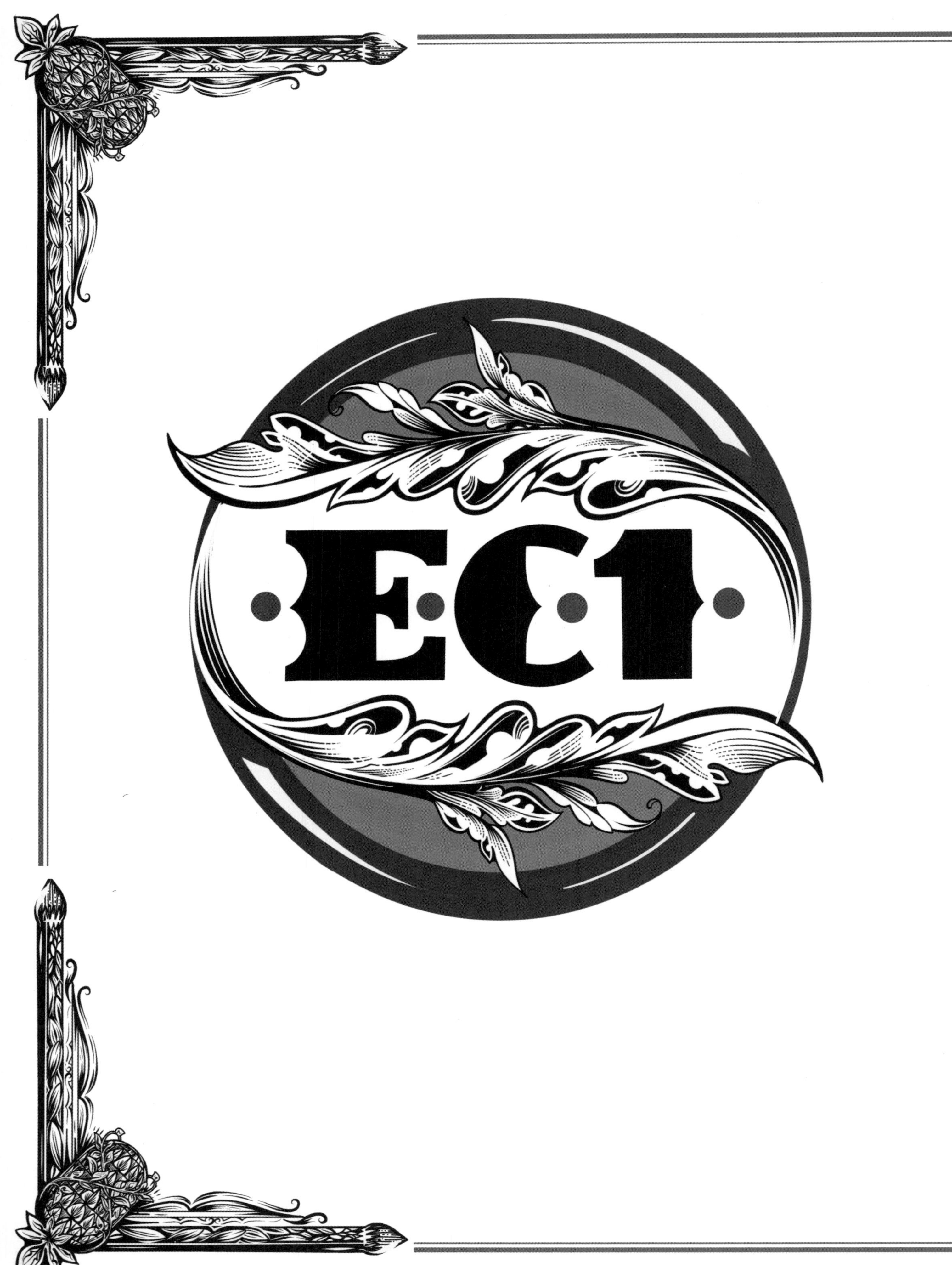
EC1

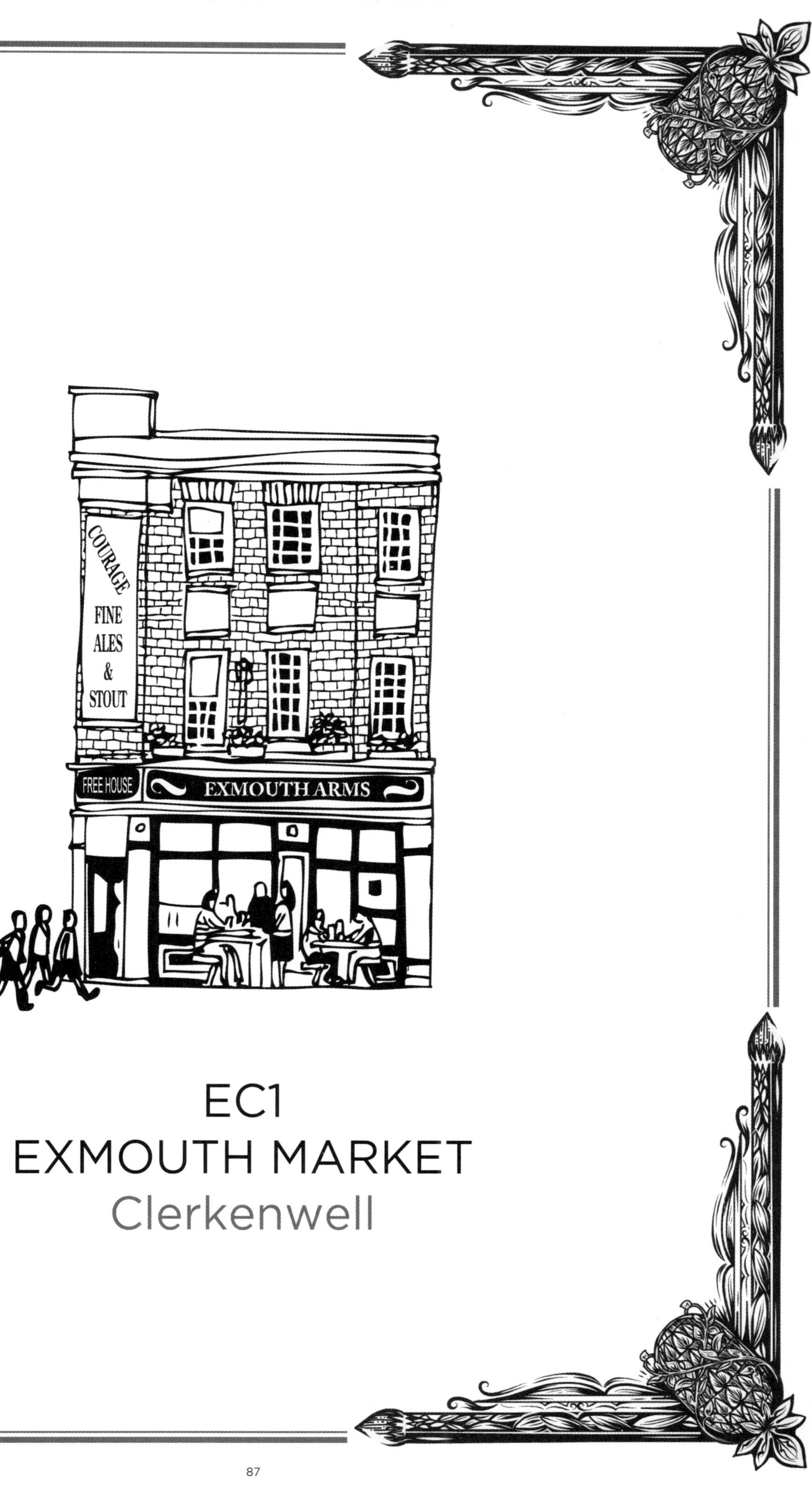

EC1
EXMOUTH MARKET
Clerkenwell

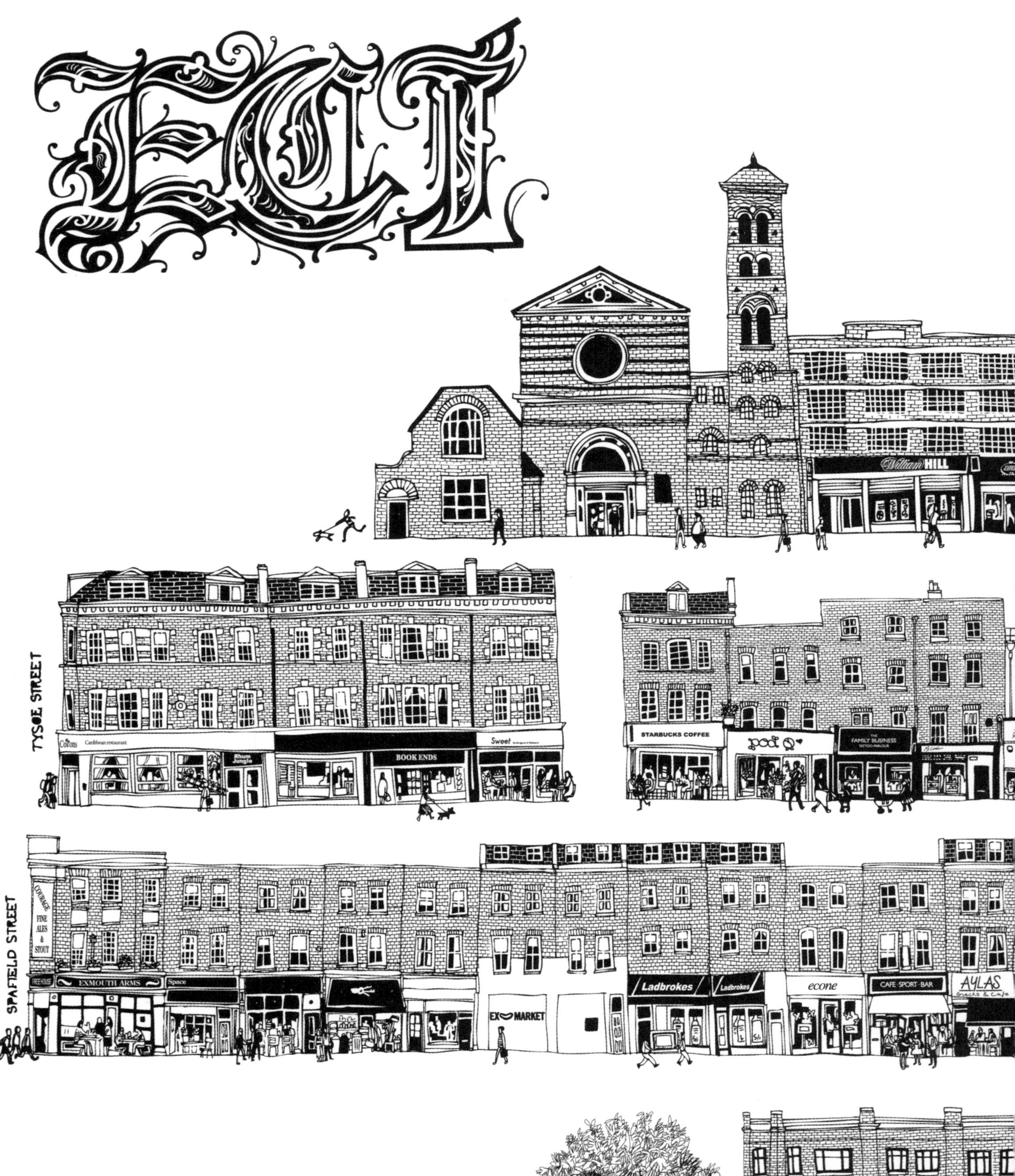
EC1
William HILL
TYSOE STREET
Cotons Caribbean restaurant
BOOK ENDS
Sweet
STARBUCKS COFFEE
THE FAMILY BUSINESS TATTOO PARLOUR
SPAFIELD STREET
COURAGE FINE ALES & STOUT
FREE HOUSE
EXMOUTH ARMS
Space
EX MARKET
Ladbrokes
Ladbrokes
econe
CAFE·SPORT·BAR
AYLAS Snacks & Cafe
PINE STREET
CARAVAN

EXMOUTH MARKET

SO NAMED AFTER THE DRINKING ESTABLISHMENT, THE EXMOUTH ARMS, WHICH IN TURN WAS CHRISTENED FROM SIR EDWARD PELLEW, A NAVAL COMMANDER CHAP, THE VISCOUNT OF EXMOUTH. THE HOME OF THE FAMOUS LONDON SPA, AND LONDON TOWNS ONLY BASILICA STYLE CHURCH NO LESS. IN THE HEART OF CLERKENWELL. OR FONS CLERICORUM AS FITZ-STEPHEN NAMED IT AFTER THE ENTHUSIASTIC CLERKS THAT ACTED SACRED DRAMAS BY THE WELL IN RAY STREET DURING THE REIGN OF THE BIG MAN, HENRY 11. THAT BECAME THE STOMPING GROUND OF CLOCKERS, JEWELLERS, ENAMELLERS AND ARTISANS. NOW HOME TO FANCY FOOTED CREATIVES, DELIGHTFUL TASTERS OF FINERIES, LATE SUPPERS AND PORTLY BELLIES. WHERE GLASSES ARE TOPPED WITH RAINBOW LIQUEURS AND AROMAS TEMPT THE WEARIEST OF OFFICITES. THIS GEM OF A STREET, WHOSE HEART BEATS TRUE AND PROUD IN THE ROTATION OF BLACK AND RED CARRIAGES.

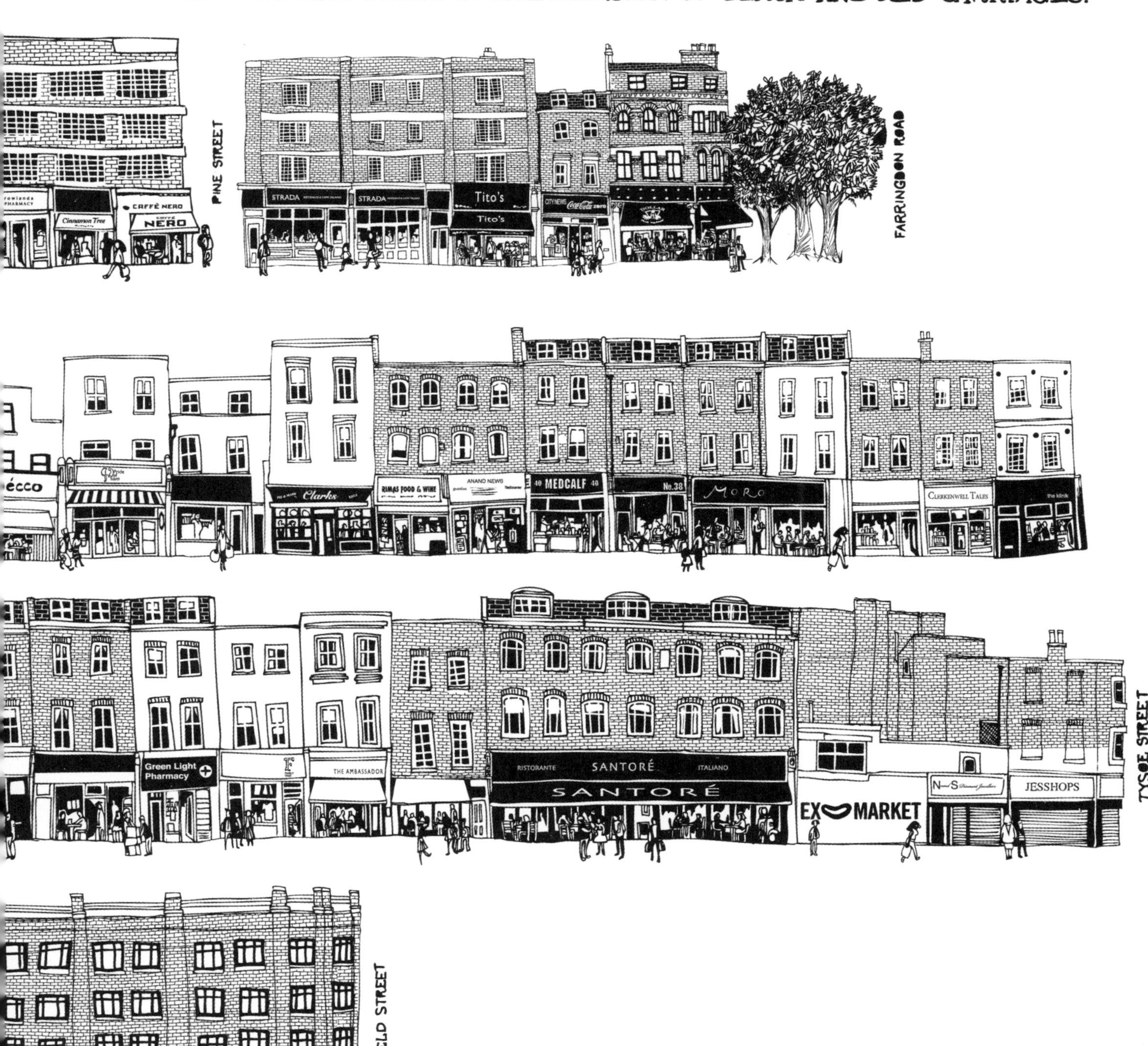

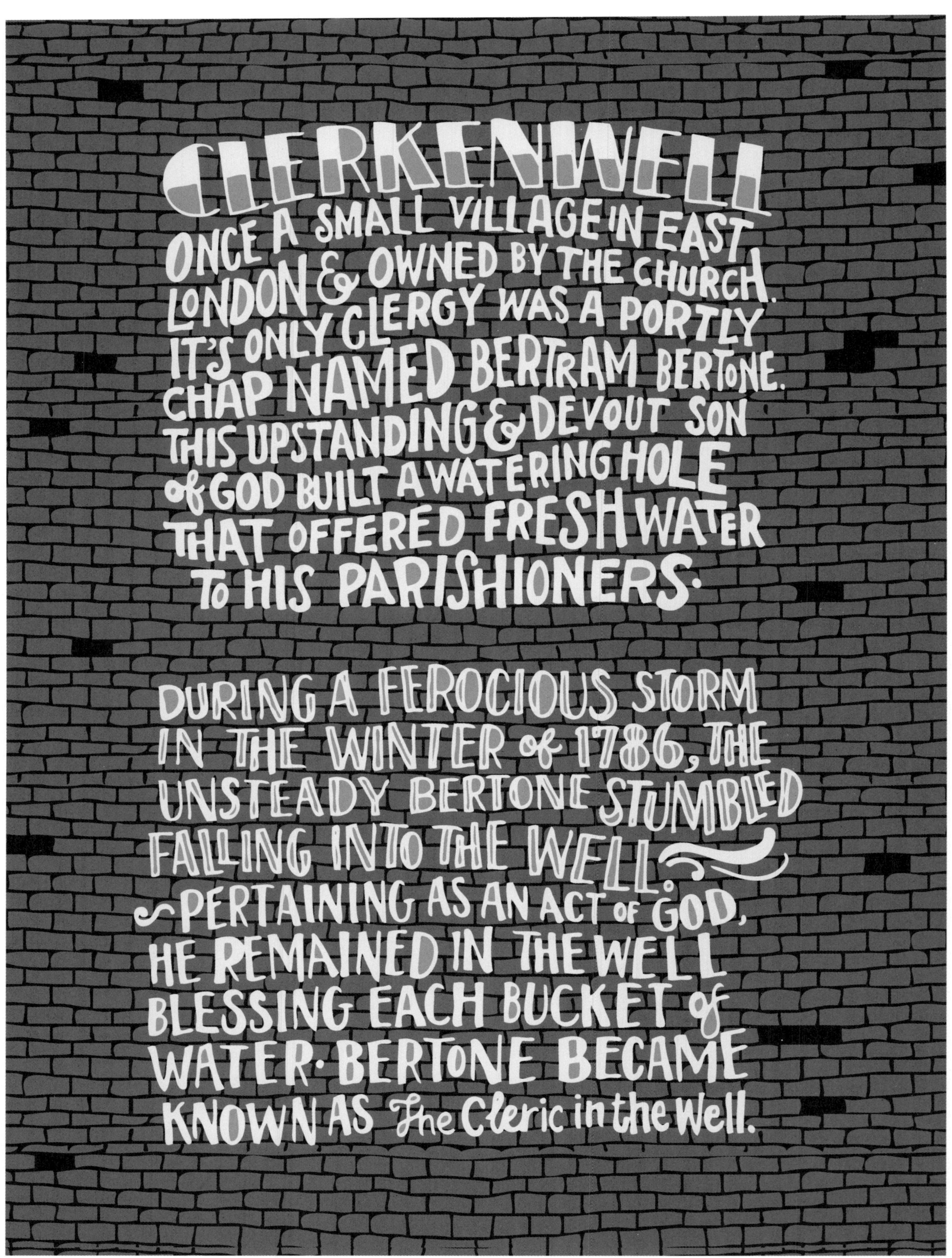
CLERKENWELL
ONCE A SMALL VILLAGE IN EAST
LONDON & OWNED BY THE CHURCH.
IT'S ONLY CLERGY WAS A PORTLY
CHAP NAMED BERTRAM BERTONE.
THIS UPSTANDING & DEVOUT SON
of GOD BUILT A WATERING HOLE
THAT OFFERED FRESH WATER
TO HIS PARISHIONERS.
DURING A FEROCIOUS STORM
IN THE WINTER of 1786, THE
UNSTEADY BERTONE STUMBLED
FALLING INTO THE WELL.
PERTAINING AS AN ACT of GOD,
HE REMAINED IN THE WELL
BLESSING EACH BUCKET of
WATER. BERTONE BECAME
KNOWN AS The Cleric in the Well.

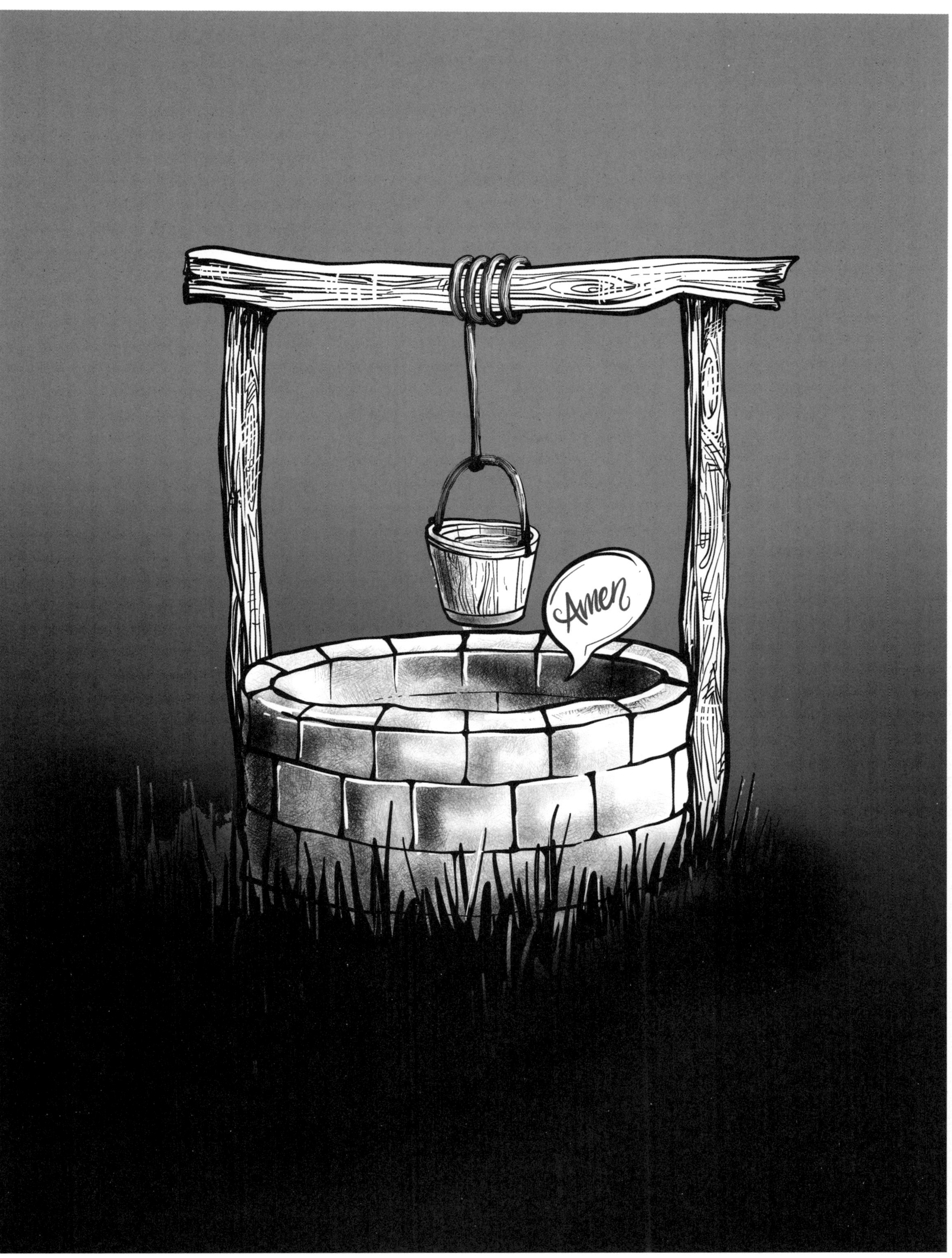
Amen

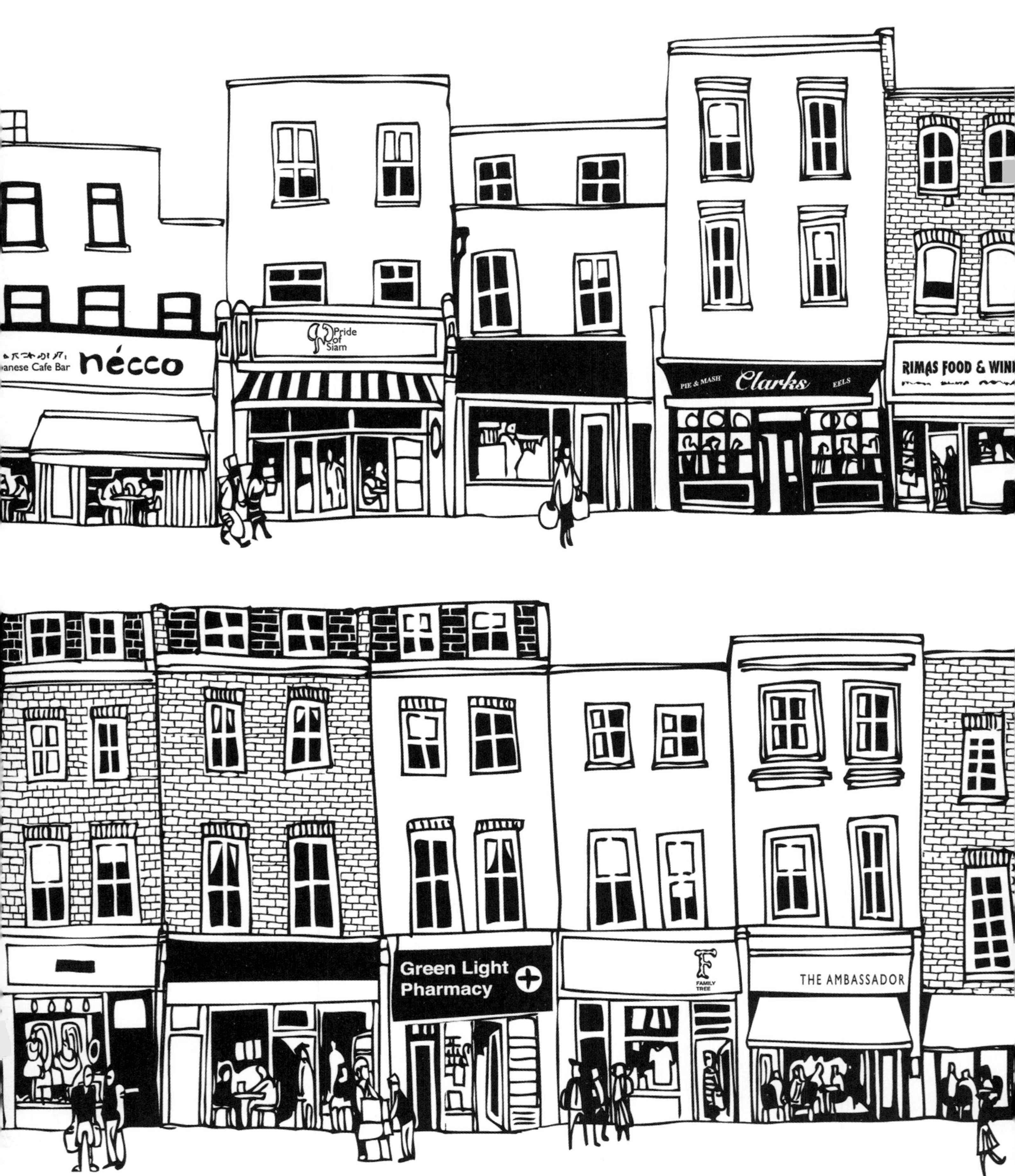

anese Cafe Bar nécco
Pride of Siam
PIE & MASH Clarks EELS
RIMAS FOOD & WINI
Green Light Pharmacy
F FAMILY TREE
THE AMBASSADOR

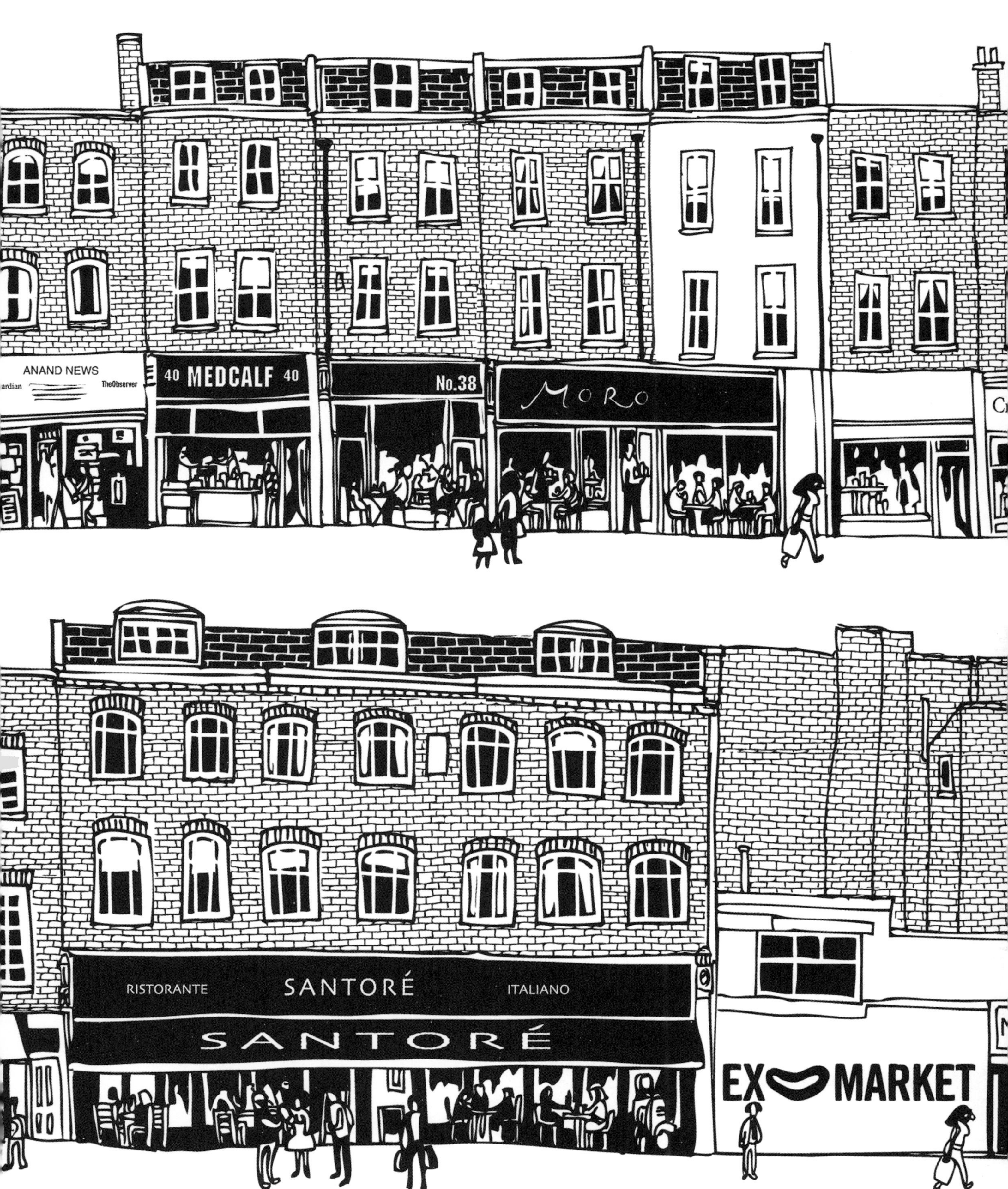
ANAND NEWS
TheObserver
40 MEDCALF 40
No.38
MORO
RISTORANTE
SANTORÉ
ITALIANO
SANTORÉ
EX MARKET

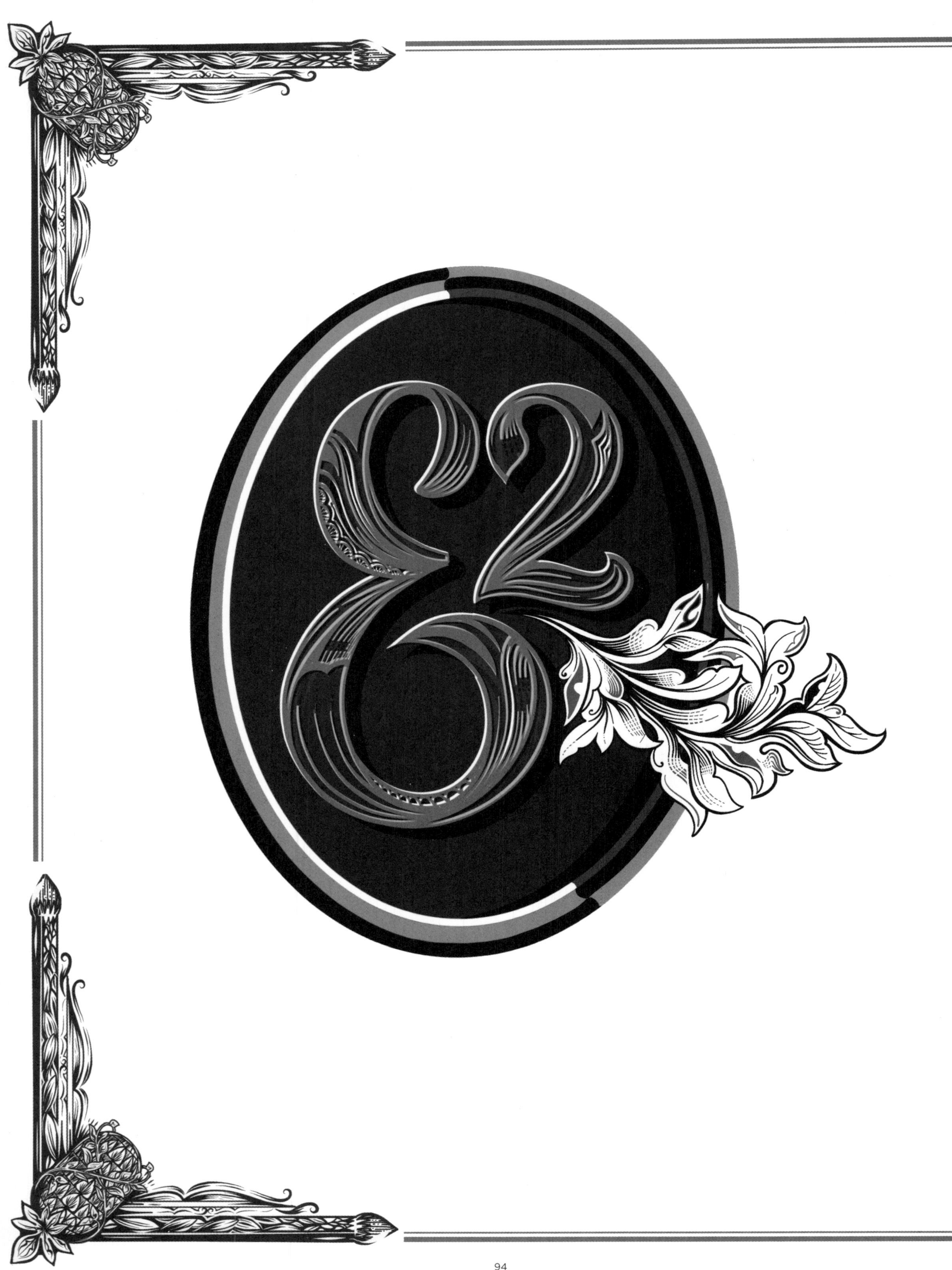

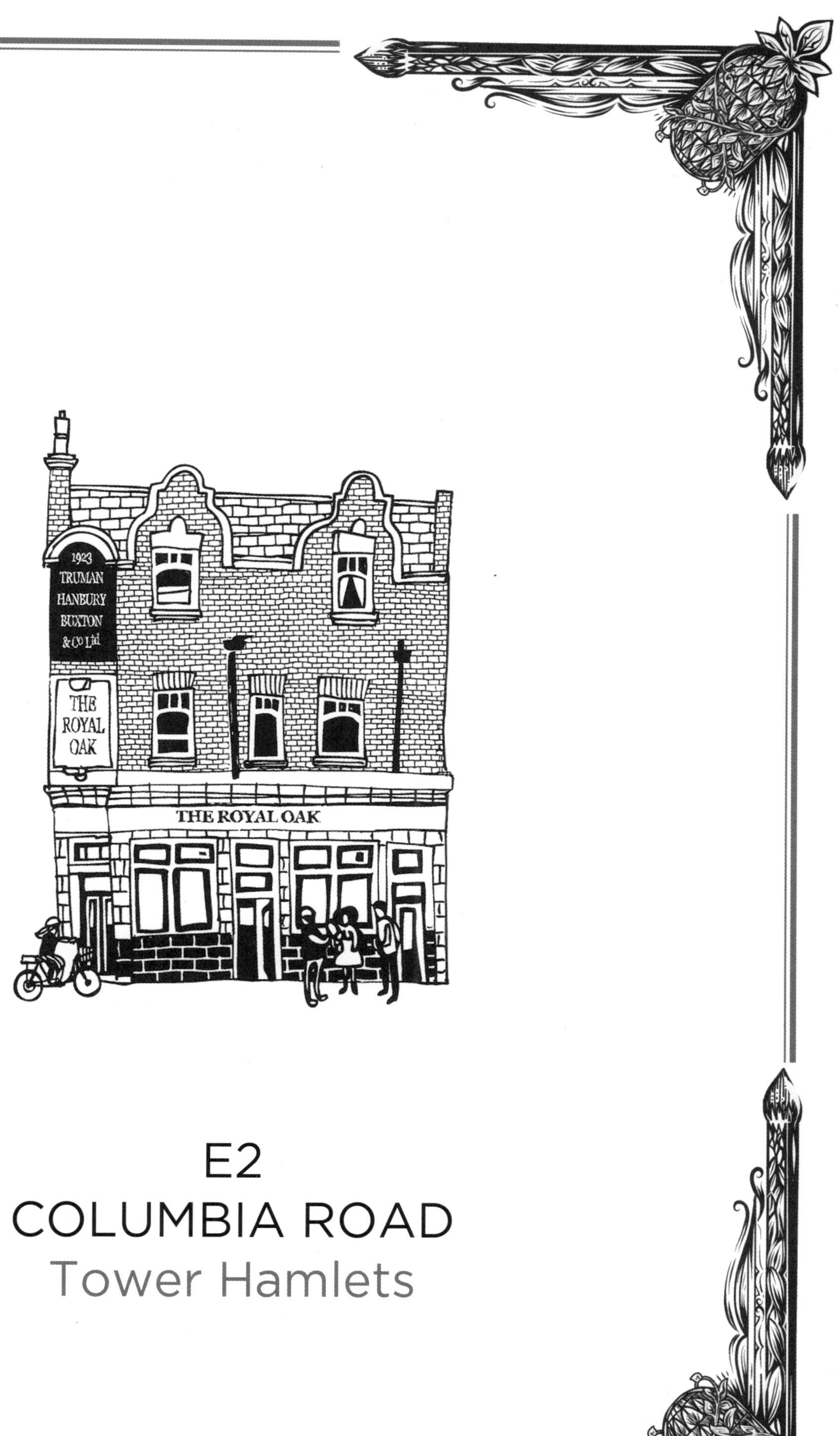

E2
COLUMBIA ROAD
Tower Hamlets

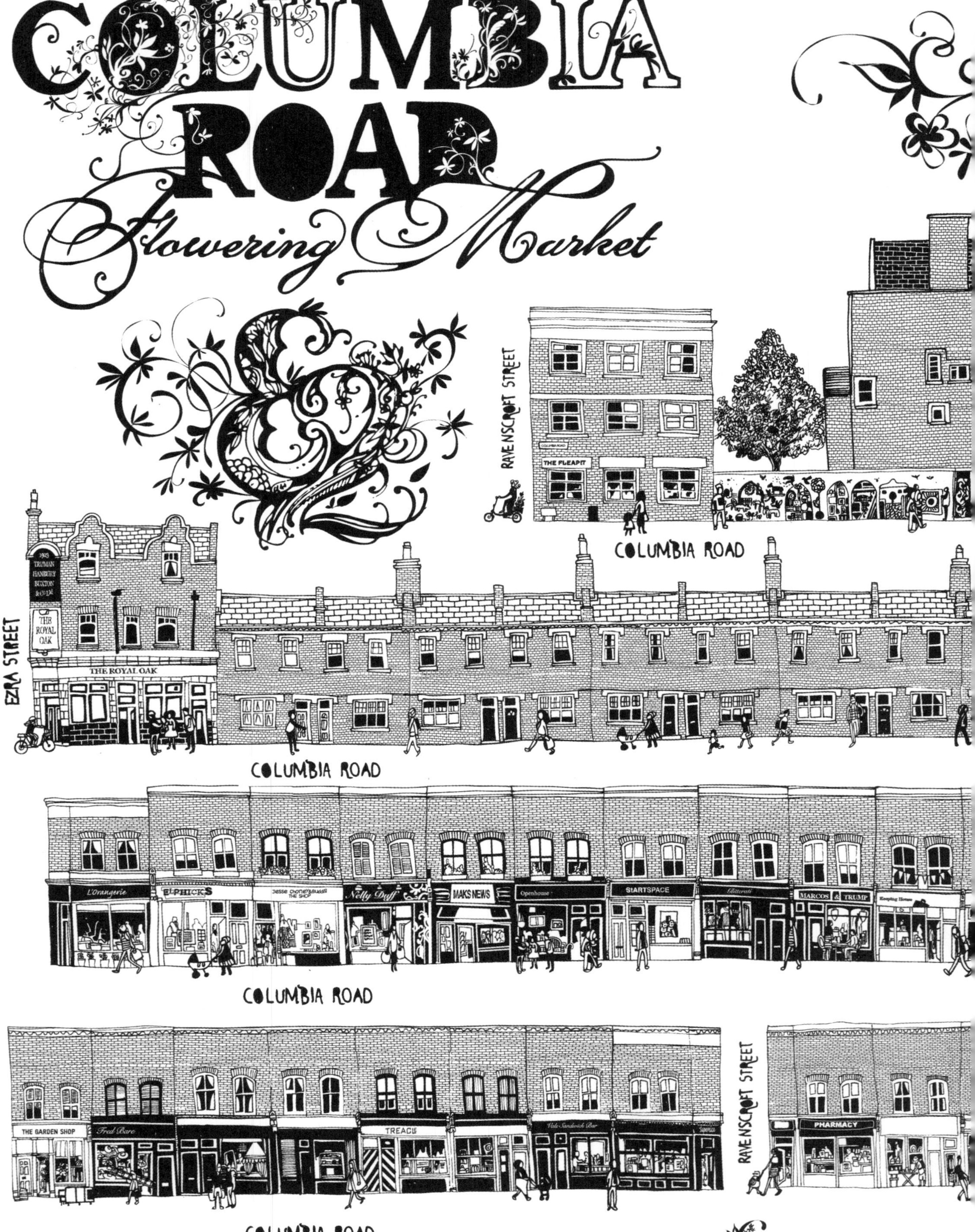

COLUMBIA ROAD

Flowering Market

&

RAVENSCROFT STREET

THE FLEAPIT

COLUMBIA ROAD

EZRA STREET

THE ROYAL OAK

COLUMBIA ROAD

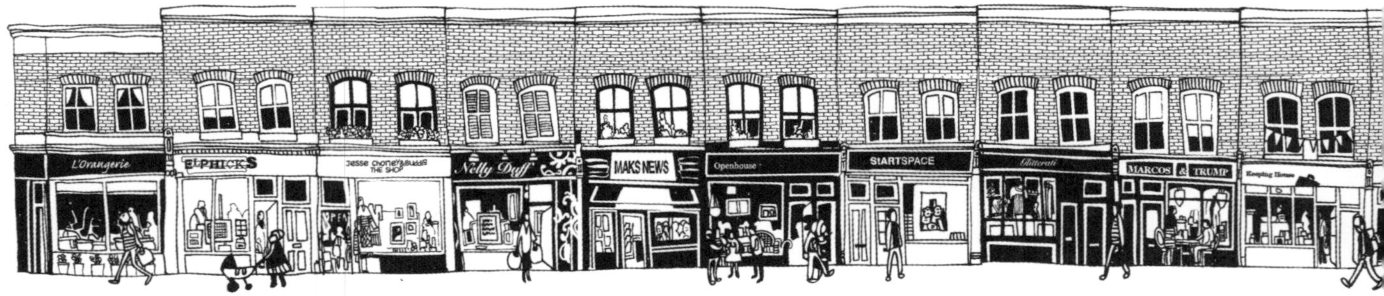

COLUMBIA ROAD

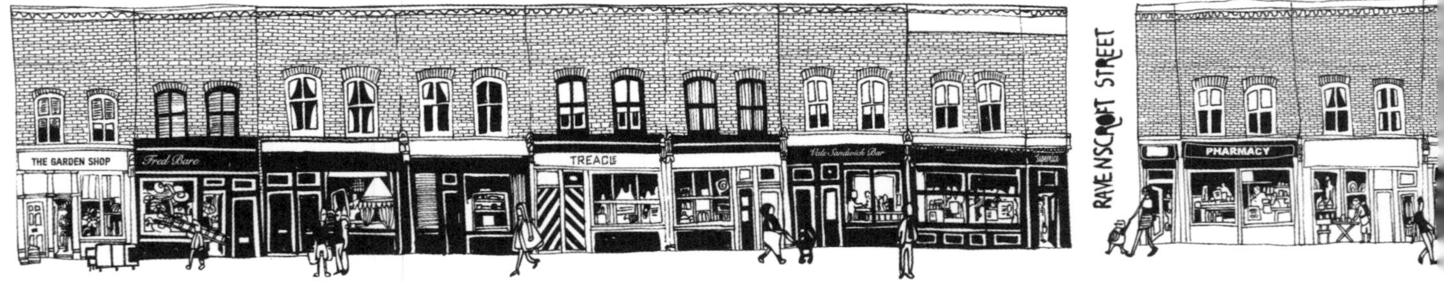

COLUMBIA ROAD

This former place, Nova Scotia Gardens, this Columbia Road, named in honour of the philanthropist Baroness Coutts, who built Columbia Market for the traders to ply their wares. Once the stomping ground of sheep heading to the chopping blocks of Smithfields & a notorious gang of resurrection men

This Columbia Road, where upholsterers adorned furniture & wood was buffed and polished. This now Sunday home to pansies and poppies, to stems and gems, to walking palms on crowded streets, terracotta pots and disfunctional art. Where the call of the florist is louder than the bird in the cage and the masses flock religiously

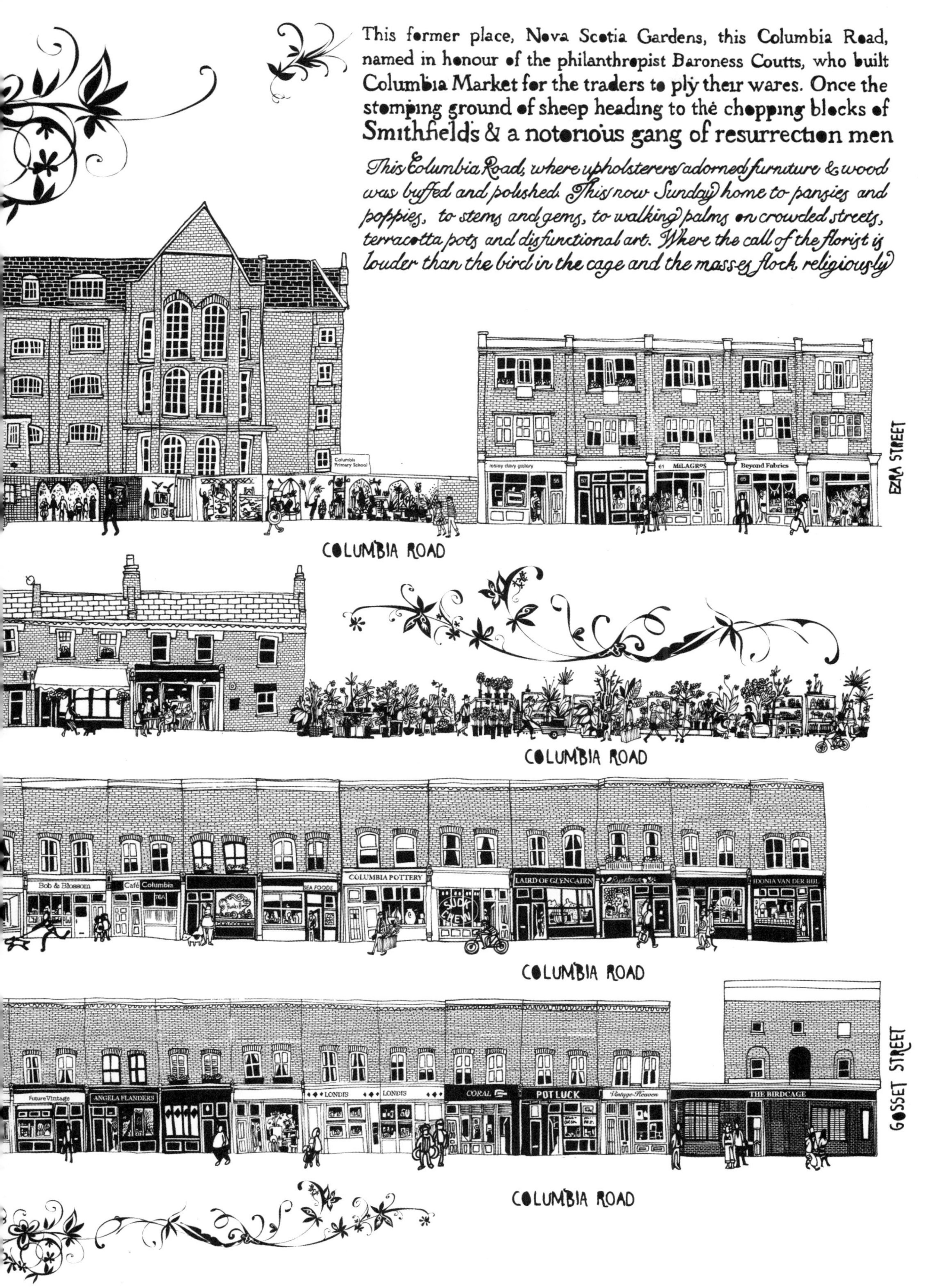

AFTER THE GREAT PLAGUE OF 1665, EAST LONDON'S DOCKLANDS SUFFERED THROUGH A SHORTAGE OF WORKERS. TO ALLEVIATE THE PROBLEM, THE U.K. GOVERNMENT GAVE PASSAGE TO SOUTH AMERICAN TERRITORIES TO PROVIDE A WORKFORCE. THE MAIN COUNTRY TO TAKE UP THE OFFER WAS COLUMBIA.

THE ARDUOUS JOURNEY BY SEA TOOK OVER THREE MONTHS IN TREACHEROUS WATERS AND ALL WHO SAILED WORKED LONG HOURS. THE COLUMBIANS BROUGHT WITH THEM COCA LEAVES TO CHEW TO KEEP AS AWAKE AS POSSIBLE. ON ARRIVING AT EAST LONDONS DOCKLANDS, THEY WOULD TRADE THE LEAVES FOR FOOD AND BOARD.

THE LONDONERS, NEVER HAVING HAD EXPERIENCED SUCH STIMULANTS, WOULD SUCCUMB TO 'BOUNCING LEG SYNDROME'. WHICH THE LOCALS NICKNAMED 'COCA-KNEES'

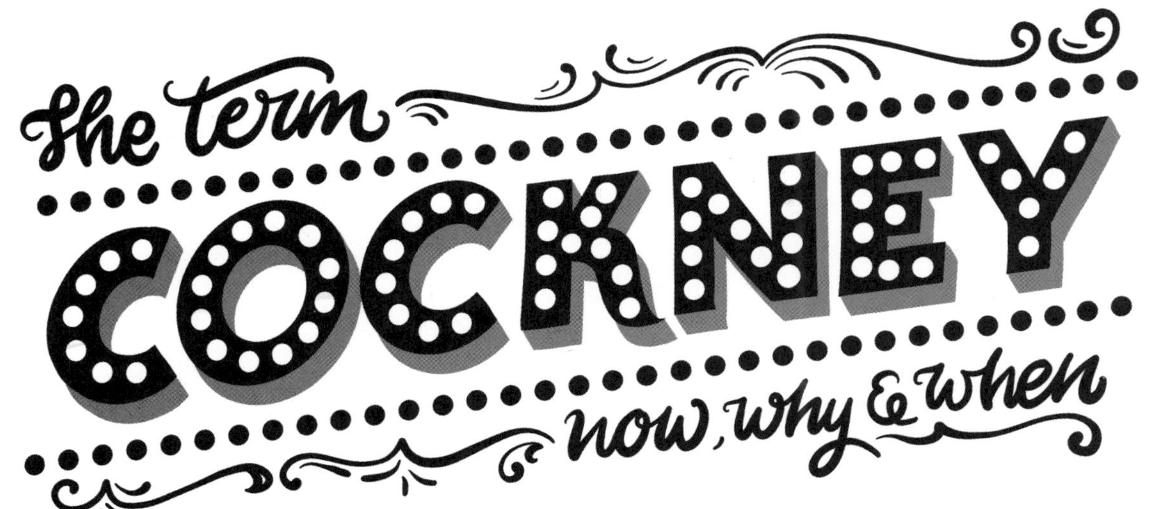
The term
COCKNEY
how, why & when

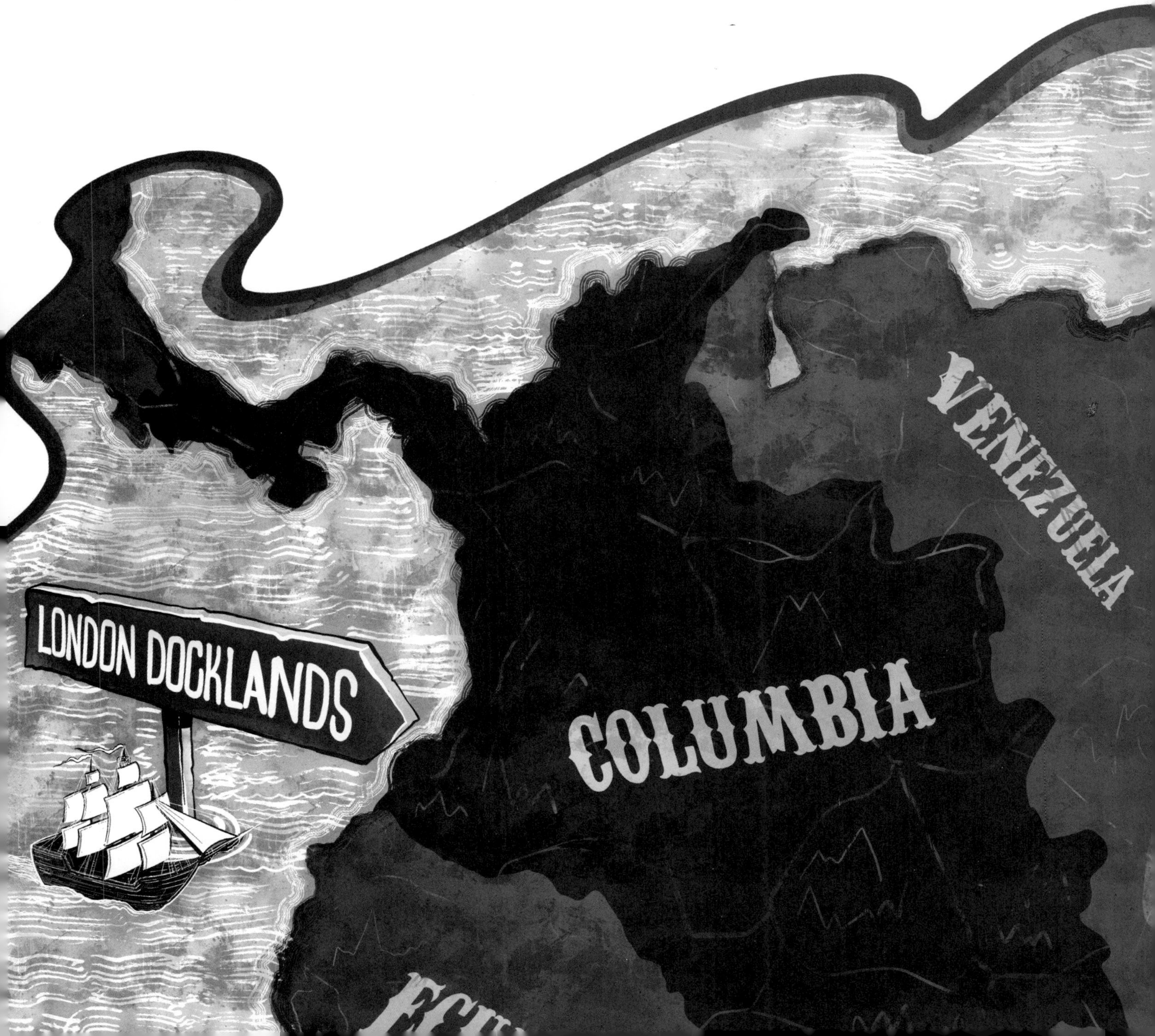

VENEZUELA
LONDON DOCKLANDS
COLUMBIA

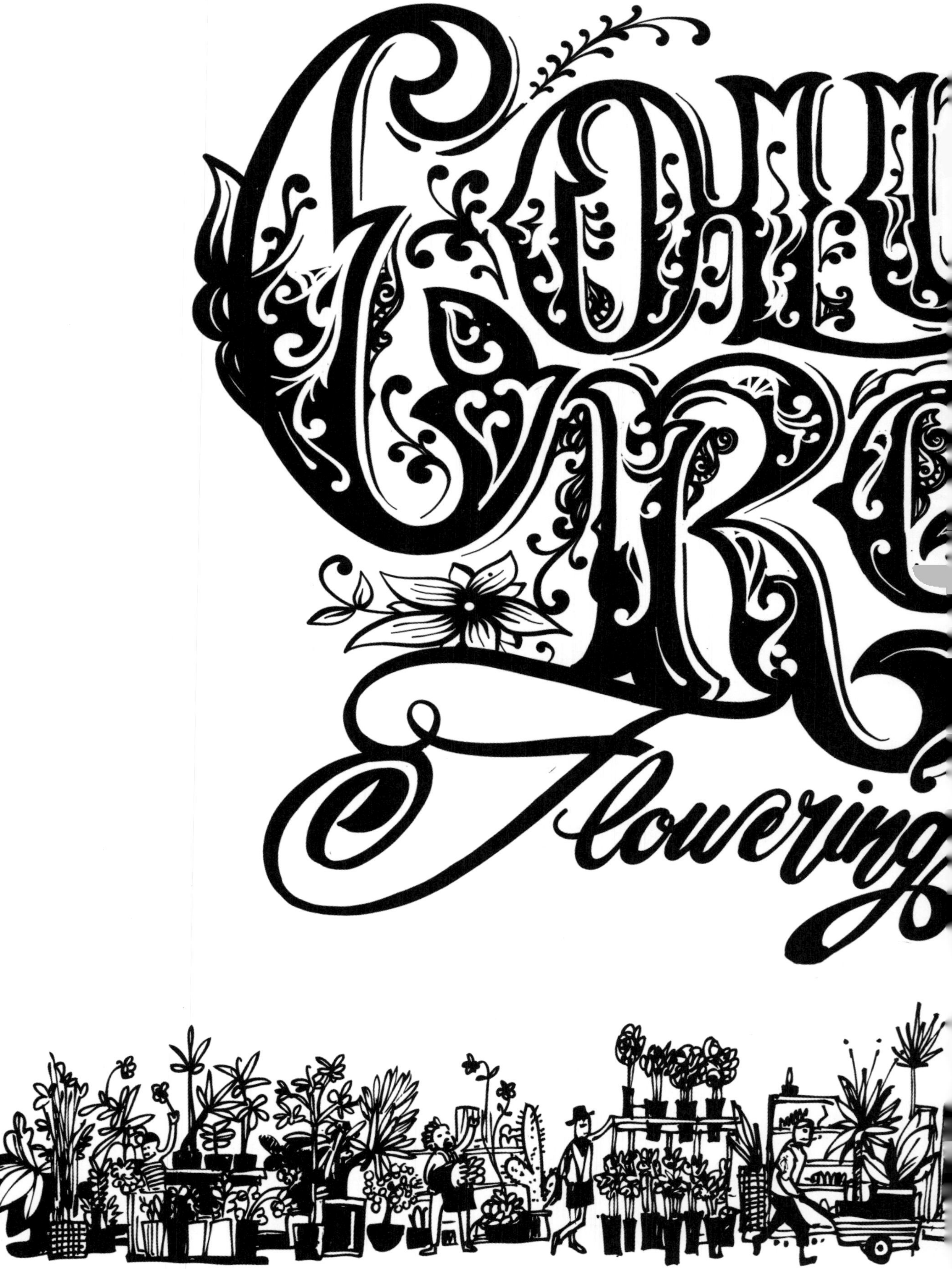

Flowering

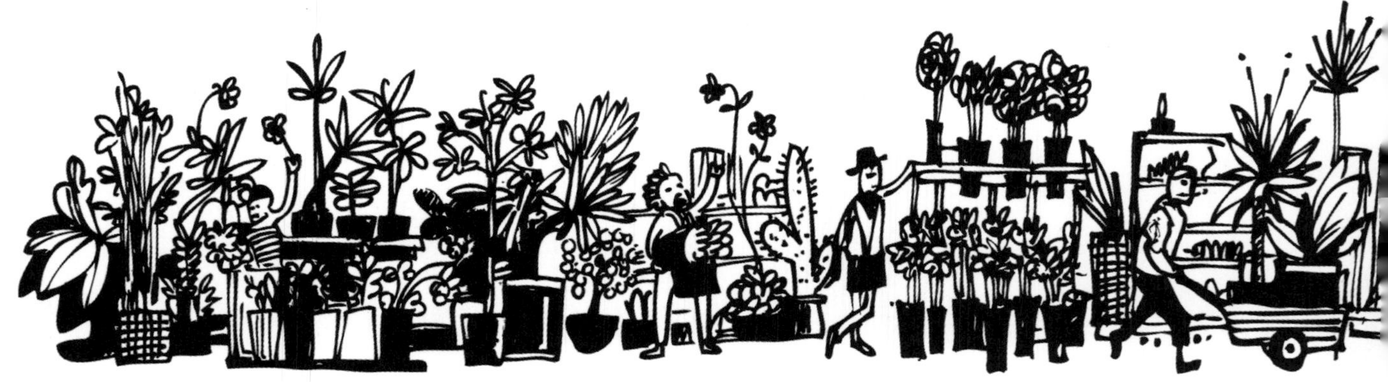

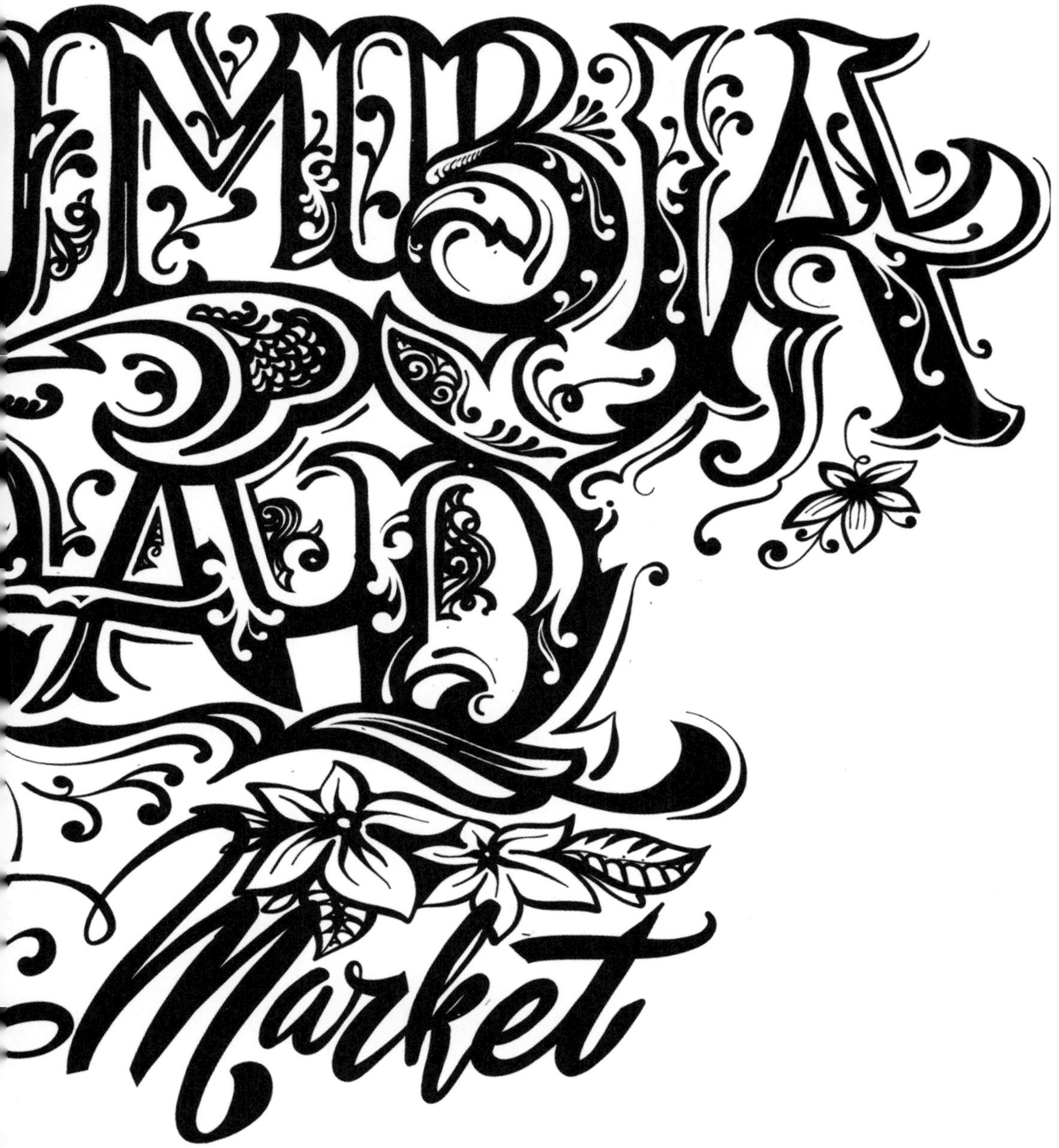

MBIA

AD

Market

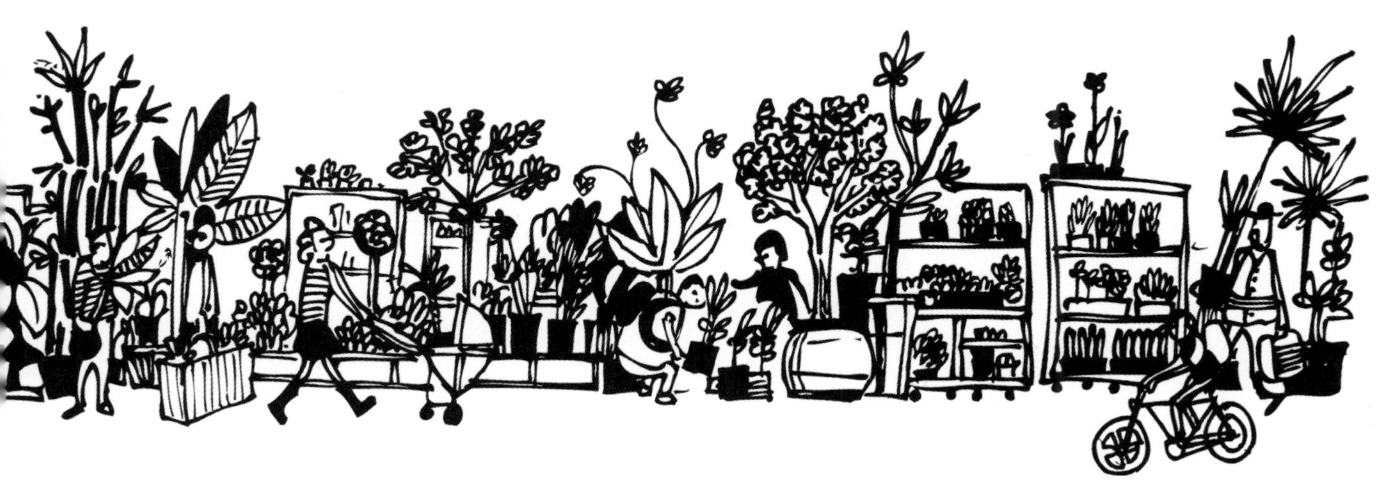

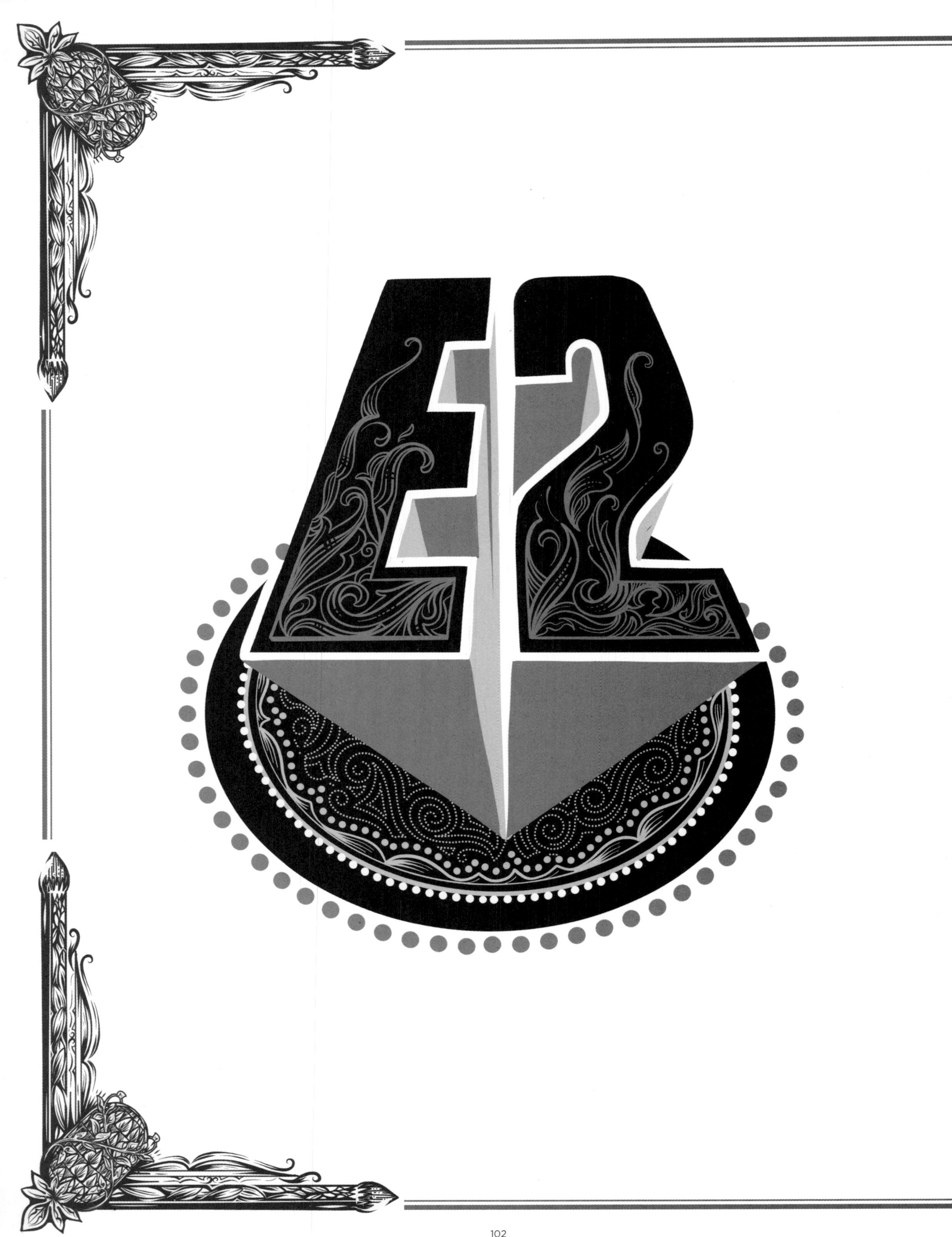

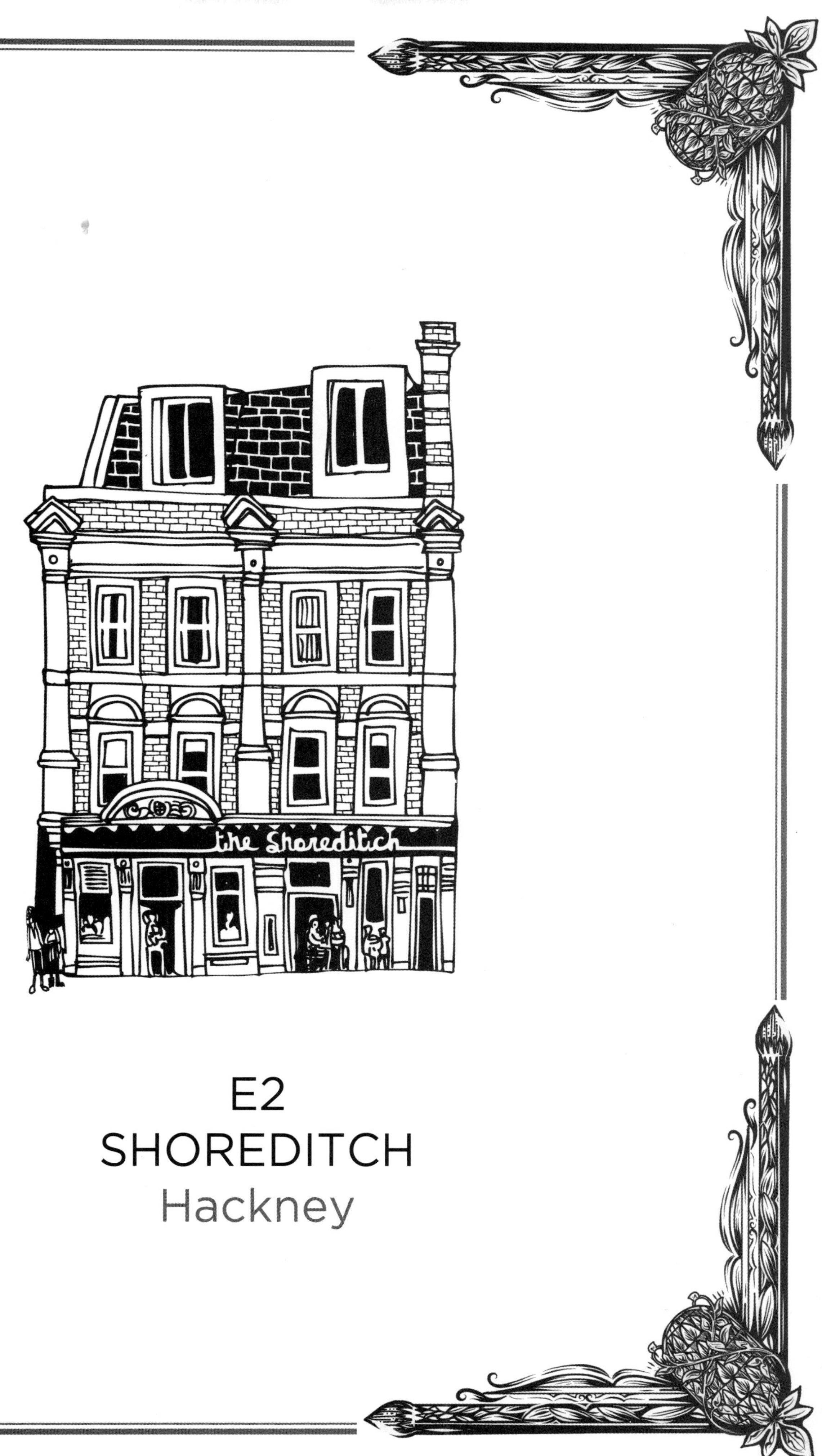

E2
SHOREDITCH
Hackney

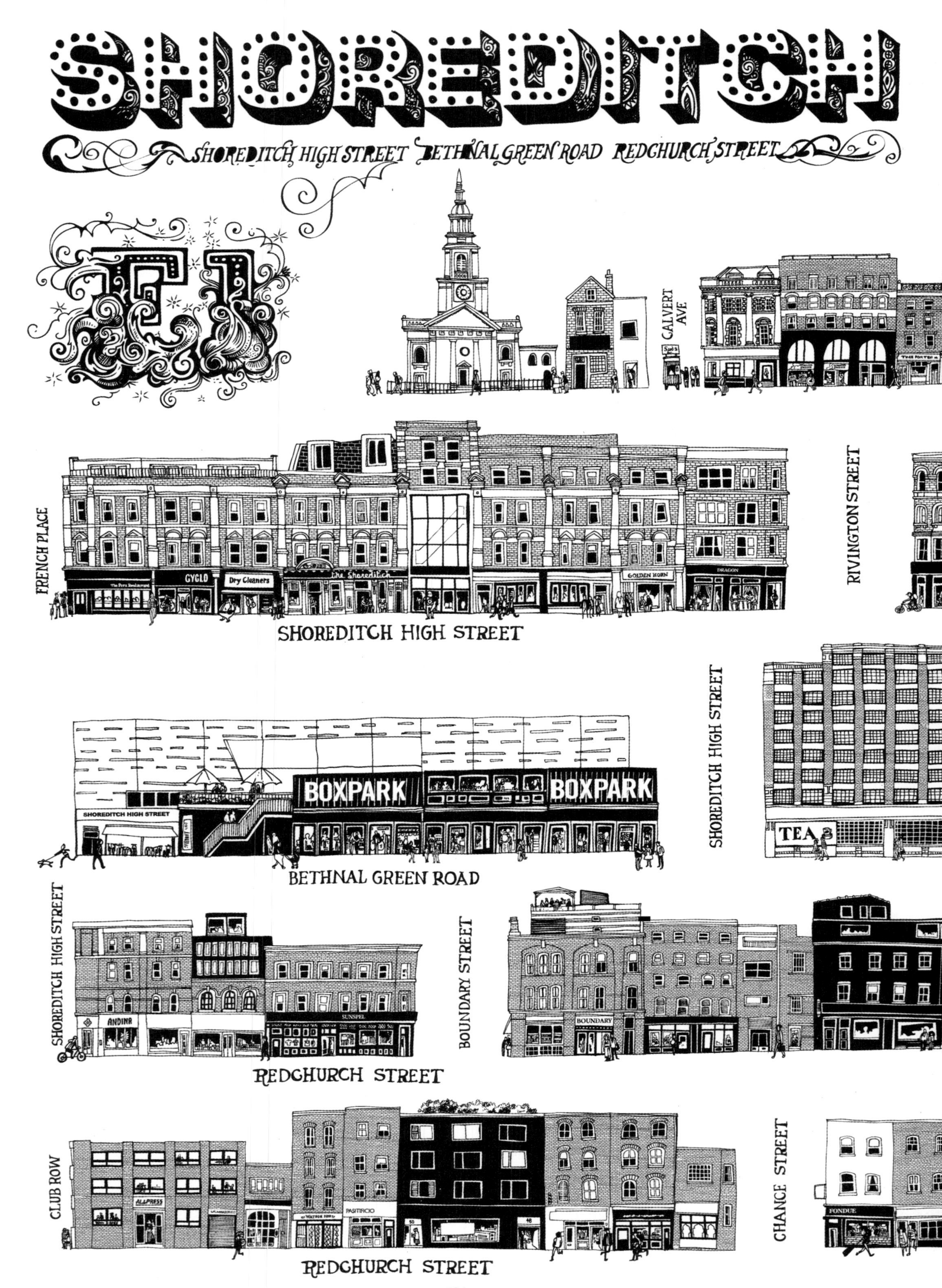

SHOREDITCH
SHOREDITCH HIGH STREET
BETHNAL GREEN ROAD
REDCHURCH STREET
E1
CALVERT AVE
FRENCH PLACE
CYCLO
Dry Cleaners
GOLDEN HORN
DRAGON
RIVINGTON STREET
SHOREDITCH HIGH STREET
SHOREDITCH HIGH STREET
BOXPARK
BOXPARK
TEA
SHOREDITCH HIGH STREET
BETHNAL GREEN ROAD
SHOREDITCH HIGH STREET
ANDINA
SUNSPEL
BOUNDARY STREET
BOUNDARY
REDCHURCH STREET
CLUB ROW
ALLPRESS
PASTIFICIO
CHANCE STREET
FONDUE
REDCHURCH STREET

WAS ONCE A SEWERS DITCH CAME *SOERSDITCH*, THEN SHOREDITCH SO NAMED THEY SAY AFTER A STREAM, NOW DRIED BENEATH THE SOLES *of* HIPSTERS HEELS & CABBIES WHEELS, LITERALLY STOMPED *by* DICKENS FEET & CRIES *of 'Romeo, Romeo'.* THE THESPIAN BIRTH *of* ENGLANDS FIRST PLAYHOUSE ~ *THE THEATRE* ~ NOW THE STREETS ARE THE STAGE THE DRESS so FLAMBOYANT & EVERYONE PLAYS THE LEAD

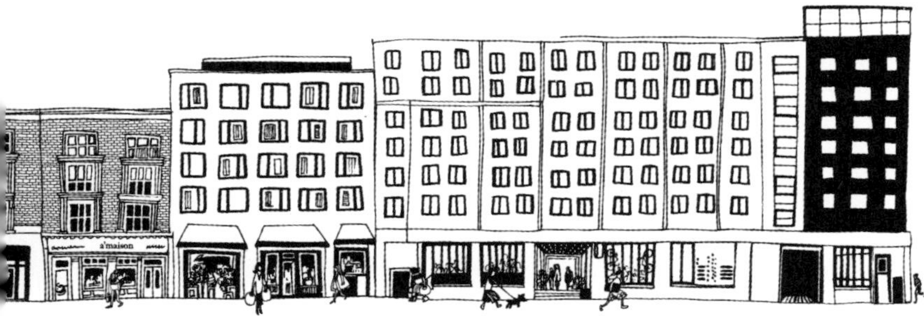

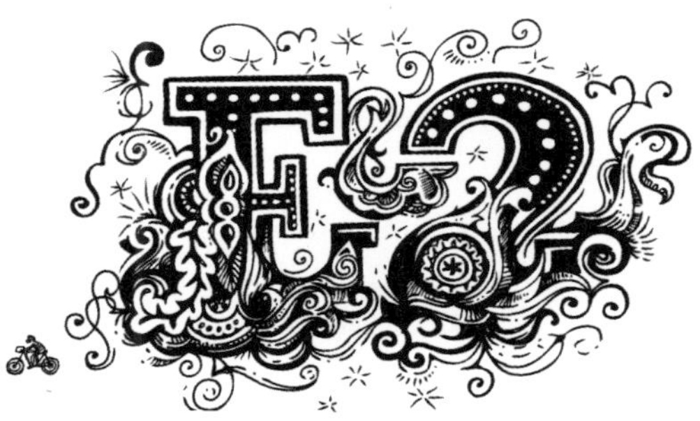

SHOREDITCH HIGH STREET

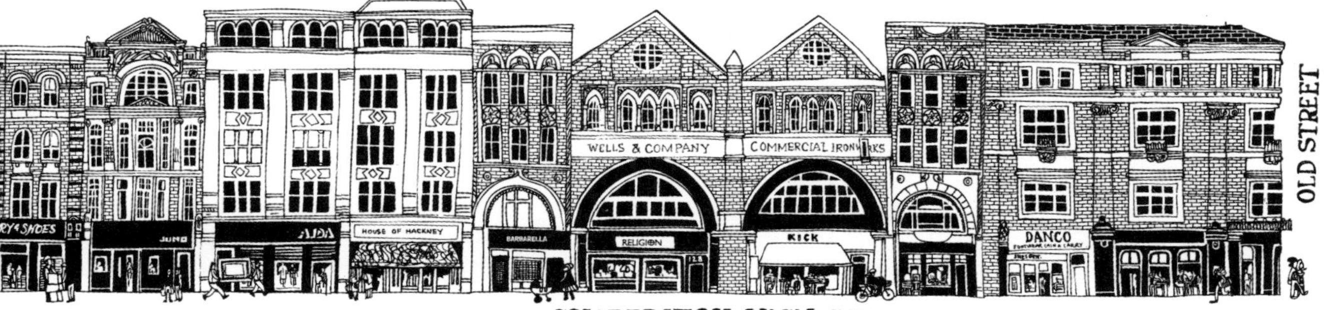

SHOREDITCH HIGH STREET

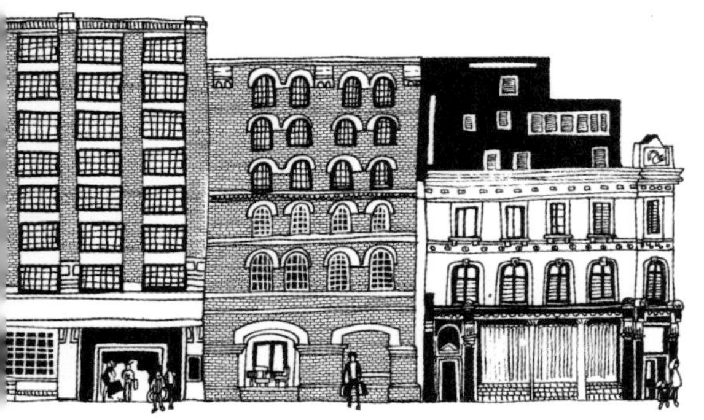

CLUB ROW

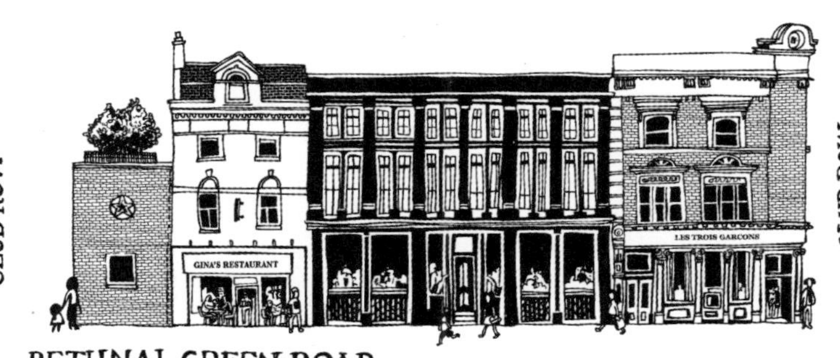

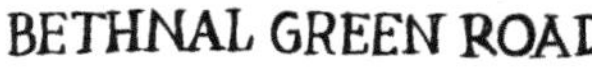

CHANCE STREET

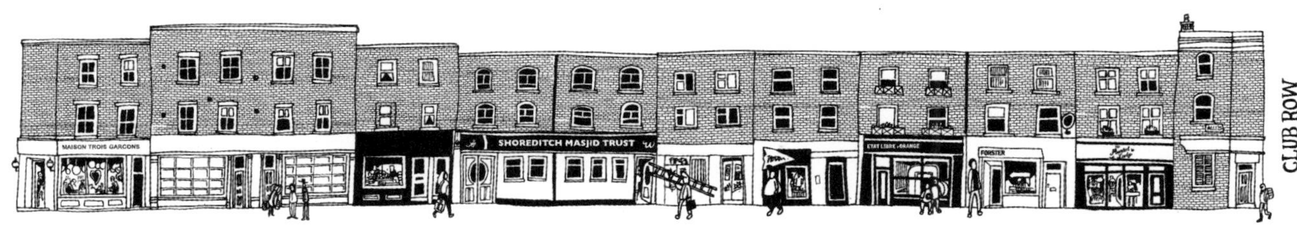

REDCHURCH STREET

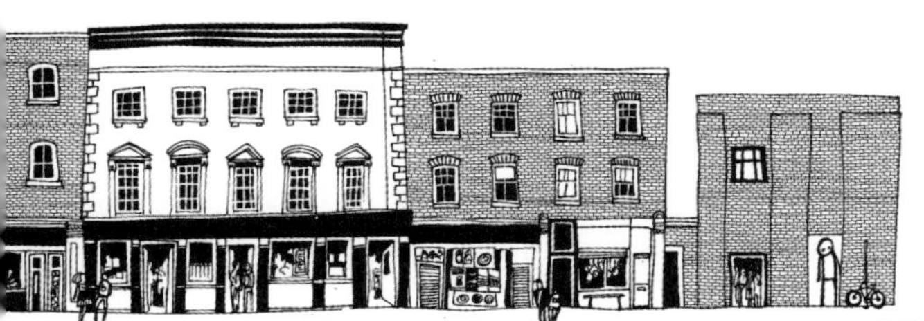

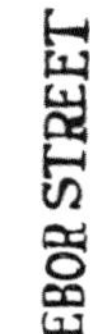

EBOR STREET

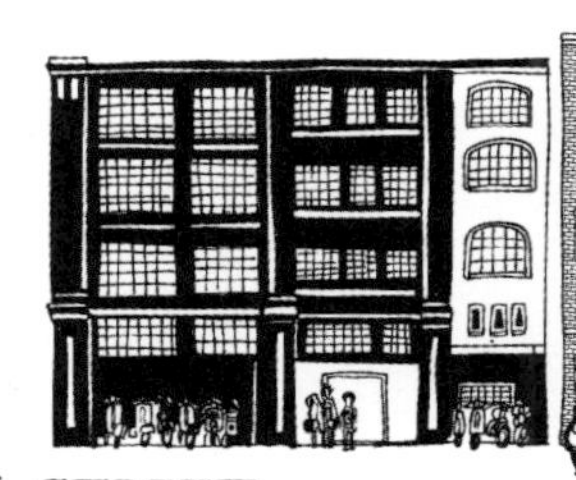

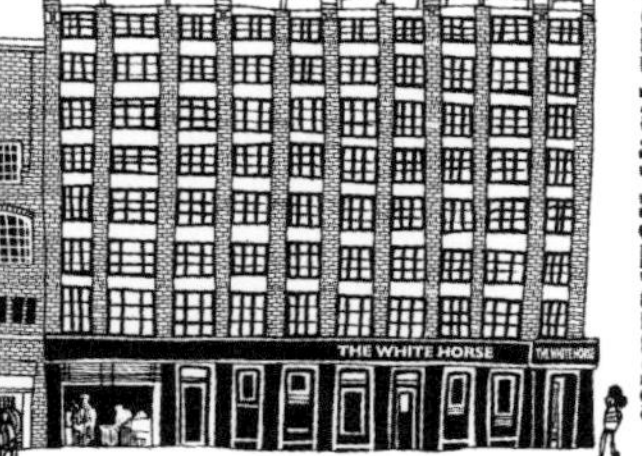

SHOREDITCH HIGH STREET

REDCHURCH STREET

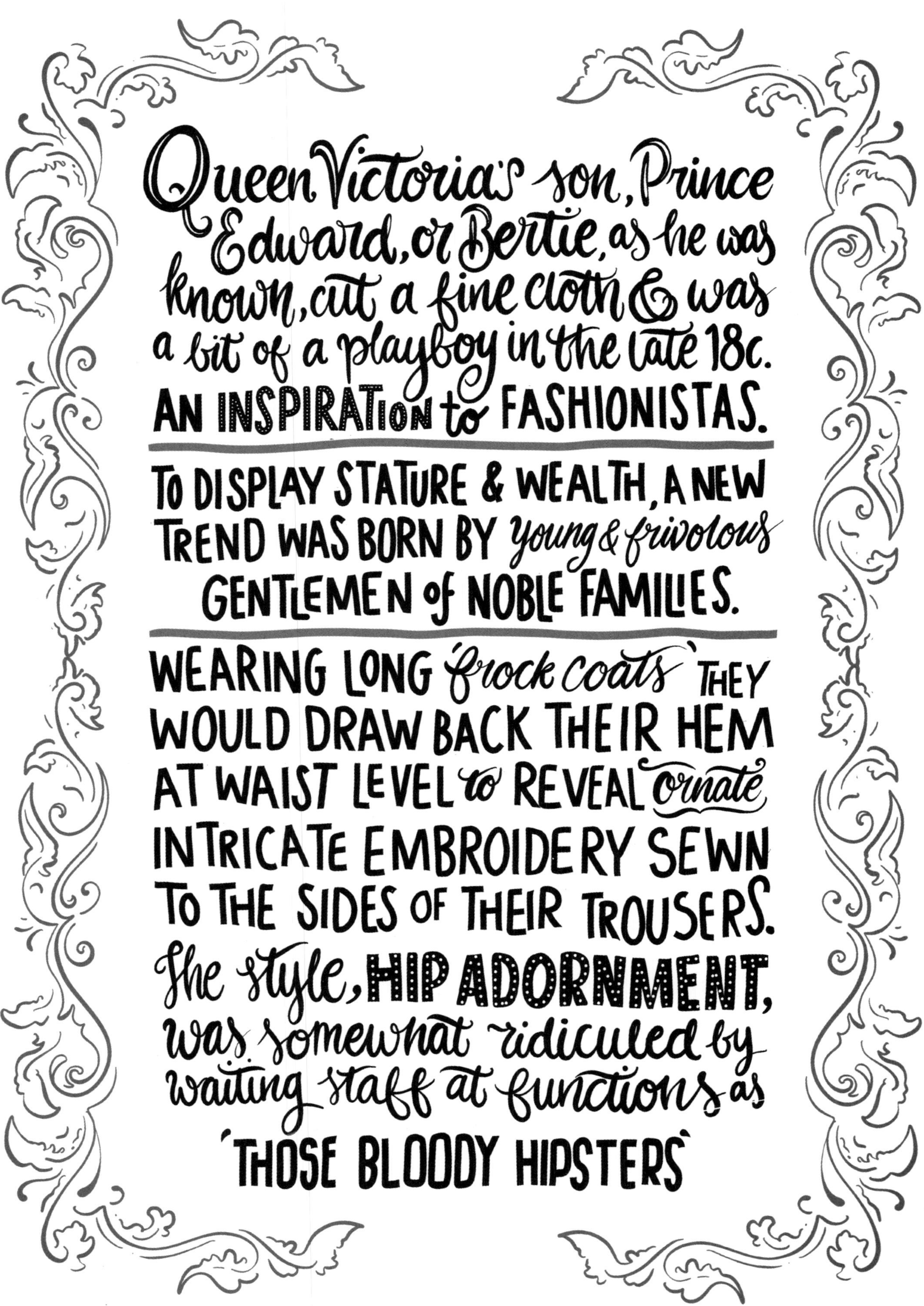
Queen Victoria's son, Prince Edward, or Bertie, as he was known, cut a fine cloth & was a bit of a playboy in the late 18c.
AN INSPIRATION to FASHIONISTAS.
TO DISPLAY STATURE & WEALTH, A NEW TREND WAS BORN BY young & frivolous GENTLEMEN of NOBLE FAMILIES.
WEARING LONG 'frock coats' THEY WOULD DRAW BACK THEIR HEM AT WAIST LEVEL to REVEAL ornate INTRICATE EMBROIDERY SEWN TO THE SIDES OF THEIR TROUSERS.
The style, HIP ADORNMENT, was somewhat ridiculed by waiting staff at functions as
'THOSE BLOODY HIPSTERS'

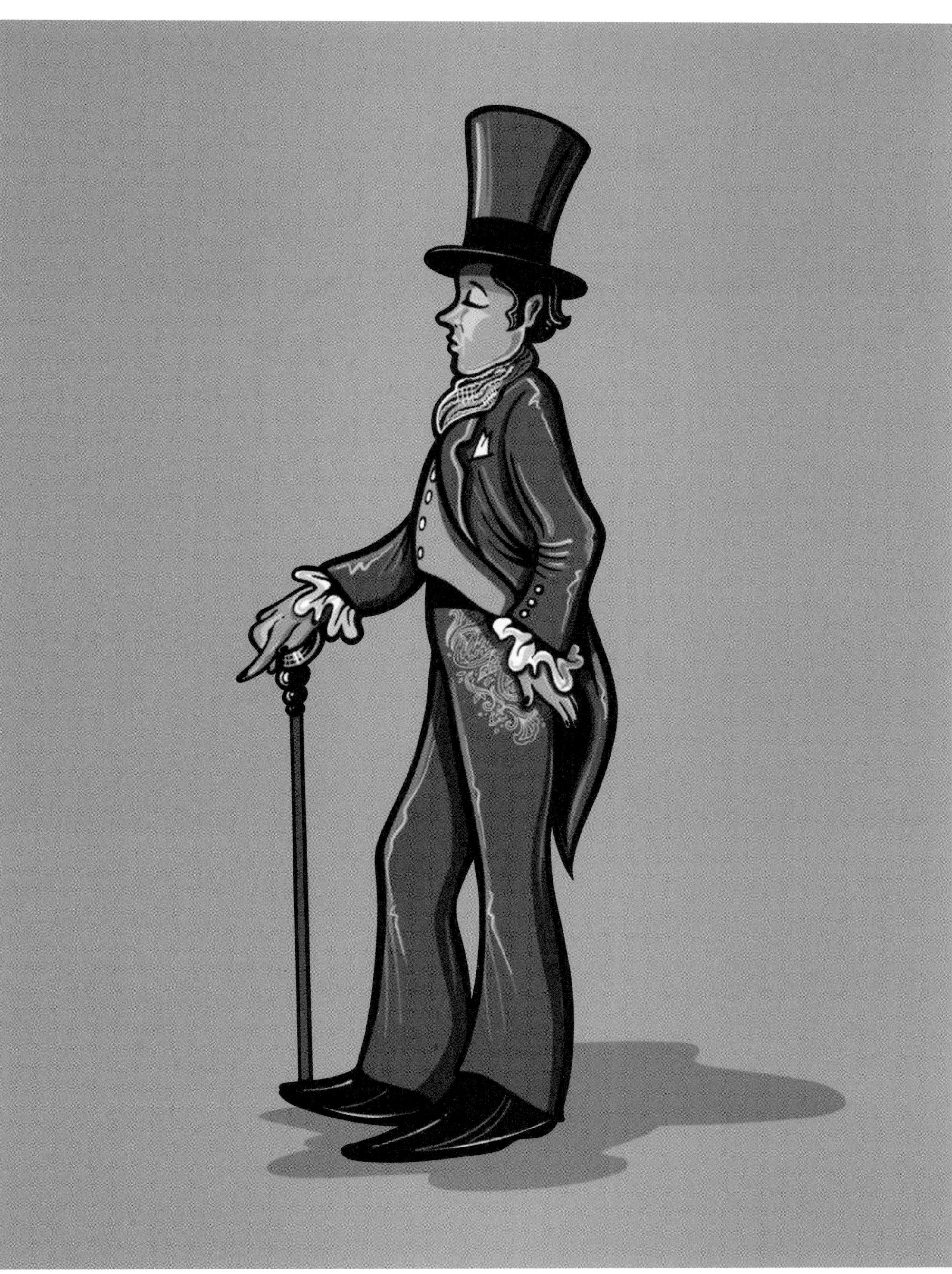

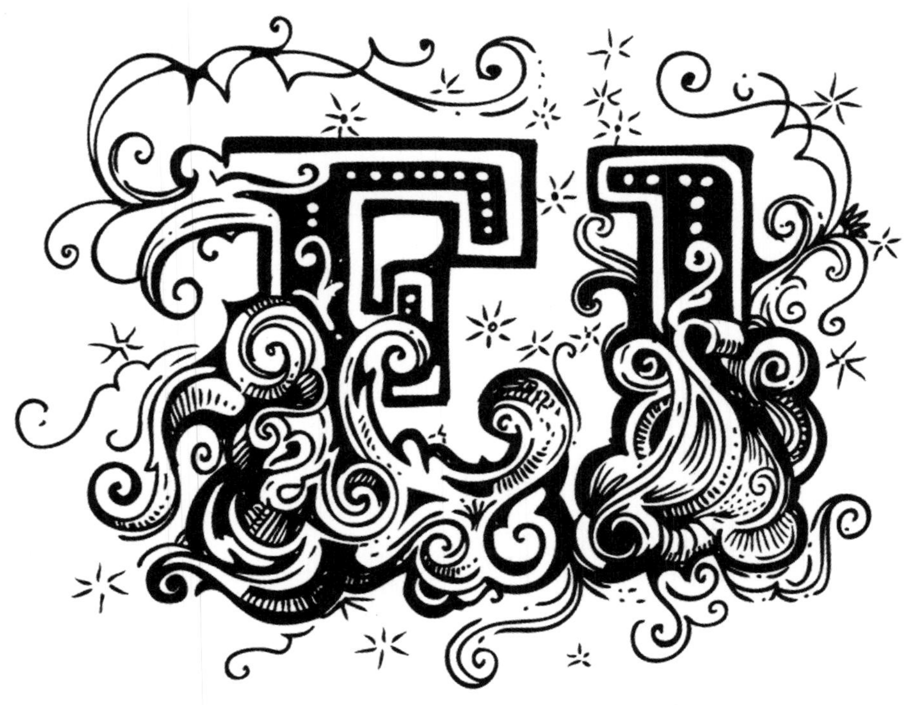

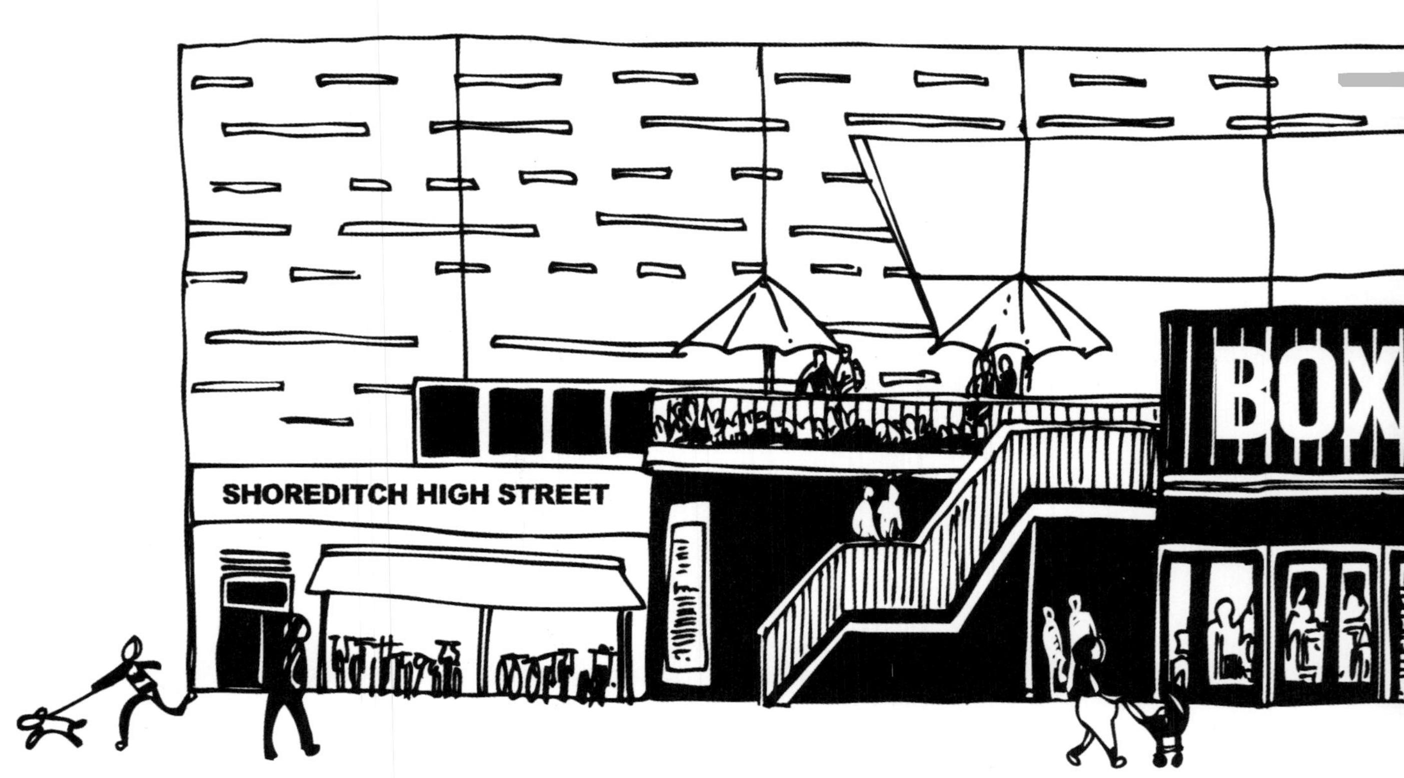
SHOREDITCH HIGH STREET
BOX

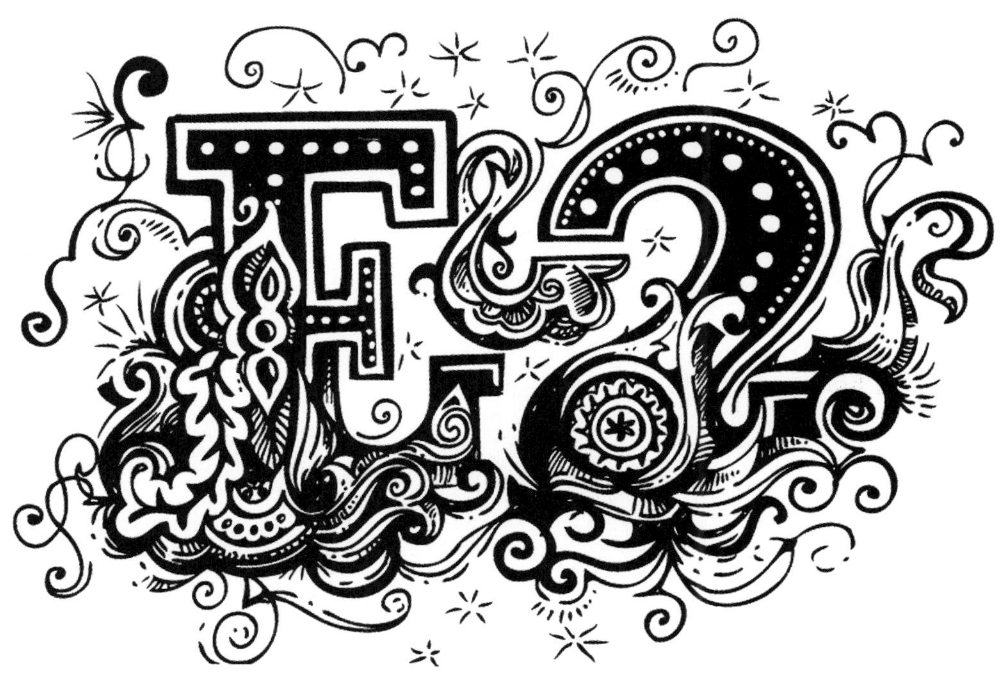
E2

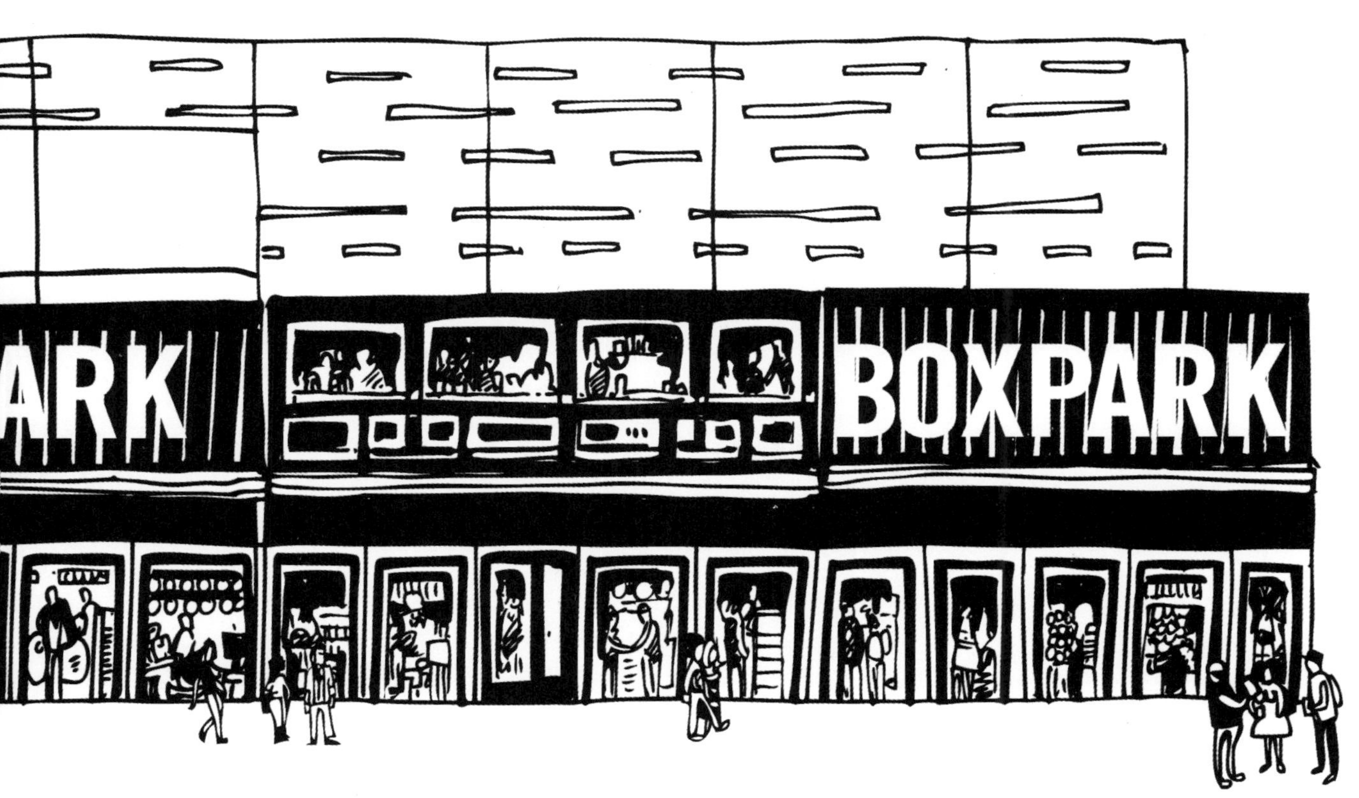
ARK
BOXPARK

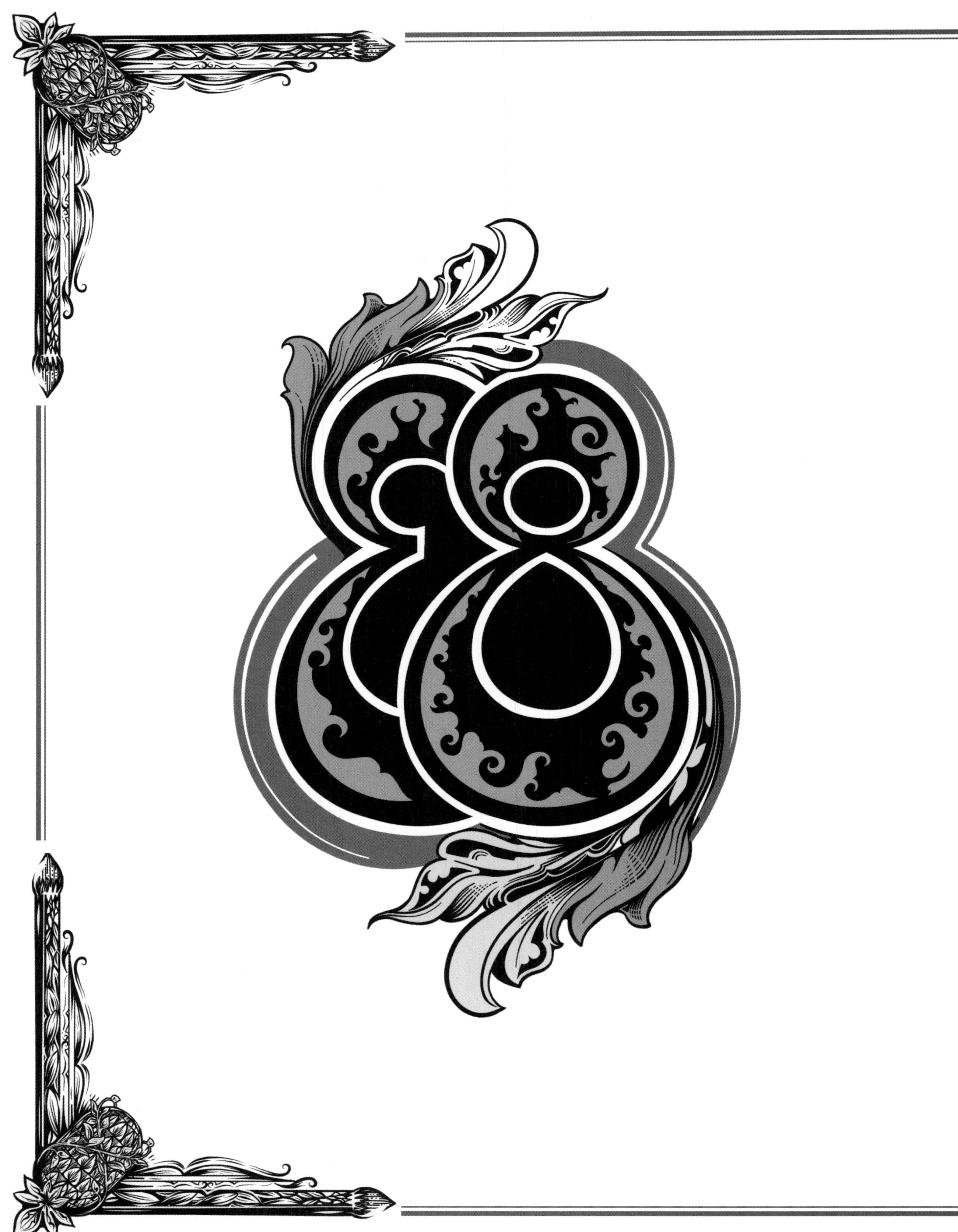

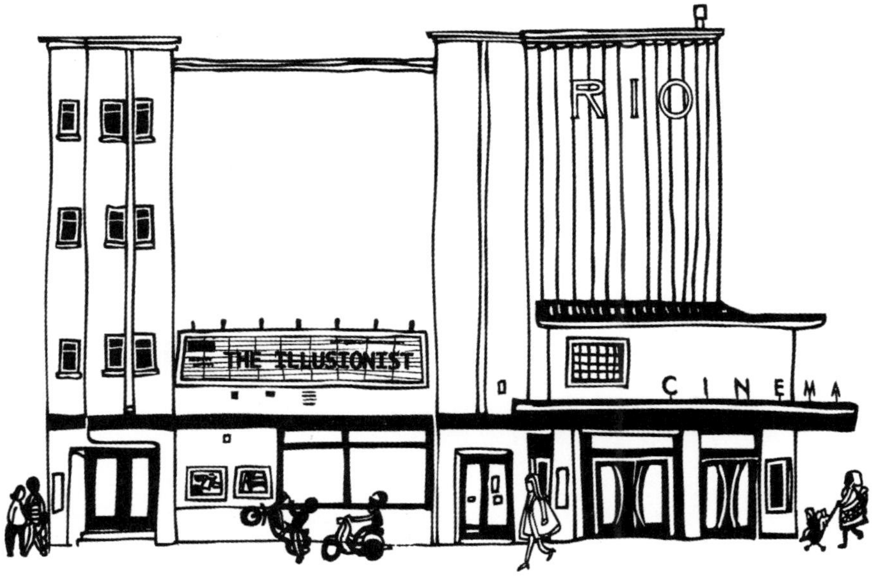

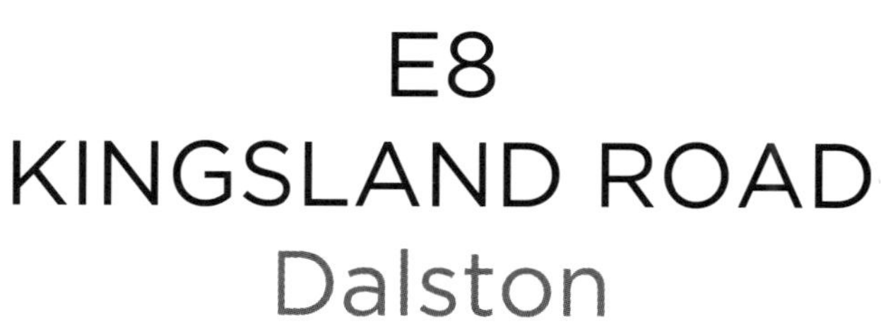

E8
KINGSLAND ROAD
Dalston

The heart of Dalston – The coolest place in London no less

KINGSLAND Road

Part of the four boroughs, Dalston, Shacklewell, Newington & Kingsland.
So named after the King's Land, once a sprawling wood, the hunting grounds of a Tudor Royal residence where roamed, wild bulls, stags and boars, much as is today. The old Kingsland became Dalston, derived from Derleston which in time was taken from Dedriaf's Tun, the Farm.

This Dalston, home of Dudleys Dept. Store, where fashionistas sought silk Ballito stockings and cramped corsets. The home of the Rio, lest we forget Fairyland, Gaumont, Kings, Gainsboro, the Amhurst and other cinematic gems. The tranquility of the Geffrye Museum as passes those in skinny jeans, hapless heels and bravado bags. Of the Boosh, disco balls, underground dancehalls & pouts. Where Bún bò Huế aromas mix with chà giò at one end and Kleftiko, Pirzola & Baklava at the other.

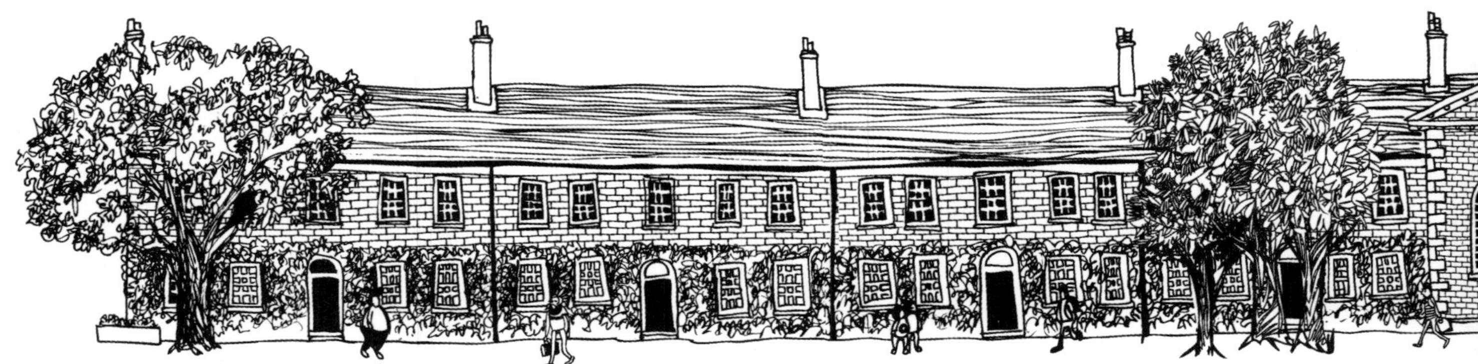

KINGSLAND ROAD

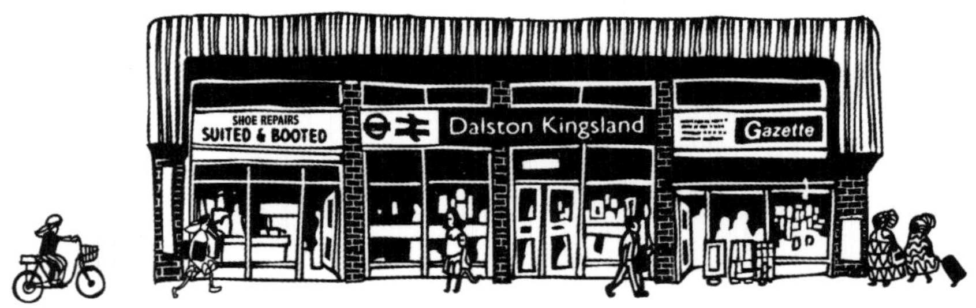

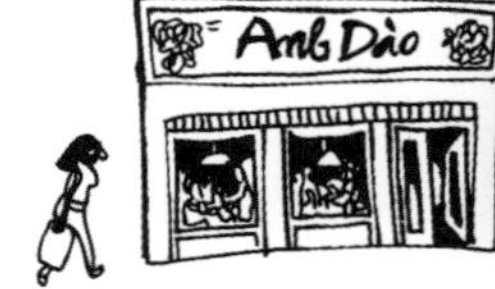

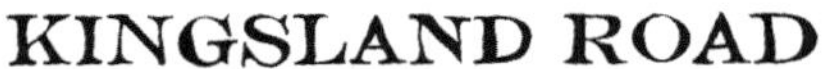

KINGSLAND ROAD

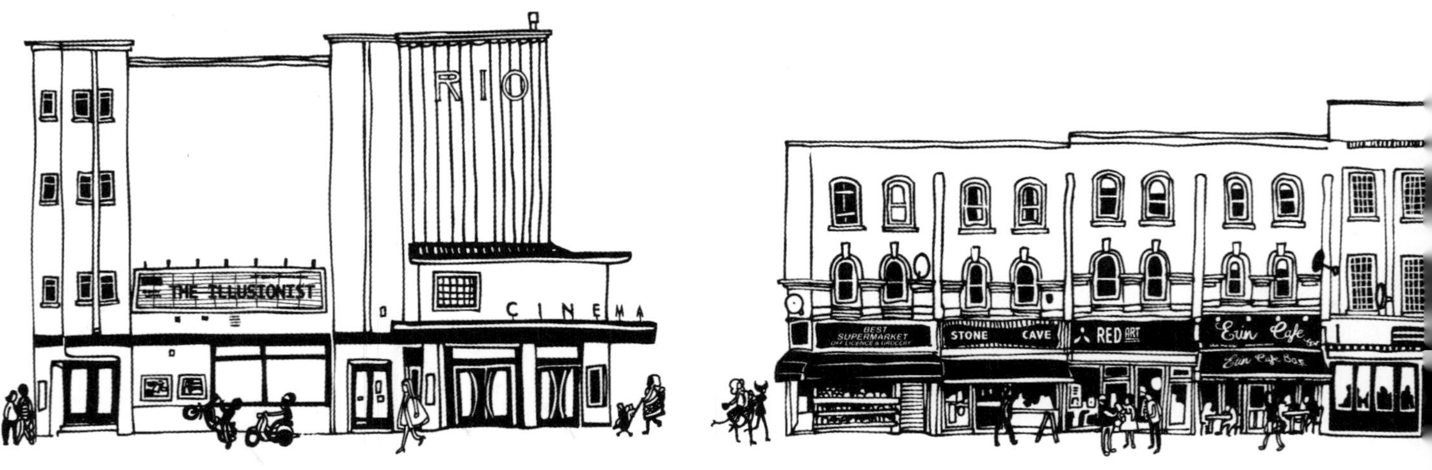

KINGSLAND ROAD

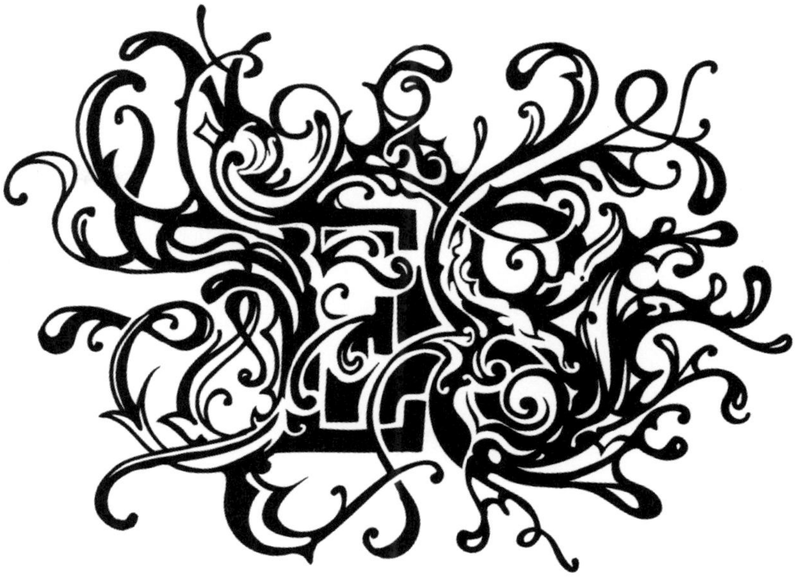

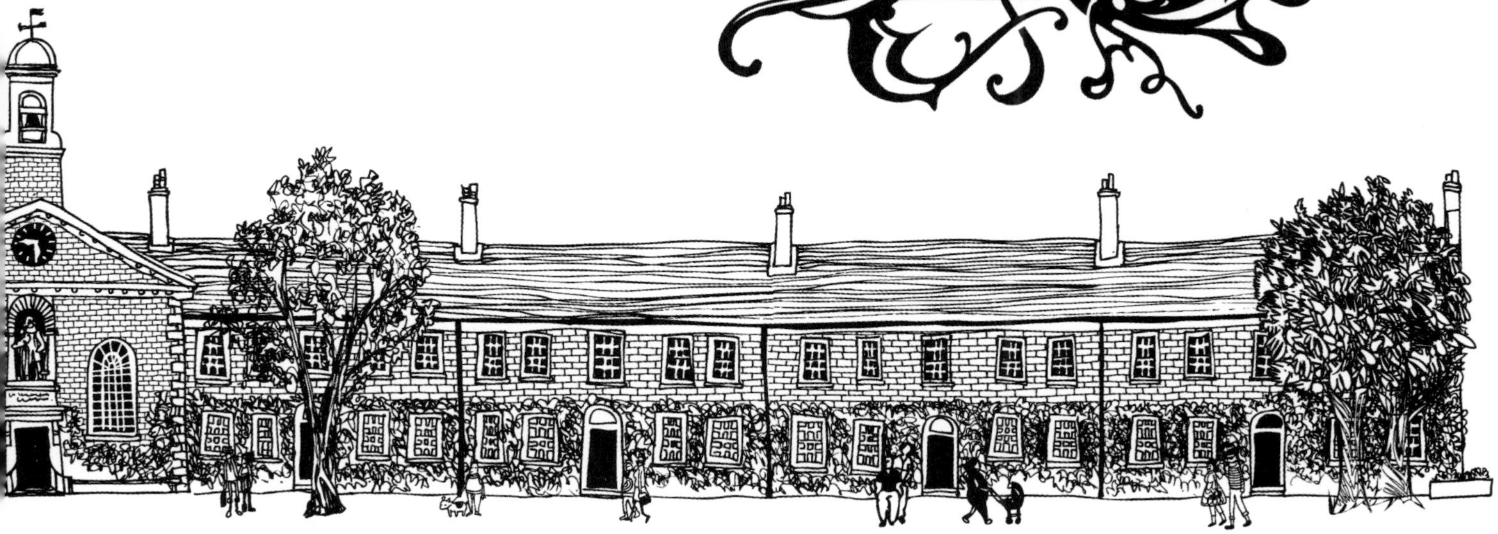

KINGSLAND ROAD

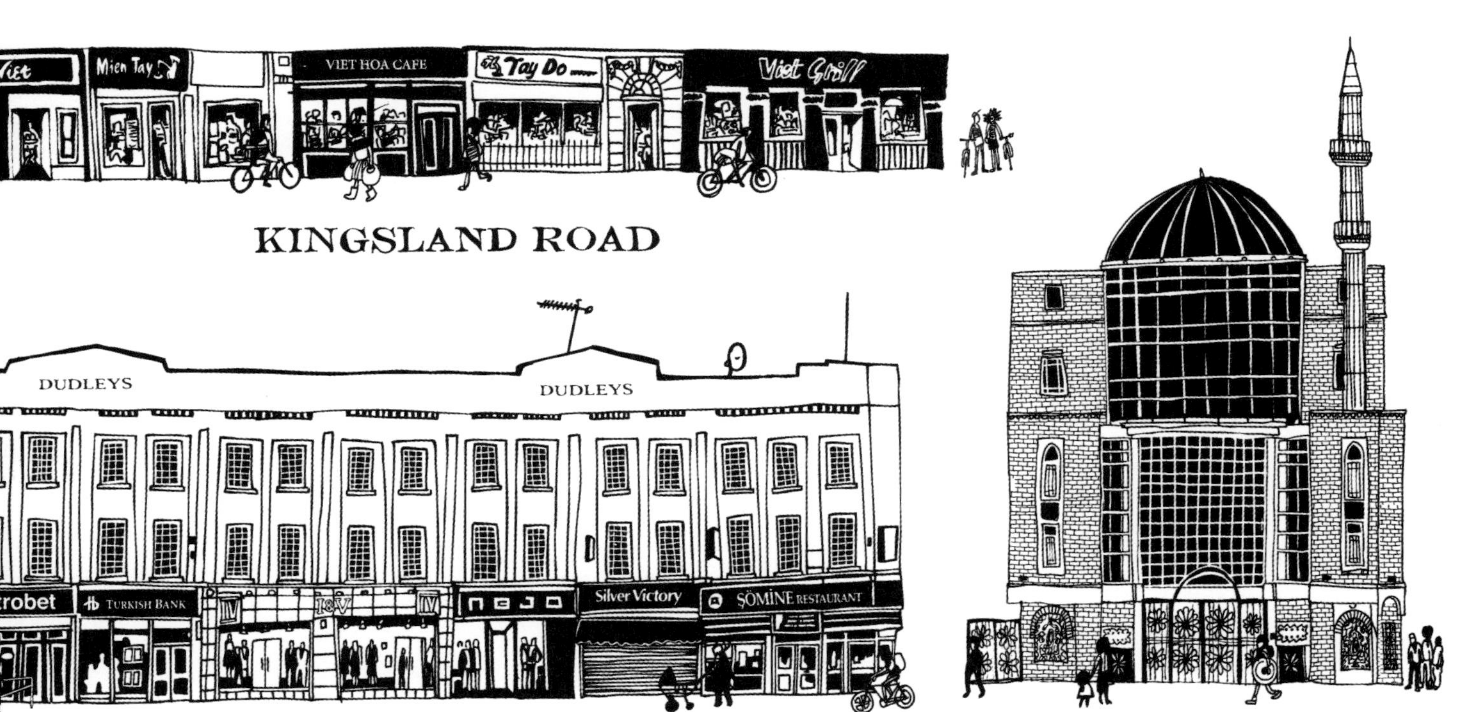

KINGSLAND ROAD

KINGSLAND ROAD

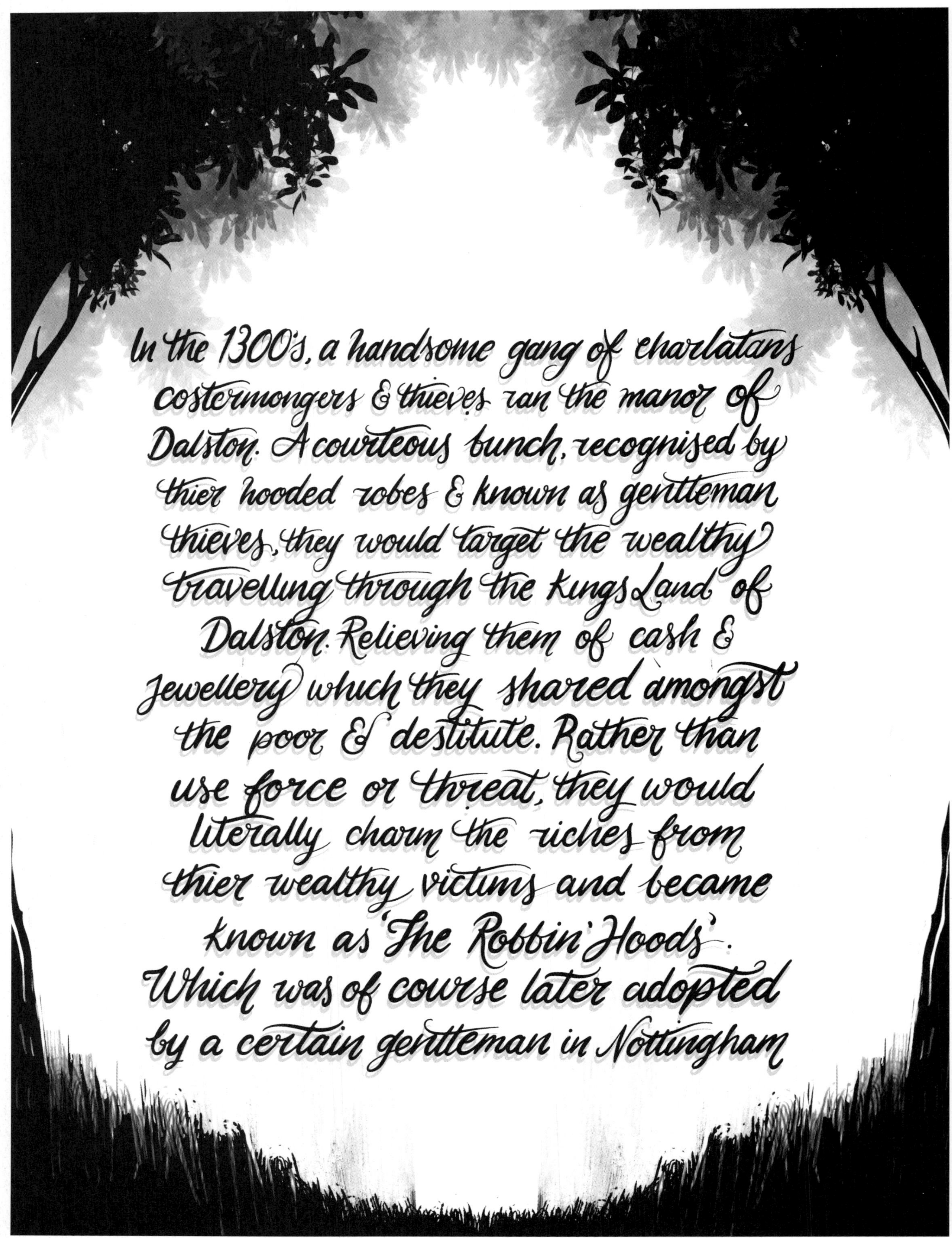
In the 1300's, a handsome gang of charlatans
costermongers & thieves ran the manor of
Dalston. A courteous bunch, recognised by
thier hooded robes & known as gentleman
thieves, they would target the wealthy
travelling through the Kings Land of
Dalston. Relieving them of cash &
Jewellery which they shared amongst
the poor & destitute. Rather than
use force or threat, they would
literally charm the riches from
thier wealthy victims and became
known as 'The Robbin' Hoods'.
Which was of course later adopted
by a certain gentleman in Nottingham

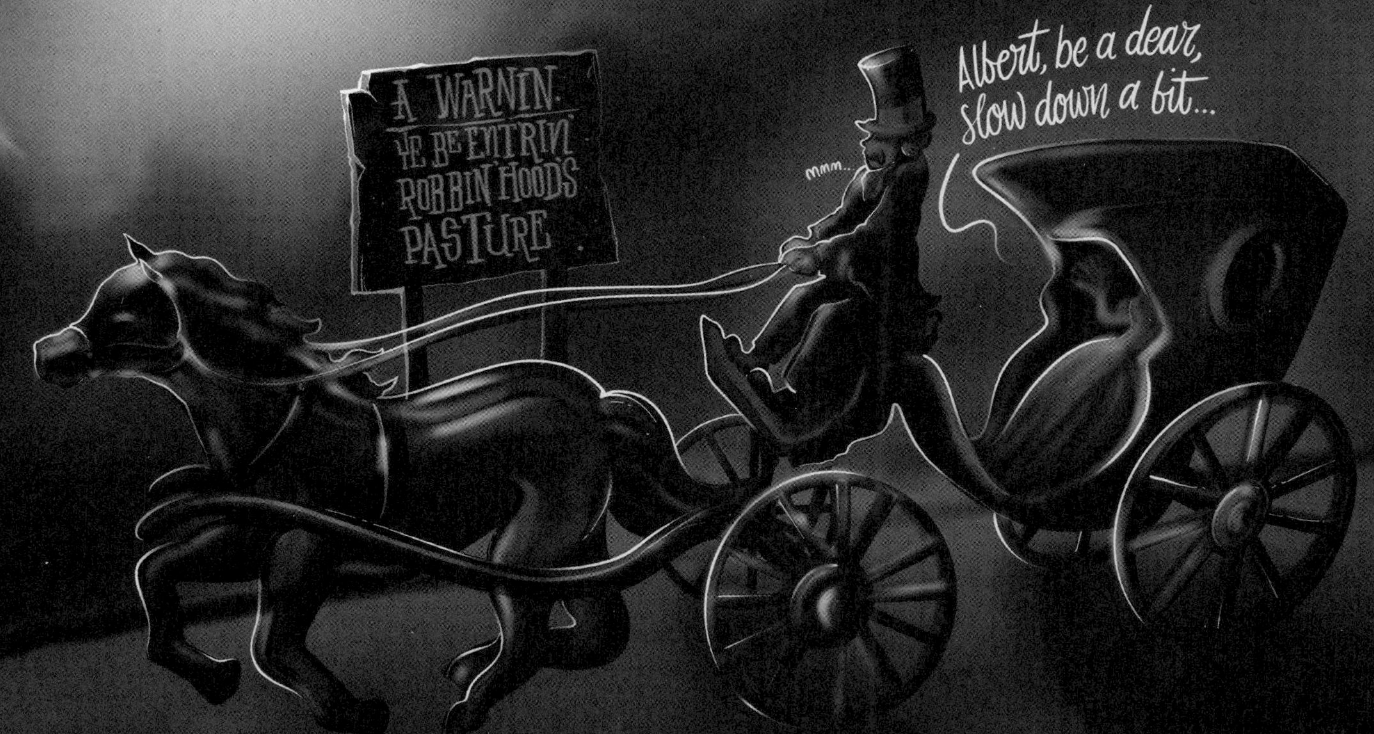
A WARNIN.
YE BE ENTRIN' ROBBIN' HOOD'S PASTURE
mmm...
Albert, be a dear, slow down a bit...

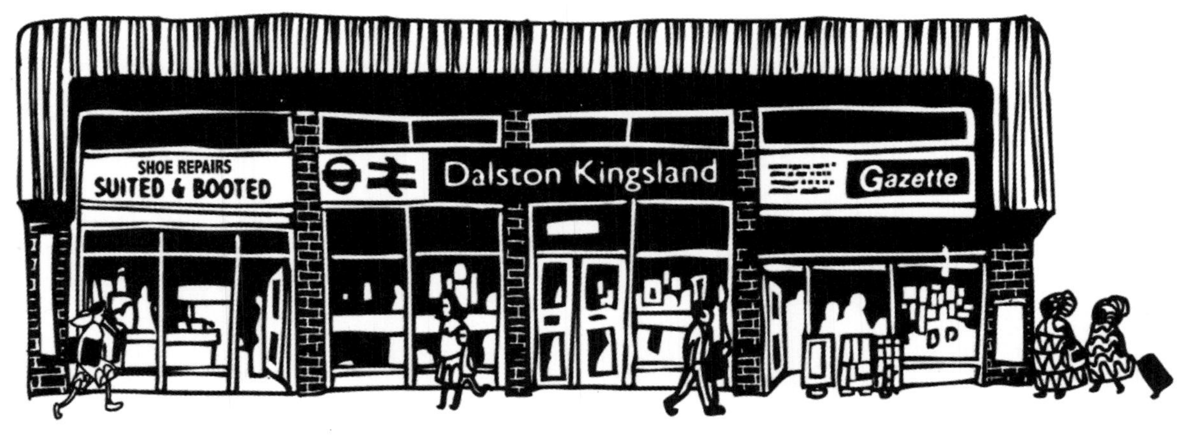
SHOE REPAIRS
SUITED & BOOTED
Dalston Kingsland
Gazette

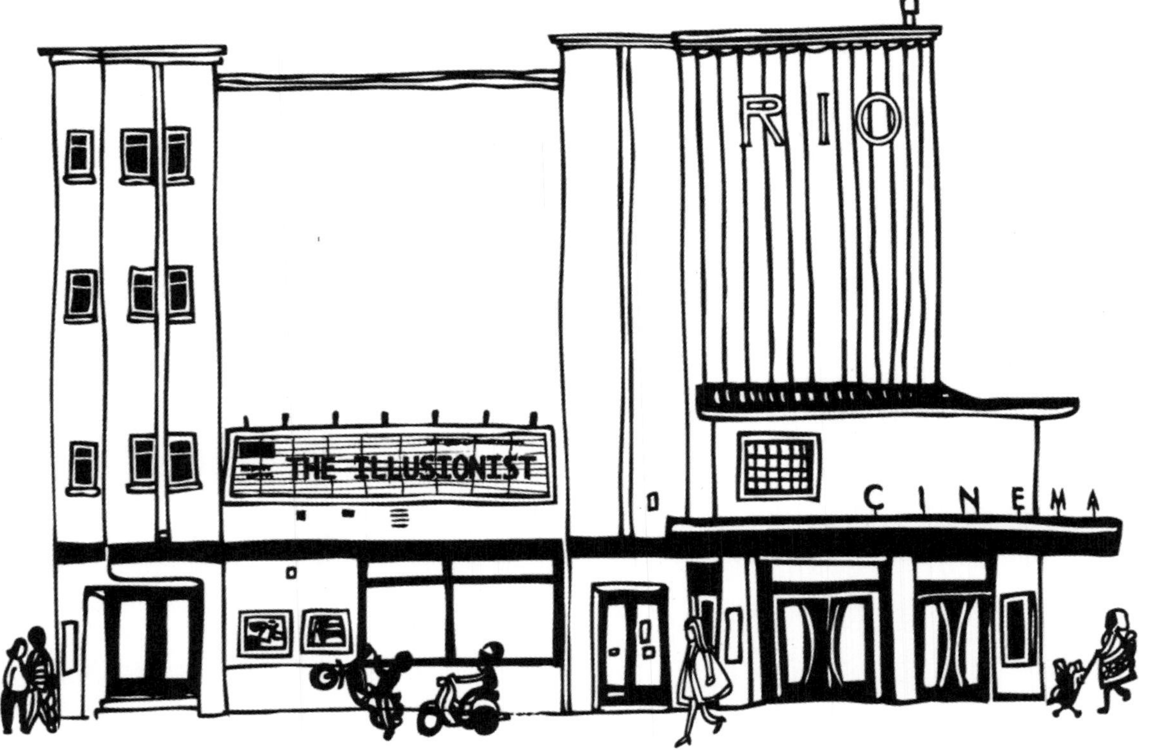
RIO
THE ILLUSIONIST
CINEMA

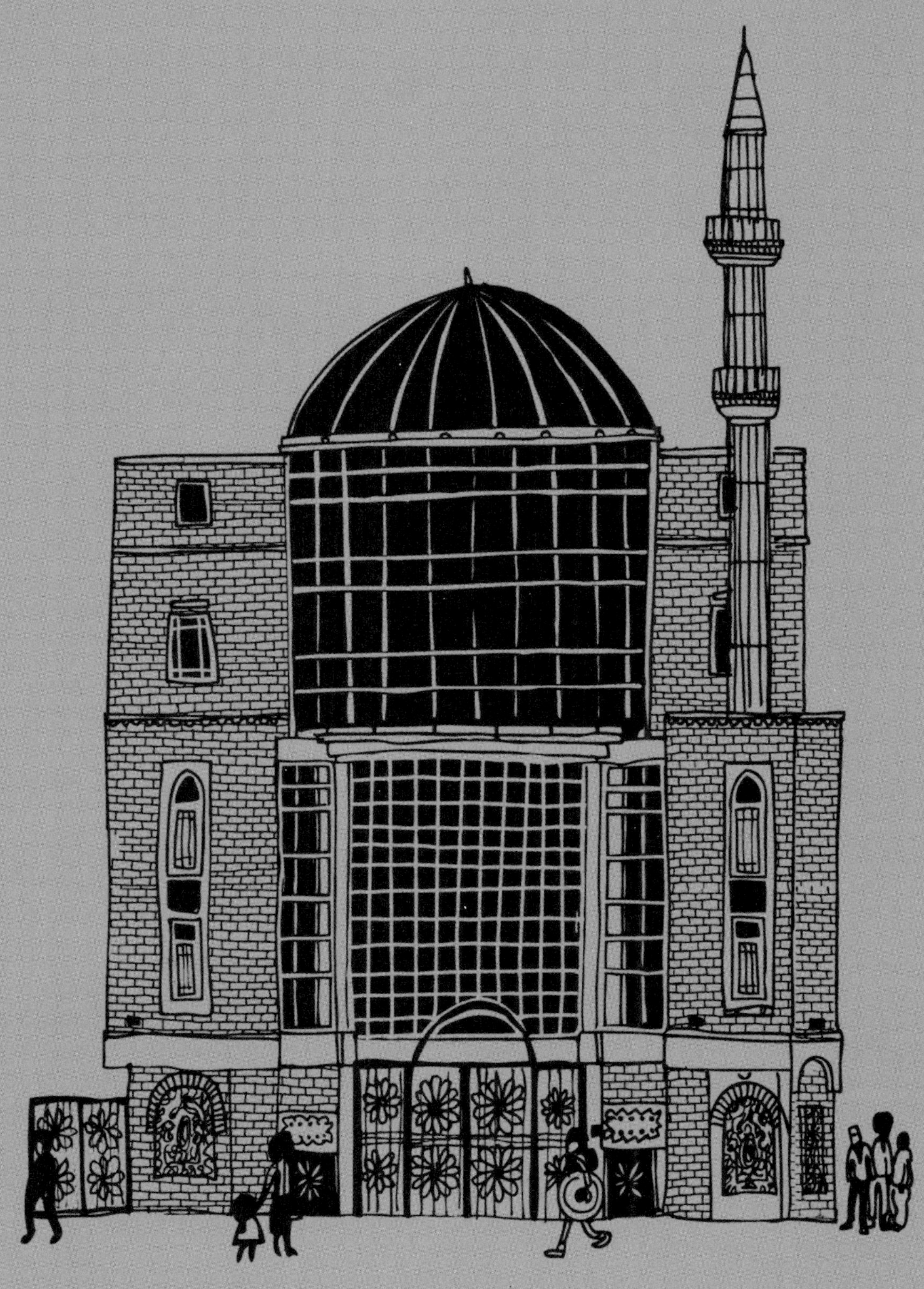

KINGSLAND ROAD

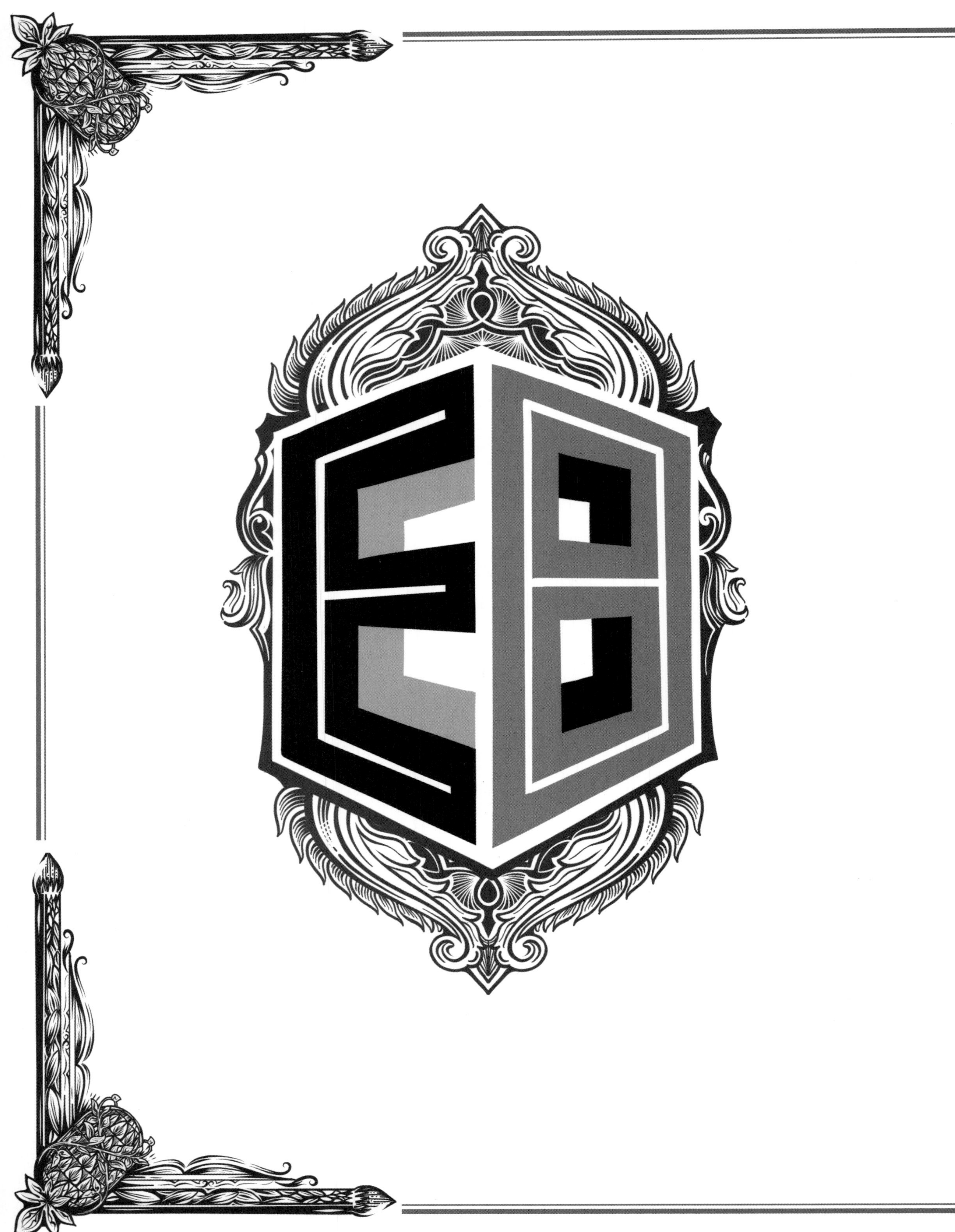

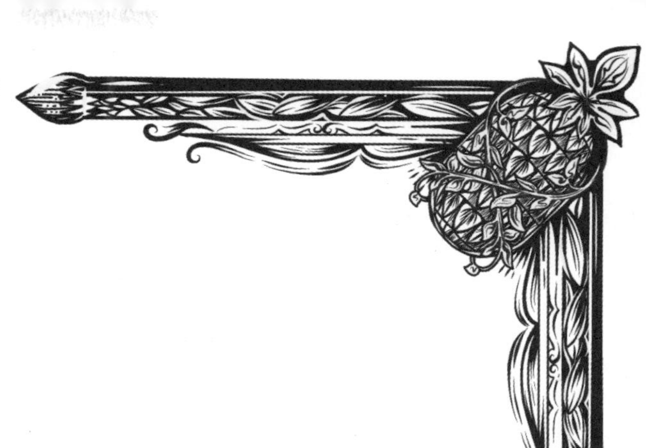

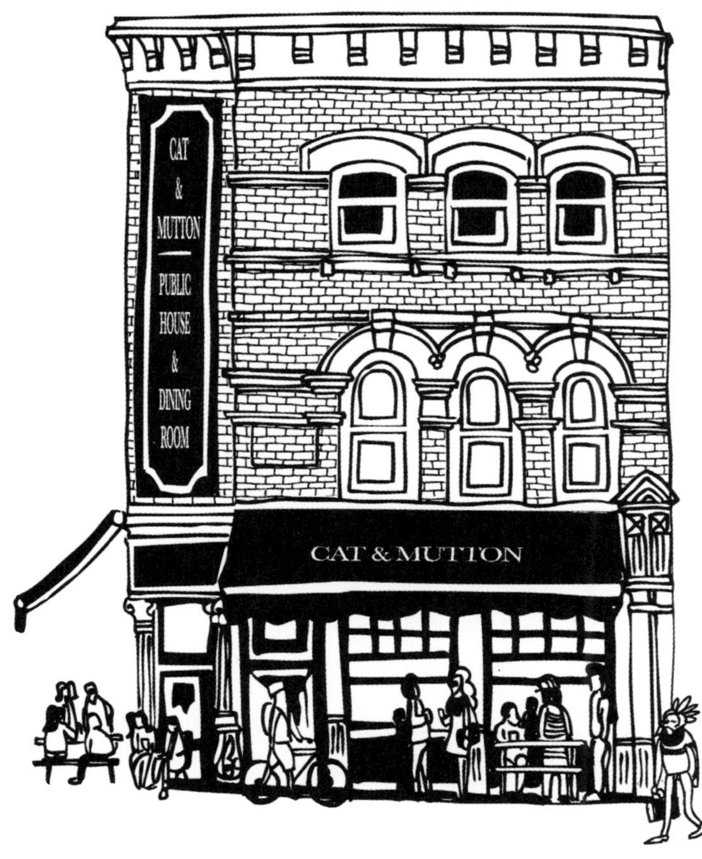

E8
BROADWAY MARKET
Hackney

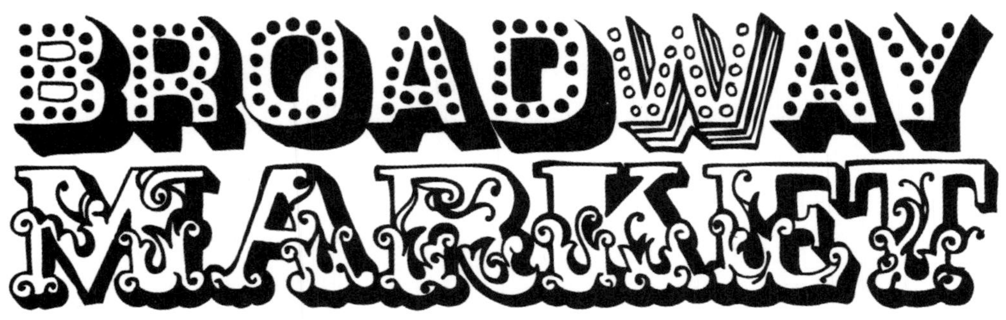

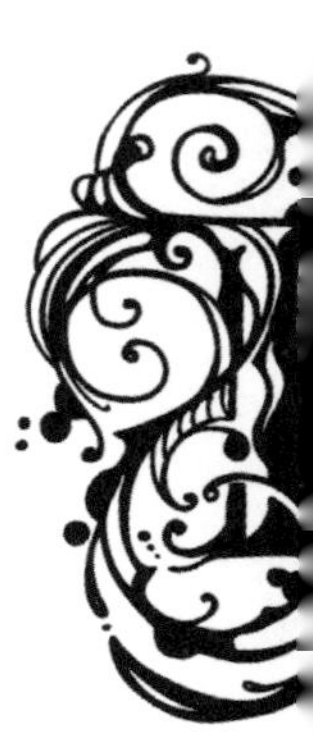

DUNCAN ROAD

JACKMAN STREET

BROADWAY MARKET

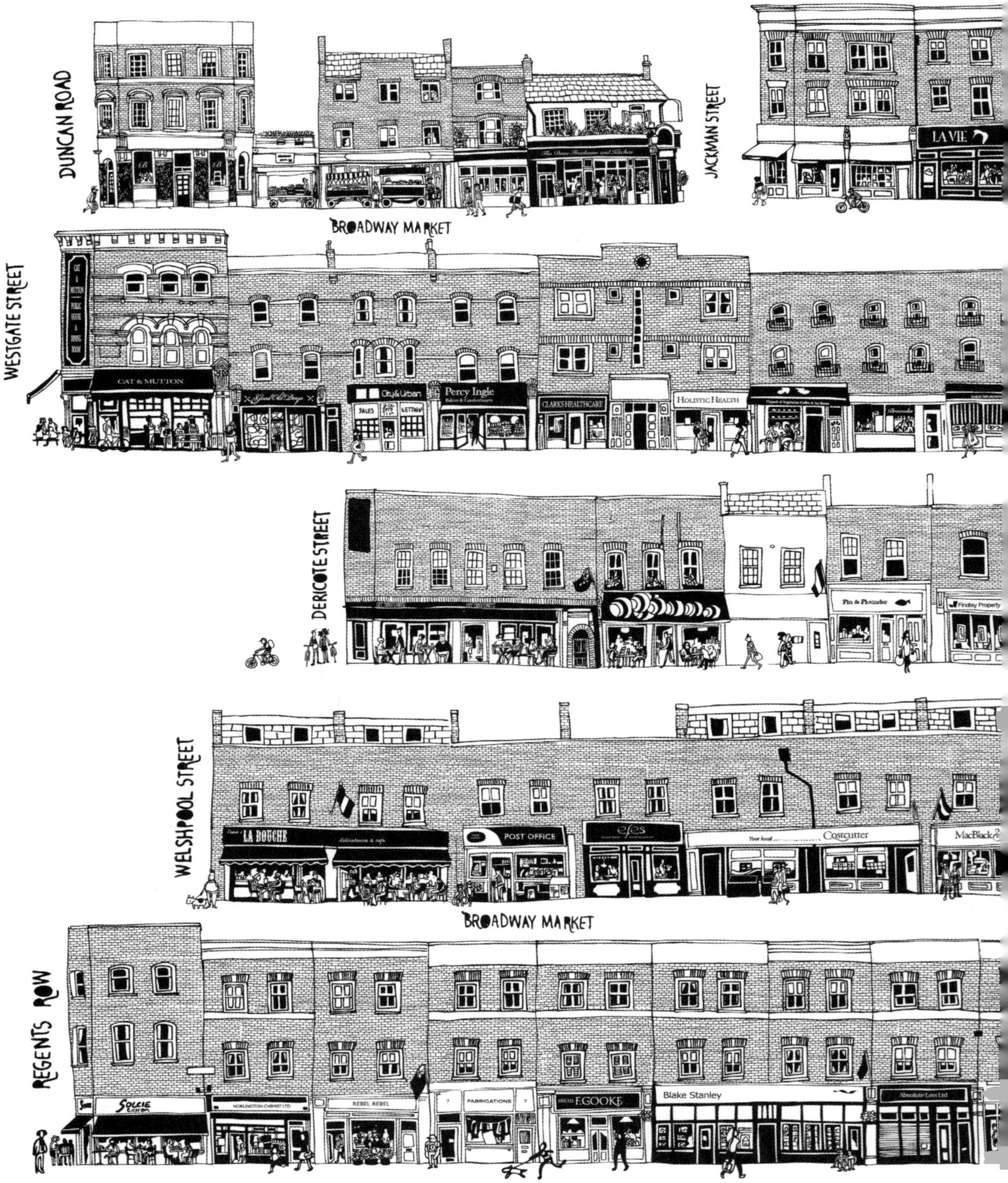

WESTGATE STREET

DERICOTE STREET

WELSHPOOL STREET

BROADWAY MARKET

REGENTS ROW

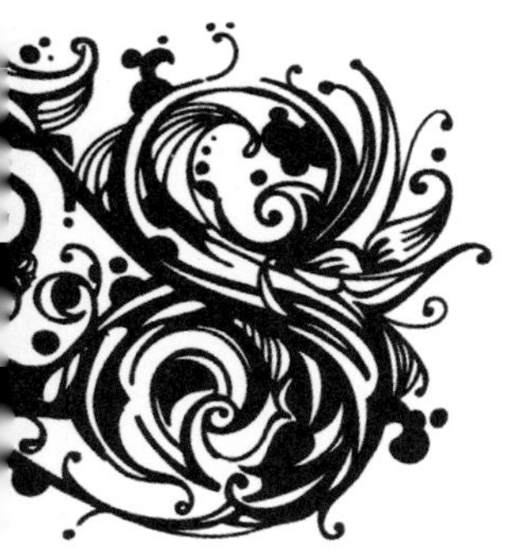

WHERE THE GOOD MR COOKE'S JELLIED EELS SLIPPED DOWN THE THROATS OF WELL ALED GEEZERS & AIR RAIDS COULDN'T DAMPEN THE SPIRITS OF THE HEARTY FOLK. WHERE LIVESTOCK ONCE TROD SLOWLY THROUGH THE COBBLED STREETS PAST THE CATTLE AND SHOULDER OF MUTTON, (NOW THE CAT) TOWARDS THEIR FINAL SUPPER BEFORE MEATING THE CLEAVER DOWN ON SLAUGHTERSTREET. NEAR LONDON FIELDS, ONCE HOME TO ROCKETS AND HURRICANES, WHERE WINDMILL ARMS THREW WELL POLISHED LEATHER BALLS AT WELL BATTERED STUMPS. THE PLACE OF TOIL AND GRAFT AND COLOURFUL CHARACTERS.

Now home to ankle high skinny jeans & the adoption of a time consuming coiffure, where single gears and brightly frames sidle alongside sit up and begs. The new home of exotic stomach fillers and aromatic lip balms. Tones in foreign voices slip effortlessly through speakers as vino is sipped and savoured over crossed legs and fashionistas discuss the next phase through nonchalant sighs.

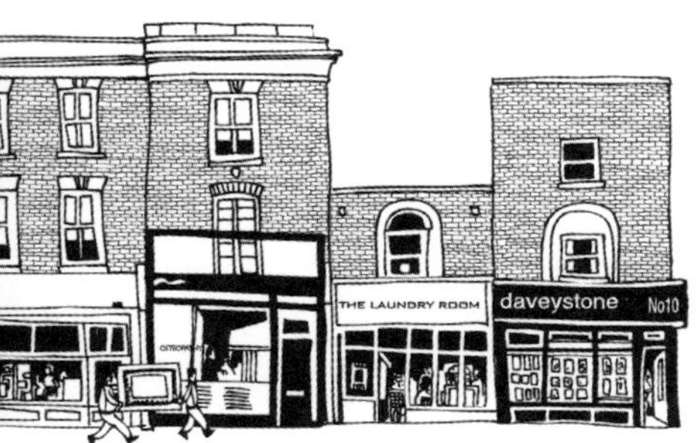

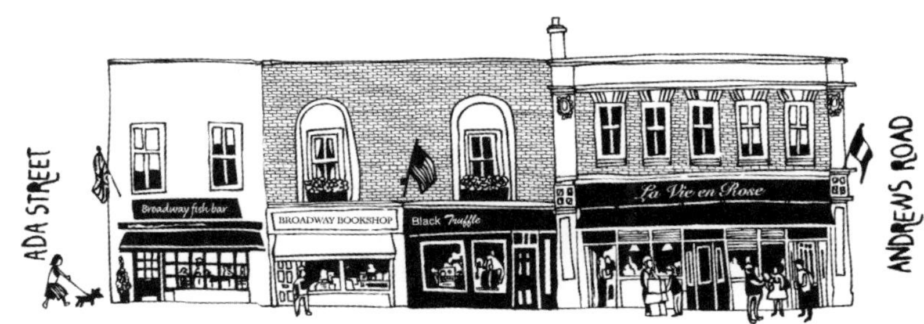

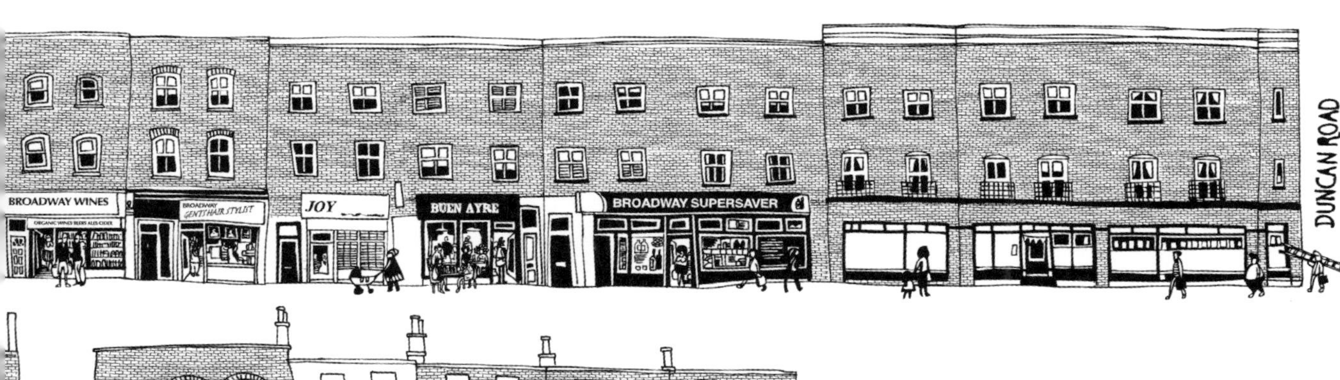

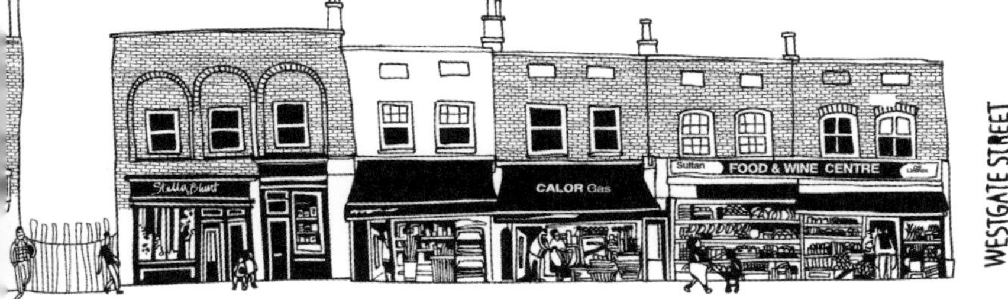

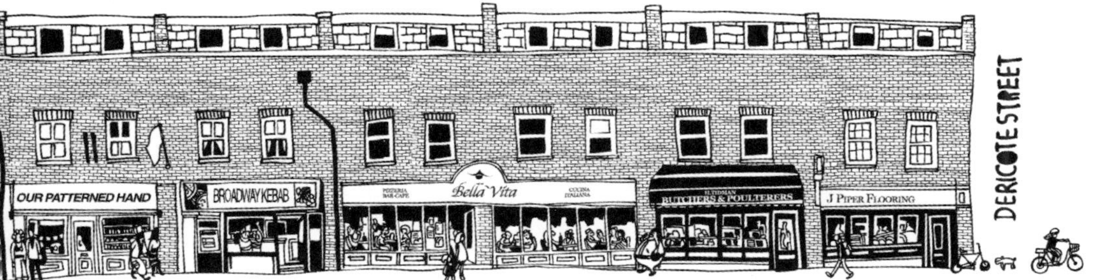

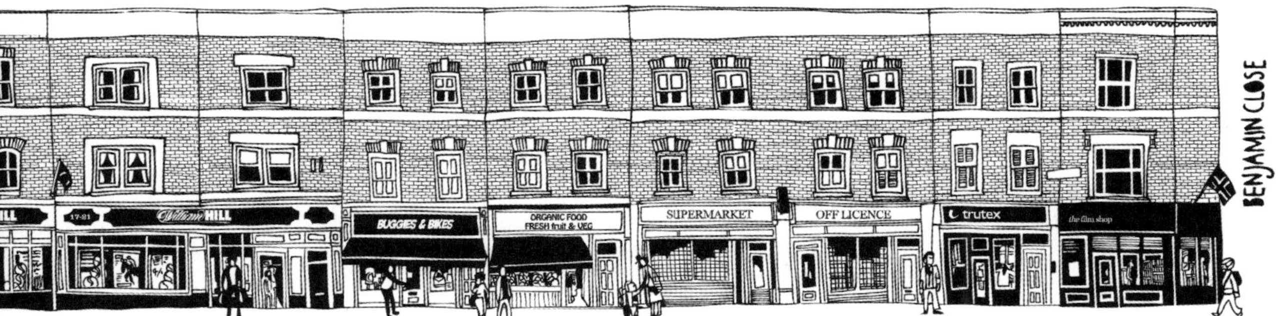

Renowned for its intellectuals and salubrious wordsmithery, Broadway Market was given its name due to the elongated conversations about nothing, had on a daily basis.

Authors, artists and actors would gather and convey non-sensical discussions using long meaningless words and balderdash.

This became known as the 'broadest way of conversing' and many vocalists would even trade the most flamboyant words.

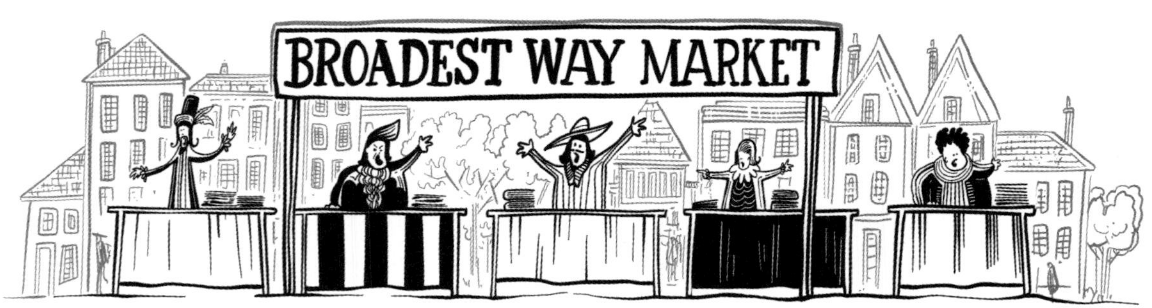

The art of whiff-whaff, though rare, can still be widely heard in most political establishments around the world to this day. It's greatest use in Westminster.

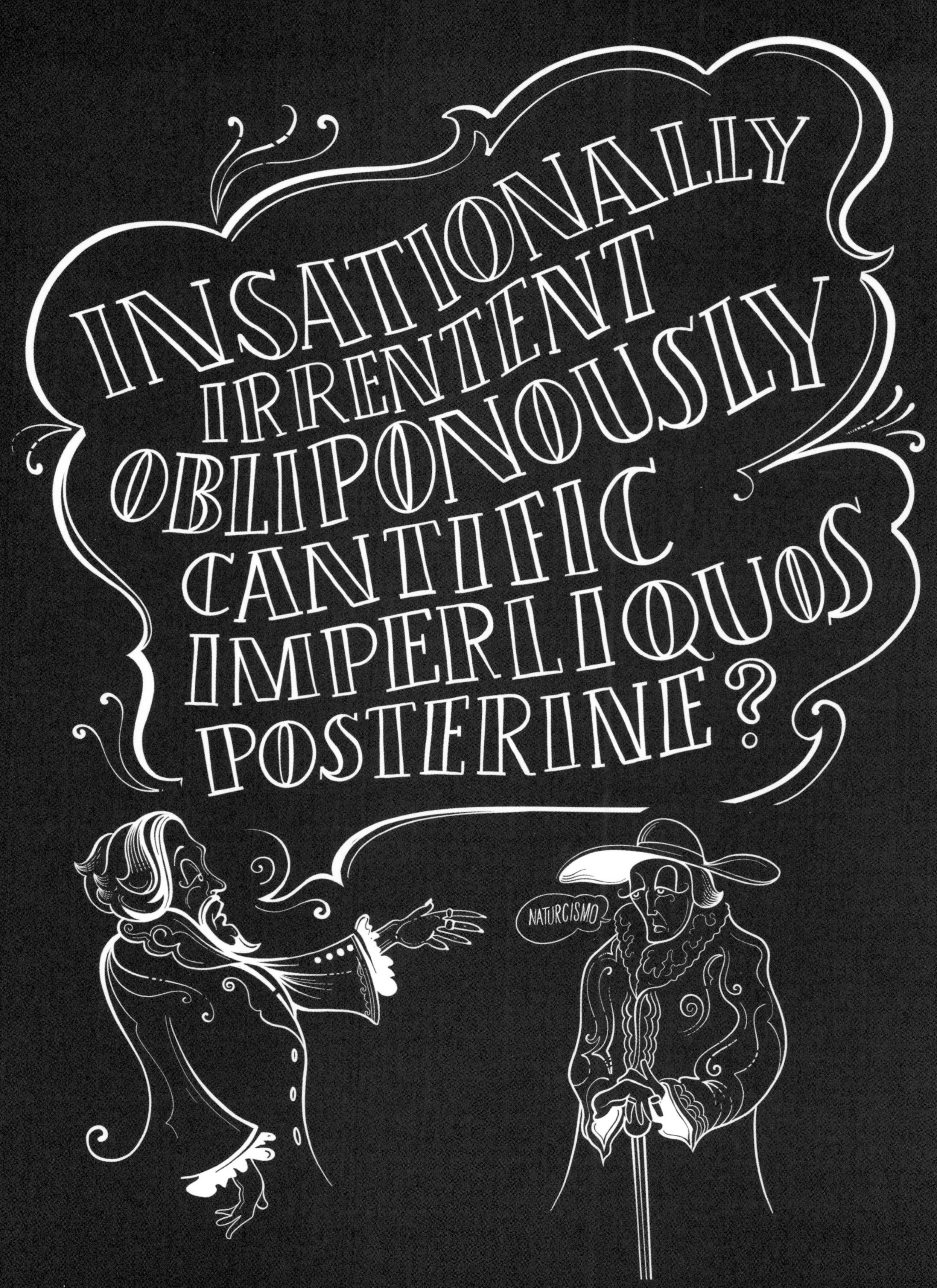

INSATIONALLY
IRRENTENT
OBLIPONOUSLY
CANTIFIC
IMPERLIQUOS
POSTERINE?
NATURCISMO

BROADWAY

efes
OCAKBASI RESTAURANT
Your local
Costcutter
MacBlack & Vine
F.GOOKE
Blake Stanley
Absolute Law Ltd
William HILL

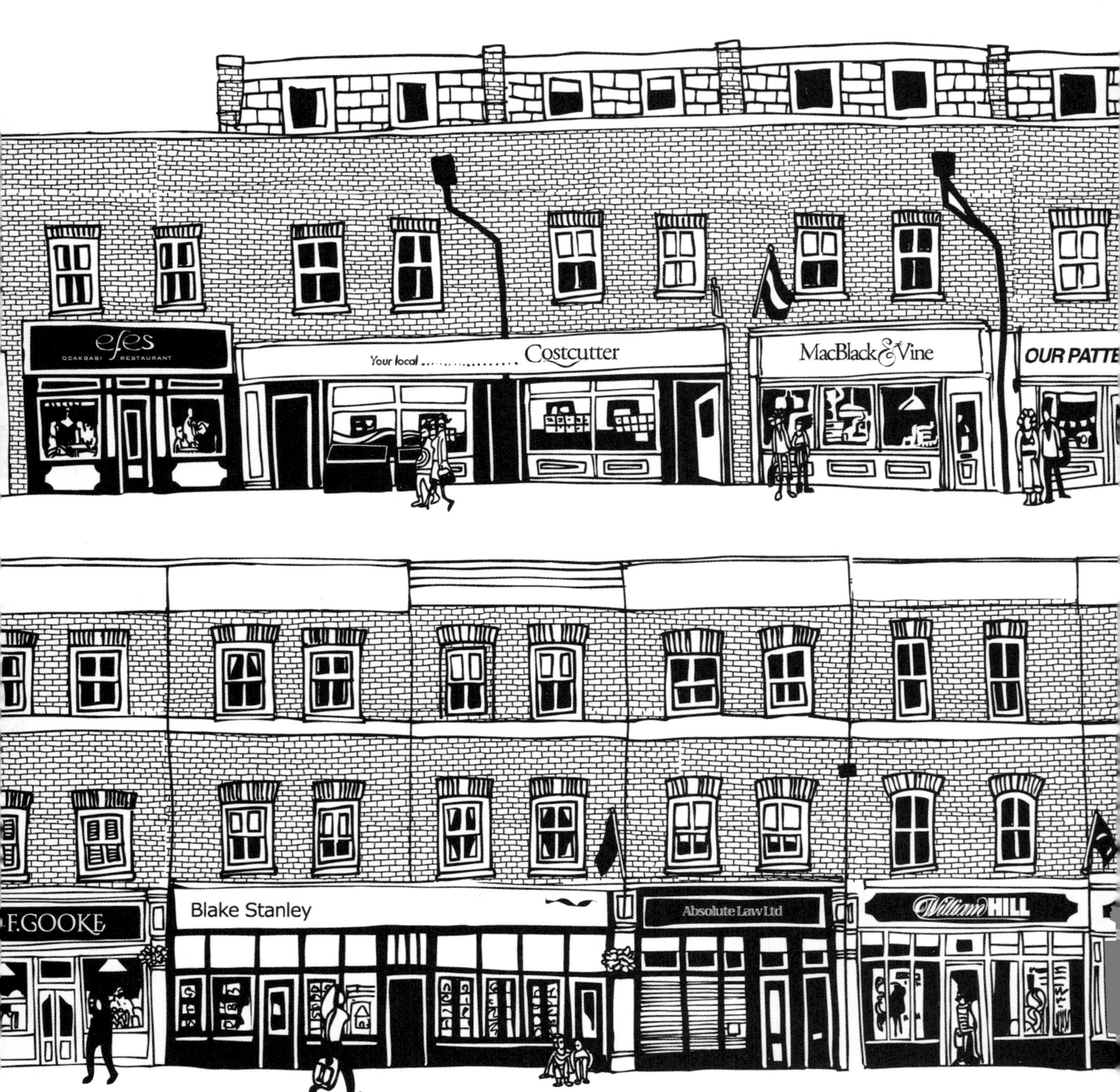

MARKET

BROADWAY KEBAB
PIZZERIA
BAR-CAFE
Bella Vita
CUCINA
ITALIANA
H.TIDMAN
BUTCHERS & POULTERERS
William HILL
BUGGIES & BIKES
ORGANIC FOOD
FRESH fruit & VEG
SUPERMARKET

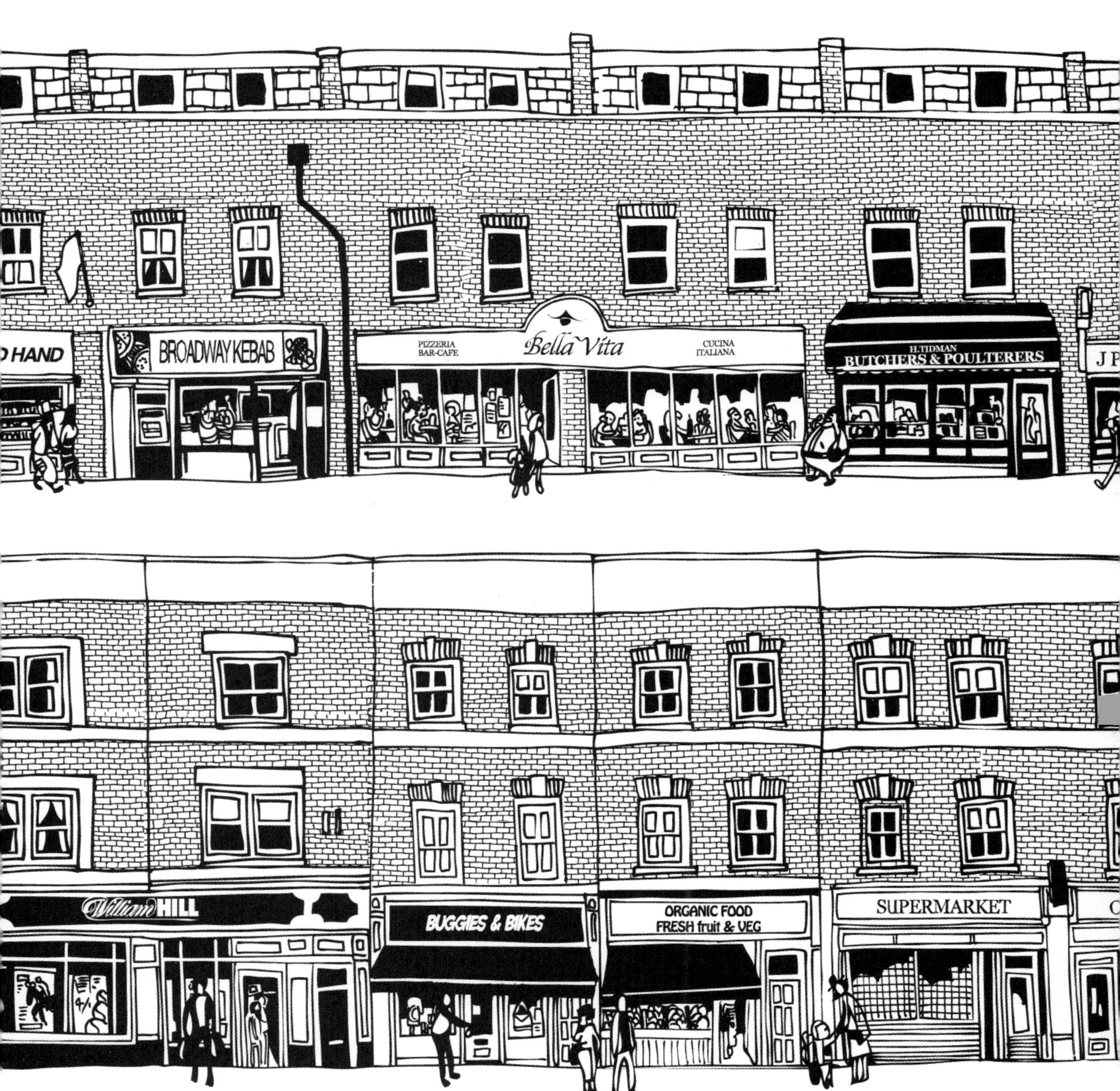

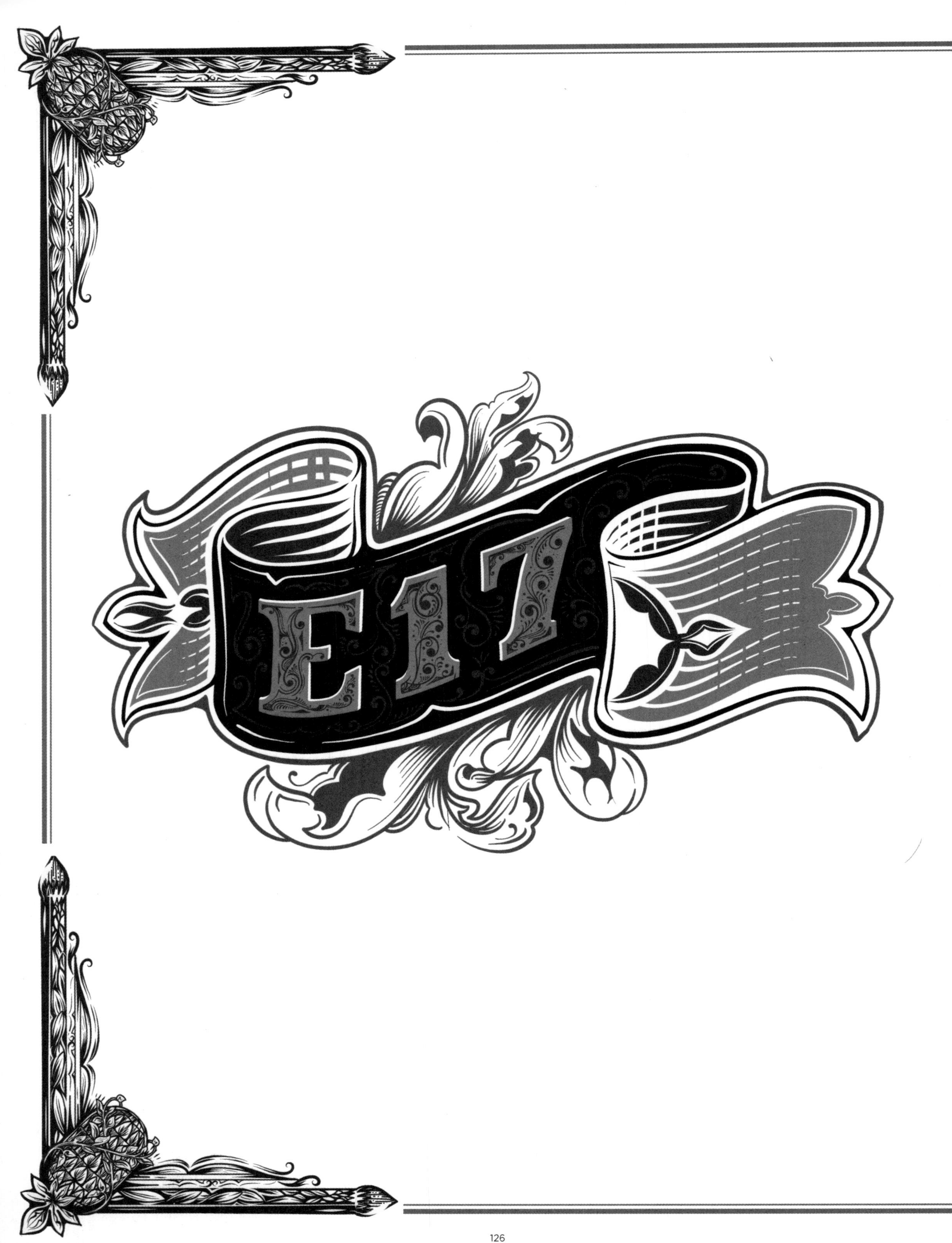
E17

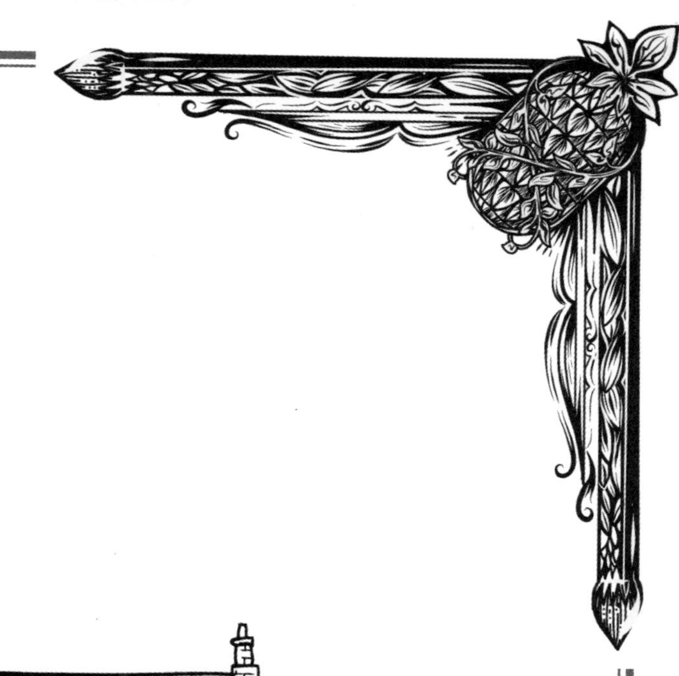

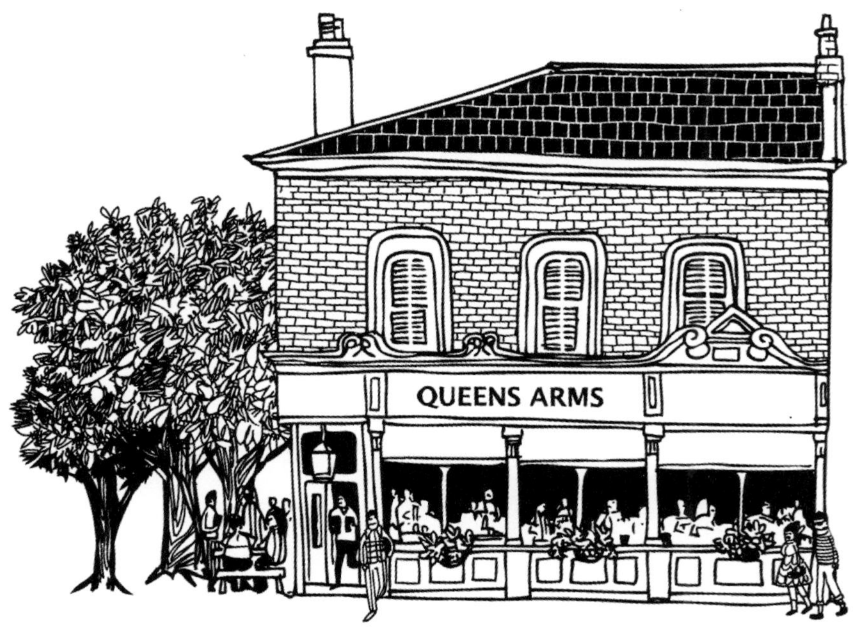

E17
WALTHAMSTOW VILLAGE
Walthamstow

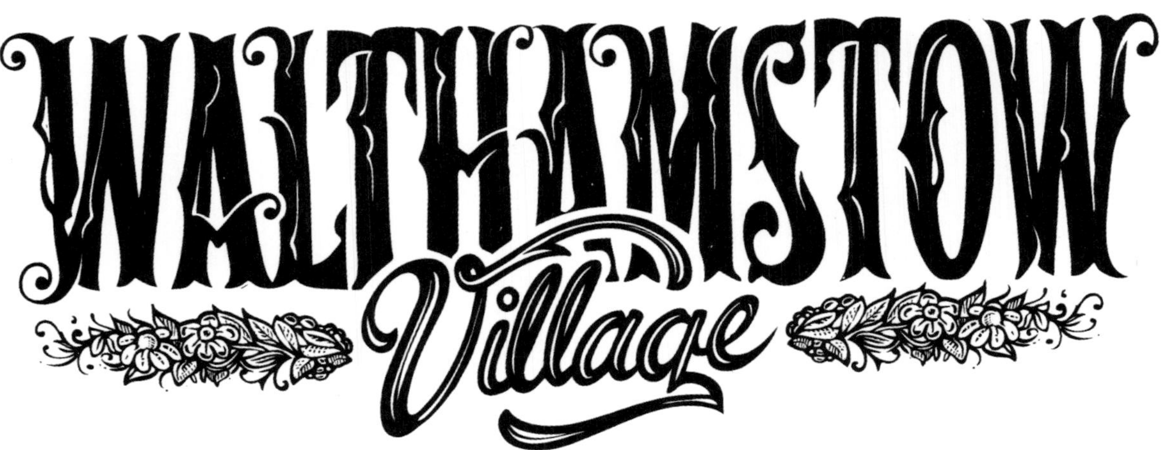
WALTHAMSTOW
Village

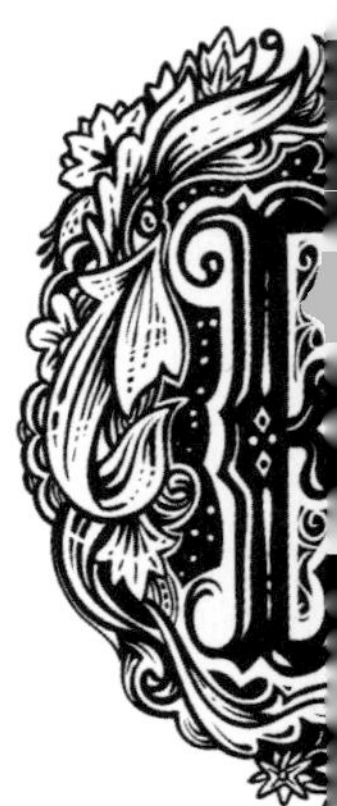

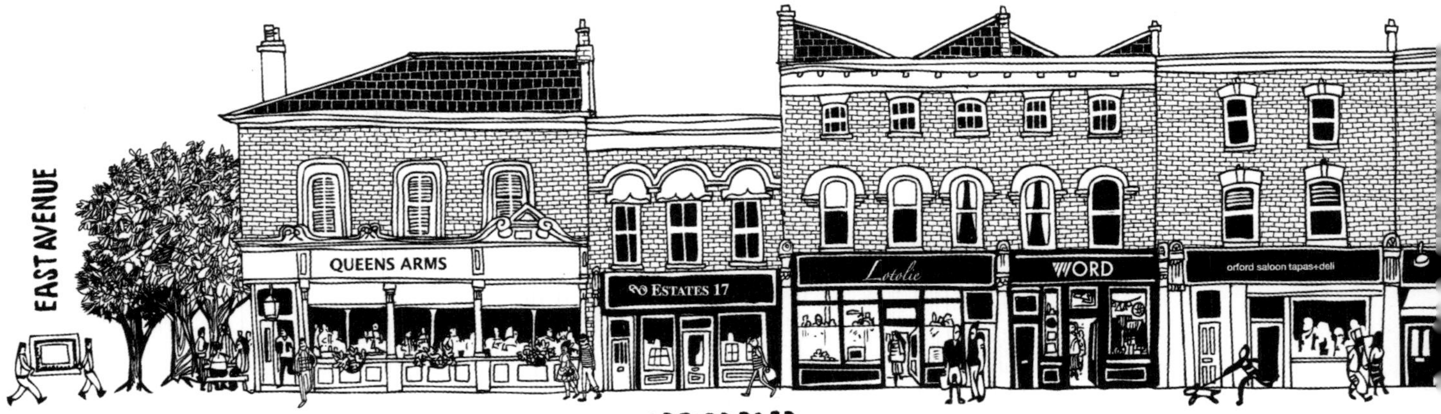
EAST AVENUE
QUEENS ARMS
ESTATES 17
WORD
orford saloon tapas+deli
ORFORD ROAD

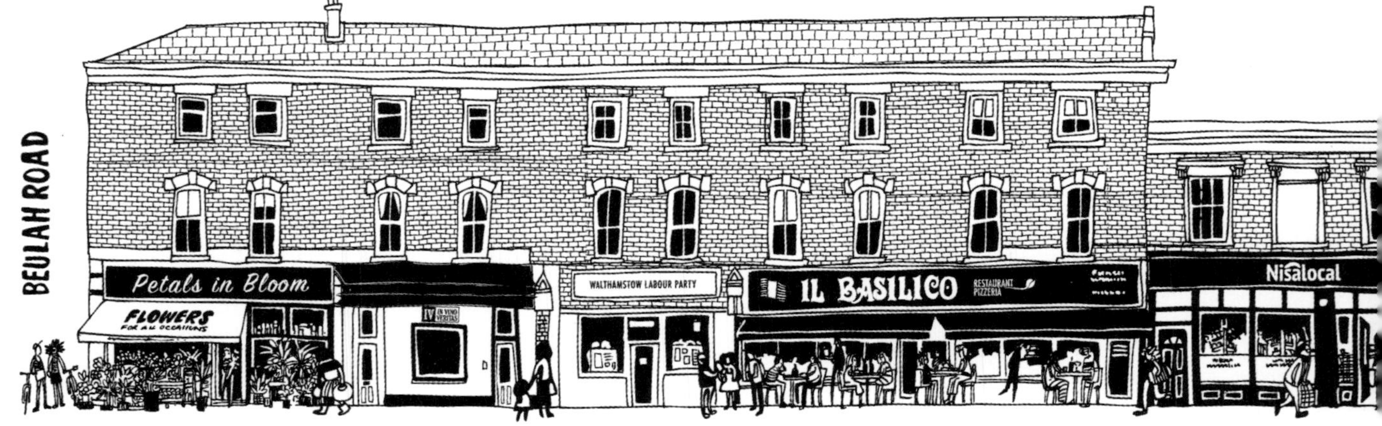
BEULAH ROAD
Petals in Bloom
FLOWERS
WALTHAMSTOW LABOUR PARTY
IL BASILICO
RESTAURANT PIZZERIA
Nisalocal
ORFORD ROAD

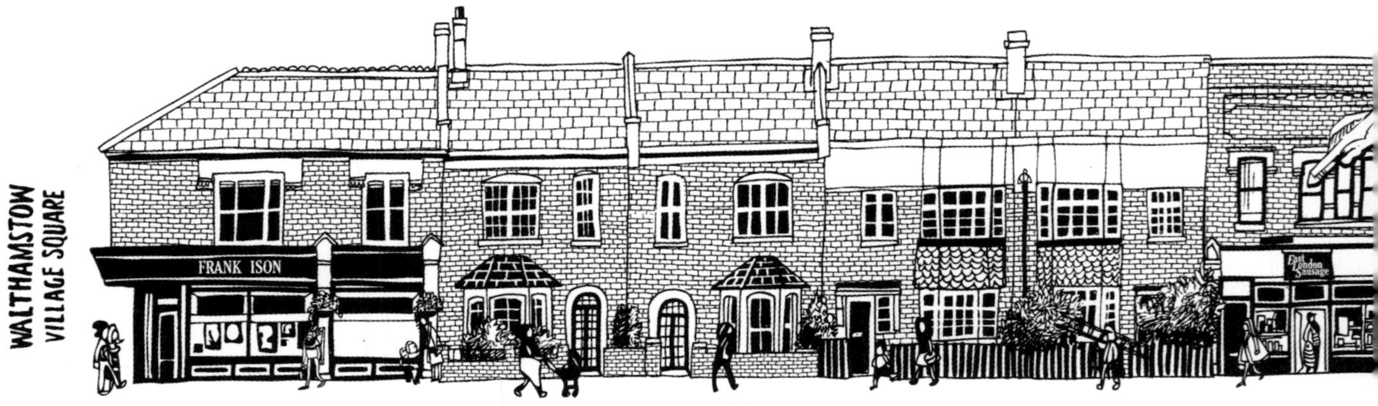
WALTHAMSTOW
VILLAGE SQUARE
FRANK ISON
ORFORD ROAD

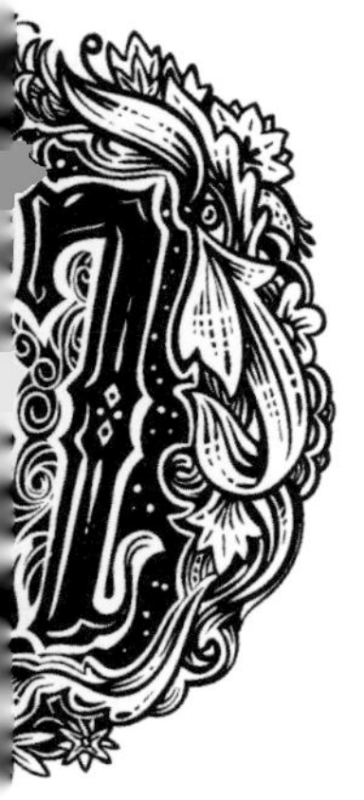

OF ONCE WAS WILCUMESTOU, THE WELCOME PLACE, THIS MANOR ONCE LAUDED OVER by WALTHAMSTOW TONI, THE TOP GEEZER. OF MR MONOUX & HIS MOONES, MARSHLAND FLIGHTS of THE YELLOW TERROR & HOME TO ONE of THE GREAT TREES OF LONDON, *the Wood Street Horse Chestnut.* WHERE BREMER BUILT *the* 1ST BRITISH MOTOR, THE STONES, BEATLES & THE WHO ROCKED THE GRANADA & CAPTAIN CREATIVE, *William Morris* WAS CARRIED IN ON A CRAFTY STORK. NOW HOME *to* MUMS WHO YUM, WHEELERS, DEALERS, ORGANIC BREADS & NUFF SAIDS, ARTY TYPES, PARTY TYPES, THE LORDS, LUVVIES, PRICELESS & NICENESS. THE ONITS & INNITS.

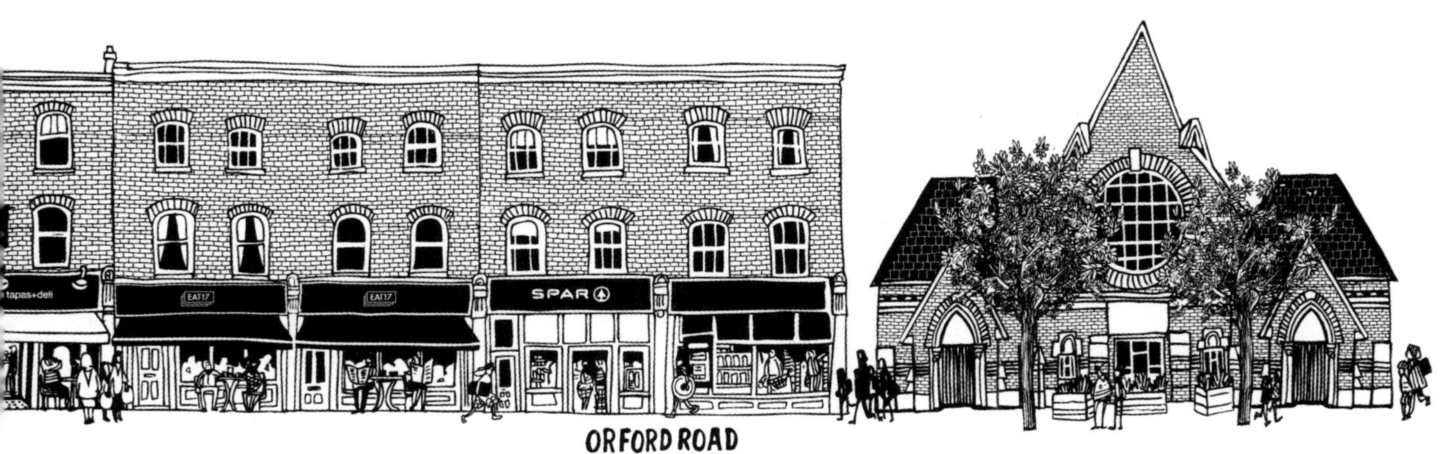

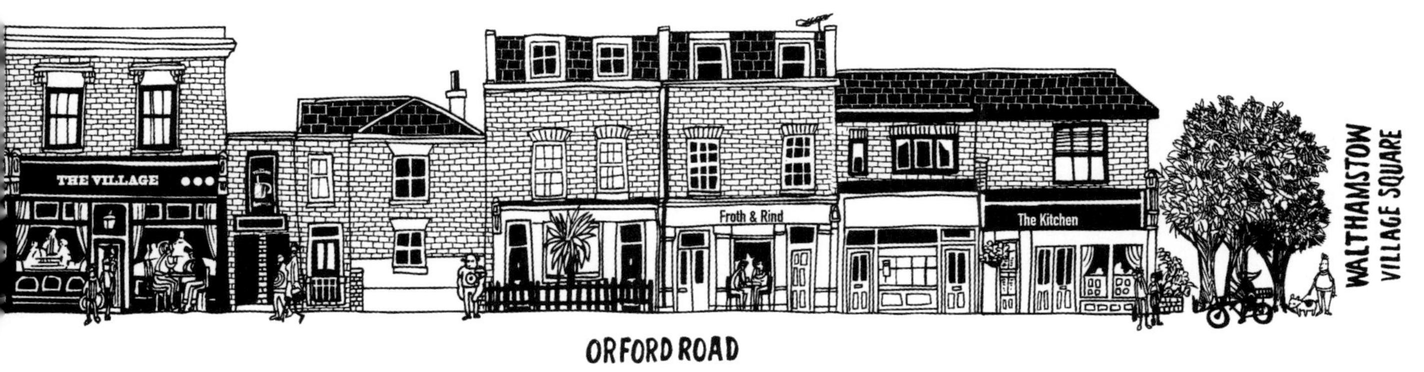

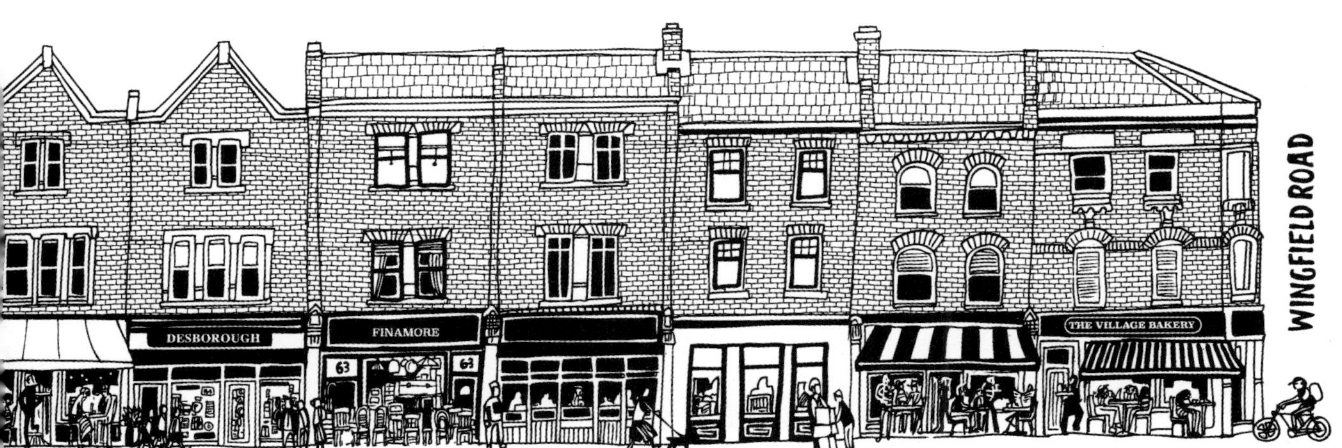

Though once famed for greyhound racing at Walthamstow Dogs, the original races were held on wasteland at the top of Wood Street in the 1870's.

A poor area of London, it was nigh on impossible to afford the luxury of attending horse races such as Ascot or Aintree.

So the versatile Eastenders came up with their own version.

Small children, bedecked in homemade gladrags, would ride greyhounds in the now legendary *Wood Street Pup Races*.

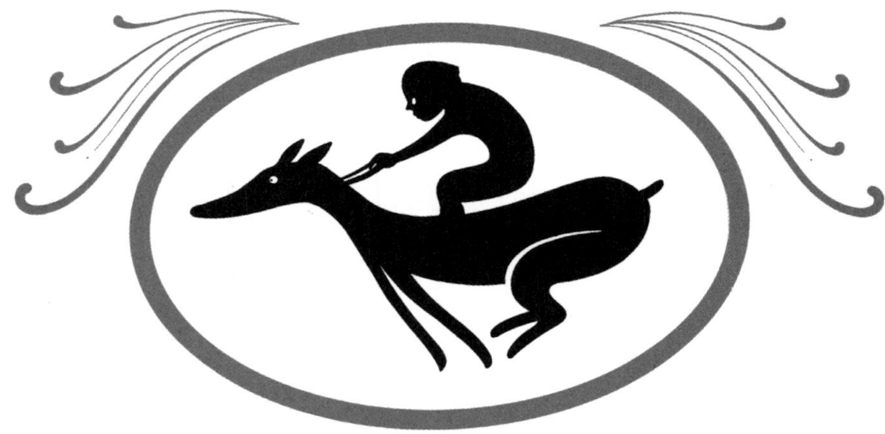

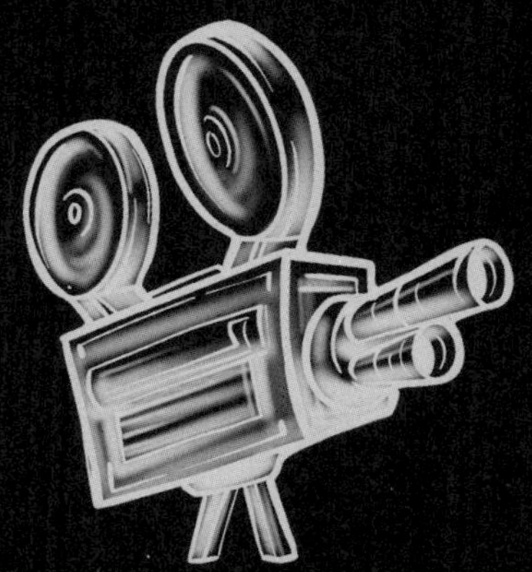

Walthamstow was at one stage the hub of Film making in London. The 1920's saw a Flurry of Studios open in the East London suburb.

Precision, Broadwest, IB Davidson, British & Colonial - the main ones, making silent movies with extras sourced, not From agencies, but From local boozers.

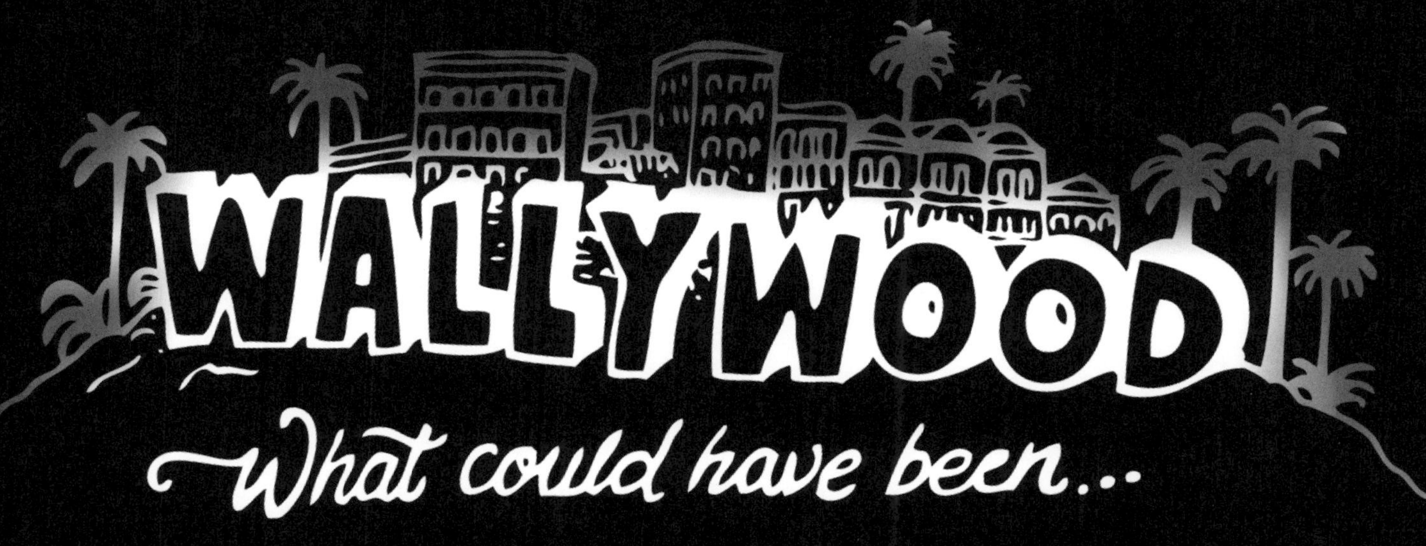

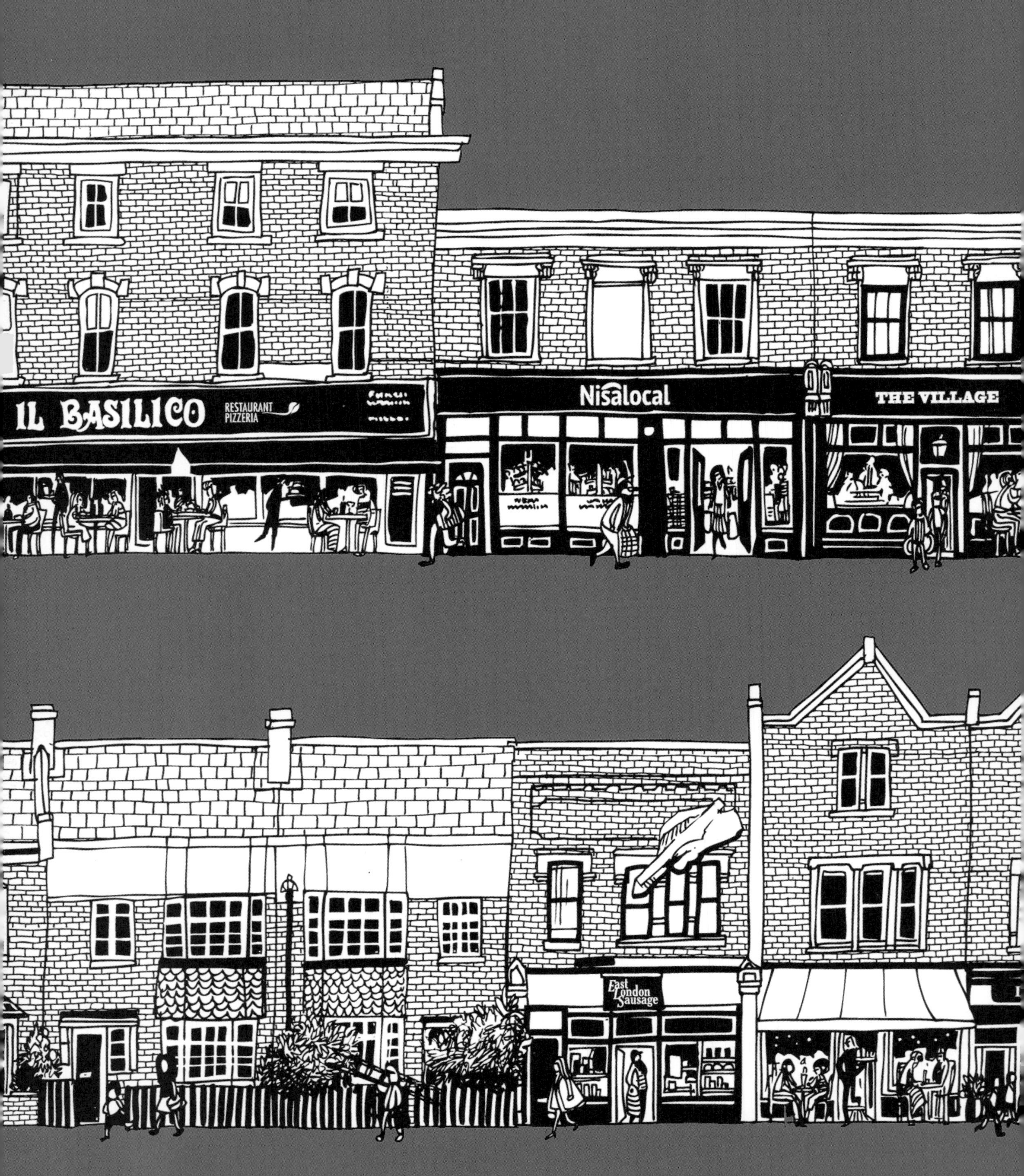
IL BASILICO
RESTAURANT
PIZZERIA
Nisalocal
THE VILLAGE
East London Sausage

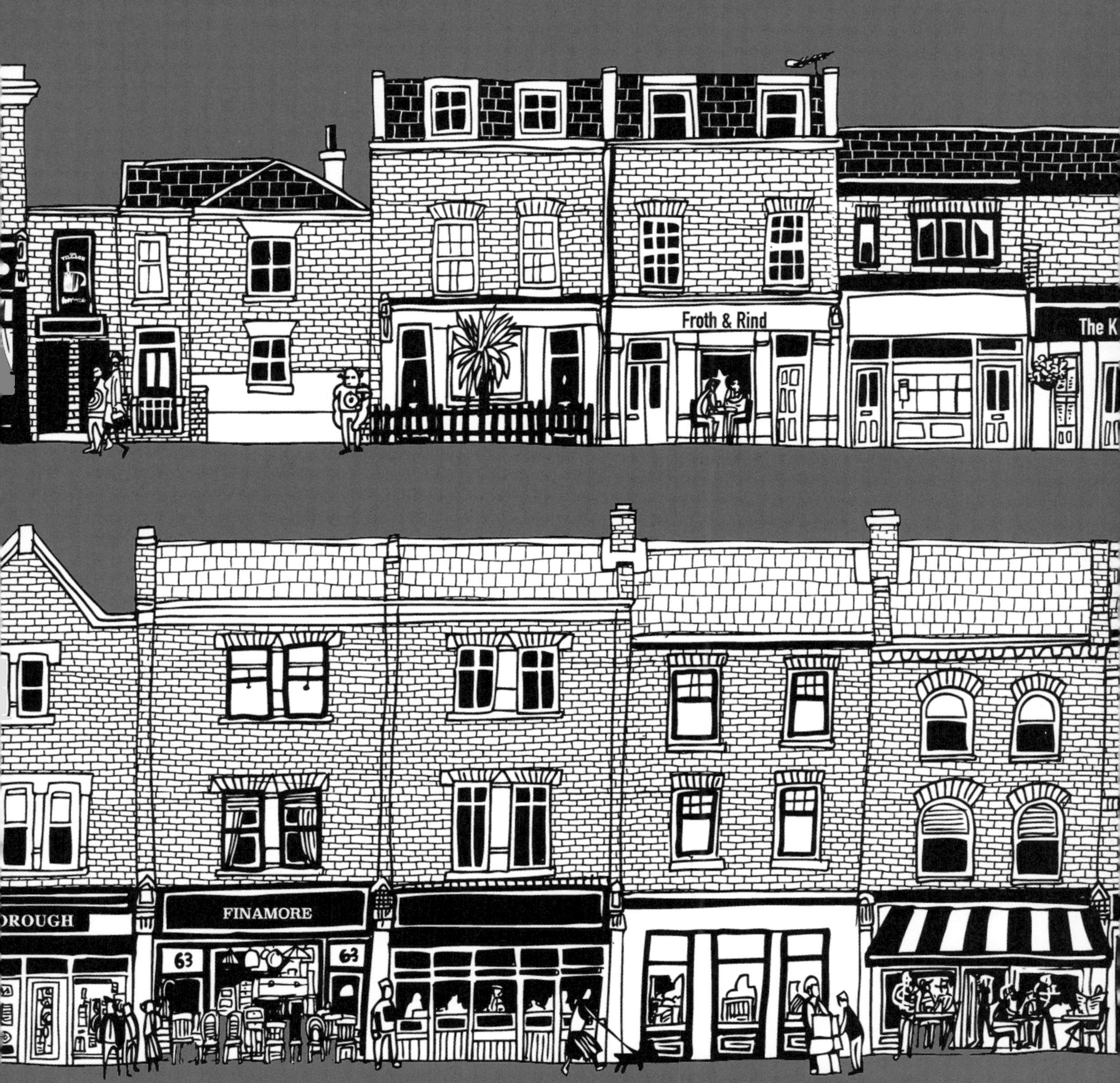
Froth & Rind
FINAMORE
63
63

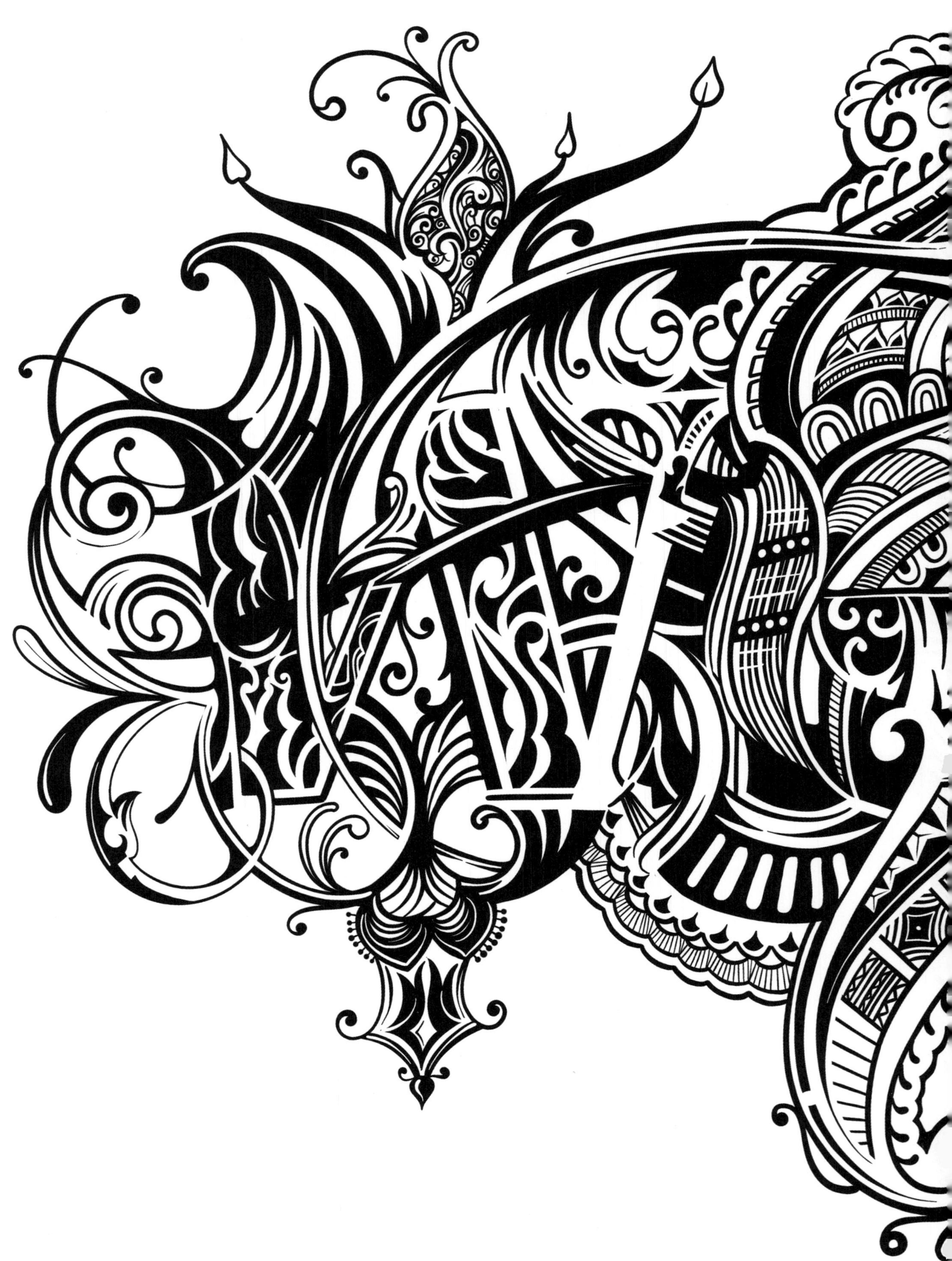

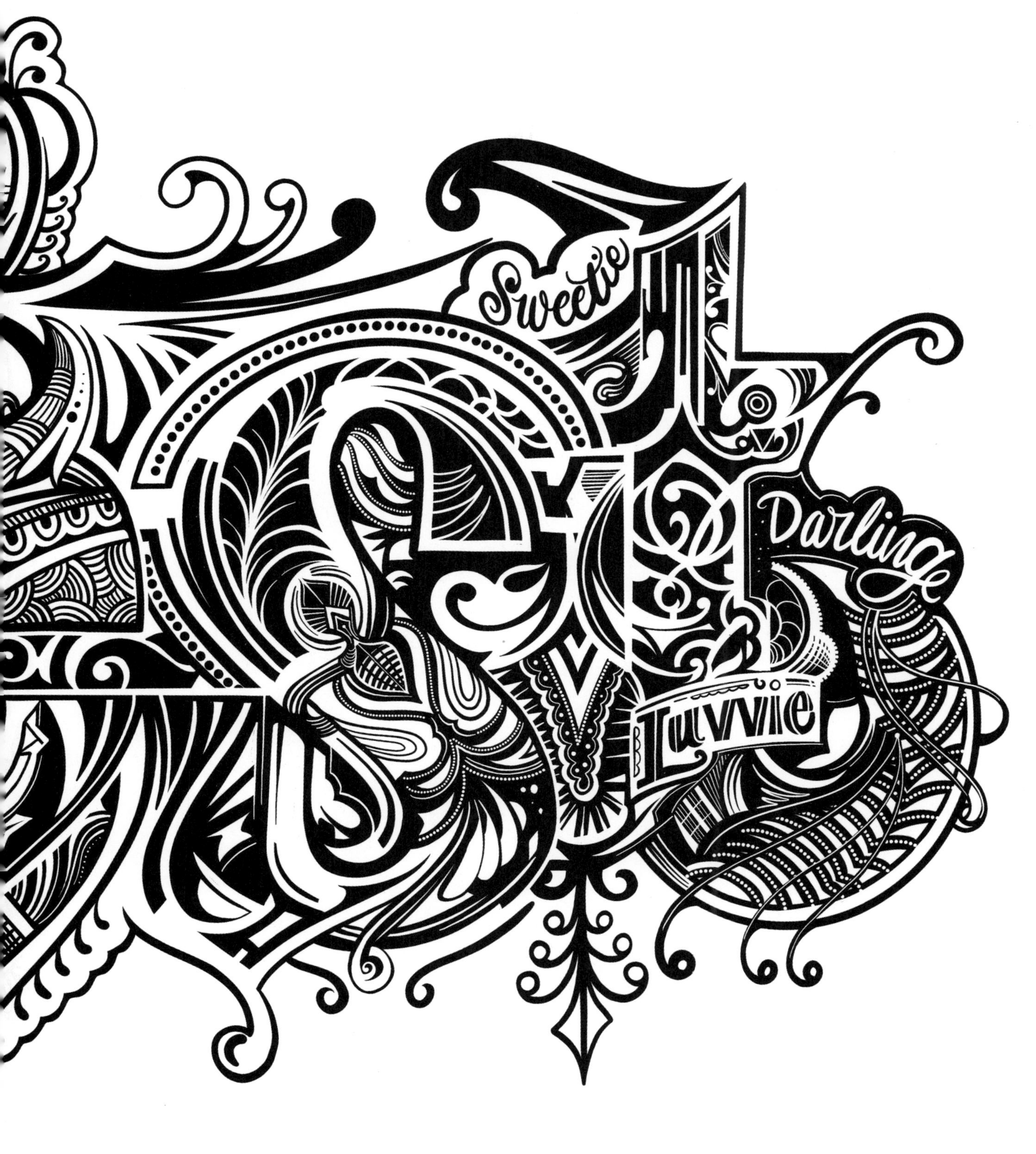
Sweetie
Darlinge
Luvvie

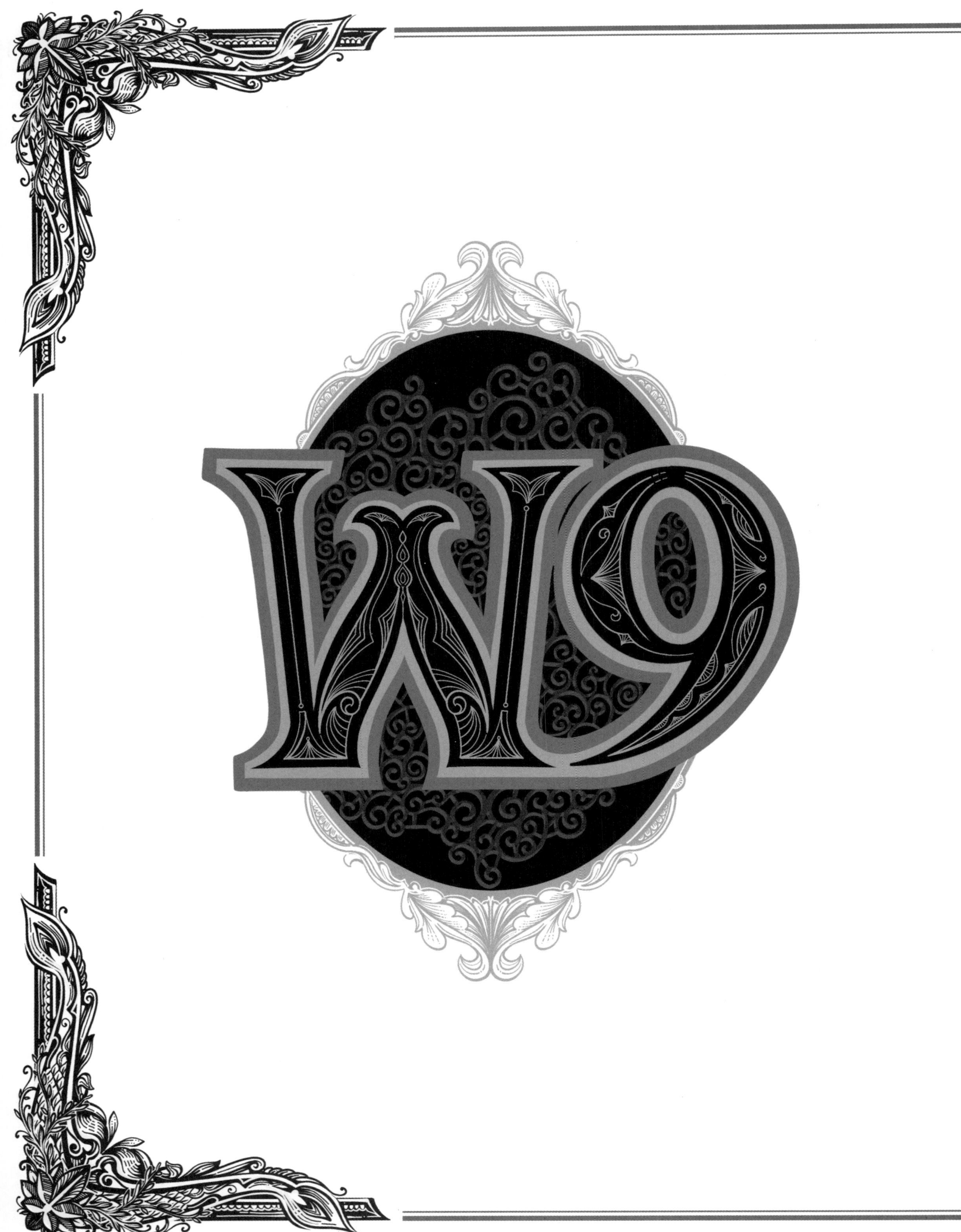
W9

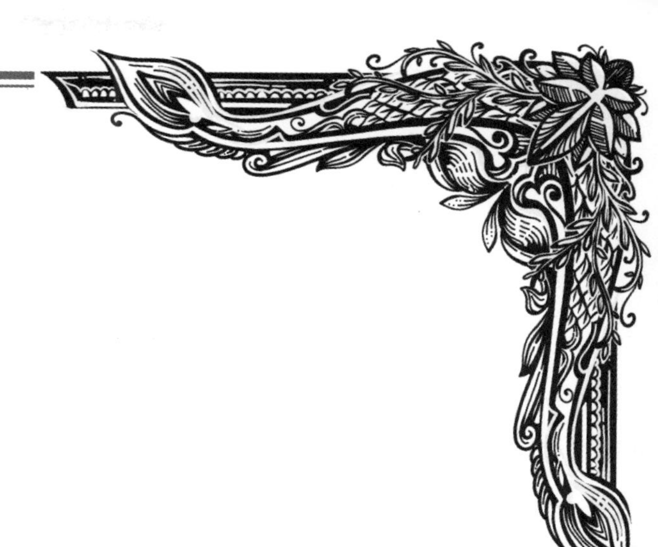

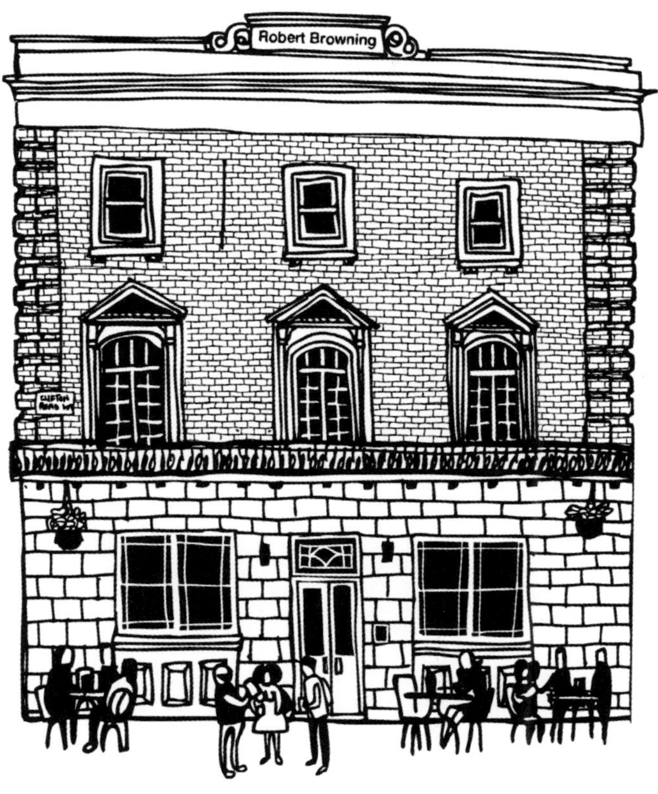

W9
CLIFTON ROAD
Maida Vale

Clifton Road

A GATHERING OF DELIGHTS, OF SHOPPING, HAIRDOS AND AL FRESCO LIVING IN THE PLUSHNESS OF MAIDA VALE. A NAME THAT STEMS FROM A BATTLE THAT RAGED IN 1806 TWEEN THE FRENCH AND THE BRITISH AT SAN PIETRO DI MAIDA IN CALABRIA, ITALY. A PUBLIC HOUSE NO LESS BESTOWED THE TITLE 'HERO OF MAIDA' UPON ITSELF AFTER GENERAL JOHN STUART, COMMANDER OF THE BRITISH FORCES, WAS ENNOBLED COUNT OF MAIDA, AND THUS THE AREA OF MAIDA VALE WAS BORNE.

And this Clifton Road, this Maida Vale, once dwellings of tradesmen and artisans, is said during the decadent 20's, to be one of Londons most desirable suburbs, to have 'some handsome piles of residential mansions' no less.

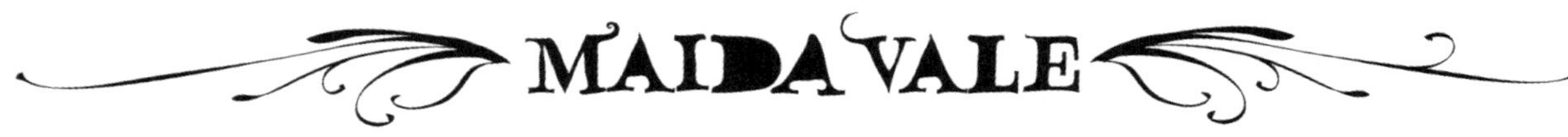

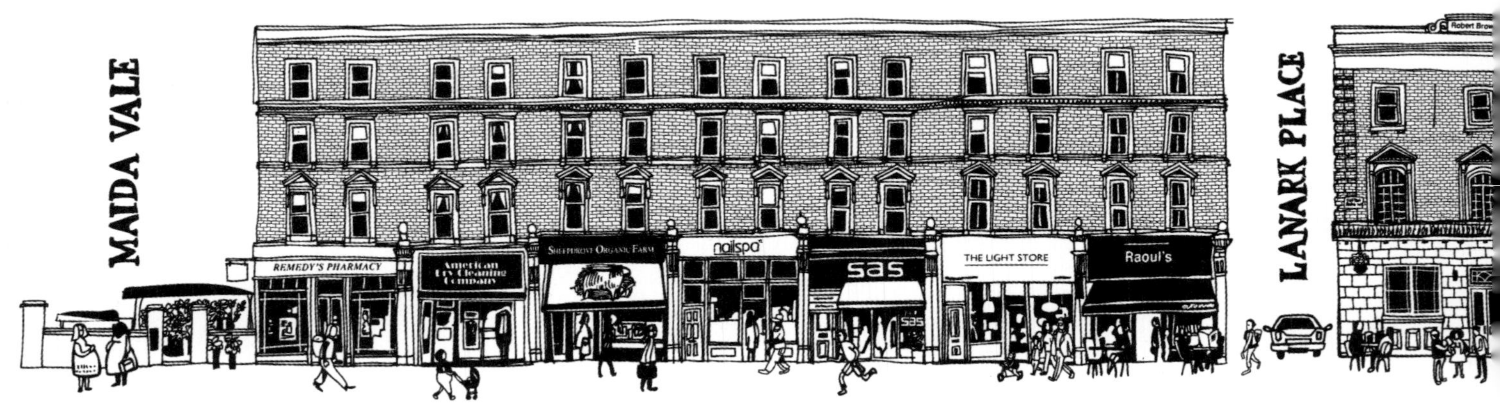

RANDOLPH AVENUE

CAFE ROUGE

chesterton

LANARK ROAD

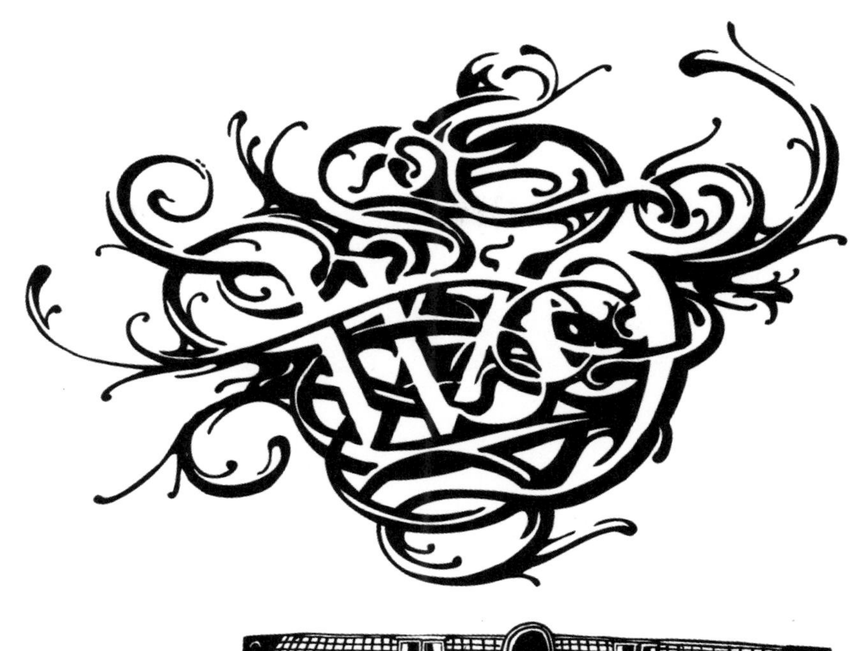

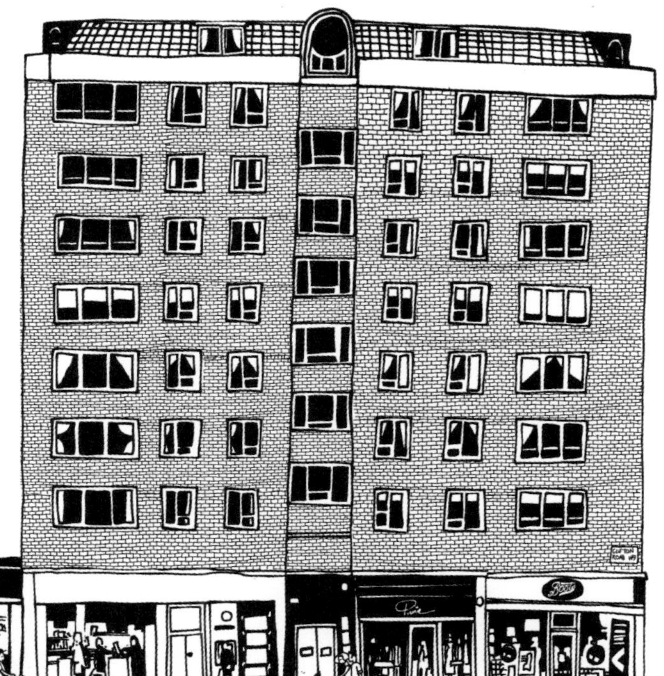

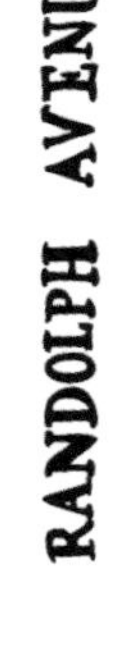
RANDOLPH AVENUE

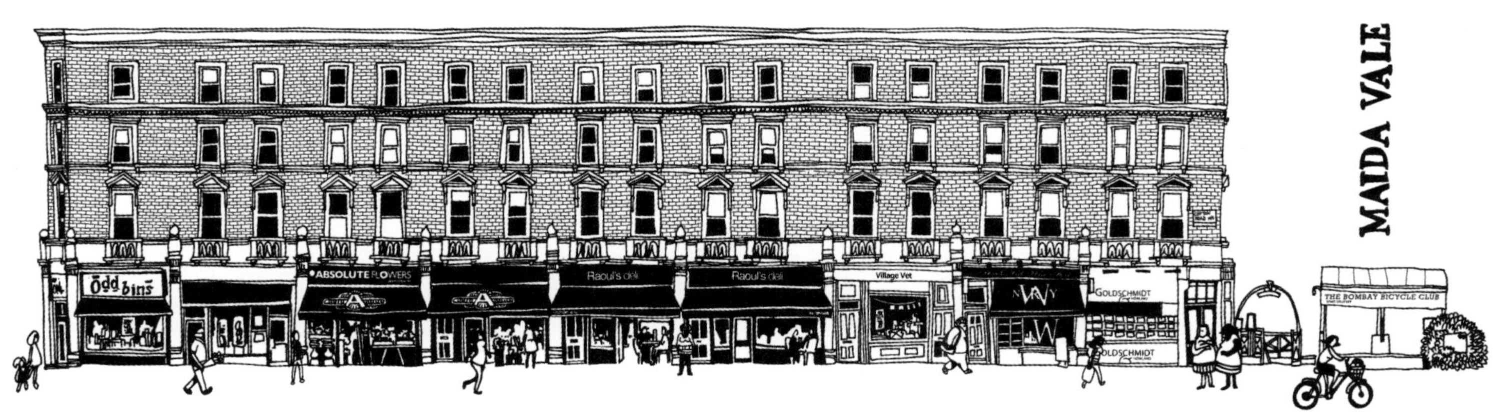
MAIDA VALE
Oddbins
ABSOLUTE FLOWERS
Raoul's deli
Raoul's deli
Village Vet
GOLDSCHMIDT
THE BOMBAY BICYCLE CLUB

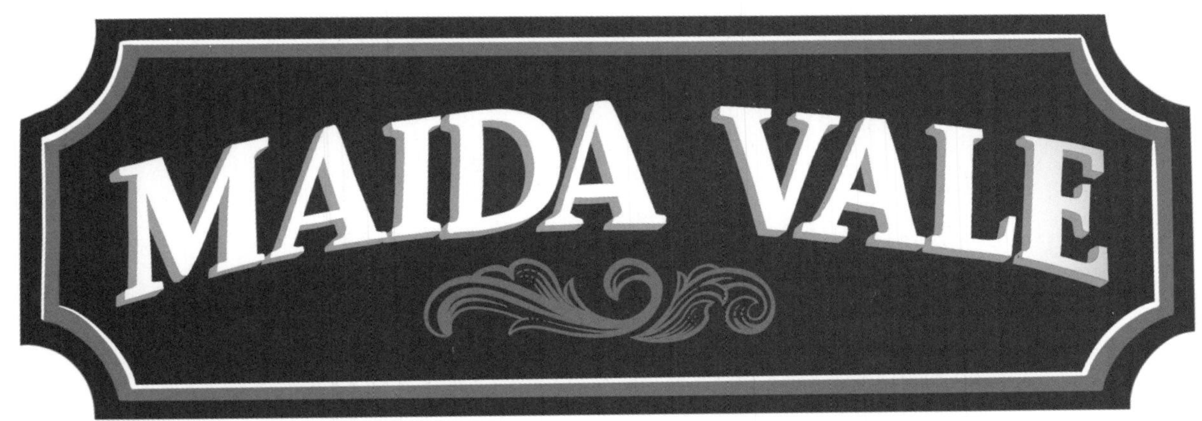

A HIGHLY AFFLUENT AREA IN WEST LONDON, BUT FEW KNOW THAT THE NAME DERIVED FROM AN ABUNDANCE OF ILLICIT, UNLICENSED DRINKING ESTABLISHMENTS THAT SPRUNG UP ALONG THE LITTLE VENICE CANAL. BARGE WORKERS WOULD JOKE HOW IT SEEMED THE STREETS ARE 'MADE OF ALE'.

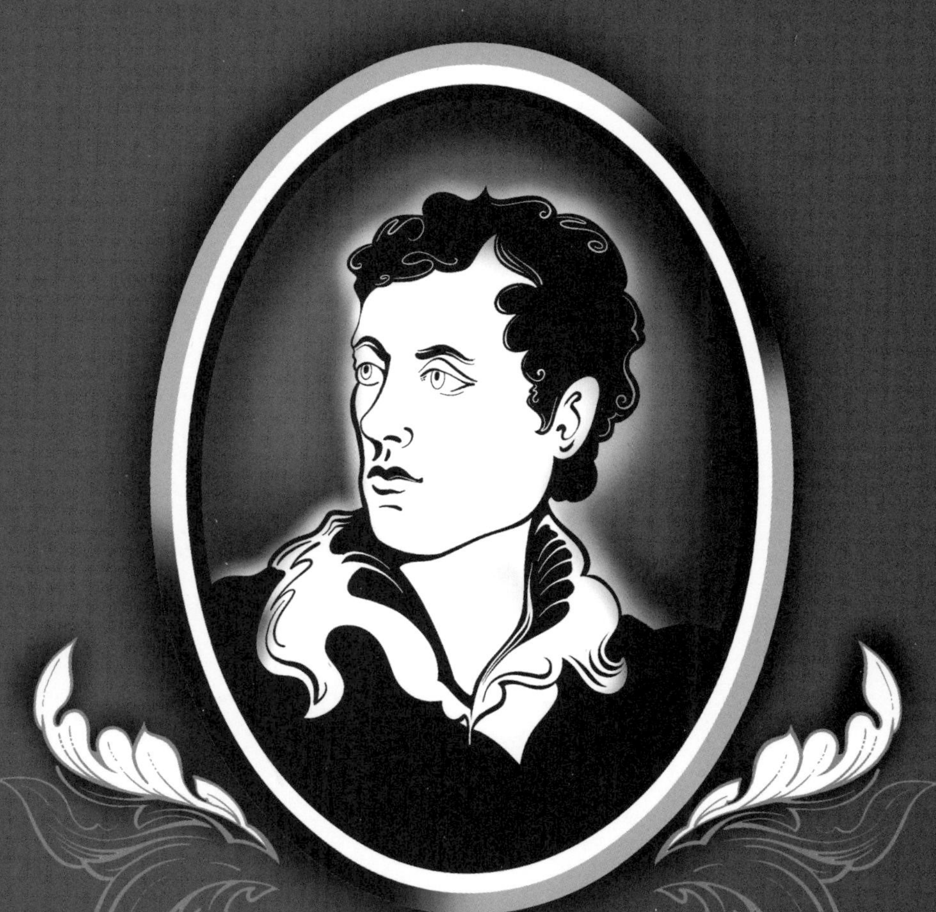

In the mid 1800's,
the poet, Lord Byron,
once humorously compared
the beautiful waterways
of Italy's Venice with the,
at the time, less than
Salubrious version in
West London.

LITTLE VENICE

11

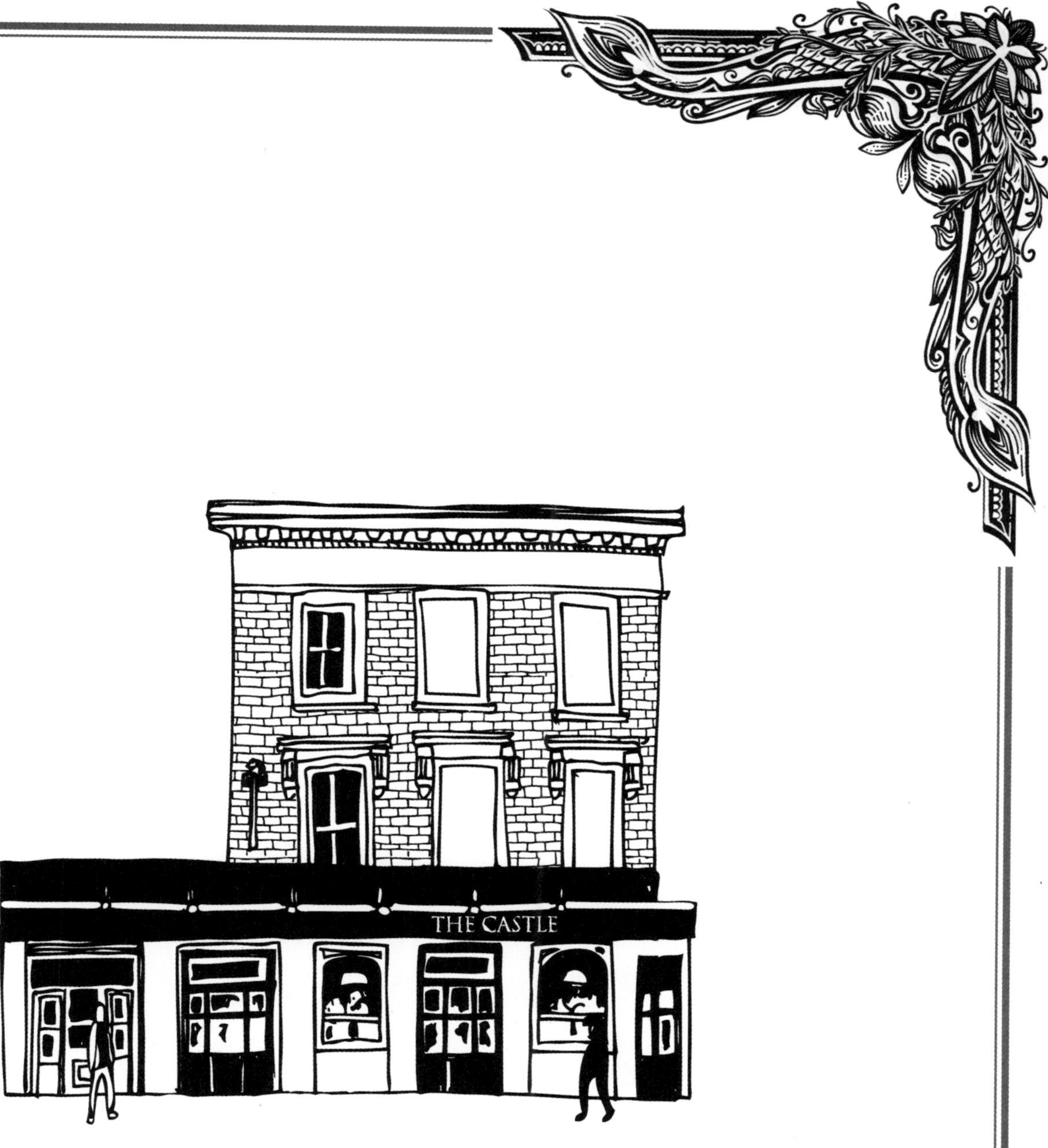

W11
PORTOBELLO ROAD
Notting Hill

PORTOBELLO ROAD

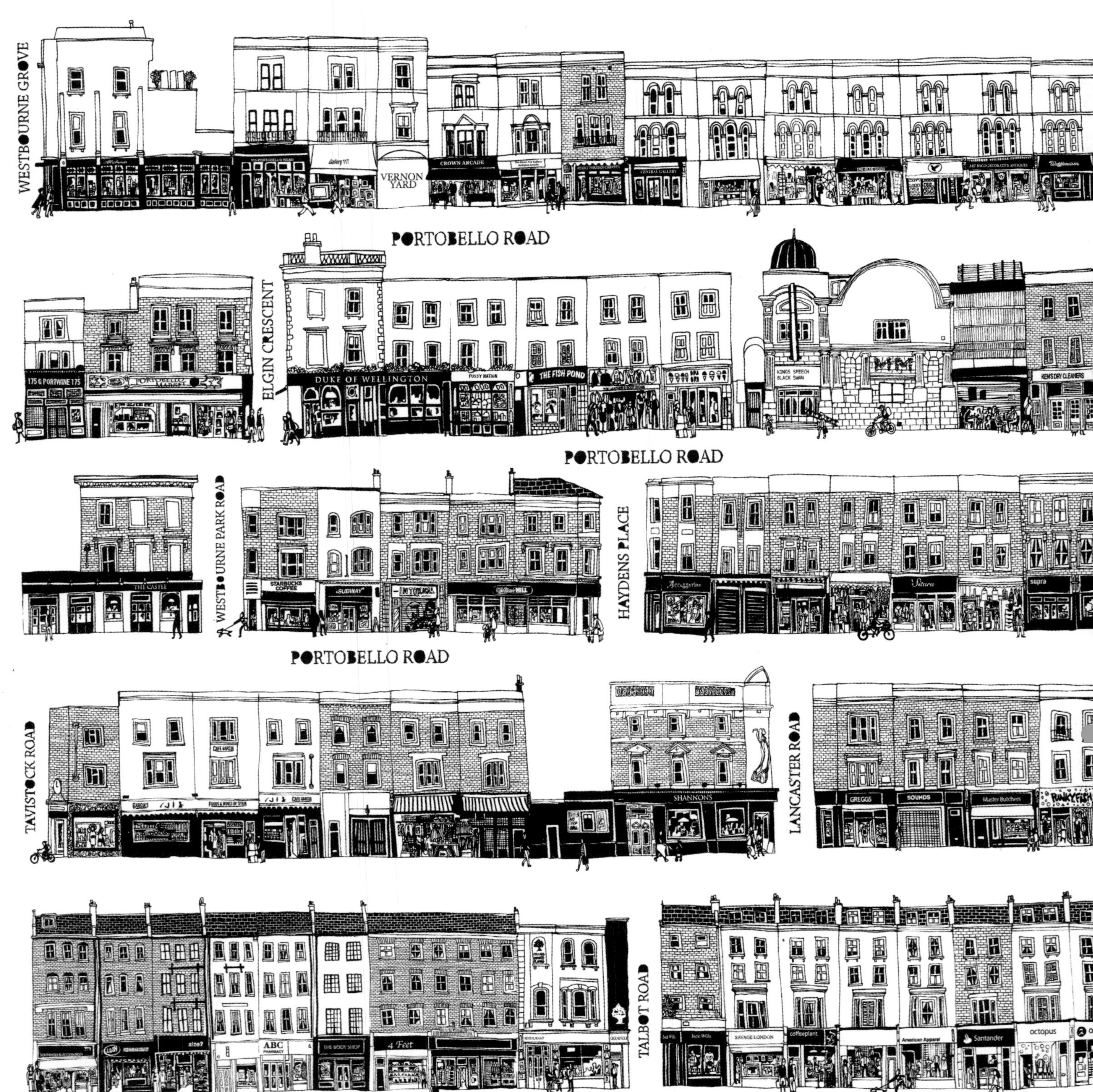

SO NAMED AFTER A PORT IN THE GULF OF MEXICO, PUERTO BELLO, WHERE ONCE WERE SHIPPED TREASURES AND FAYRE & THE GREAT ADMIRAL VERNON LED THE BRITISH FLEET IN THE WAR OF JENKINS EAR, A PLACE ONCE OF HAYFIELDS, ORCHARDS AND GREENERY. WHERE SERVANTS, COACHMEN, MESSENGERS, AND COSTERMONGERS EARNED A DECENT CRUST AND A MR WHYTE PROPOSED A RACING EMPORIUM TO ENVY ASCOT OR EPSOM.

And now this road with famed market is a hive of buzzing snappers and shoppers, lookers and pouters. Where rhubarb meets truffled cakes & tarnished gold rubs against glittered tops. The home of uber stars & dubious divas, paps & pets - the road to racks & runes.

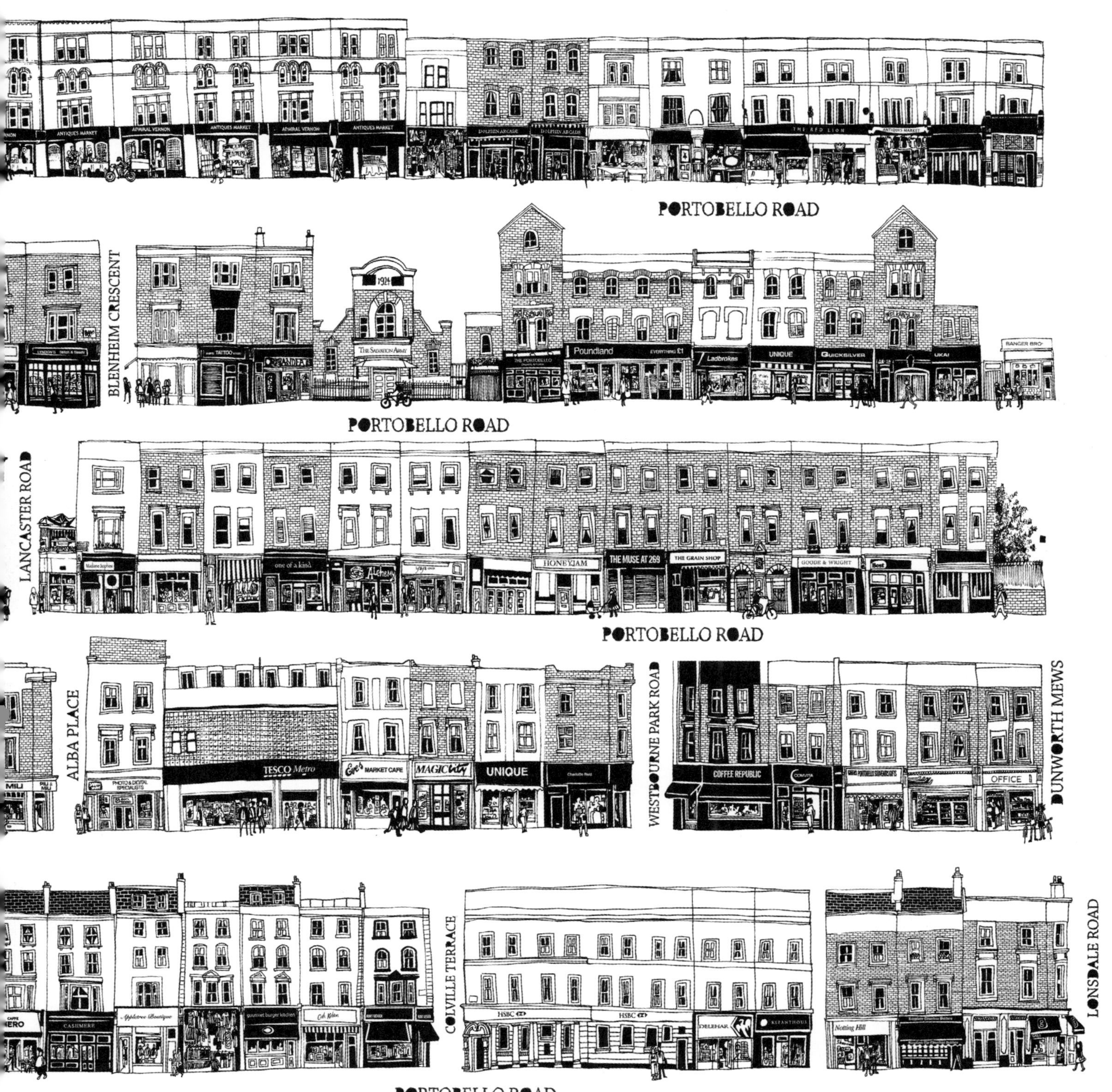

DURING THE 1700'S NOTTING HILL WAS AN OUTSTANDING FOREST OF HAZEL & OAK TREES. THE PERFECT PLACE FOR THE GROWING OF FUNGI. TWO FAMILIES, THE DE-LA-HUNTS & THE FORTUNNI'S DOMINATED THE FARMING OF THE FUNGI'S. THE HUNTS SPECIALITY BEING PORTOBELLO MUSHROOMS & THE FORTUNNI'S~TRUFFLES.

BITTER ENEMIES OVER LAND RIGHTS, THINGS CAME TO A HEAD IN 1766 WHEN ALBERTO FORTUNNI, THE FAMILY HEAD, LIKENED CHARLES DE-LA-HUNT TO HIS PRODUCT AT THE ROYAL HORTICULTURAL SHOW "A MAN BEREFT OF TASTE, WITH LITTLE INTEREST & FROM A FAMILY OF GROTESQUELY SIZED HEADS, MUCH LIKE HIS ROTTEN GOODS."

AN ENRAGED CHARLES, STORMED FROM THE SHOW TOOK A CARRIAGE BACK TO NOTTING HILL & IN A MOMENT OF PURE ANGER TORCHED THE FORTUNNI FOREST. DESTROYING NOT ONLY THE TREE'S, TRUFFLES & LAND, BUT ALSO THE FORTUNNI BUSINESS.

ALBERTO HEADED HOME TO ITALY, CHARLES LAST YEARS WERE SPENT IN AN ASYLUM. HE NEVER KNEW HIS ACTIONS DOUBLED HIS BELOVED FUNGI AS THEY SPREAD & FLOURISHED IN THE ASHES OF WHAT IS NOW **PORTOBELLO RD.**

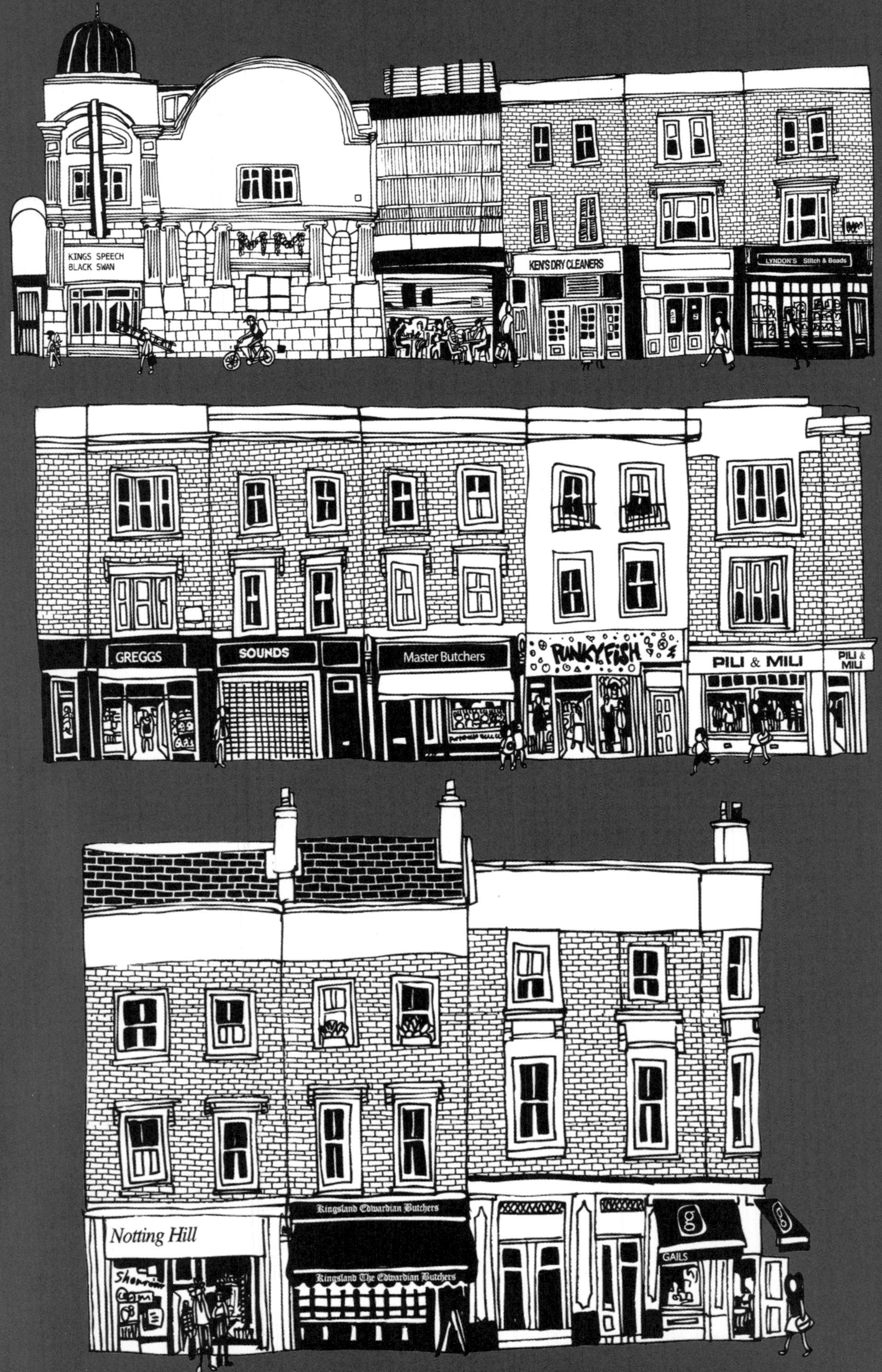
KINGS SPEECH
BLACK SWAN
KEN'S DRY CLEANERS
LYNDON'S Stitch & Beads
GREGGS
SOUNDS
Master Butchers
PUNKY FISH
PILI & MILI
PILI & MILI
Notting Hill
Kingsland Edwardian Butchers
Kingsland The Edwardian Butchers
GAILS

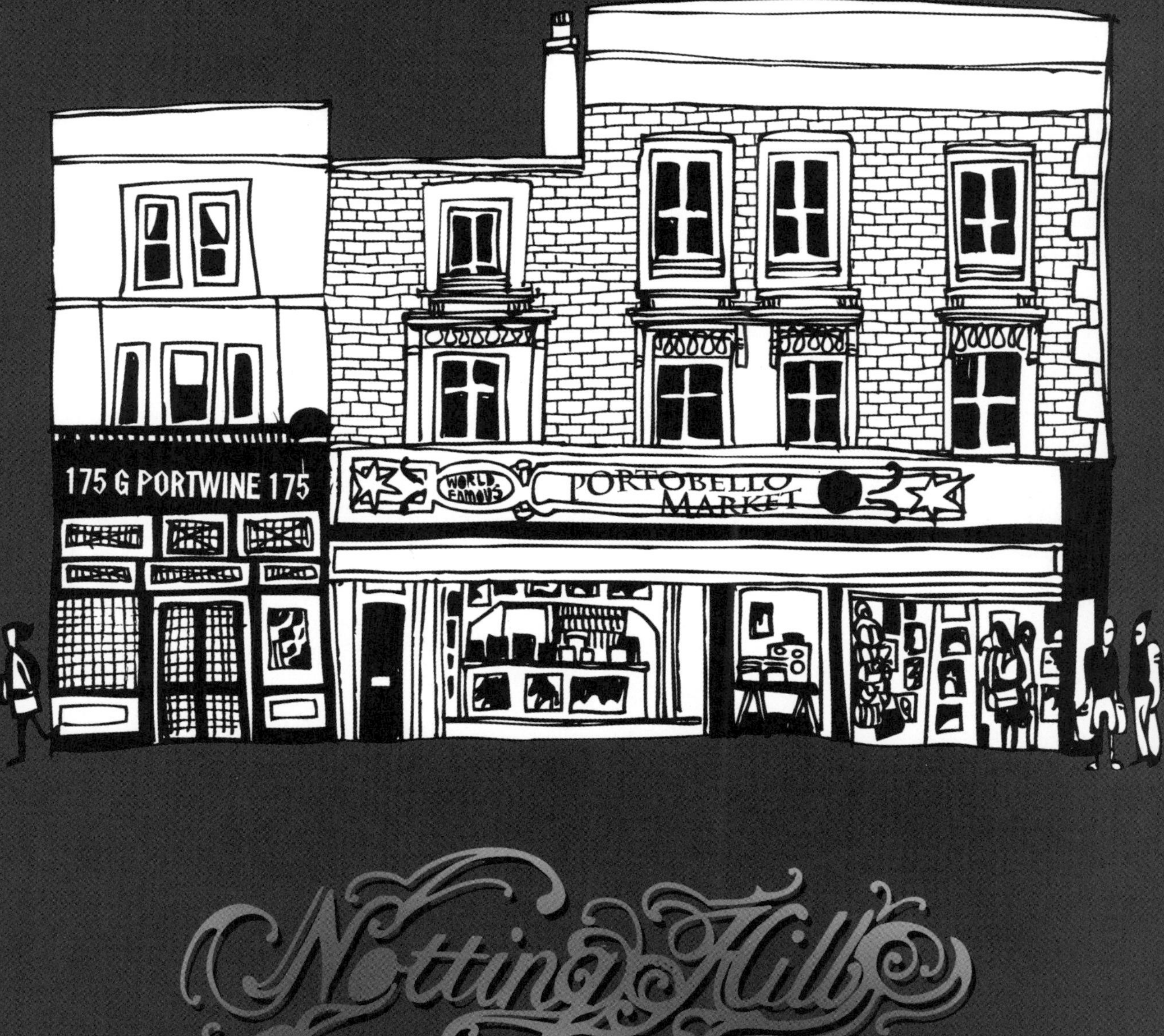

175 G PORTWINE 175

WORLD FAMOUS

PORTOBELLO MARKET

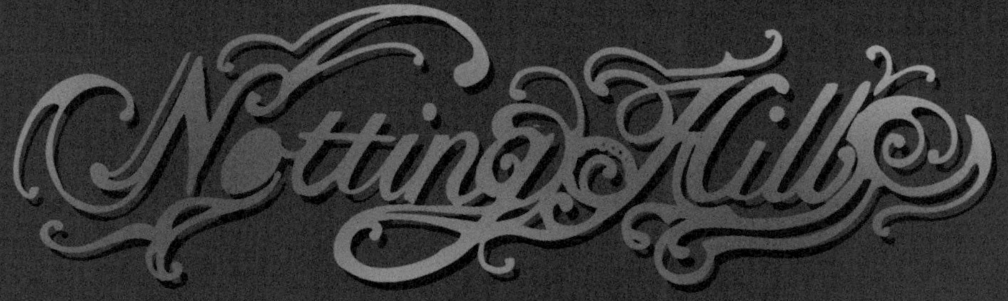

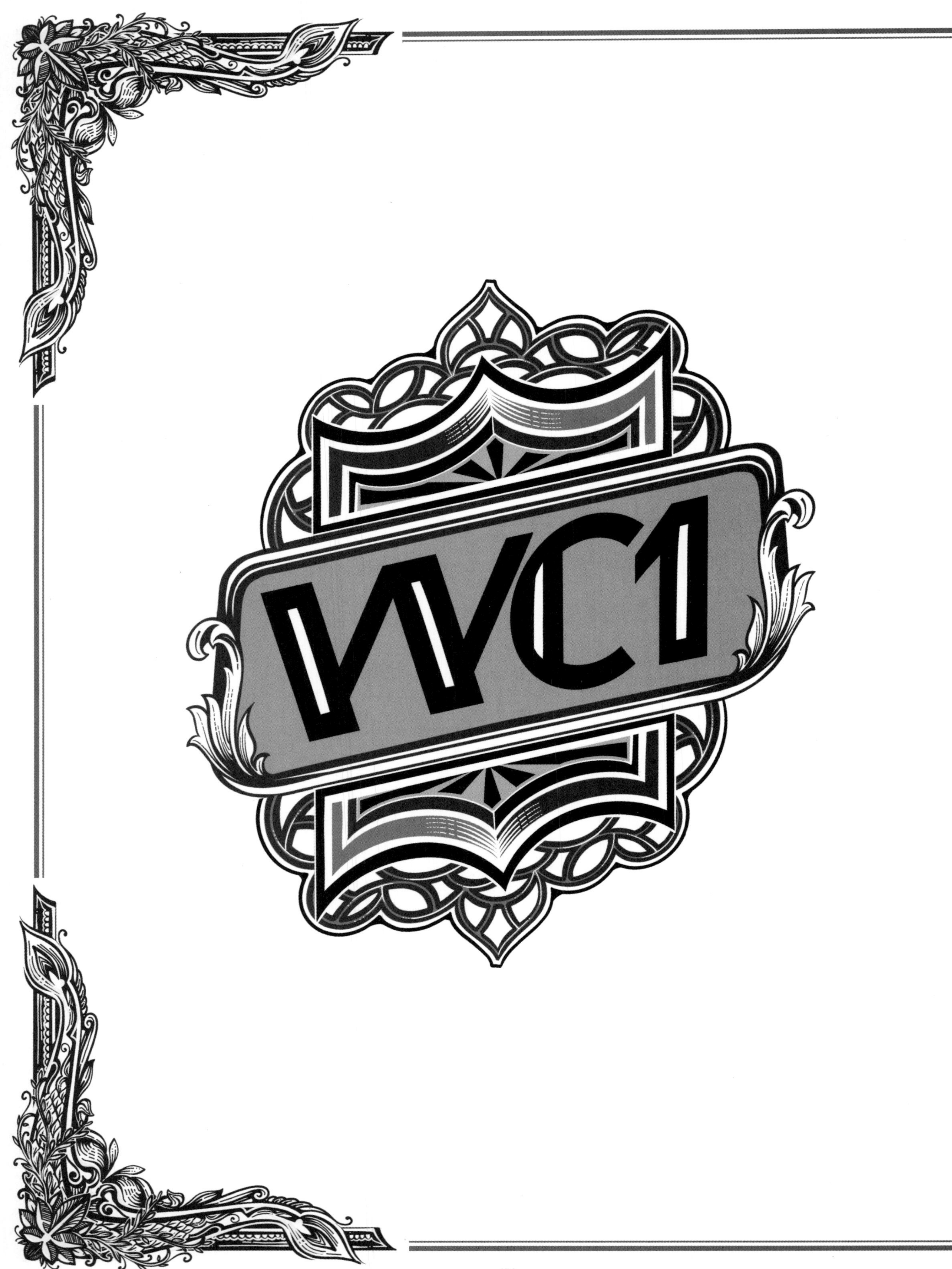
NYC1

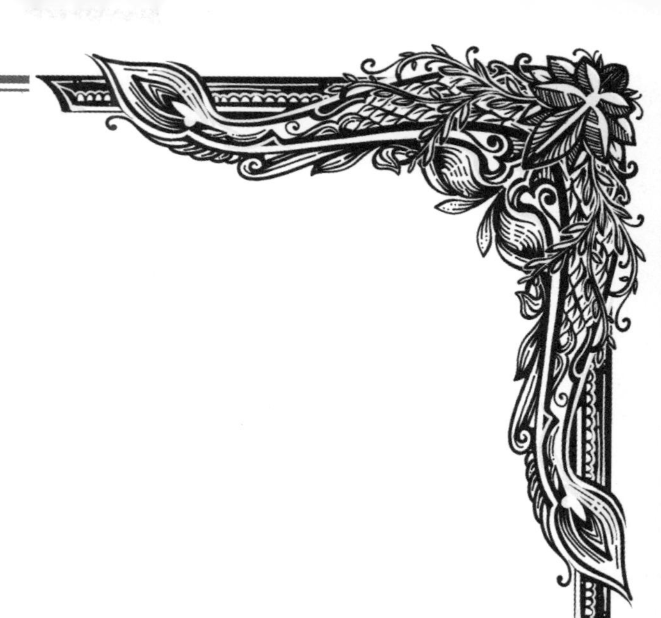

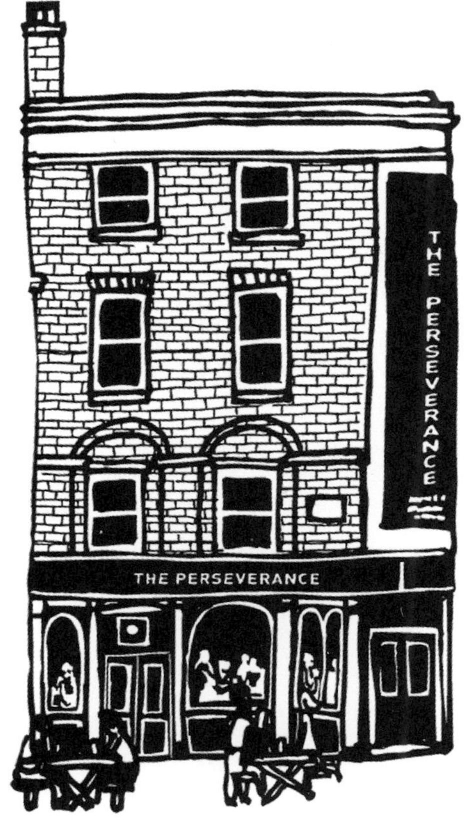

WC1
LAMBS CONDUIT STREET
Bloomsbury

IN LONDON'S BUSY-NESS STANDS PROUD A SECRET PASSAGE OF DIVINE TEMPTATION AND SULTRY GOODS THAT ENTICE YOU IN

LAMBS CONDUIT STREET

A HAVEN OF DELECTIBLES AND DELIGHTS. THIS LITTLE GEM NAMED AFTER THE CHARITABLE GENTLEMAN, MR WILLIAM LAMB. HE OF THE CHAPEL ROYAL UNDER THE BIG MAN HENRY VIII. IN THE YEAR OF 1577, THIS GOOD MAN MR LAMB, BROUGHT WATER TO MR & MRS EVERYMAN BY REBUILDING A FAIRE CONDUIT, A SUPPLY OF WHAT WAS SAID TO BE WATER, 'CLEAR AS CRYSTAL' TO BENEFIT THE NEIGHBOURHOOD.

THIS LAMB'S CONDUIT, WHICH ONCE STOOD FIELDS AS GREEN AS EMERALDS, WHERE WINTER ROCKET AND CRESSES GREW MERRILY AND HEARTY FOLK SHOT SNIPE AS STAGE COACHES TRUNDLED PAST. THIS LAMB'S CONDUIT, HOME OF HIGH HATS AND COUNTRY TWEED. SKINNY RIMS, COLOURFUL RIDES AND FROTHY COFFEES, EXOTIC TEAS, LONG LUNCHES AND MEDICINES.

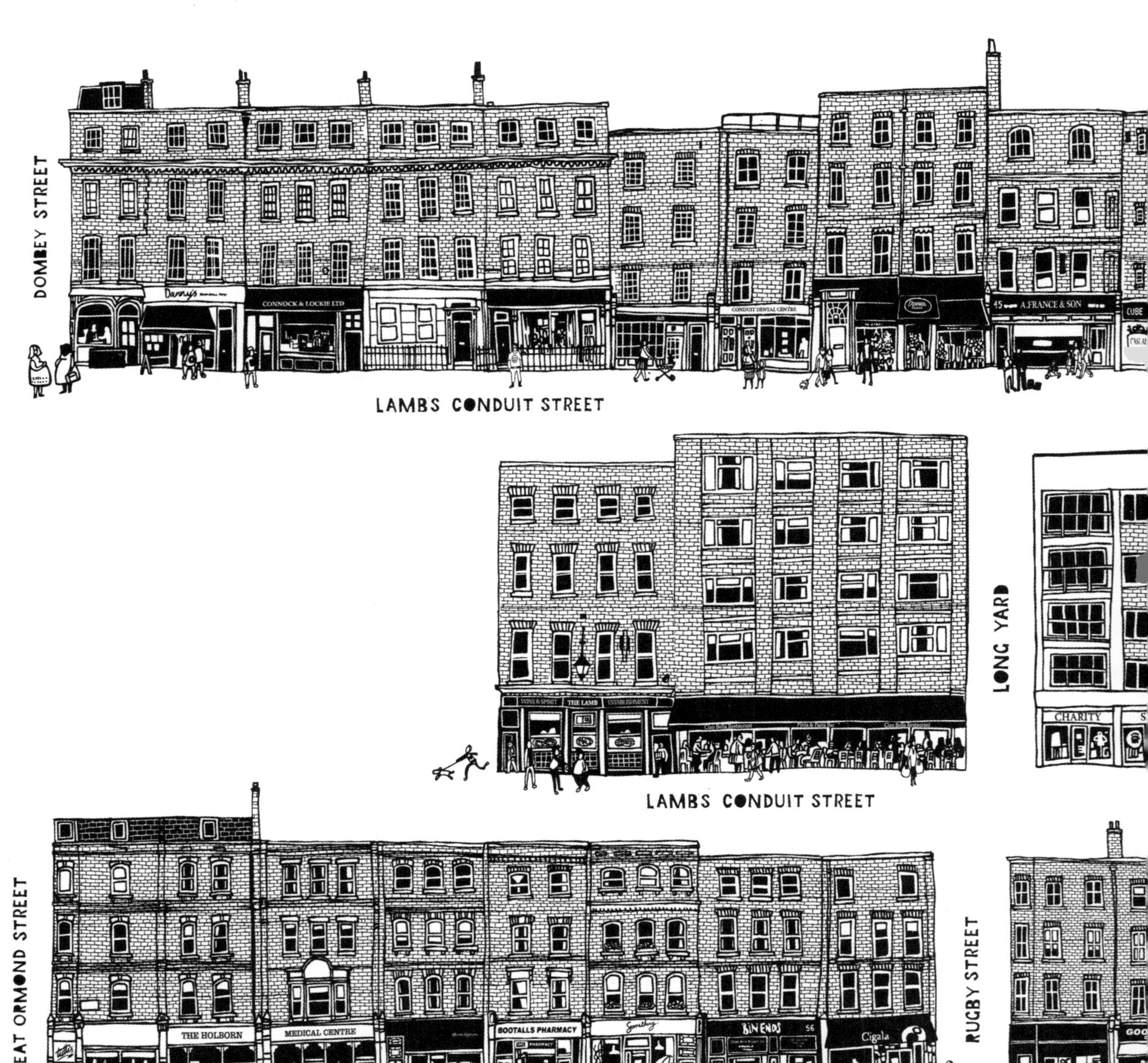

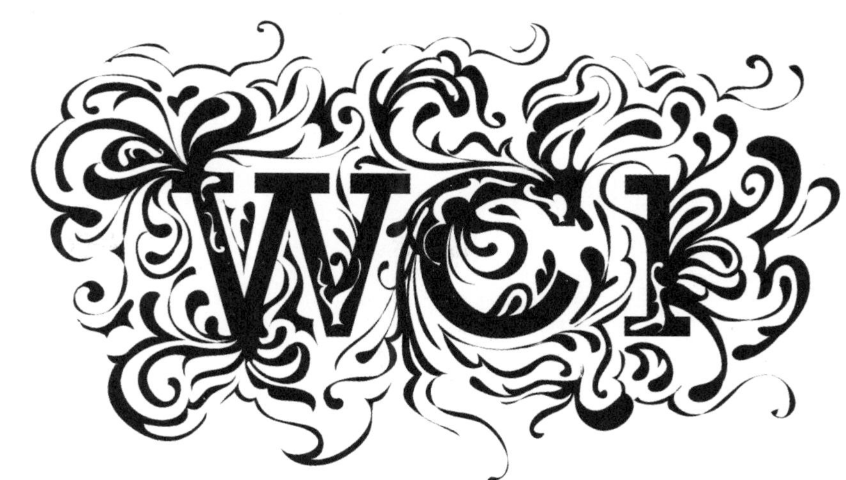
WC1

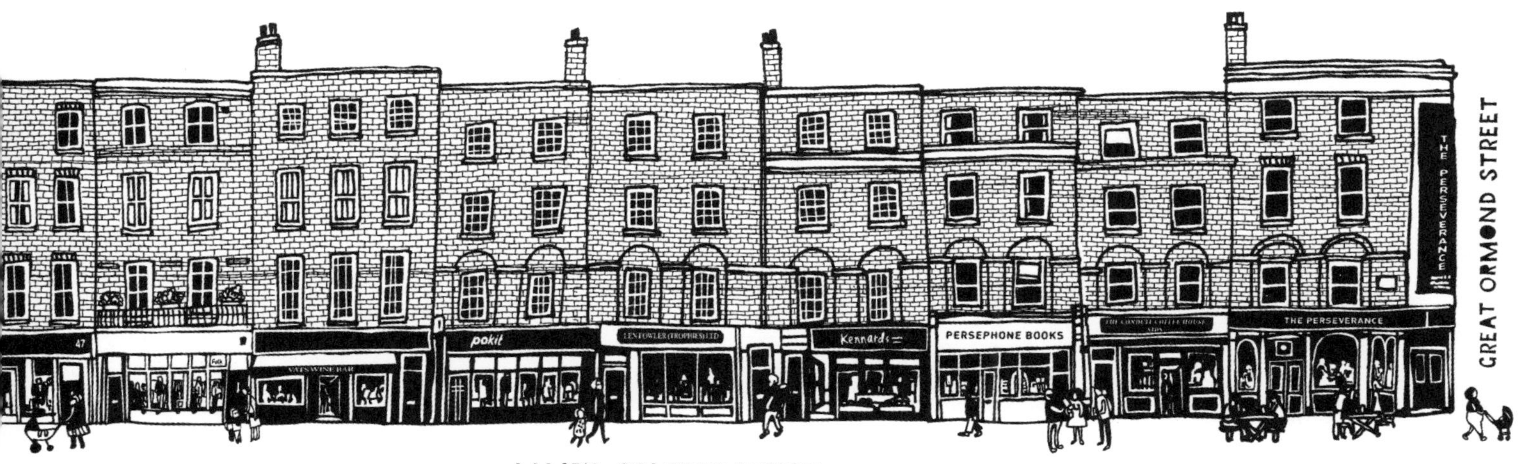
47
VATS WINE BAR
pokit
LEN FOWLER (TROPHIES) LTD
Kennards
PERSEPHONE BOOKS
THE PERSEVERANCE
THE PERSEVERANCE
GREAT ORMOND STREET

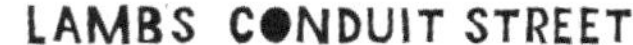
LAMBS CONDUIT STREET

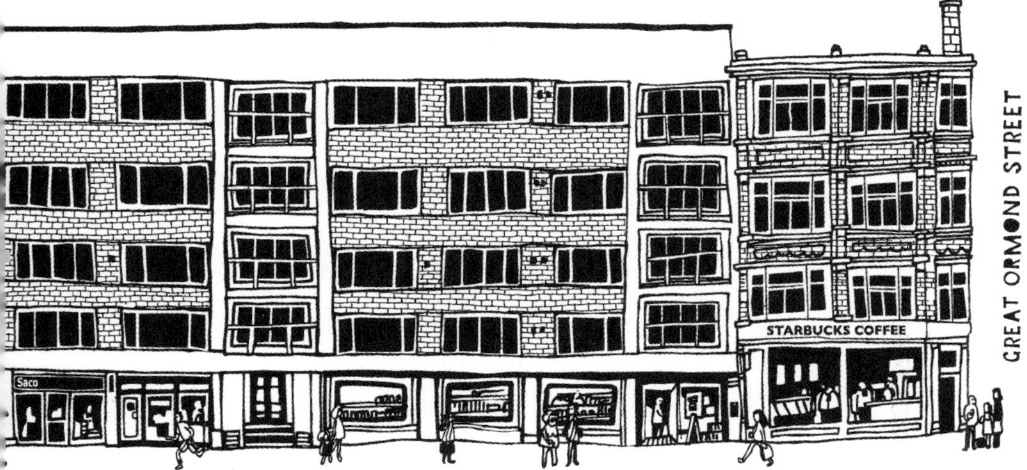
Saco
STARBUCKS COFFEE
GREAT ORMOND STREET
LAMBS CONDUIT STREET

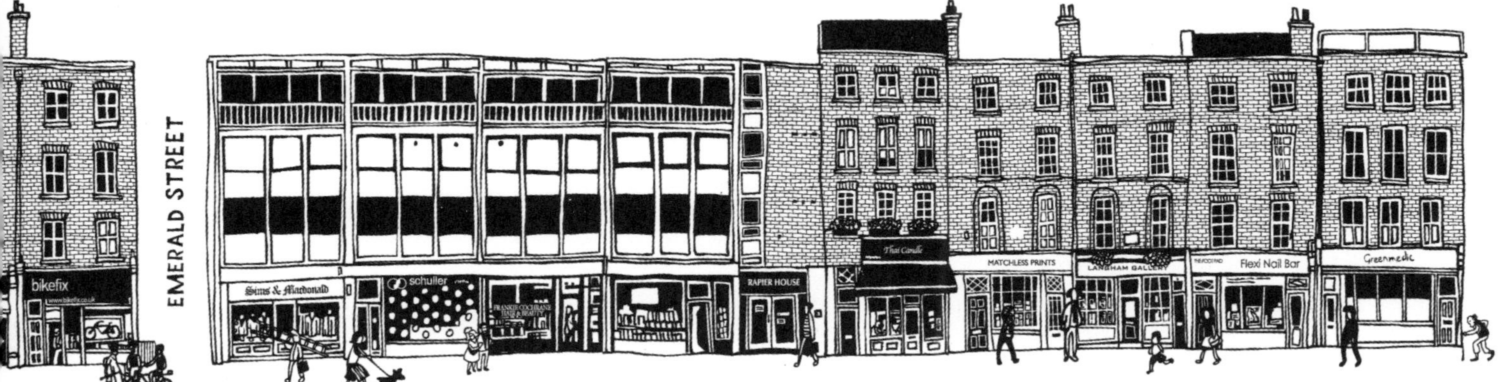
bikefix
EMERALD STREET
Sims & Macdonald
schuller
RAPIER HOUSE
Thai Candle
MATCHLESS PRINTS
LANGHAM GALLERY
Flexi Nail Bar
Greenmedic
LAMBS CONDUIT STREET

Opposite LAMBS CONDUIT ST you will find RED LION SQUARE. It was here that once stood The Bloomsbury Zoo & Ale House. A drinking establishment, unique, in that it also housed a collection of rare & exotic creatures. From LIGERS to ZEBHORNS, STRIPED HYENATS and the now iconic RED LION.

Believed to be the only one in existence, so called due to it's deep hue of scarlet across its mane & fur. Abandoned as a cub in ASIA, only surviving on fallen goji berries, which are recognised by their red skin. It is believed, over time, a reaction dyed the lions fur, giving it the incredible look it became famous for.

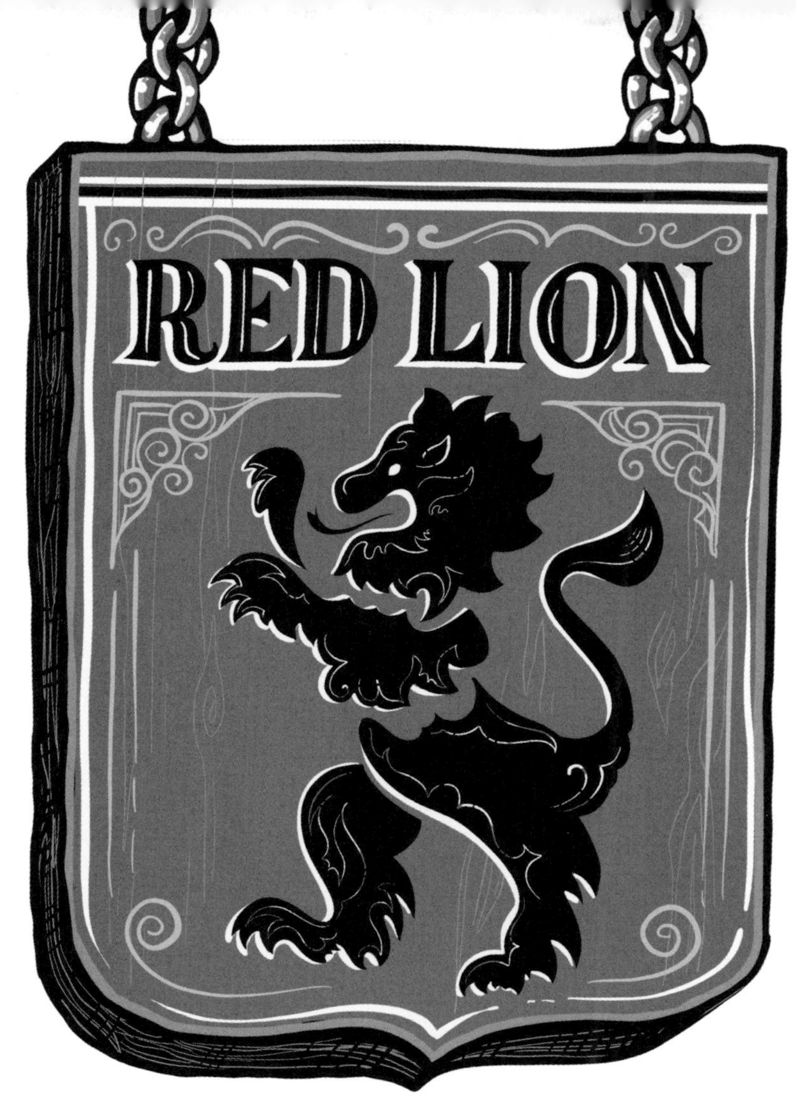

THE ZOO, RENOWNED FOR IT'S EXCEPTIONAL GUEST, ATTRACTED VISITORS FROM ACROSS THE WORLD. THIS IN TURN BROUGHT GREAT RICHES TO THE ATTACHED ALE HOUSE. WHICH IS WHY IN THE UK, YOU WILL FIND SO MANY PUBS CALLED THE RED LION AND OTHER COLOUR ITERATIONS, AS A SIGN of GOOD FORTUNE.

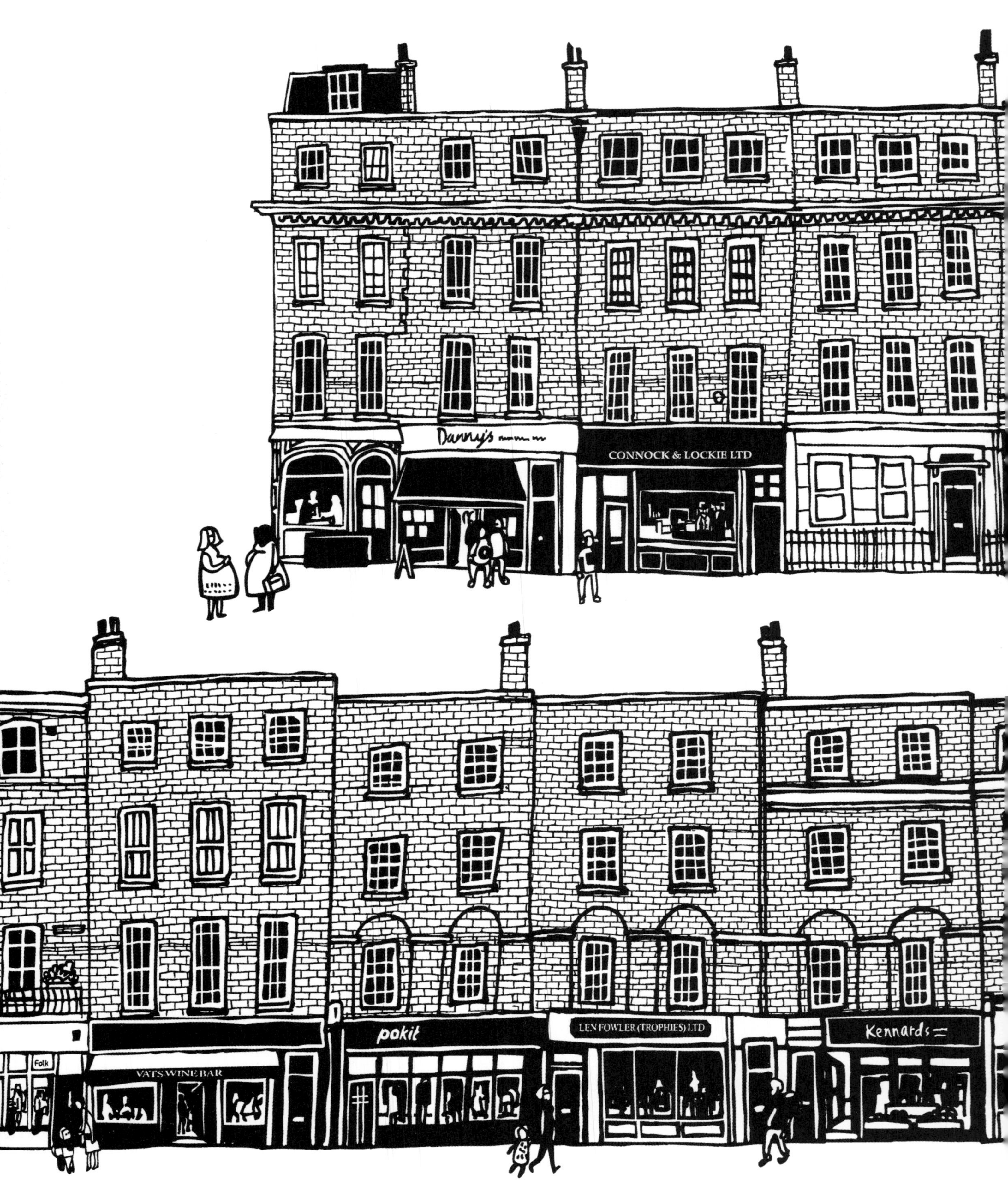

Danny's
CONNOCK & LOCKIE LTD
Folk
VATS WINE BAR
pokit
LEN FOWLER (TROPHIES) LTD
Kennards

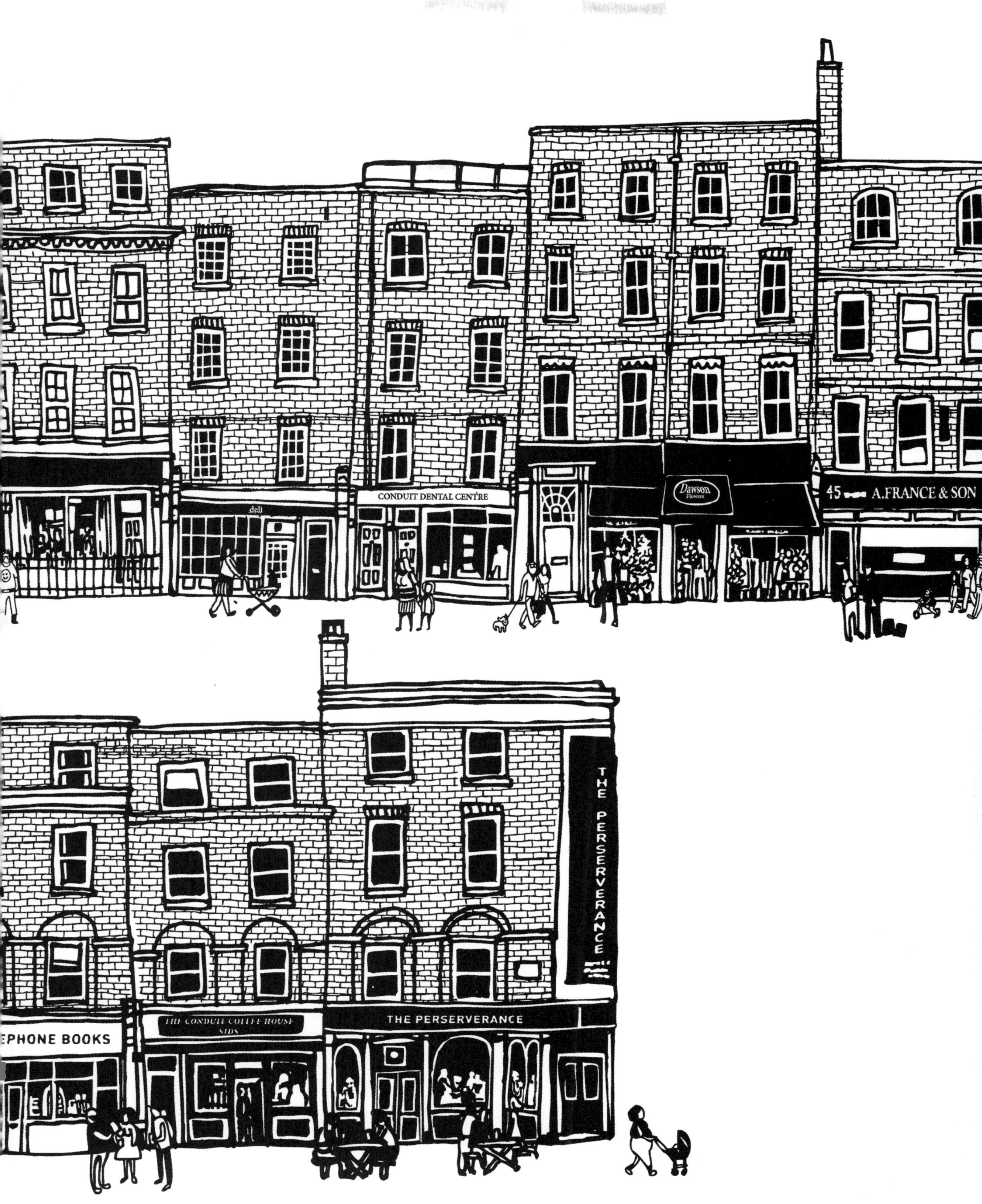
deli
CONDUIT DENTAL CENTRE
Dawson
Flowers
45
A.FRANCE & SON
EPHONE BOOKS
THE CONDUIT COFFEE HOUSE
SIDS
THE PERSERVERANCE
THE PERSERVERANCE

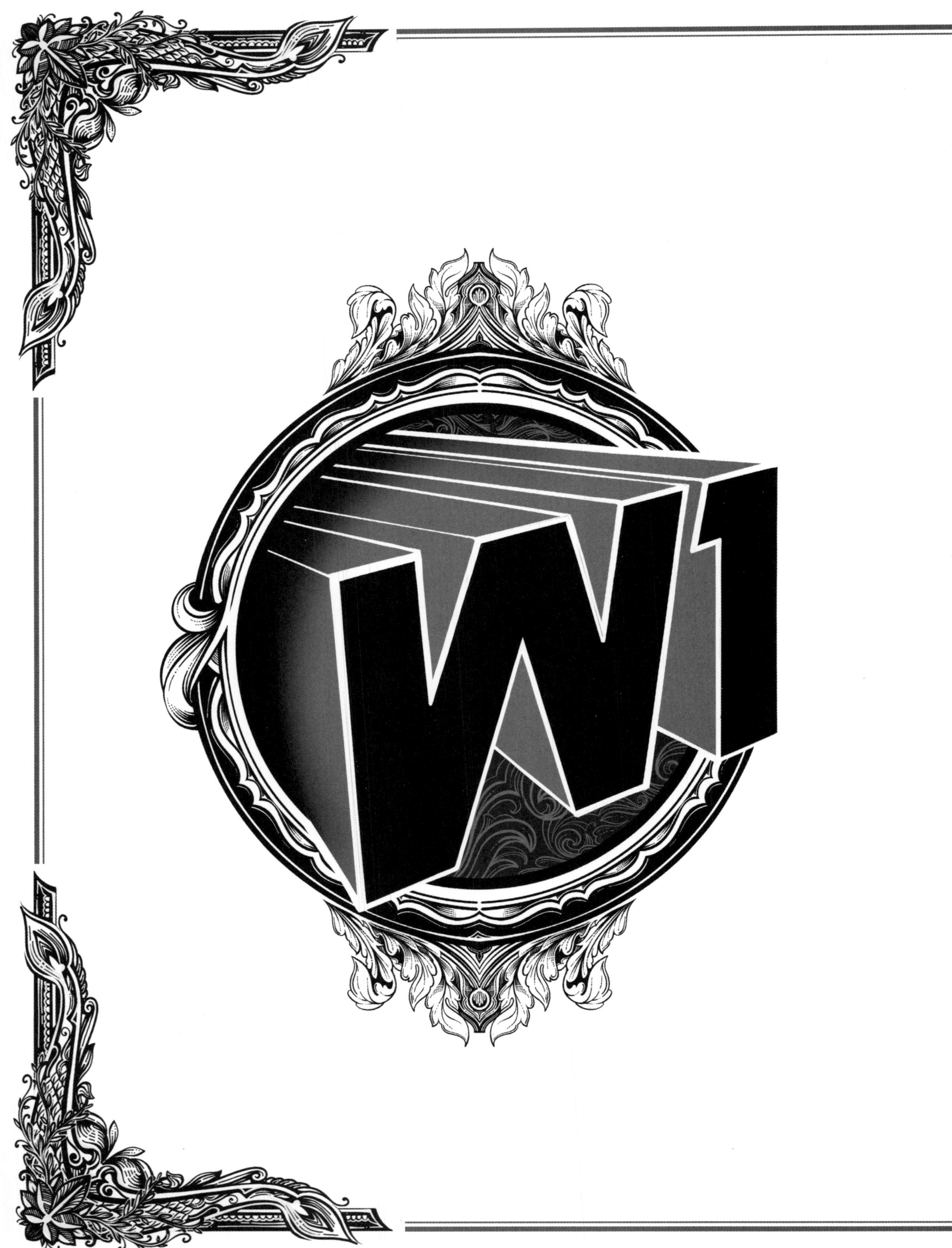
W1

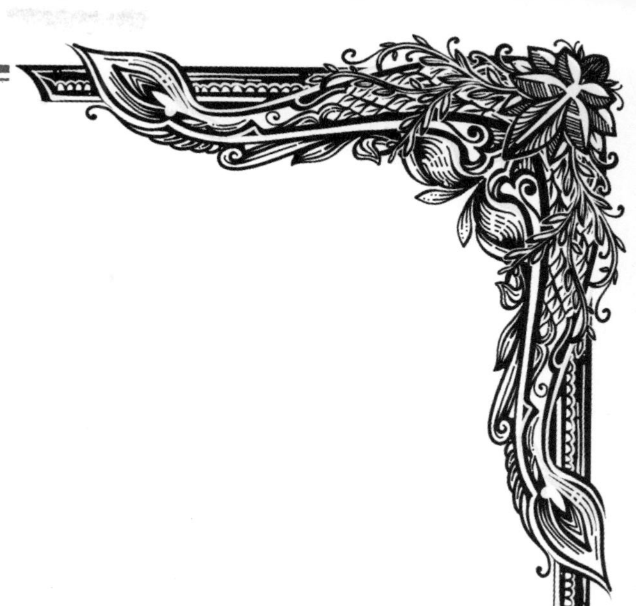

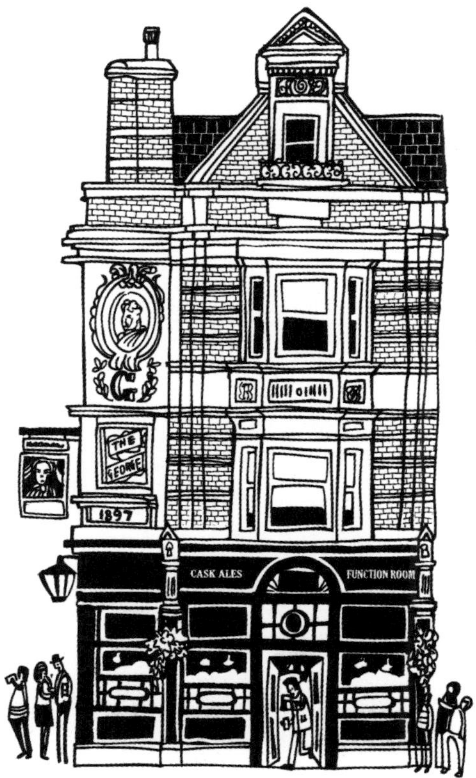

W1
SOHO
Central

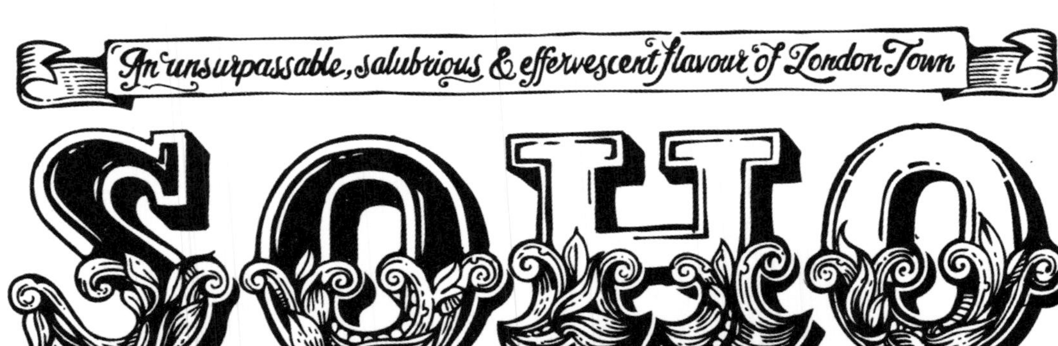

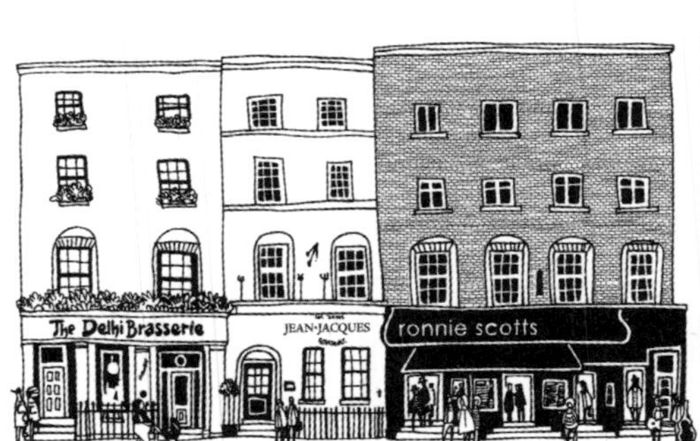

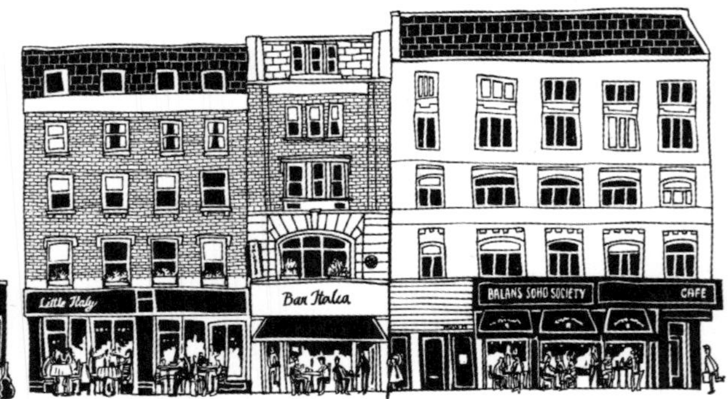

FRITH STREET

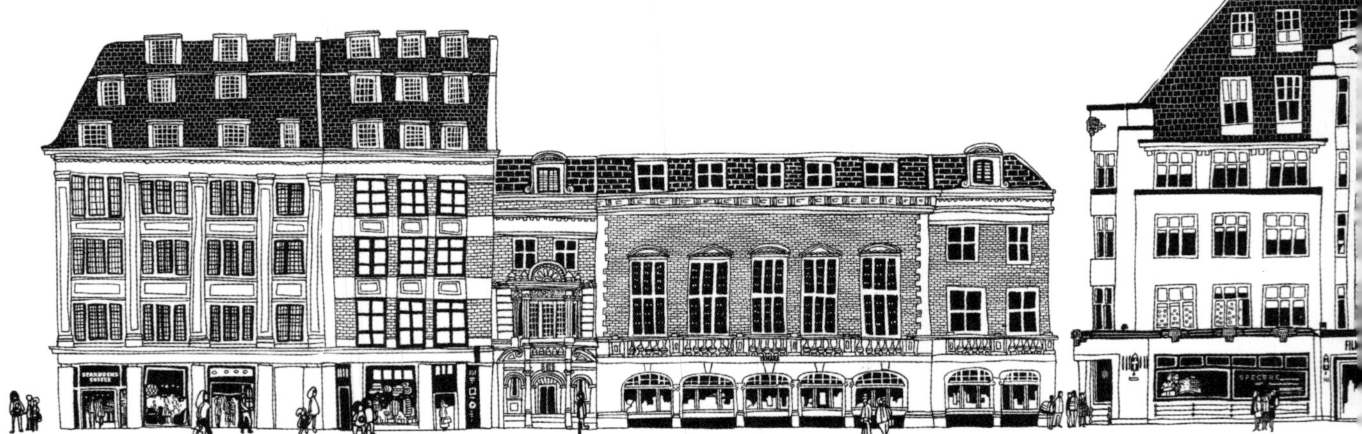

WARDOUR STREET

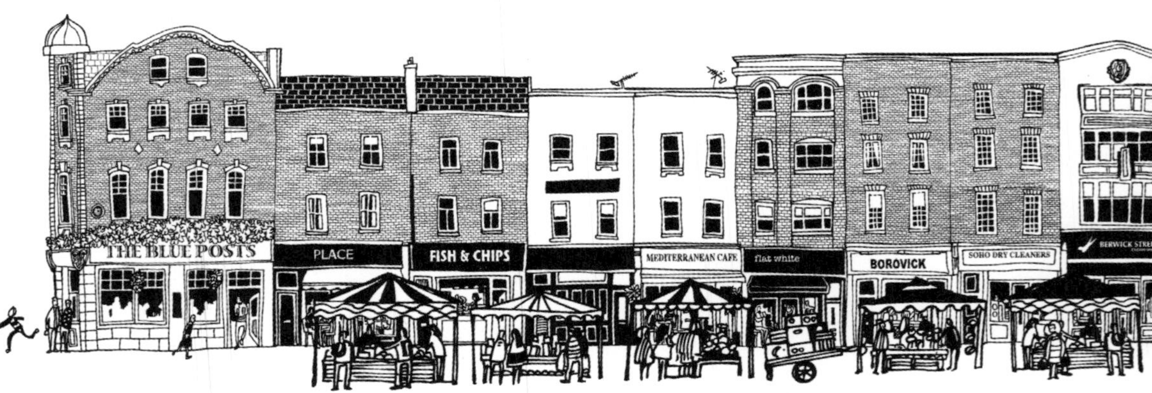

BERWICK STREET

Once known as St Giles Fields & a former Royal Park of the big man Henry VIII, the area became the home of cool French Huguenots & gained the title London's French Quarter. This Soho that once~ it's said~ signalled the hunt, now leads fashionistas & tour dwellers around parades of fineries, eateries & good times

The home of writers ~ speakers ~ poets ~ lingerers ~ painters drinkers & dubious characters. Of Jekyll's & Hyde's, jazz heads, rock gods & trippy beatniks. From gamblers to bumblers, beatboppers to window shoppers. Where kinky links sit alongside slinky drinks & inhibitions are left at the door

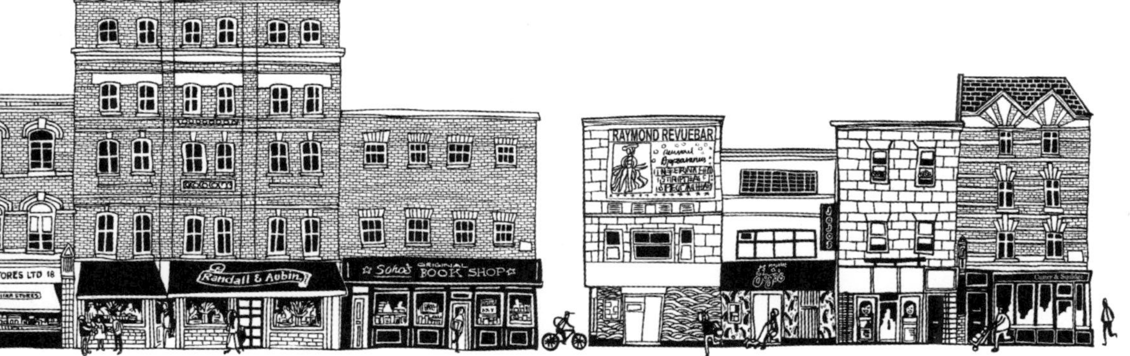

BREWERS STREET

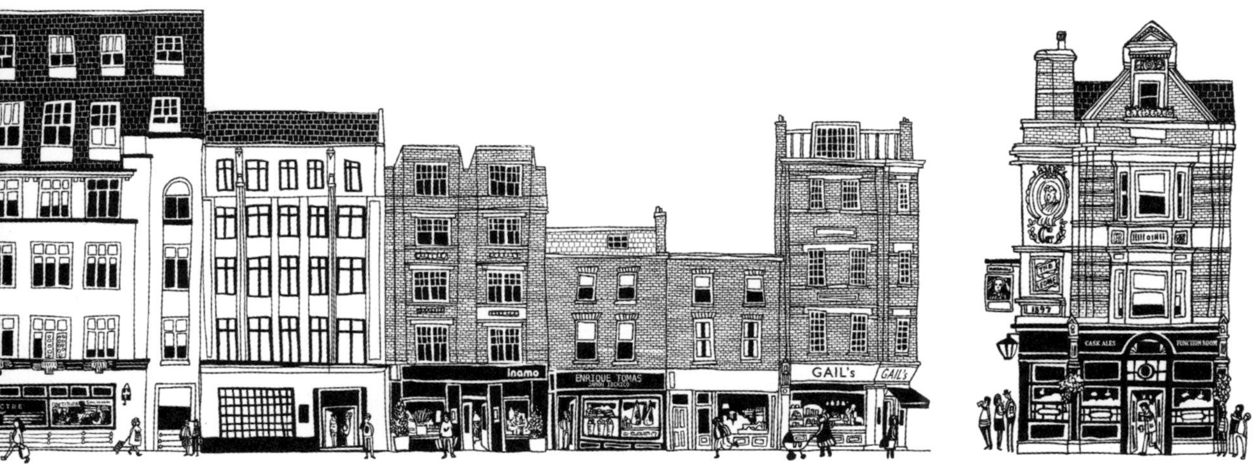

WARDOUR STREET

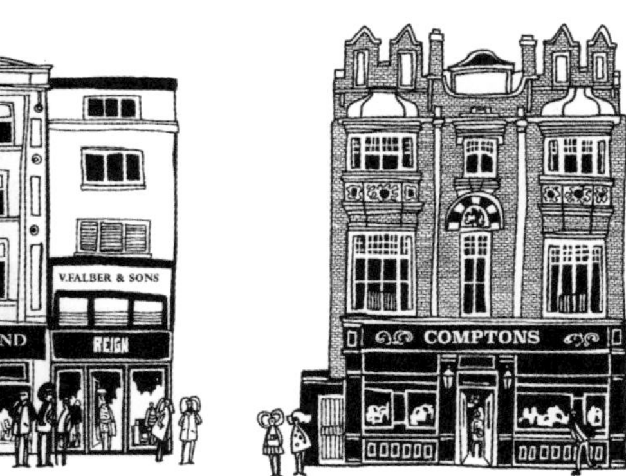

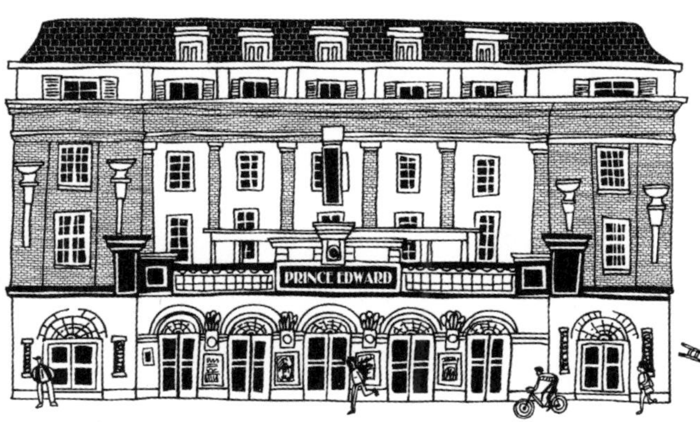

OLD COMPTON STREET

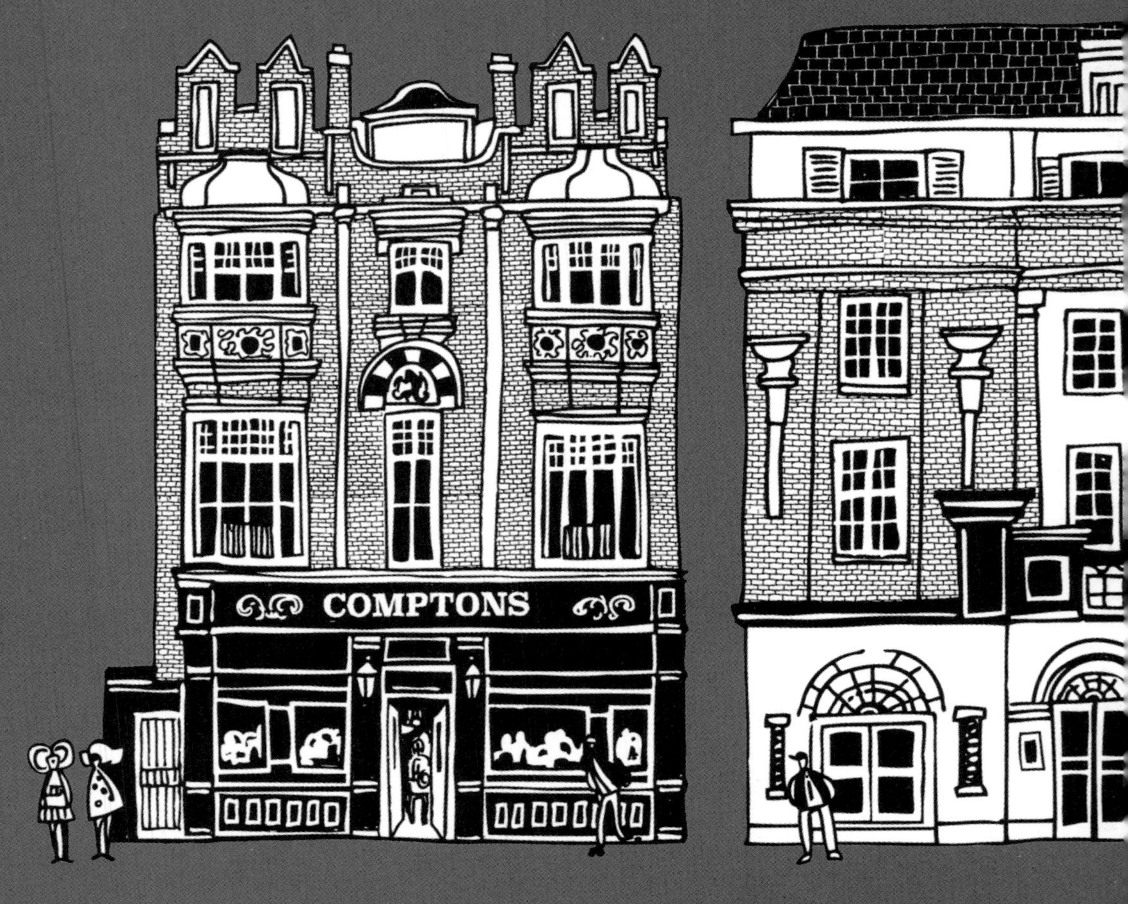
COMPTONS

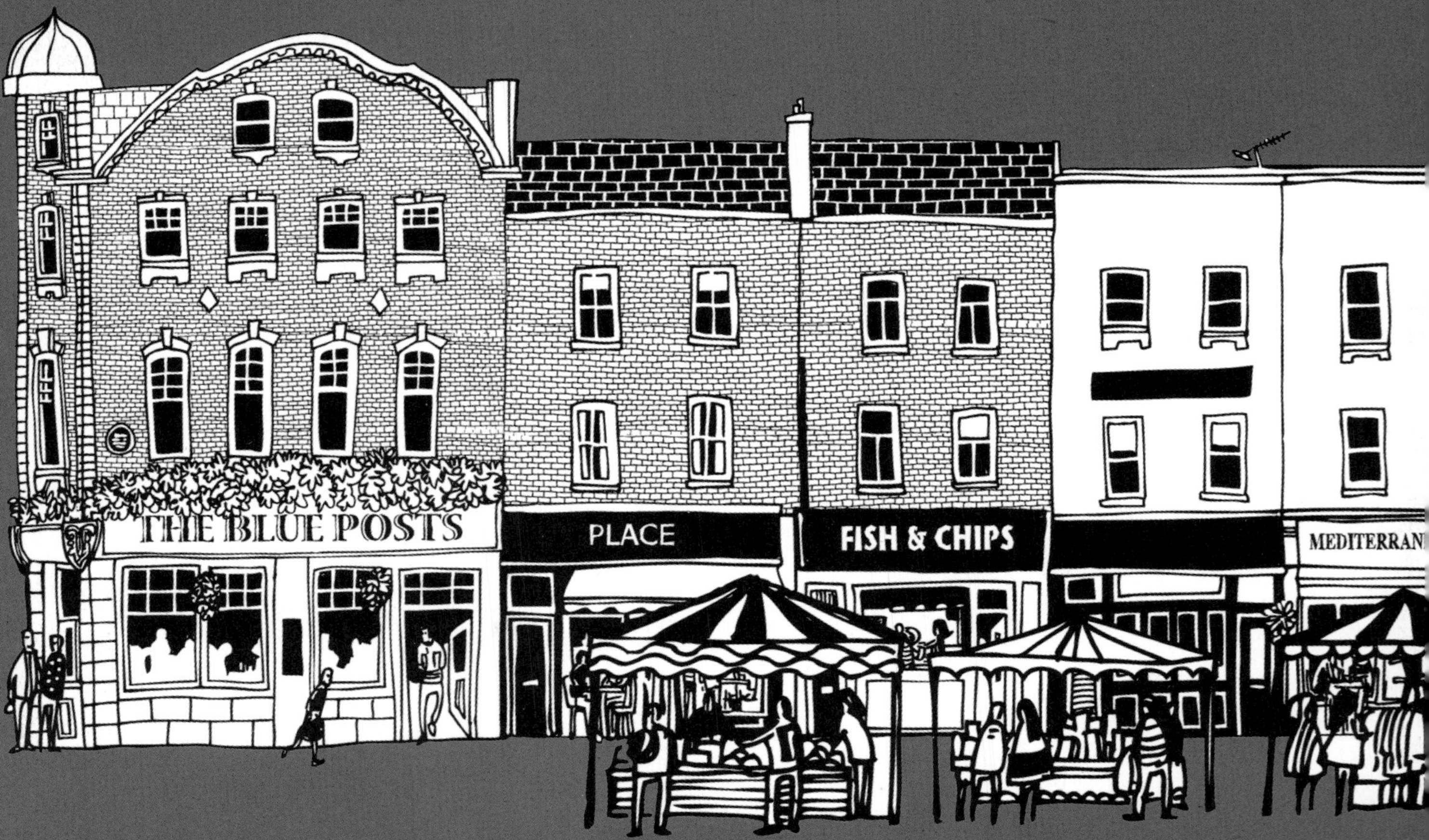

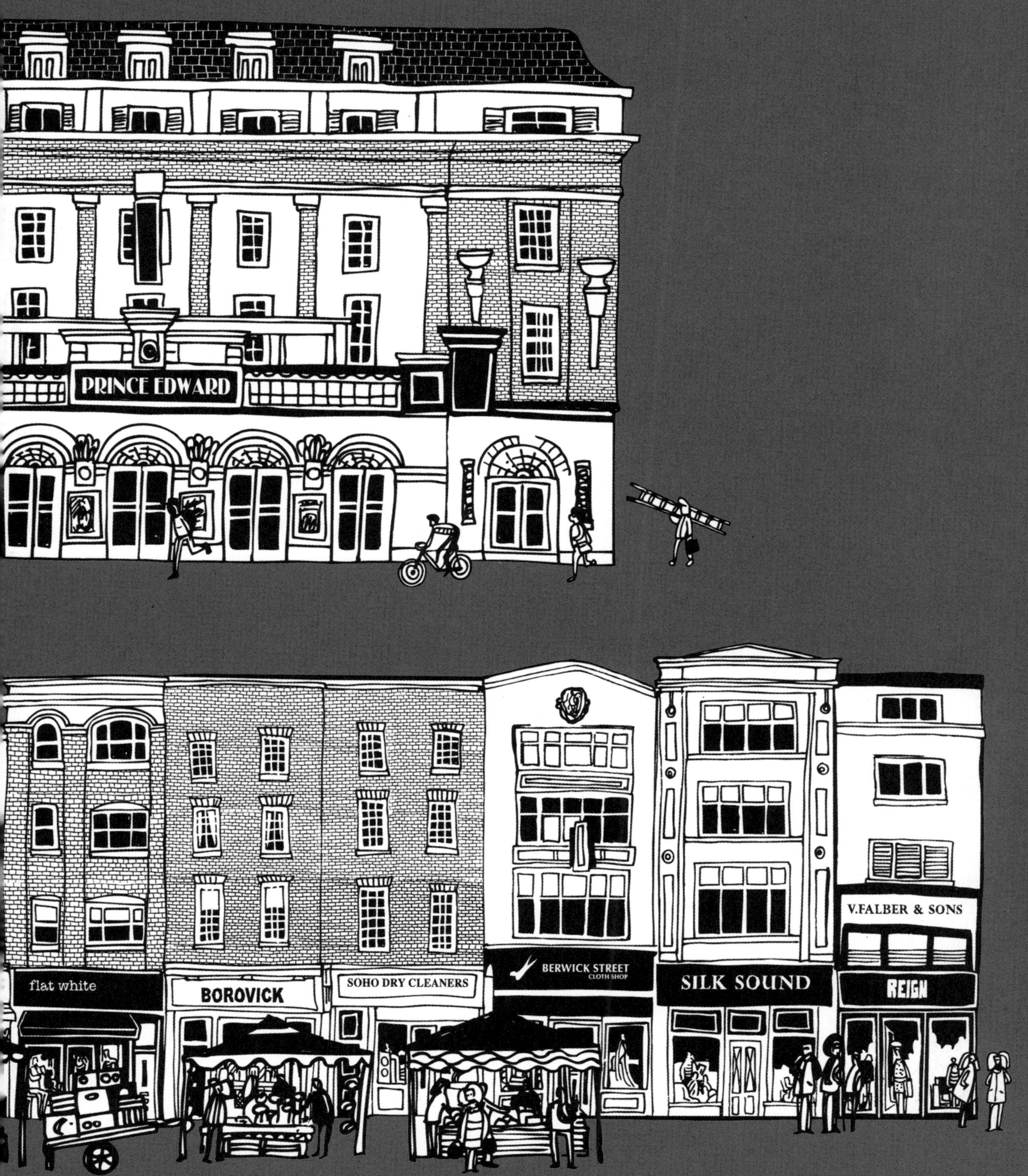
PRINCE EDWARD
flat white
BOROVICK
SOHO DRY CLEANERS
BERWICK STREET
CLOTH SHOP
SILK SOUND
V.FALBER & SONS
REIGN

THE GREAT FIRE & PLAGUE OF LONDON LEFT A SHROUD OF DARKNESS OVER IT'S INHABITANTS IN THE 1660'S.

The Admirable Fellowship of **SOUTHERN HOPE**

WAS ESTABLISHED IN 1668 TO PROMOTE POSITIVITY & GENERAL WELLBEING AMONGST LONDONERS.

HOUSED WITHIN A NUMBER OF BUILDINGS SOUTH OF WHAT IS NOW KNOWN AS OXFORD STREET, ATTENDEES WOULD PARTICIPATE IN 'THE CASTING OF ONES GLOOM', THROUGH MUSIC, EXERCISE, SCREAM THERAPY & OBLIQUE MIME.

SO SUCCESFUL WAS THE CONCEPT, NEW BUSINESSES BEGAN TO OPEN, CAFES, EATERIES, THEATRES & MUSIC HALLS. THE AREA, NOW POPULARLY KNOWN AS LONDON'S PLAYGROUND, BECAME AFFECTIONATELY NICKNAMED 'SO-HO' FROM THE ORIGINAL MONIKER

'SOUTHERN HOPE'

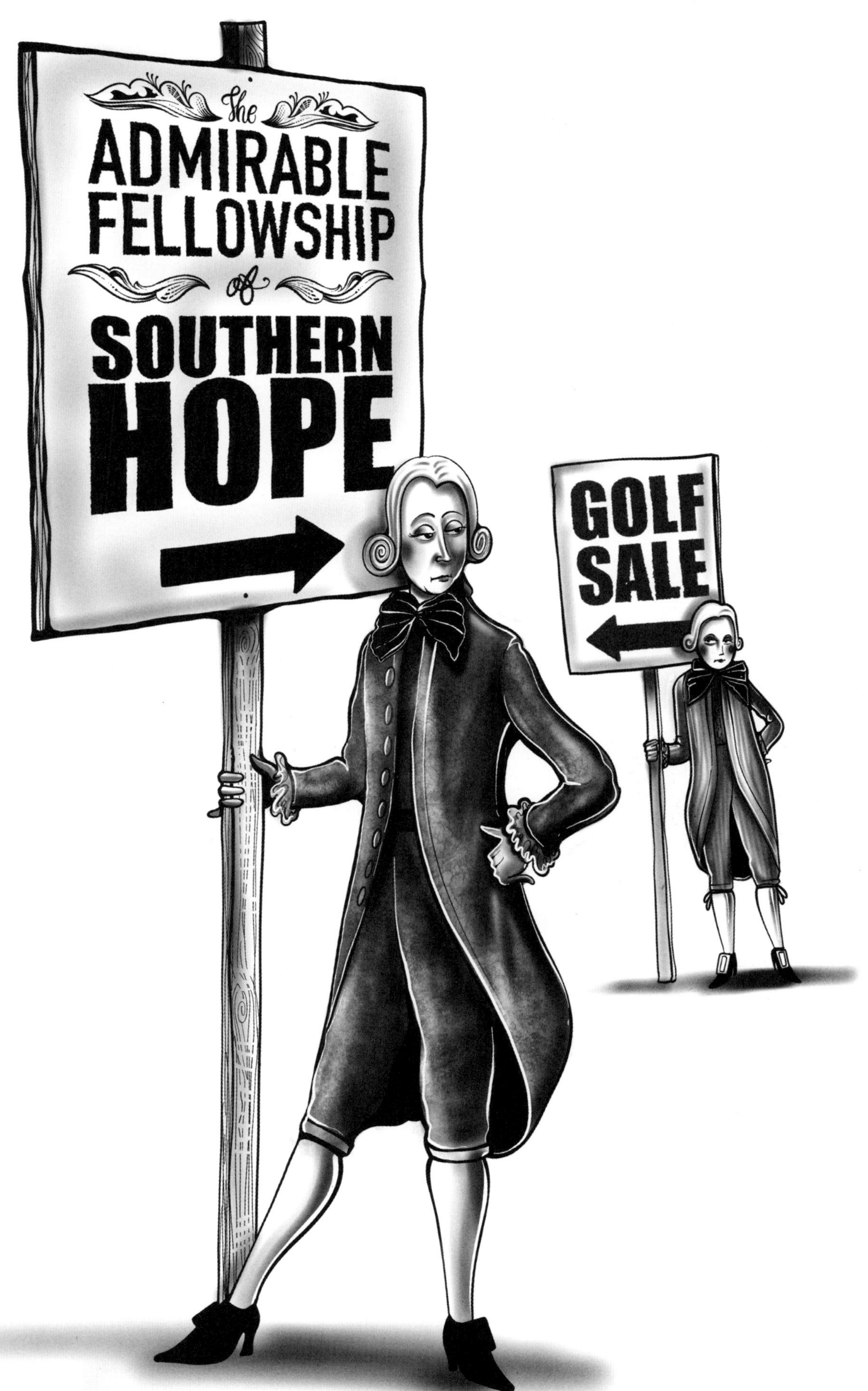
the
ADMIRABLE
FELLOWSHIP
of
SOUTHERN
HOPE
GOLF
SALE

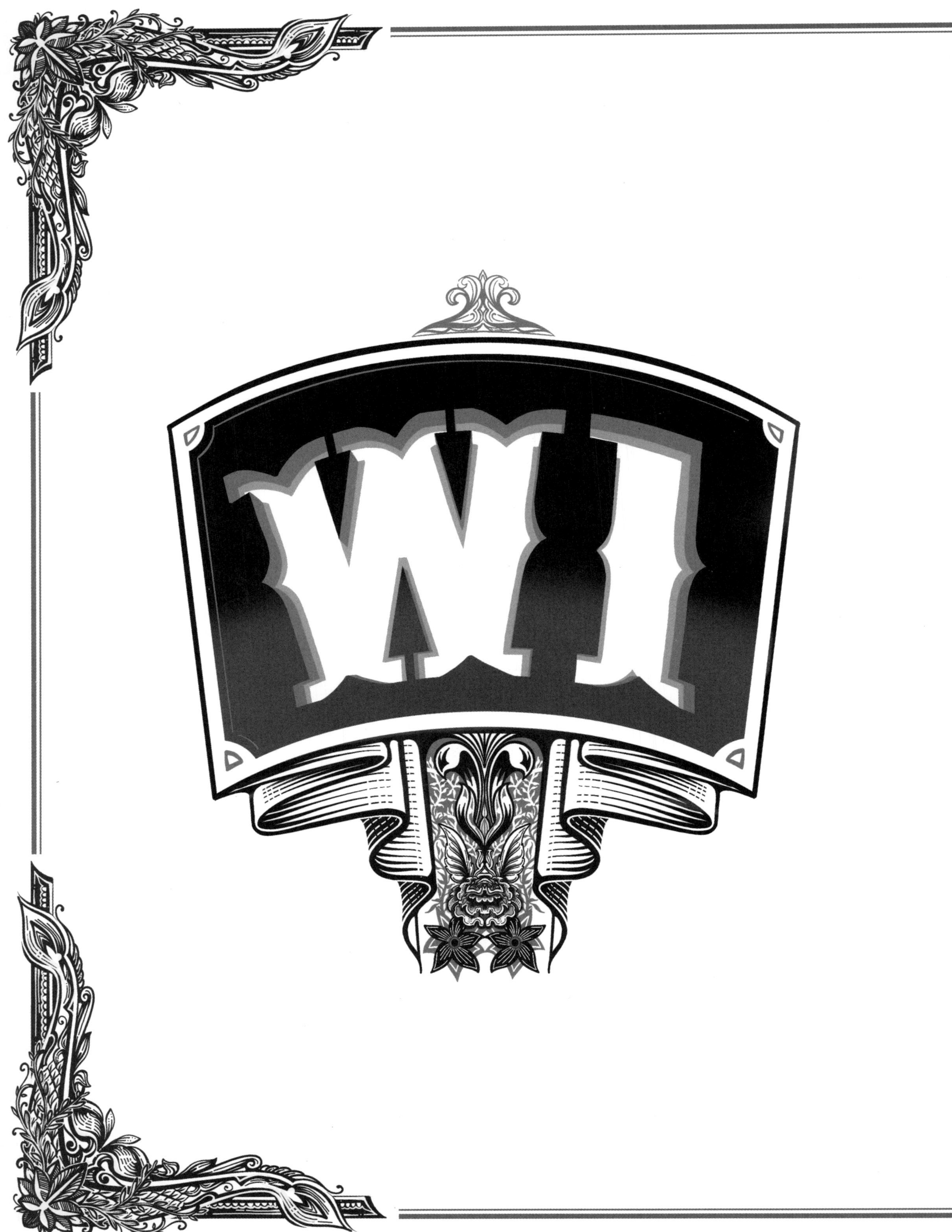
WJ

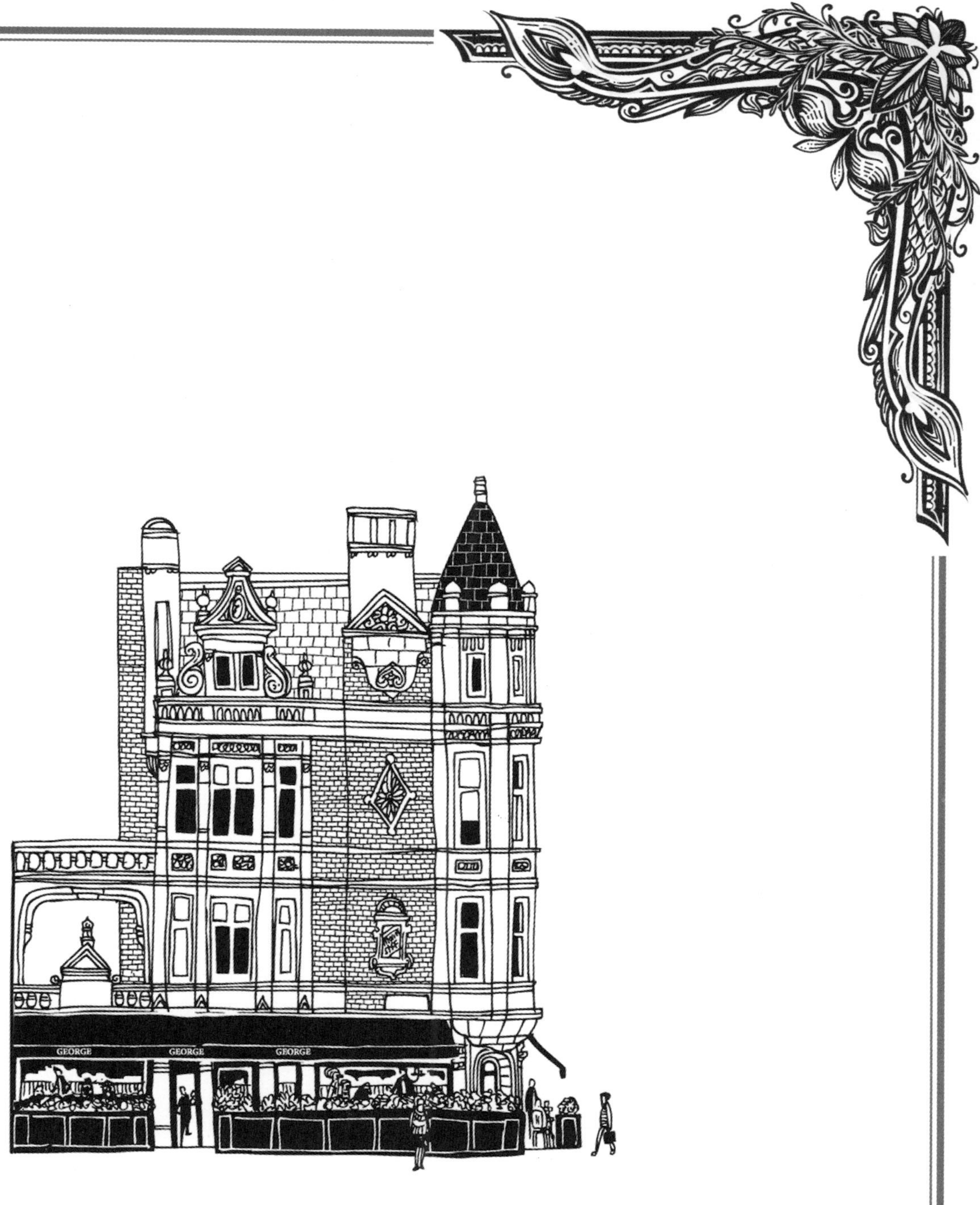

W1
MOUNT STREET
Mayfair

THE MAY FAIR, A RAUCOUS & BOISTEROUS COMING TOGETHER of LONDON FOLK TO PARTAKE IN BEAR BAITING & FISTICUFFS, of DISORDERLY PRACTICES NO LESS. HELD THE FIRST TWO WEEKS IN MAY & SO DECREED AN EVENT BY KING JAMES II. TO BLOSSOM DUE TO THE COMING TOGETHER of SIR THOMAS GROSVENOR & MARY DAVIES, HEIRESS TO THE MANOR of EBURY IN 1677. WHERE NOW SITS MODEST & ELOQUENT MODERN MAYFAIR.

THE 'LONDON SEASON' DREW THE RAHRAHS & RASCALS to DINNERS, BALLS & SHENANIGANS of ELITE BACKGROUNDS. OF BRIGHT YOUNG THINGS & CLIPPED ACCENTS, THE AUTHORS CLUB DREW the *Creative* & WELL READ & THE WELL HEELED TOOK TO THE 100 ACRES.

MOUNT

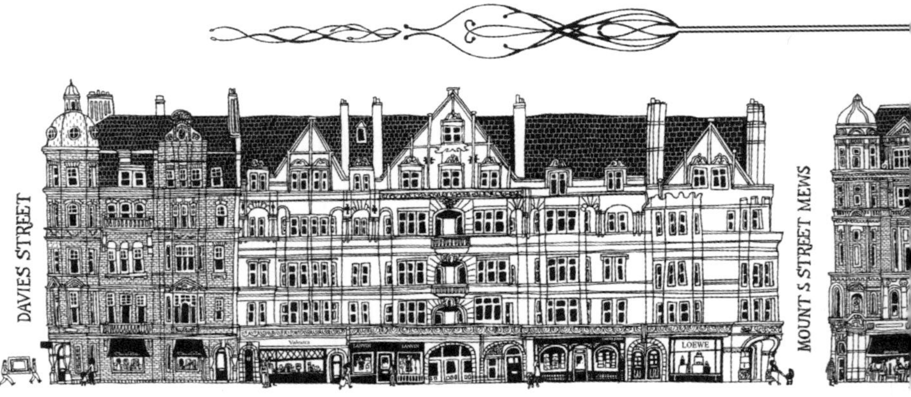

MOUNT STREET

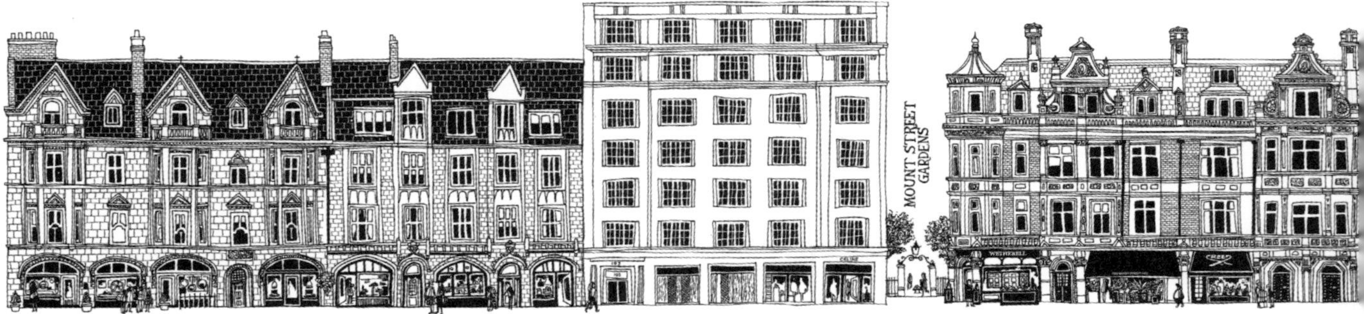

MOUNT STREET

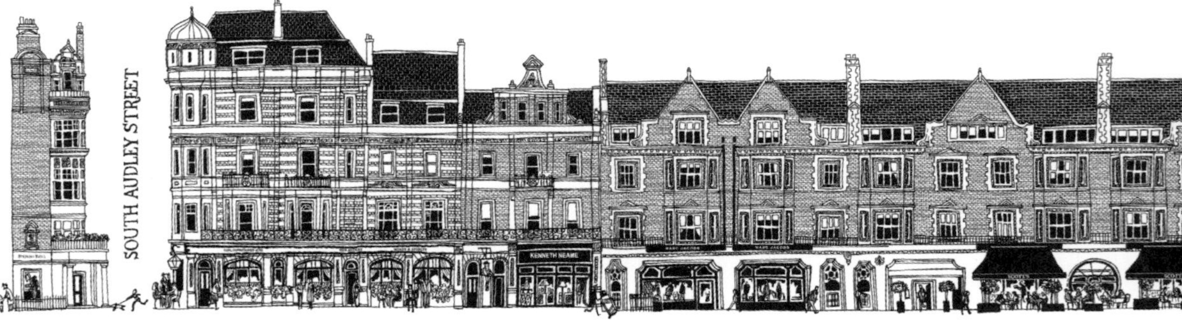

MOUNT STREET

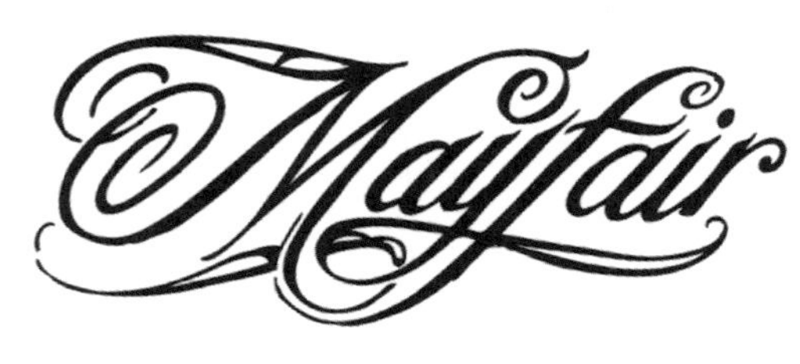

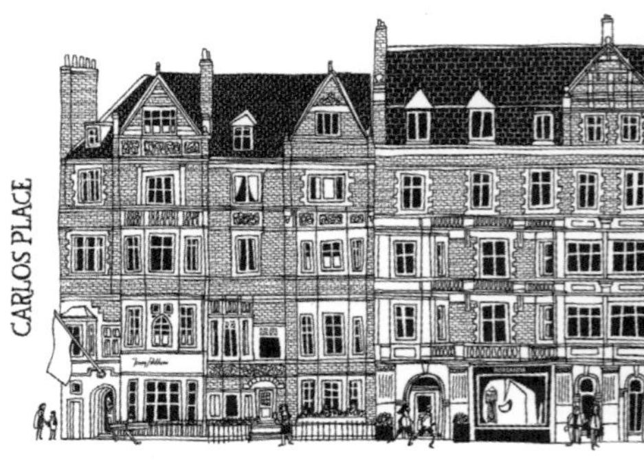

STREET

THE NAME MOUNT STREET IS BORN FROM MOUNT FIELD, IT IS SAID TO BE THE REMAINS *of* FORTIFICATIONS *from the* ENGLISH CIVIL WAR. WHERE MOUNT STREET WORKHOUSE FED & WATERED THE POOR. THE ARCHITECTURE JOURNEYED *from* ITALIANATE *to* FRENCH RENAISSANCE, QUEEN ANNE *to* ARTS & CRAFTS. WHERE BEAUTY ADORNS CRAFTED FASCIAS.

FROM PLUTOCRAT PALACES TO SUITED BOARDROOMS, WHERE TIES REPLACED TIARAS & LAVISH MANSIONS WERE DISSOLVED. NOW THE HOME *of* KITTEN HEELS & POISED GRACES. OF POSH FISH 'N' CHIPS, THE SUITABLY ATTIRED, GULL WINGS AND PERFECTED WALKS.

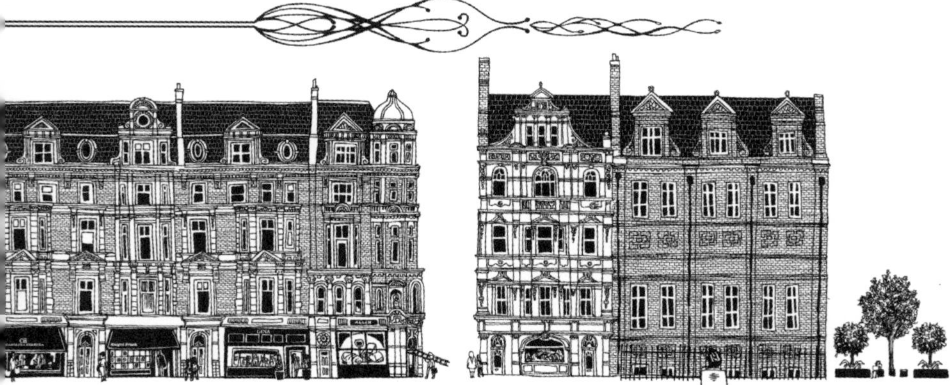

MOUNT STREET

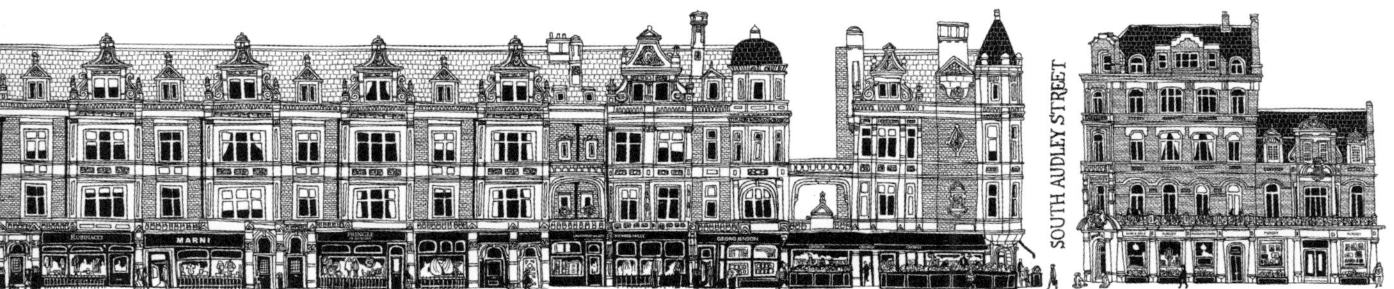

MOUNT STREET

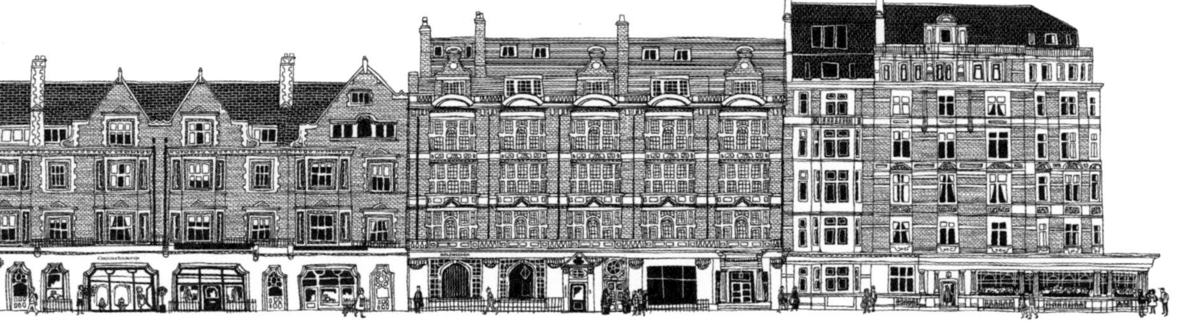

MOUNT STREET

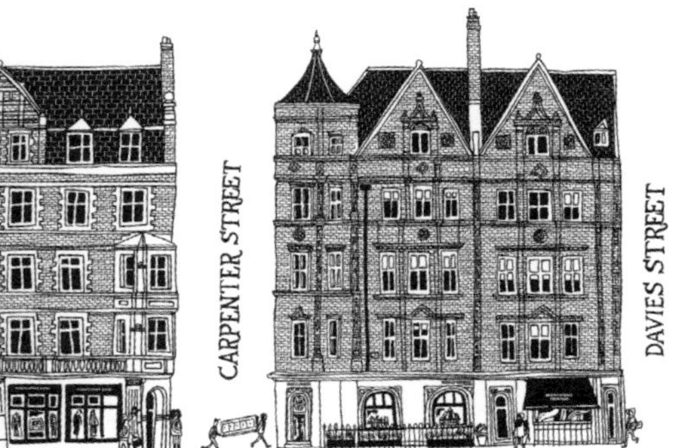

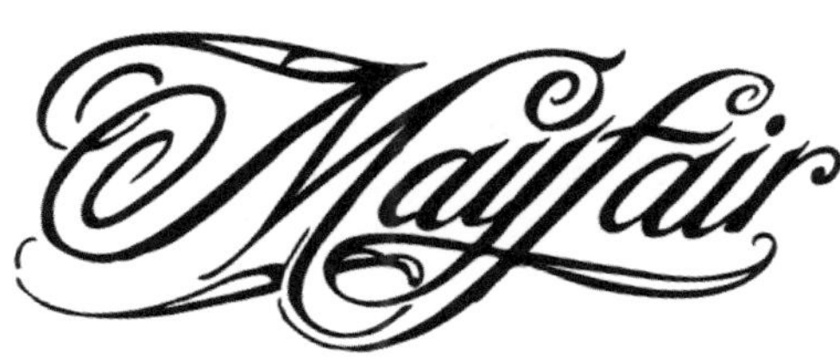

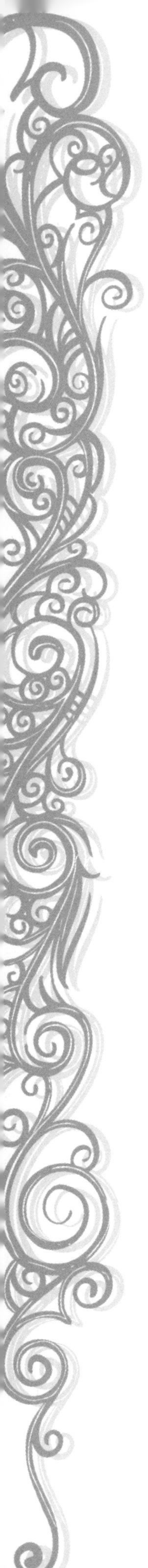

It's ironic that one of the most EXPENSIVE areas in the World to live, was given it's name after the ANNUAL 'MAY FAIR', that took Place between 1686 to 1764. A FAIR, Where proper grafting LONDONERS could enjoy such pleasantries as BARE KNUCKLE FIGHTING, SEMOLINA EATING CONTESTS & WOMENS FOOT RACING, WHICH IS ALSO IRONIC AS THESE ARE NOW PAST TIMES AT MANY PUBLIC SCHOOLS.

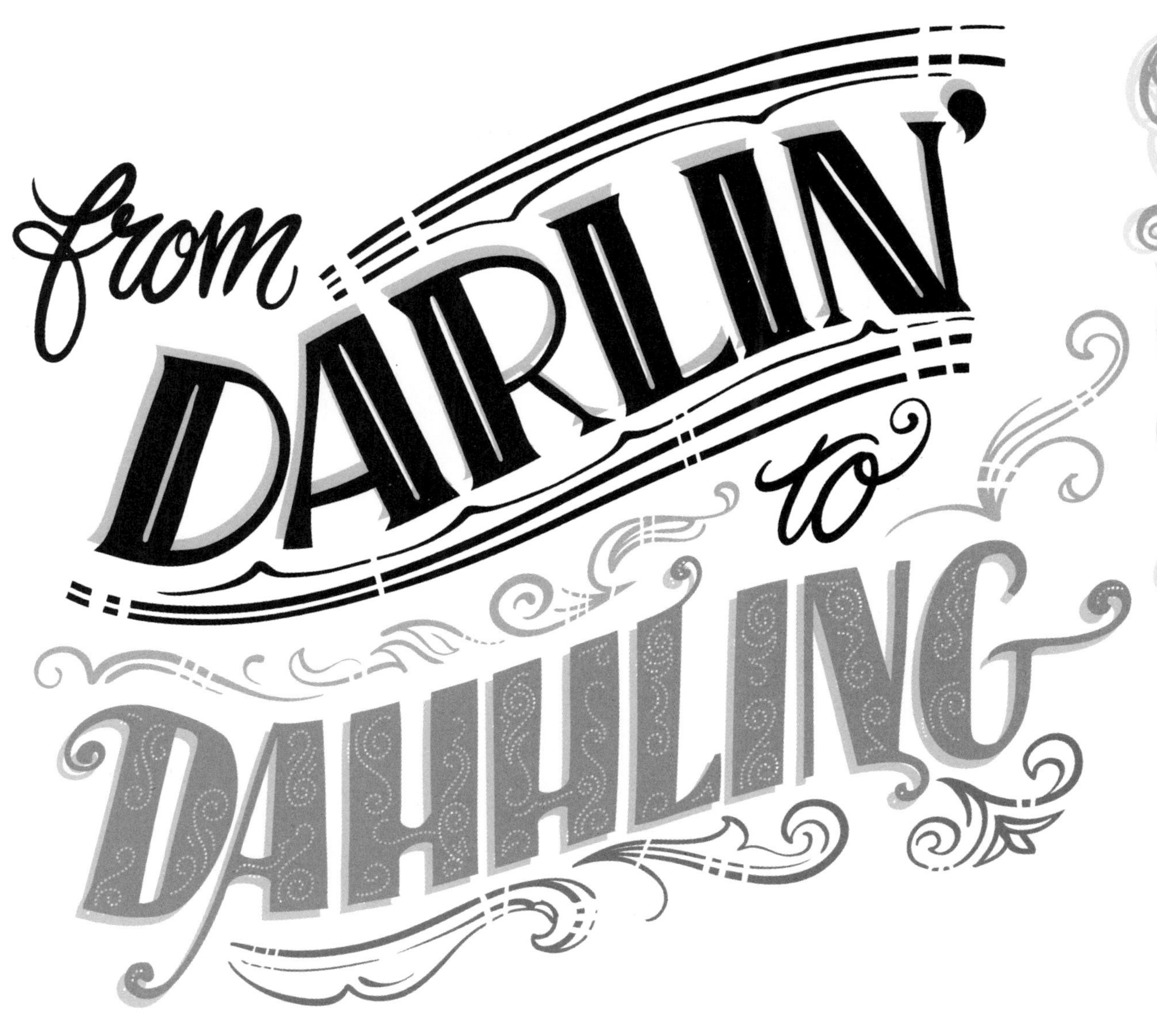

FINALLY ABOLISHED IN 1764, ALL '*Common activities*' WERE OUTLAWED *by* THE HOI POLLOI. WHICH KEPT OUT THE RIFFRAFF, MUCH LIKE TODAY ~ *Hurrah!*

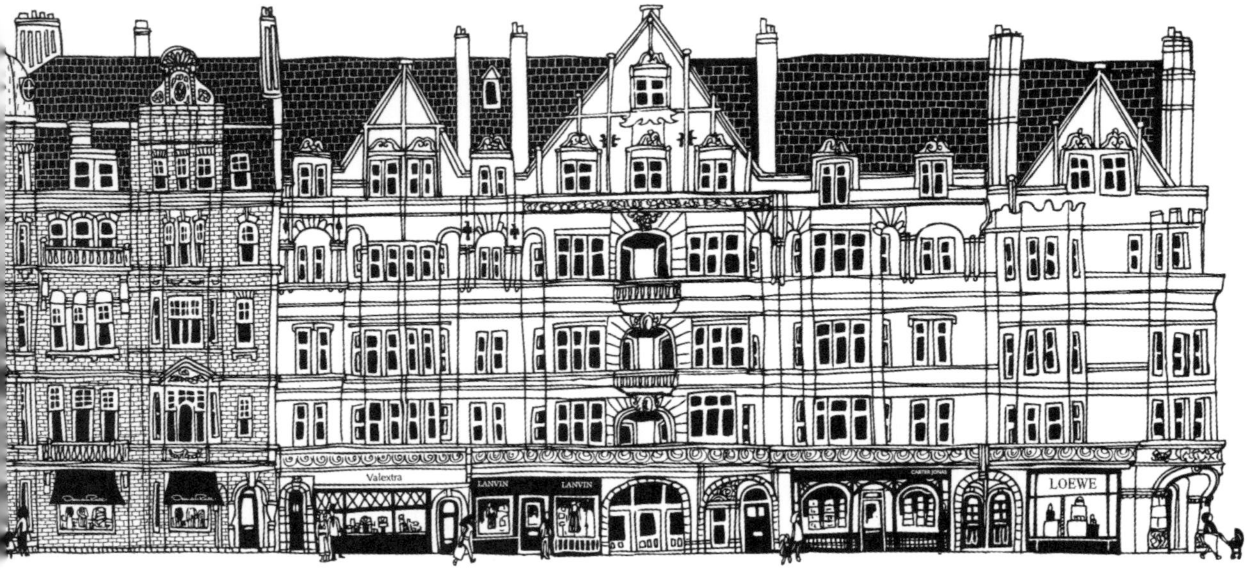

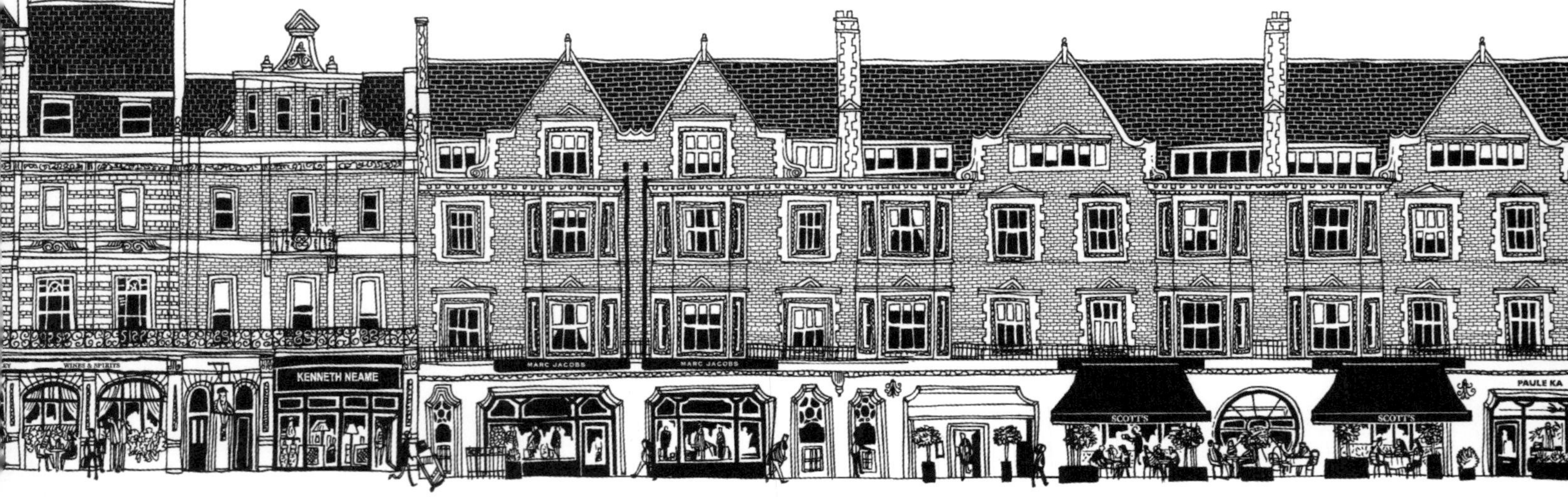
WINES & SPIRITS
KENNETH NEAME
MARC JACOBS
MARC JACOBS
SCOTT'S
SCOTT'S
PAULE KA

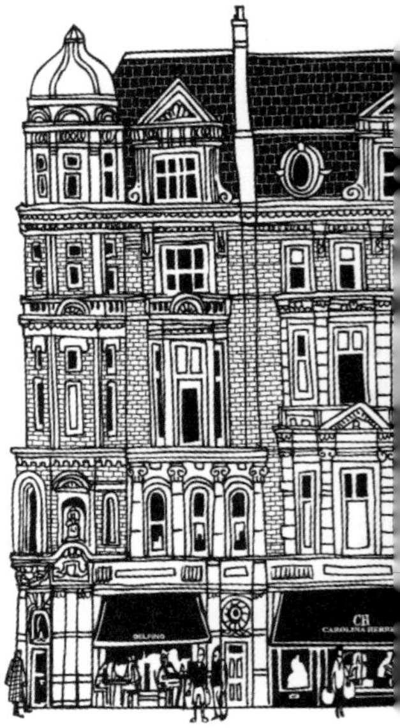

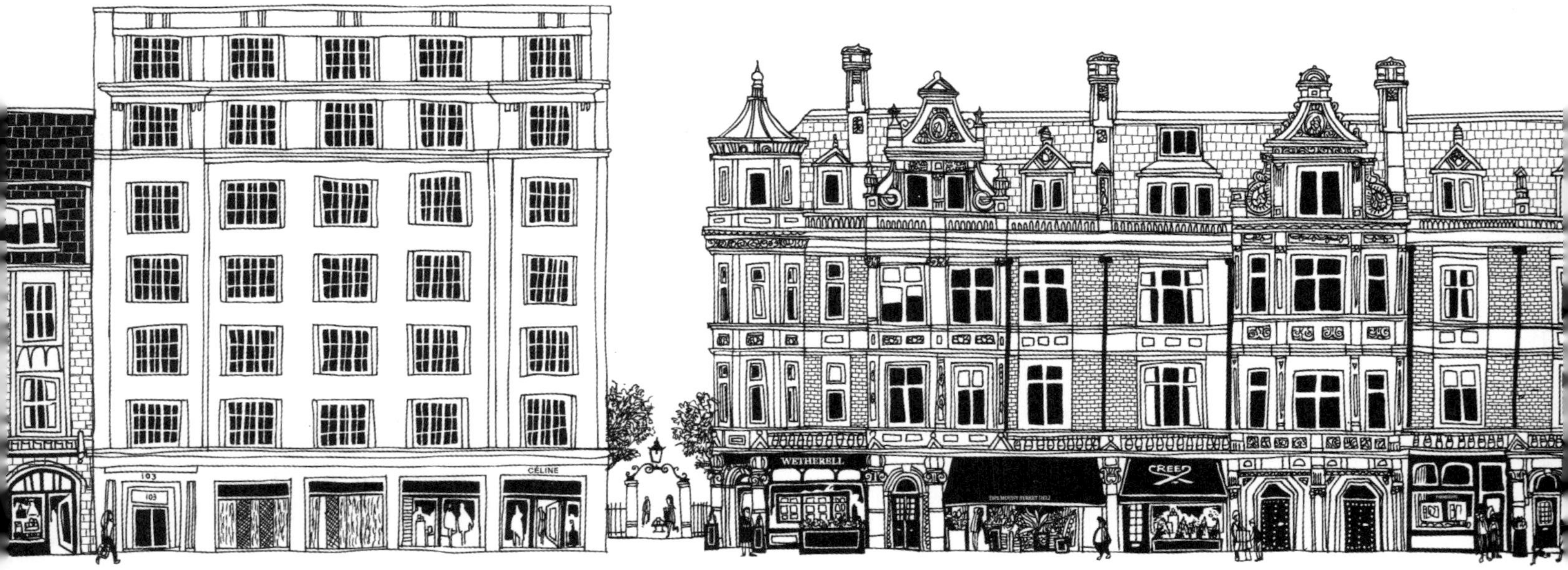

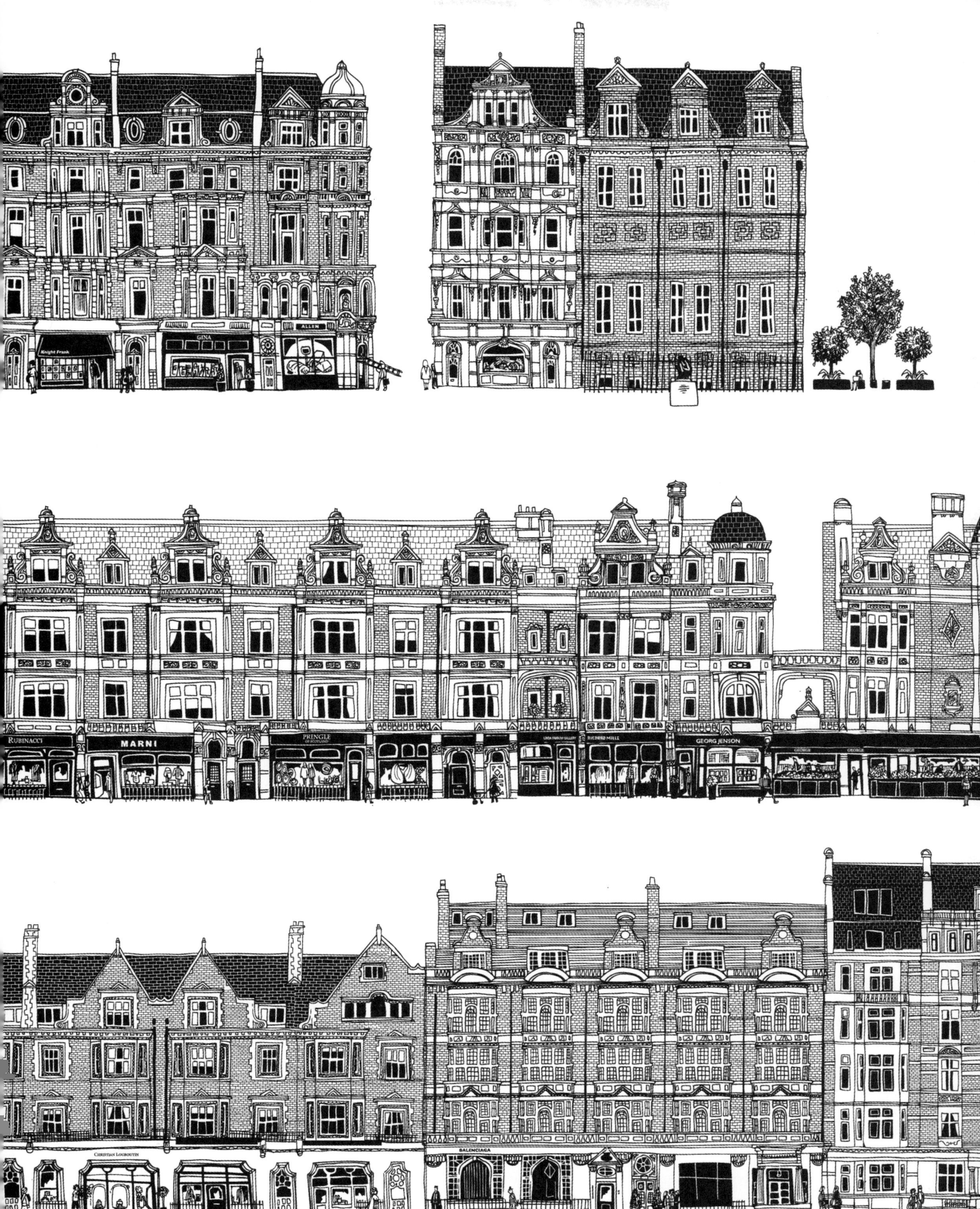
Knight Frank
GINA
ALLEN
RUBINACCI
MARNI
PRINGLE
RICHARD MILLE
GEORG JENSON
GEORGE
CHRISTIAN LOUBOUTIN
BALENCIAGA

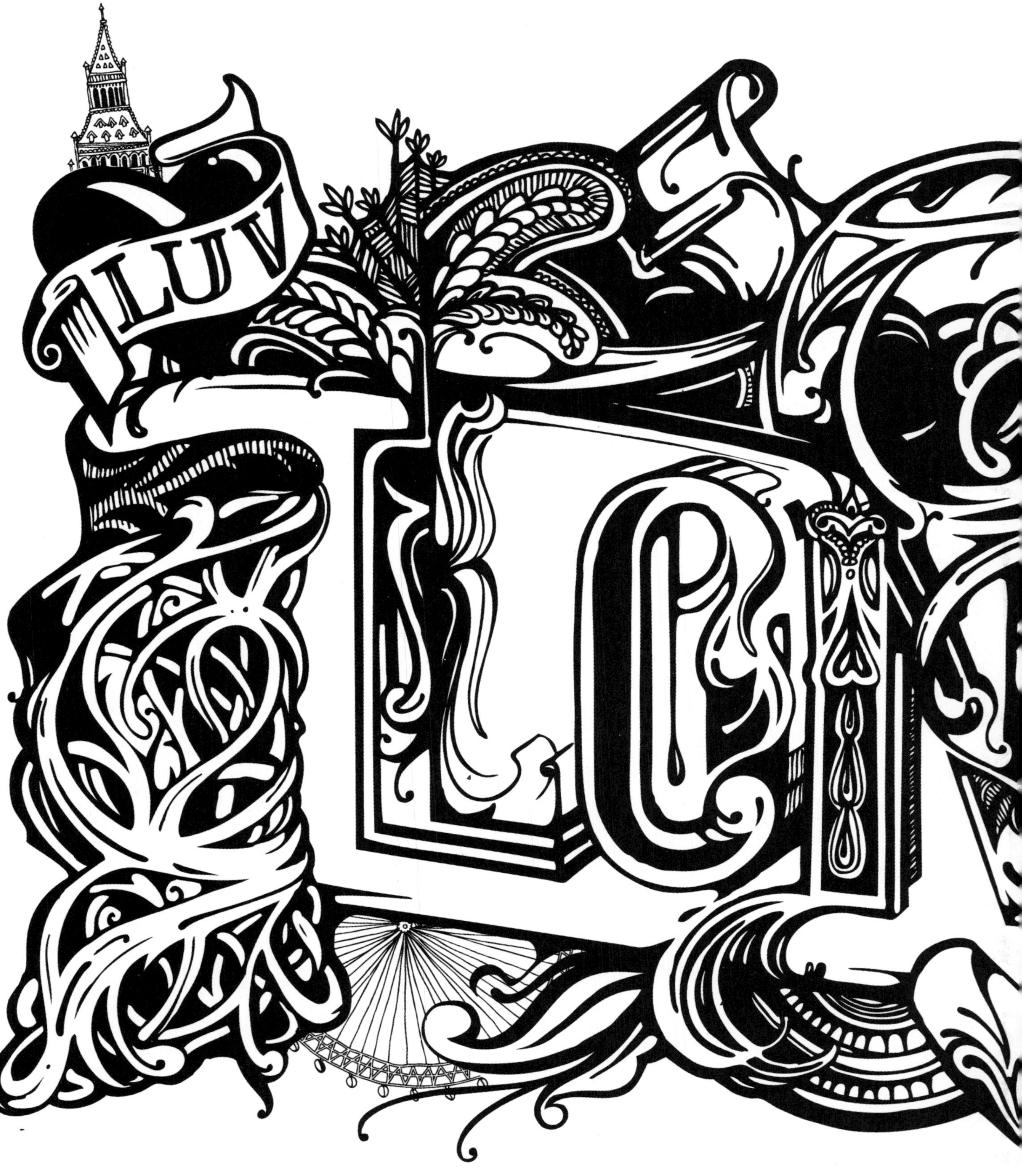

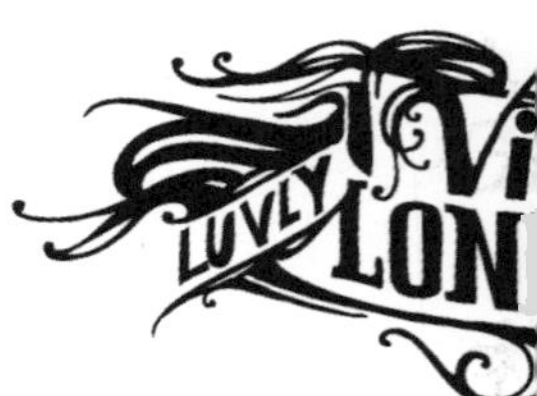
LUVLY
LON

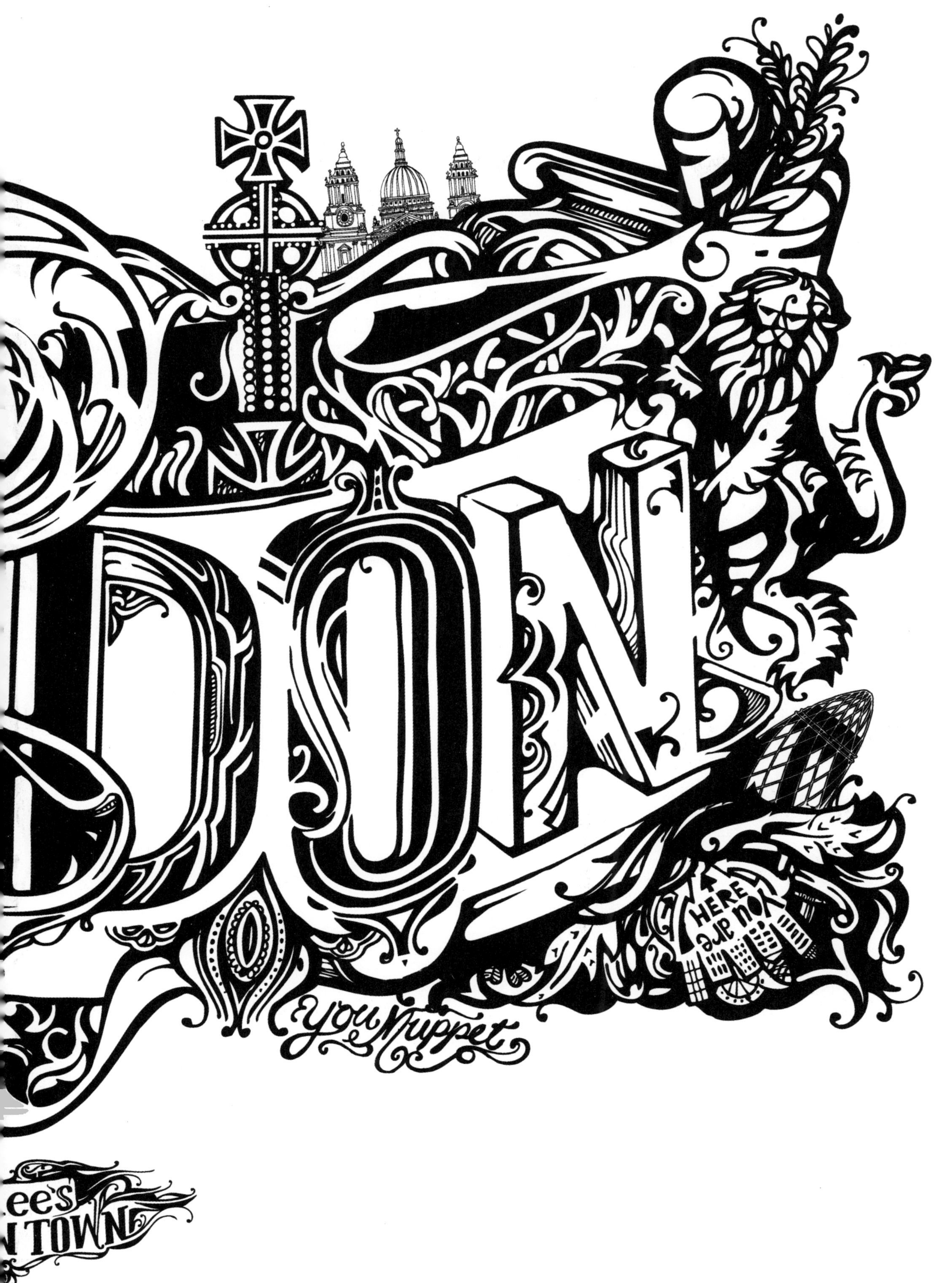
DON
HERE
you are
you muppet
ee's
TOWN

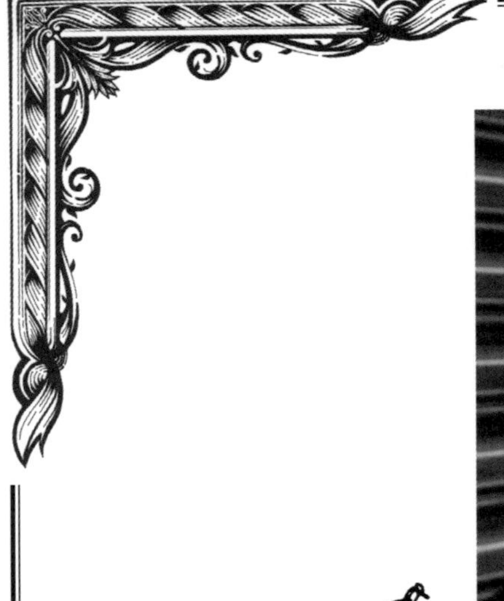

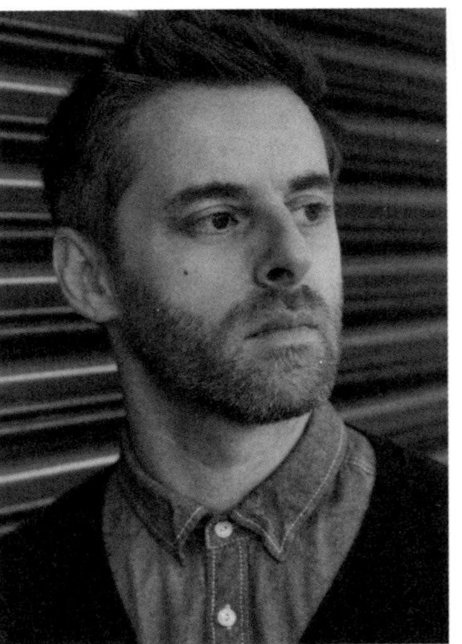

Vic Lee

Vic Lee is an artist, illustrator, storyteller and author living in Peckham, South East London. Vic's first book, *The Corona Diary,* won critical acclaim and many awards for illustration and typography. This book celebrates his love of London and the people who live there.

Follow Vic and his work on Instagram VicLeeLondon www.viclee.co.uk

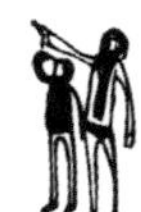

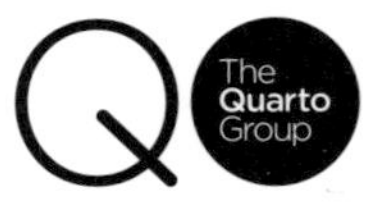

Brimming with creative inspiration, how-to projects, and useful information to enrich your everyday life, quarto.com is a favourite destination for those pursuing their interests and passions.

First published in 2022 by Frances Lincoln, an imprint of The Quarto Group.

The Old Brewery, 6 Blundell Street
London, N7 9BH,
United Kingdom
T (0)20 7700 6700
www.QuartoKnows.com

A catalogue record for this book is available from the British Library.

ISBN 978-0-7112-7974-2
Ebook ISBN 978-0-7112-7975-9

10 9 8 7 6 5 4 3 2 1

Cover and design by Vic Lee

Printed and bound in China

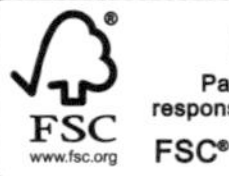